OLD LONDON
The Tower and East End

**THE
'VILLAGE LONDON'
SERIES
from
THE ALDERMAN PRESS**

OLD LONDON

The Tower and East End

by

WALTER THORNBURY

THE ALDERMAN PRESS

British Library Cataloguing in Publication Data.

Thornbury, Walter
    Old London: the Tower and East End.
    1. London (England) ———— History
    I. Title   2. Thornbury, Walter. Old and new London
    942.1   DA677

ISBN 0-946619-24-7

This edition published 1986
The Alderman Press, 1/7 Church Street,
Edmonton, London N9 9DR

Printed and bound in Great Britain
by The Camelot Press Ltd., Southampton.

CONTENTS.

— ❖ —

CHAPTER I.

FISHMONGERS' HALL AND FISH STREET HILL.

CHAPTER II.

LONDON BRIDGE.

CHAPTER III.

UPPER THAMES STREET.

CHAPTER IV.

UPPER THAMES STREET (continued).

CHAPTER V.

LOWER THAMES STREET.

CHAPTER VI.

THE TOWER

CHAPTER VII.

THE TOWER (continued).

CHAPTER VIII.

THE TOWER (continued).

CONTENTS.

CONTENTS.

CHAPTER XX.
BISHOPSGATE.

CHAPTER XXI.
BISHOPSGATE (*continued*).

CHAPTER XXII.
CORNHILL, GRACECHURCH STREET, AND FENCHURCH STREET.

LIST OF ILLUSTRATIONS.

—————⚬—————

CHAPTER I.

FISHMONGERS' HALL AND FISH STREET HILL.

The First Fishmongers' Hall—William Walworth—The Wealth and Power of the Old Fishmongers—Their Quarrels—Their Records—The present Hall—Walworth's Dagger—Walworth's Pall—Fish Street Hill—The Churchyard of St. Leonard's—Goldsmith and Monument Yard.

HERE Fishmongers' Hall, that handsome Anglo-Greek building at the west side of the foot of London Bridge, still stands, this rich semi-marine Company have had a stronghold ever since the reign of Edward III. It was in this convenient spot, also, that that most warlike and eminent of Fishmongers, Sir William Walworth, himself resided during the reign of Richard II., the monarch whose crown he saved by a single blow of his prompt sword.

Mr. Herbert, who took great pains about this question, says that there were originally five tenements on the site of Fishmongers' Hall. The frontage towards Thames Street was 120 feet, and the depth to the river about 200 feet. The plot of ground stood in Upper Thames Street, between the Water-Gate and Old Swan Lane, and lay in three parishes. It was parted into six great slips by five stairs to the Thames, as seen in "The Exact Survey of the Ruins of London after the Fire of 1666." The stairs were—Water Gate (originally called Oyster Hill, and afterwards the Gully Hole), the site of the old water works, Churchyard Alley, Fleur de Luce Alley,

Black Raven Alley, and Ebgate, (Old Swan Lane), and, after the Fire, Wheatsheaf Alley.

Henry III., in order to increase his queen's customs at Queenhithe (Thames Street), prohibited any fish being landed from fishing-vessels except at that port. This led to a great London fish-market being established in Old Fish Street (near Doctors' Commons), and Knightrider Street soon became famous, as Stow tells us, for fish dinners. The stalls soon grew into houses, and this is why St. Nicholas Coleabbey contained the tombs of so many celebrated Fishmongers.

Edward I., finding the old restrictions work badly, restored the Fishmongers to their ancient liberty, and in the next reign they removed to Bridge Street, thenceforward called New Fish Street. Here the Fishmongers could correspond with Billingsgate, and their other colonies at Fish Wharf, Oyster Gate, and Eastcheap. " The topping men," says Stow, " lived in Bridge Street." The Stock Market was also an early fish-market; in 1545 there were 25 fishmongers there, and only 18 butchers. After the change of market all the great Fish-monger mayors and aldermen were buried at St. Magnus' and St. Botolph's, while the Stock Fish-mongers took a fancy to the cool vaults of St. Michael's, Crooked Lane.

Herrings, says Herbert, are mentioned soon after the Conquest, and in the 31st of Edward III. they had become fish of such importance, that a special Act of Parliament was passed relating to them. Whales accidentally stranded on our inhospitable coasts in that reign were instantly salted down and sent to the king for his consumption. As for porpoises, they were favourites with English cooks till after Elizabeth's reign.

Edward I. seems to have been a fish-loving king, for he fixed a tariff of prices. The edict limits the best soles to 3d. a dozen; the best turbot to 6d.; the best mackerel, in Lent, to 1d. each; the best pickled herrings to twenty the penny; fresh oysters to 2d. per gallon; a quarter of a hundred of the best eels to 2d.; and other fish in propor-tion. " Congers, lampreys, and sea-hogs " are enu-merated.

The same King Edward, the born plague of fish-mongers and Scotchmen, forbade all partnerships with foreign fishmongers, and all storing fish in cellars to retail afterwards at exorbitant rates. No fishmonger was to buy before the king's pur-veyors, and no fish (unless salted) was to be kept in London beyond the second day. The City had limited the profit of the London fishmonger to a penny in the shilling; moreover, no one was to sell fish except in the open market-place, and no

one was permitted to water fish more than twice, under pain of fines and the market-place stocks.

In the reign of Edward II. all the London fish-mongers had their stalls in Bridge Street, a market of a later date than Billingsgate and Old Fish Street. In the reign of Richard II. the Stock Fish-mongers formed a new company, and had a hall of their own to the east of the Fishmongers'. The two companies united in the reign of Henry VI., and held their meetings at Lord Fairhope's house in Thames Street. The restless Stock Fishmongers again seceded in the reign of Henry VII.; but in the reign of Henry VIII. the two companies were again finally fused together, and on this occasion Lord Fairhope's hall saw cups of wine drained to the happy union.

The great tenant of Fishmongers' Hall in the reign of Edward III. was John Lovekyn, who was several times Lord Mayor of London. At the death of Lovekyn's wife the celebrated William Walworth lived there, and carried on his honest but unheroic business of stock fishmonger, a great trade in Catholic times, when fish was in demand for frequent fast-days. To Walworth succeeded William Askham, one of his apprentices, and twice Mayor of London. The building is then spoken of as having a wharf, a loft, and a tower which Walworth had built.

The Fishmongers must have been wealthy in the reign of Edward III., when they contributed £40 towards the expenses of the French wars—only one pound less than the Mercers, the grandest Company; and two years later they again con-tributed the same sum. In the 50th Edward III. the Fishmongers ranked the fourth Company, as at present, and returned six members to the Common Council, the greatest number that any guild sent.

In spite of Walworth's " swashing blow " and loyal service, the reign of Richard II. proved a vexatious one to the Fishmongers. John de Northampton, Mayor in 1380, obtained an Act of Parliament to entirely throw open the trade, and compelled the Fishmongers to admit that their occu-pation was no craft, and unworthy to be reckoned among the mysteries. He also went further, for in the year 1382 Parliament, indignant at the frauds of Billingsgate, enacted that in future no Fishmonger should be admitted Mayor of London. This prohibition was removed next year, when the Fishmongers pleaded their own cause in Parlia-ment. During this discussion the Fishmongers prayed for the king's protection from " corporal hurt," and ascribed malice to their accusers. Upon which John Moore, a Mercer, angrily charged Walter Sybell, a spokesman of the Fishmongers, with having let the rebels of Kent and Essex, Wat Tyler's followers, into the City. This same Walter, a violent and rash man, was, by-the-bye, afterwards fined 500 marks for slandering Robert de Vere, Earl of Oxford. Even in 1383 the anti-Fishmonger agitation still continued, for we find John Cavendish, a Fishmonger, challenging the Chancellor for taking a bribe of £10 in the fore-named case. The Chancellor freed himself by oath on the Sacrament, and John Cavendish, being found guilty, was

appointed—namely, the chapel on London Bridge, Baynard's Castle, and Jordan's Key." This was to prevent their going and meeting the boats before their arrival at London. "No fish were to be brought in any boat without first being landed at the chapel on the bridge; fresh fish was only to be sold after mass, and salt fish after prime." Eight years later—viz., in 1298—the Company displayed their great wealth by meeting the brave king, Edward I., on his return from Scotland, with

THE NEIGHBOURHOOD OF LONDON BRIDGE. *From Hollar's View.* (*See page 4.*)

sentenced to pay the Chancellor 1,000 marks, and was also sent to prison.

Herbert says that the Fishmongers were amongst the earliest of the metropolitan guilds. They were one of those amerced in the reign of Henry II.; and we have seen that charters were granted to them not only by Edward II., Edward III., and Richard II., but by Edward I. They were fined 500 marks as a guild, in the 18th of the latter prince, for forestalling, contrary to the laws and constitutions of the City; and it was soon afterwards found necessary to make fresh regulations for them, which are to be found in the "Liber Horn." These, amongst other things, ordain "that no fishmonger shall buy fish beyond the bounds

very splendid retinue and costly trappings. We have already (Vol. I., p. 305) noticed a great affray which took place between the Fishmongers and the Skinners, in the midst of Cheapside, in 1340, which ended in the apprehension and execution by the mayor of several of the ringleaders. These quarrels were common amongst the great companies in early times; and in the above, and most other instances, arose from disputed claims about precedency, which were uniformly settled by the Court of Aldermen. Stow's allusion to the ancient amity between the Fishmongers and Goldsmiths, which he charges the former with ignorance for not knowing, but which he himself has not explained, was the consequence of one of these decisions, which were always accompanied by orders for them alternately to take precedence, dine together, exchange livery hoods, and other methods calculated to make them friends, as will be shown to have been the case in both instances. The Fishmongers and Goldsmiths have no commemoration of this amity at present; but the Skinners (who were similarly reconciled after the above affray, of which a notice will also be seen in our account of that Company), when members of their courts dine with each other, drink as toasts the "Merchant Taylors and Skinners," and "Skinners and Merchant Taylors."

When Alderman Wood, as prime warden of the Company, was examined before the Commissioners of Municipal Inquiry, he stated that till the year 1830 only eight liverymen were made a year, but that year (for election purposes) 400 liverymen had been elected, on signing a declaration foregoing all rights to dine in hall. The fee for coming on the livery was then £25, the purchase-money of the freedom £105; and for translation from another Company double that sum.

The Fishmongers' books do not extend far enough back to give any account of their ancient livery. For many years the Goldsmiths and Fishmongers, as proof of amity, exchanged each others' liveries.

Every year, on the festival of their patron saint, St. Peter, all the brethren and "sistern" of the fraternity went in their new livery to St. Peter's Church, Cornhill, and there heard a solemn mass in the worship of God and St. Peter, and offered at offering-time whatever their devotion prompted them. They kept three priests to celebrate obits, which was one more than is mentioned in any other Company. The ancient custom of electing wardens is still retained by this Company. A sort of cap, fronted with a metal plate, is placed successively on the head of each new warden.

The second Fishmongers' Hall, though usually ascribed to Sir Christopher Wren, was built by a Mr. Jerman, who was also the architect of Drapers' Hall and the second Royal Exchange. Old Fishmongers' Hall was a stately structure, particularly the front towards the river, of which it commanded a very fine view. The Thames Street front was a mere cluster of houses; the entrance, however, was pleasing. It was ornamented with sculptured pilasters, sustaining an open pediment, which had the Company's arms carved in bold relief. The buildings environed a square court, handsomely paved. The dining-hall formed the south side of the court, and was a spacious and lofty apartment, having, besides the usual accompaniment of a screen of Grecian architecture, a capa-

cious gallery running round the whole interior, and a statue of Sir William Walworth, said by Walpole to have been carved by an artist named Pierce. The rooms for business lay on the west side of the court, and those for courts and withdrawing at entertainments on the east; they were ornamented with many rich decorations, and paintings of a great variety of fish, not easy to be described.

In Hollar's large four-sheet view of London, 1647, we perceive two courtyards, evidently formed by running a dining-hall, or refectory—high-roofed and turreted, like that of Westminster—across the original quadrangle. This view also affords a good representation of the Thames front, which appears of an irregular form and unornamental, but to have been at one time regular and handsome. It consists of two wings and a receding centre, the latter having a balcony at the first floor, double rows of windows, a lofty octagonal tower or staircase rising above the roof, and crowned with a sort of cupola; there was also a large arched doorway leading to a small terrace on the Thames, similar to the present house. The wings were evidently, when perfect, uniform square towers, harmonising with the centre; but only the western one here remains in its original state, the eastern one being modernised and roofed like a common house.

In De Hogenberg's earlier plan of London, Fishmongers' Hall appears as a square pile of masonry, with embattled parapets, towers at the angles, a central gateway, and steps leading from the river to one of the side towers.

In no worse spot in all London could the Great Fire have broken out than Pudding Lane. It found there stores of oil, hemp, flax, pitch, tar, cordage, hops, wines, brandies, and wharves for coal and timber. Fishmongers' Hall was the first great building consumed, when, as Dryden says, in two splendid lines,

    "A key of fire ran all along the shore,
      And frightened all the river with a blaze."

The building on the river-side was reduced to a shell. Even the hall itself, which was at the back, with a high roof and turret, was entirely destroyed, as well as two sets of stairs, and the houses round the Old Swan and Black Raven Alley. After the Fire, the building committee met at Bethlehem Hospital. Sir William Davenant (Shakespeare's supposed son), describing this part of London before the Great Fire, says: "Here a palace, there a wood-yard; here a garden, there a brewhouse; here dwelt a lord, there a dyer; and between both duomo commune." A strange, picturesque spot, half Dutch, half Venetian, this part of the river-side must have been before the Great Fire.

The present Fishmongers' Hall, at the north-west foot of London Bridge (says Timbs), was re-built by Roberts in 1830–33, and is the third of the Company's halls nearly on this site. It is raised upon a lofty basement cased with granite, and contains fire-proof warehouses, which yield a large rental. The river front has a balustraded terrace, and a Grecian-Ionic hexastyle and pedi-ment. The east or entrance front is enriched by pilasters and columns, and the arms of the Company and crest. The entrance-hall is separated from the great staircase by a screen of polished Aberdeen granite columns ; and at the head of the stairs is Pierce's statue of Sir William Walworth, a Fish-monger, who carries a dagger. In his hand was formerly a real dagger, said to be the identical weapon with which he stabbed Wat Tyler ; though, in 1731, a publican of Islington pretended to possess the actual poniard. Beneath the statue is this inscription :—

> "Brave Walworth, Knight, Lord Mayor, yᵗ slew
> Rebellious Tyler in his alarmes ;
> The King, therefore, did give in liew
> The dagger to the City armes,
> In the 4th year of Richard II., Anno Domini 1381."

A common but erroneous belief was thus propa-gated ; for the dagger was in the City arms long before the time of Sir William Walworth, and was intended to represent the sword of St. Paul, the patron saint of the Corporation. The reputed dagger of Walworth, which has lost its guard, is preserved by the Company. The workmanship is no doubt that of Walworth's period. The weapon now in the hand of the statue (which is somewhat picturesque, and within recollection was coloured *en costume*) is modern.

Amongst celebrated Fishmongers and their friends we must mention Isaac Pennington, the turbulent Lord Mayor of the Civil War under Charles I. ; and Dogget, the comedian and Whig, who bequeathed a sum of money for the purchase of a "coat and badge," to be rowed for every 1st of August from the "Swan" at London Bridge to the "Swan" at Battersea, in remembrance of George I.'s accession to the throne.

In Fishmongers' Hall there is an original drawing of a portion of the pageant exhibited by the Fish-mongers' Company on the 29th of October, 1616, on the occasion of Sir John Leman, a member of the Company, entering on the office of Lord Mayor of the City of London, and the following portraits : William III. and queen, by Murray ; George II. and queen, by Schakleton ; Dukes of Kent and

Sussex, by Beechey ; Earl St. Vincent (the admiral), by Beechey ; Queen Victoria, by Herbert Smith ; the Margrave of Anspach and Margravine, by G. Rowney ; the late Lord Chancellor Hatherley, by Wells.

"The Fishmongers," says Herbert, "have no wardens' accounts or minutes of an earlier date than 1592, their more ancient ones having been either destroyed in the Fire of London or other-wise lost. The title-deeds of their various estates commence as far back as 9 Edward III., and are finely preserved, as are also their Book of Ordi-nances and some other ancient documents relating to the Company. The minutes remaining—or, as they are termed in this Company, 'court ledgers' —consist of eight folio volumes, separately dated."

The Fishmongers' greatest curiosity is their pall, commonly although erroneously described as "Walworth's pall ;" it is in three pieces, like the famous pall of the Merchant Taylors, and exactly resembles in shape one belonging to the Saddlers' —namely, that of a cross. It consists of a centre slip, about 12 feet long and 2½ feet wide, and two shorter sides, each 8 feet 11 inches long by 1 foot 4 inches wide, and when laid over a corpse must have totally enveloped the coffin, but without corner falls, like our modern palls. In the style of orna-ment, workmanship, and materials, this is one of the most superb works of its kind of ancient art, and in this country, as a relic of the old Catholic faith, has probably no parallel. The pattern of the second part is a sprig, or running flower, which is composed of gold network, bordered with red, and the whole of which reposes on a smooth, solid ground of cloth of gold. The end pieces and side borders to this middle slip are worked in different pictures and representations. The end pieces con-sist of a very rich and massy wrought picture, in gold and silk, of the patron, St. Peter, *in pontificalibus*. He is seated on a superb throne, his head crowned with the sacred tiara. One hand holds the keys ; the other is in the position of giving the bene-diction. On each side of the saint is a kneeling angel, censing him with one hand, and holding a sort of golden vase with the other. Each of these end pieces is perfectly similar ; and the materials, which are beautifully worked, are of gold and silk. The angels' wings, according to the old custom in such representations, are composed of peacocks' feathers, in all their natural vivid colours. The outer robes are gold, raised with crimson ; their under-vests white, shaded with sky-blue. The faces are finely worked in satin, after nature ; and they have long yellow hair. St. Peter's vest, or under-robe, is crimson, raised with gold ; the inside of the hanging sleeve of his outer robe, or coat, azure, powdered with gold stars. A golden nimbus, or rather glory, encircles his head; and in his lap is placed an open book, having the following inscription in old English black-letter on a silver ground: "Credo in Deum patrem, Omnipotentem," at the one end piece; and at the other similarly, "Credo in Deum Patrem, omnium." The pictures of the side pieces are divided into three compartments. The centre is Christ delivering the

Claves Regum Cœlo'm." Both figures stand in a beautiful arched recess, within Gothic-pinnacled buildings and ornaments. On each side of this middle picture, which is the same on both sides, the decorations are made up of the Fishmongers' arms, richly and properly emblazoned. The supporters (merman and mermaid) are worked in their natural colours. The merman wears gold armour. The mermaid's body is of white silk thread, beautifully worked; her long tresses of golden thread.

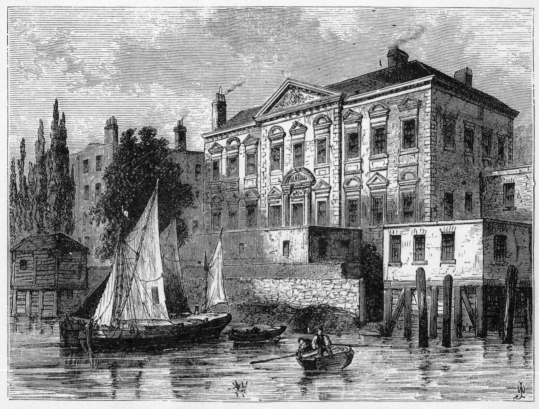

THE SECOND FISHMONGERS' HALL (see page 4).

keys to Peter, the latter of whom is kneeling, and habited as in the end pieces, but with only a glory encircling the head, and no crown (he not being crowned Prince of the Apostles). The Saviour is habited agreeably to the usual representations of him as regards costume. His robe is crimson, raised with gold; the inner vesture purple, and very rich. Around the head is a superb circular glory, jewelled and coronetted. He graciously stoops to deliver the two golden keys of heaven and hell with one hand; while with the other he poises the golden orb of sovereignty, surmounted with the cross. A label proceeding from the mouth has inscribed, in black-letter and on a silver ground, as before: "Tibi dabo

A superb jewel hangs by a gold chain from her neck. Her mirror reflects a head like that of Christ or St. Peter. The entire pall has a fringe two inches deep of gold and purple silk threads, and is lined inside with black silk. The weight of the whole, owing to the quantity of gold and silver worked into it, is very considerable; and it is in the finest preservation.

The Saddlers' Company also still have a valuable pall, though not so costly. It is of crimson velvet. The centre is of yellow silk, forming an elegant sprig pattern. On one side of the pall there are embroidered in raised work of gold thread, in the old English character, the words, "In te Domine speravi;" and on the other side, worked in like

LONDON BRIDGE, 1756.   *From an Old View, taken shortly before the Demolition of the Houses.*

manner, the words, "Ne me confunde in æternum." The head and foot of the pall have embroidered on them the arms of the Company, and four kneeling angels surrounding the letters I.H.S. encircled by a glory. The whole is bordered with a broad gold fringe.

"A curious relic of the old shows," says Mr. Herbert, "is kept by the Fishmongers. It is the original drawing for the mayoralty procession of their member, Sir John Leman, in 1616, and which, from containing allusions in it to the story of Walworth and Wat Tyler, has been called, in the most modern accounts of London, 'The Procession of Sir William Walworth in 1380.' The representation occupies a roll of strong paper several feet in length, filled with characters and objects six or seven inches high, well drawn, and all properly coloured, emblazoned, and gilt. The pageants have inscriptions over them in the handwriting of the time, from which we learn that it was the custom to suspend them from the roof of the hall when done with, for future solemnities. Several of the Companies still possess remains of their old shows, in particular the Grocers. The scenes were painted like those of the theatres, in distemper, and the animals, or 'beasts which drew the pageants,' were fabricated so like what are used there, that there seems little doubt that the latter specimens, at least, were the work of theatrical artists. Those who had no pageants (which were confined to the twelve) have many of them other articles which were used in their processions. We saw in the old pageant-chamber at Brewers' Hall the fittings-up of their state barge, with various other relics; and in a corner of the room stood silk banners and streamers, covered with dust and dropping from their staves—a melancholy memento of former splendour."

Fish Street Hill was formerly called New Fish Street. The Black Prince once lived there, according to Stow. "Above Crooked Lane end, upon Fish Street Hill," he says, "is one great house, for the most part built of stone, which pertained some time to Edward the Black Prince, son of Edward III., who was in his lifetime lodged there. It is now altered to a common hostelry, having the 'Black Bell' for a sign." Here, too, was the scene of Jack Cade's utmost fury, when he let slip the dogs of war, and, according to Shakespeare, shouted out his cruel commands of "Up Fish Street! Down St. Magnus' corner! Kill and knock down! Throw them into Thames!"

The churchyard of St. Leonard marks the site of a church of no interest destroyed by the Great Fire. Many of the Doggets were buried there.

In Ben Jonson's time King's Head Court, near the Monument, was a tavern, celebrated for its wine, and much resorted to by roysterers. He mentions it in that wretched play of his paralytic old age, *The Magnetic Lady;* and "Fish Street dinners" are especially noted as luxurious things in one of the Roxburghe ballads.

Any spot in London that can be connected with the name of Goldsmith becomes at once ennobled. It was in Monument Yard that the poor poet, on his return from his foreign tour, served as shopman to a chemist. "He went among the London apothecaries," says Mr. Forster, "and asked them to let him spread plaisters for them, pound in their mortars, run with their medicines; but they asked him for a character, and he had none to give. 'His threadbare coat,' says the 'Percy Memoir,' 'his uncouth figure, and Hibernian dialect, caused him to meet with repeated refusals.' At last a chemist of the name of Jacob took compassion upon him; and the late Conversation Sharp used to point out a shop at the corner of Monument Yard, on Fish Street Hill, shown to him in his youth as this benevolent Mr. Jacob's." Of his struggles at this time Goldsmith himself tells us, in his "Vicar of Wakefield." "Upon my arrival in town, sir," he says, in his delightful novel, "my first care was to deliver your letter of recommendation to our cousin, who was himself in little better circumstances than I. My first scheme, you know, sir, was to be usher at an academy, and I asked his advice on the affair. Our cousin received the proposal with a true sardonic grin. 'Ay,' cried he, 'this is indeed a very pretty career that has been chalked out for you. I have been an usher at a boarding-school myself; and may I die by an anodyne necklace, but I had rather be under-turnkey in Newgate. I was up early and late; I was browbeat by the master, hated for my ugly face by the mistress, worried by the boys within, and never permitted to stir out to receive civility abroad. But are you sure you are fit for a school? Let me examine you a little. Have you been bred apprentice to the business?' 'No.' 'Then you won't do for a school. Can you dress the boys' hair?' 'No.' 'Then you won't do for a school. Have you had the smallpox?' 'No.' 'Then you won't do for a school. Can you lie three in a bed?' 'No.' 'Then you will never do for a school. Have you got a good stomach?' 'Yes.' 'Then you will by no means do for a school.'"

It was from his rough training here that Goldsmith was afterwards enabled to start as a humble physician, taking care to hide the holes in the front of his coat with his hat when he paid his visits.

CHAPTER II.

LONDON BRIDGE.

"Old Moll"—Legend of John Overy—The Old Wooden Bridge—The First Stone Bridge—Insults to Queen Eleanor—The Head of Wallace—Tournament on London Bridge—Welcome to Richard II.—Murderers' Heads—Return of Henry V.—The Poet Lydgate—Funeral of Henry V.—Brawls on London Bridge—Accident to a Ducal Barge.—Lollards' Heads on the Bridge—Entry of Henry VI.—Fall of the End Tower—Margaret of Anjou—Jack Cade and his Ruffianly Crew—Falconbridge—Other Heads on the Bridge—Bishop Fisher—Sir Thomas More—Wyatt's Rebellion—Restoration in Elizabeth's Reign—Fire on the Bridge—Removal of the Houses—Temporary Wooden Bridge—Smeaton's Repairs—Rennie's New Bridge—Laying the First Stone—Celebrated Dwellers on the Old Bridge—The Force of Habit—Jewish Tradition about London Bridge—Average Number of Passengers over the Bridge.

THERE are few spots in London where, within a very limited and strictly-defined space, so many historical events have happened, as on Old London Bridge. It was a battle-field and a place of religious worship, a resort of traders and a show-place for traitors' heads. Its Nonsuch House was one of the sights of London in the reign of Elizabeth; and the passage between its arches was one of the exploits of venturous youth, down to the very time of its removal. Though never beautiful or stately, London Bridge was one of those sights that visitors to the metropolis never forgot.

There is no certain record of when the first London Bridge was built. It is true that Dion Cassius, writing nearly two hundred years after the invasion of Britain by Claudius, speaks vaguely of a bridge across the Thames in the reign of that emperor; but it is more probable that no bridge really existed till the year 994, the year after the invasion of Olaf the Dane, in the reign of King Ethelred. It is at least certain that in the year 1008, in the reign of Ethelred II., the Unready, there was a bridge, for, according to Snorro Sturlesonius, an Icelandic historian, Olaf the Norwegian, an ally of Ethelred, attacking the Danes who had fortified themselves in Southwark, fastened his vessels to the piles of London Bridge, which the Danes held, and dragged down the whole structure. This Olaf, afterwards a martyr, is the patron saint from whom the church now standing at the south-east corner of London Bridge, derived its Christian name. Tooley Street below, a word corrupted from Saint Olave, also preserves the memory of the Norwegian king, eventually slain near Drontheim by Knut, King of Denmark.

Still, whenever the churchwardens and vestry of St. Mary Overie's, Bankside, meet over their cups, the first toast, says an antiquary who has written an exhaustive history of London Bridge, is to their church's patron saint, "Old Moll." This Old Moll was, according to Stow, Mary, the daughter of a ferryman at this part of the river, who left all her money to build a house of sisters, where the east part of St. Mary Overie's now stands. In time the nunnery became a house of priests, who erected the first wooden bridge over the Thames. There is still existing at the Church of St. Mary Overie's a skeleton effigy, which some declare to be that of Audery, the ferryman, father of the immortal Moll. The legend was that this John Overy, or Audery, was a rich and covetous man, penurious, and insanely fond of hoarding his hard-earned fees. He had a pious and beautiful daughter, who, though kept in seclusion by her father, was loved by a young gallant, who secretly wooed and won her. One day the old hunks, to save a day's food, resolved to feign himself dead for twenty-four hours, vainly expecting that his servants, from common decency, would fast till his funeral. With his daughter's help he therefore laid himself out, wrapped in a sheet, with one taper burning at his feet, and another at his head. The lean, half-starved servants, however, instead of lamenting their master's decease, leaped up overjoyed, danced round the body, broke open the larder, and fell to feasting. The old ferryman bore all this as long as flesh and blood could bear it; but at last he scrambled up in his sheet, a candle in each hand, to scold and chase the rascals from the house; when one of the boldest of them, thinking it was the devil himself, snatched up the butt-end of a broken oar, and struck out his master's brains. On hearing of this unintentional homicide, the lover came posting up to London so fast that his horse stumbled, and the eager lover, alas! broke his neck. On this second misfortune, Mary Overy, shrouding her beauty in a veil, retired into a cloister for life. The corpse of the old miser was refused Christian burial, he being deemed by the clergy a wicked and excommunicated man; the friars of Bermondsey Abbey, however, in the absence of their father abbot, were bribed to give the body "a little earth, for charity." The abbot on his return, enraged at the friars' cupidity, had the corpse dug up and thrown on the back of an ass, that was then turned out of the abbey gates. The patient beast carried the corpse up Kent Street, and shook it off under the gibbet near the small pond once called St. Thomas à Waterings, where it was roughly interred. The ferryman's effigy referred to before is really, as Gough, in his "Sepulchral Monuments," says most of such figures are, the work of the fifteenth century. Now the real Audery, if he lived at all, lived long before the Conquest, for the first wooden bridge was, it is thought, probably built to stop the Danish pirate-vessels.

The first wooden bridge was destroyed by a terrific flood and storm, mentioned in the "Chronicle of Florence of Worcester," which, in the year 1090, blew down six hundred London houses, and lifted the roof off Bow Church. In the second year of Stephen a fire, that swept away all the wooden houses of London from Aldgate to St. Paul's, destroyed the second wooden bridge.

The first London Bridge of stone was begun in 1176, by Peter, a priest and chaplain of St. Mary Colechurch, a building which, till the Great Fire made short work of it, stood in Conyhoop Lane, on the north side of the Poultry. There long existed a senseless tradition that pious Peter of the Poultry reared the arches of his bridge upon woolpacks; the fact, perhaps, being that Henry II. generously gave towards the building a new tax levied upon his subjects' wool. Peter's bridge, which occupied thirty-three years in its construction, boasted nineteen pointed stone arches, and was 926 feet long, and 40 feet wide. It included a wooden drawbridge, and the piers were raised upon platforms (called starlings) of strong elm piles, covered by thick planks bolted together, that impeded the passage of barges. On one of the piers was erected a two-storeyed chapel, forty feet high and sixty feet long, to St. Thomas à Becket. The lower chapel could be entered either from the chapel above or from the river, by a flight of stone stairs. The founder himself was buried under the chapel staircase. Peter's bridge was partly destroyed by a great fire in 1212, four years after it was finished, and while its stones were still sharp and white. There were even then houses upon it, and gate-towers; and many people crowding to help, or to see the sight, got wedged in between two fires by a shifting of the wind, and being unable to escape, some three thousand were either burnt or drowned.

King John, after this, granted certain tolls, levied on foreign merchants, towards the bridge repairs. Henry III., according to a patent-roll dated from Portsmouth, 1252, permitted certain monks, called the Brethren of London Bridge, with his especial sanction, to travel over England and collect alms. In this same reign (1263) the bridge became the scene of great scorn and insult, shown by the turbulent citizens to Henry's queen, Eleanor of Provence, who was opposed to the people's friends, the barons, who were still contending for the final settlement of Magna Charta. As the queen and her ladies, in their gilded barge, were on their way to Windsor, and preparing to shoot the dangerous bridge, the rabble above assailed her with shouts and reproaches, and casting heavy stones and mud into her boat, at her and her bright-clothed maidens, drove them back to the Tower, where the king was garrisoned. Towards the end of the same year, when Simon de Montfort, Earl of Leicester, marched on London, the king and his forces occupied Southwark, and, to thwart the citizens, locked up the bridge-gates, and threw the ponderous keys into the Thames. But no locks can bar out Fate. The gates were broken open by a flood of citizens, the king was driven back, and Simon entered London. After the battle of Evesham, where the great earl fell, the king, perhaps remembering old grudges, took the half-ruinous bridge into his own hands and delivered it over to the queen, who sadly neglected it. There were great complaints of this neglect in the reign of Edward I., and again the Holy Brothers went forth to collect alms throughout the land. The king gave lands also for the support of the bridge—namely, near the Mansion House, Old Change, and Ivy Lane. He also appointed tolls—every man on foot, with merchandise, to pay one farthing; every horseman, one penny; every pack carried on horseback, one halfpenny. This same year (1281) four arches of London Bridge were carried away by the same thaw-flood that destroyed Rochester Bridge.

The reign of Edward I. was disgraced by the cruel revenge taken by the warlike monarch on William Wallace. In August, 1305, on Edward's return from the fourth invasion of Scotland, "this man of Belial," as Matthew of Westminster calls Wallace, was drawn on a sledge to Smithfield, there hanged, embowelled, beheaded, quartered, and his head set on a pole on London Bridge. An old ballad in the Harleian Collection, describing the execution of Simon Fraser, another Scotch guerilla leader, in the following year, concludes thus—

" Many was the wives-chil' that looked on him that day,
    And said, Alas ! that he was born, and so vilely forlorn,
    So fierce man as he was.
    Now stands the head above the town bridge,
    Fast by Wallace, sooth for to say."

The heads of these two Scotch patriots were, no doubt, placed side by side on the gate at the north or London end of the bridge.

The troublous reign of the young profligate, Richard II., brought more fighting to the bridge, for

Wat Tyler and his fierce Kentish and Surrey men then came chafing to the gates, which the Lord Mayor, William Walworth, had chained and barred, pulling up the drawbridge. Upon this the wild men shouted across to the wardens of the bridge to let it down, or they would destroy them all, and from sheer fear the wardens yielded. Through that savage crowd the Brethren of the Bridge, as Thomas of Walsingham says, came passing with processions and prayers for peace.

In 1390 fighting of a gayer and less bloodthirsty kind took place on the bridge. No dandy modern tournament this, but a genuine grapple with spear, sword, and dagger. Sir David Lindsay, of Glenesk, who had married a daughter of Robert II., King of Scotland, challenged to the joust Lord Wells, our ambassador in Scotland, a man described by Andrew of Wyntoun, a poetical Scotch chronicler, as being

"Manful, stout, and of good pith,
And high of heart he was therewith."

Sir David arrived from Scotland with twenty-nine attendants and thirty horses. The king presided at the tournament. The arms which Lindsay bore on his shield, banner, and trappings were gules, a fesse chequé argent and azure; those of Wells, or, a lion rampant, double queué, sable. At the first shock the spears broke, and the crowd shouted that Lindsay was tied to his saddle. The earl at that leaped off his charger, vaulted back, and dashed on to the collision. At the third crash Wells fell heavily, as if dead. In the final grapple Lindsay, fastening his dagger into the armour of the English knight, lifted him from the ground and dashed him, finally vanquished, to the earth. According to Andrew of Wyntoun, the king called out from his "summer castle," "Good cousin Lindsay, do forth that thou should do this day;" but the generous Scotchman threw himself on Wells and embraced him till he revived. Nor did he stop there; during Wells's sickness of three months Lindsay visited him in the gentlest manner, even like the most courteous companion, and did not omit one day. "For he had fought," says Boethius, "without anger, and but for glory." And to commemorate that glorious St. George's day, the Scotch knight founded a chantry at Dundee, with a gift of forty-eight marks (£32) yearly, for seven priests and divers virgins to sing anthems to the patron saint of England.

In 1392, when Richard II. returned to London, reconciled to the citizens, who had resented his reckless extravagance, London Bridge was the centre of splendid pageants. At the bridge-gate the citizens presented the handsome young scapegrace with a milk-white charger, caparisoned in cloth of gold and hung with silver bells, and gave the queen a white palfrey, caparisoned in white and red; while from every window hung cloths of gold and silver. The citizens ended by redeeming their forfeited charter by the outrageous payment of £10,000.

In 1396, when Richard had lost his first queen, Anne of Bohemia, and married the child-daughter of Charles VI. of France, the crowd was so great to welcome the young queen, that at London Bridge nine persons were crushed to death in the crowd. The reign of Richard II. was indeed a memorable one for London Bridge.

The year when Richard II. was deposed, Henry of Lancaster laid rough hands on four knights who had three years before smothered the old Duke of Gloucester, by the commands of the king, his nephew. The murderers were dragged to Cheapside, and there had their hands lopped off at a fishmonger's stall. The heads were then spiked over the gate of London Bridge, and the bodies strung together on a gibbet. Nor did these heads long remain unaccompanied, for in 1407–8 Henry Percy, Earl of Northumberland, was beheaded, while Lord Bardolf, one of his adherents who had joined in a northern insurrection, was quartered, and the earl's head and a flitch of unfortunate Bardolf were set up on London Bridge.

There was a great rejoicing on London Bridge when Henry V. returned with his long train of French captives from the red field of Agincourt, in November, 1415. The Mayor of London, with all the aldermen and crafts, in scarlet gowns and red and white hoods, welcomed him back to his capital; and on the gate-tower stood a male and a female giant, the former having the keys of the City hanging from a staff, while trumpeters with horns and clarions sounded welcome to the conqueror of the French. In front of the gate was written, "The King's City of Justice." On a column on one side was an antelope, with a shield of the royal arms hanging round his neck, and holding a sceptre, which he offered to the king, in his right foot. On the opposite column stood a lion rampant, with the king's banner in his dexter claw. At the foot of the bridge rose a painted tower, with an effigy of St. George in complete armour in the midst, under a tabernacle. The saint's head was crowned with laurel interwoven with gems, and behind him spread a tapestry emblazoned with escutcheons. The turrets, embossed with the royal arms, were plumed with banners. Across the tower ran two scrolls, with the mottoes, "To God only be honour and glory," and "The streams of the river make glad the city of God." In the house adjoining stood bright-faced children singing welcome to the king, accompanied by the melody of organs. The hero of Agincourt rode conspicuous above all on a courser trapped with parti-colours, one-half blue velvet embroidered with antelopes, the arms of the De Bohun family, having large flowers springing between their horns. These trappings were afterwards utilised as copes for Westminster Abbey.

Lydgate, that Suffolk monk who succeeded

Seven years after this rejoicing day, the corpse of the young hero, aged thirty-four, was borne over the bridge on its way from Vincennes to Westminster Abbey. On a bier covered with red silk and beaten gold lay a painted effigy of the king, robed and crowned, and holding sceptre, ball, and cross. Six richly-harnessed horses drew the chariot, the hangings blazoned with the arms of St. George, Normandy, King Arthur, St. Edward the Confessor, France, and France and England

REMAINS OF THE CHAPEL OF ST. THOMAS, OLD LONDON BRIDGE (*page* 10).   *From a View taken during its demolition.*

Chaucer in the bead-roll of English poets, wrote a poem on this day's celebrations. "Hail, London!" he makes the king exclaim at the first sight of the red roofs; "Christ you keep from every care." The last verse of the quaint poem runs thus :—

> "And at the drawbridge that is fast by
> Two towers there were up pight ;
> An antelope and a lion standing hym by,
> Above them Saint George our lady's knight,
> Beside him many an angel bright ;
> 'Benedictus,' they gan sing,
> 'Qui venit in nomine Domini, Godde's knight.
> Gracia Dei with you doth spring.'
> Wot we right well that thus it was—
> Gloria tibi Trinitas."

quarterly. A costly canopy was held over the royal bier ; and ten bishops, in their pontificals, with mitred abbots, priests, and innumerable citizens, met the corpse and received it with due honour, the priests singing a dirge. Three hundred torch-bearers, habited in white, surrounded the bier. After them came 5,000 mounted men-at-arms, in black armour, holding their spears reversed ; and nobles followed, bearing pennons, banners, and bannerolls; while twelve captains preceded, carrying the king's heraldic achievement. After the body came all the servants of the household, in black, James I. of Scotland as chief mourner, with the princes and lords of the royal blood clad in sable ; while at the distance of two miles followed Queen Katherine and her long train of ladies.

Readers of Shakespeare will remember, in the first part of *Henry VI.*, how he makes the serving-men of the Protector Gloucester wrangle with the retainers of Cardinal Beaufort, till tawny coat beats blue, and blue pommels tawny. Brawls like this took place twice on London Bridge, and the proud and ambitious cardinal on one occasion assembled

a weaver of Abingdon, who had threatened to make priests' heads "as plentiful as sheep's heads," was spiked upon the battlements. The very next year the child-king, Henry VI., who had been crowned at Notre Dame in 1431, entered London over this bridge. Lydgate, like a true laureate, careless who or what the new king might be, nibbed his ready pen, and was at it again with ready verse. At the drawbridge there was a tower, he says, hung with silk and arras, from

LONDON BRIDGE. (*From a Print dated* 1796.)

his archers at his Bankside palace, and attempted to storm the bridge.

The dangers of "shooting" London Bridge were exemplified as early as 1428 (in the same reign—Henry VI.). "The barge of the Duke of Norfolk, starting from St. Mary Overie's, with many a gentle-man, squire, and yeoman, about half-past four of the clock on a November afternoon, struck (through bad steering) on a starling of London Bridge, and sank." The duke and two or three other gentlemen fortunately leaped on the piles, and so were saved by ropes cast down from the parapet above ; the rest perished.

Several Lollards' heads had already adorned the bridge ; and in 1431 the skull of a rough reformer,

which issued three empresses—Nature, Grace, and Fortune.

> "And at his coming, of excellent beauty,
>   Benign of part, most womanly of cheer,
>   There issued out empresses three,
>   Their hair displayed, as Phœbus in his sphere,
>   With crownets of gold and stones clear,
>   At whose outcoming they gave such a light
>   That the beholders were stonied in their sight."

With these empresses came fourteen maidens, all clad in white, who presented the king with gifts, and sang a roundel of welcome.

If Old London Bridge had a fault, it was, perhaps, its habit of occasionally partly falling down. This it did as early as 1437, when the great stone gate and tower on the Southwark end, with two arches, subsided into the Thames.

There was another gala day for the bridge in 1445, when the proud and impetuous William de la Pole, afterwards Duke of Suffolk, brought over Margaret, daughter of René (that weak, poetical monarch, immortalised in "Anne of Geierstein"), as a bride for the young King of England, and the City welcomed her on their river threshold. The Duke of Gloucester, who had opposed the match, preceded her, with 500 men clad in his ducal livery, and with gilt badges on their arms ; and the mayor and aldermen rode on in scarlet, followed by the City companies in blue gowns and red hoods. Again Lydgate tuned his ready harp, and produced some certainly most unprophetic verses, in which he called the savage Margaret—

"The dove that brought the branch of peace,
    Resembling your simpleness, Columbyne."

In 1450, and the very month after Margaret's favourite, De la Pole, had been seized in Dover Roads, and his head brutally chopped off on the side of a boat, the great insurrection under Jack Cade broke out in Kent. After routing a detachment of the royal troops at Sevenoaks, Cade marched towards London, and the commons of Essex mustering threateningly at Mile End, the City, after some debate, admitted Cade over London Bridge. As the rebel passed over the echoing drawbridge, he slashed in two the ropes that supported it. Three days after, the citizens, irritated at his robberies, barred up the bridge at night, and penned him close in his head-quarters at Southwark. The rebels then flew to arms, and tried to force a passage, eventually winning the drawbridge, and burning many of the houses which stood in close rows near it. Now the battle raged by St. Magnus's corner, now at the bridge-foot, Southwark side, and all the while the Tower guns thundered at the swarming, maddened men of Kent. At nine the next morning both sides, faint and weary, retired to their respective quarters. Soon afterwards Cade's army melted away ; Cade, himself a fugitive, was slain in a Kentish garden where he had hid himself; and his grim, defaced head was placed on the very bridge-gate on which he had himself but recently, in scorn and triumph, placed the ghastly head of Lord Say, the murdered Treasurer of England. Round Cade's head, when the king re-entered London, were placed the heads of nine of his captains.

At the entry of Edward IV. into London, in 1461, before his coronation, he passed over London Bridge, escorted by the mayor and his fellows, in scarlet, and 400 commoners, "well horsed and clad in green."

In 1471, when Henry was a prisoner in the Tower, the Bastard of Falconbridge, one of the deposed king's piratical partisans, made a dash to plunder London. While 3,000 of his men attacked Aldgate and Bishopsgate, the rest set fire to London Bridge, and burnt thirteen houses. But the citizens, led by Ralph Jocelyn, a brave Draper, made a gallant defence, drove off the filibusters, and chased them to Blackwall.

In 1481 another house on the bridge fell down, drowning five of its inhabitants.

The reign of Henry VII. brought more terrible trophies to London Bridge ; for in 1496 Flamock, a lawyer, and Joseph, a farrier of Bodmin, leaders of a great Cornish insurrection, contributed their heads to this decorative object. But Henry VII. was not half such a mower off of heads as that cruel Blue-beard, his son. Henry VIII., what with the wives he grew tired of, and what with the disbelievers in his ecclesiastical supremacy, kept the headsman's axe very fairly busy. First came the prior and several unfortunate Charter House monks, and then the good old Bishop of Rochester, John Fisher. The parboiled head of the good old man who would not bow the knee to Rimmon was kept, that Queen Anne Boleyn might enjoy the grateful sight. The face for a fortnight remained so ruddy and life-like, and such crowds collected to see the so-called miracle, that the king, in a rage, at last ordered the head to be thrown down into the river. The next month came the head of a far greater and wiser man, Sir Thomas More. This sacred relic More's daughter, Margaret Roper, bribed a man to remove, and drop into a boat in which she sat ; and the head was, long after, buried with her, in a vault under St. Dunstan's, Canterbury.

In Queen Mary's reign there was again fighting on London Bridge. In the year 1554, when rash Sir Thomas Wyatt led his 4,000 Kentish men to London, to stop the impending Spanish marriage, the rebel found the drawbridge cut away, the gates of London Bridge barred, and guns planted ready to receive him. Wyatt and his men dug a trench at the bridge-foot, and laid two guns. The night before Wyatt retreated to Kingston, to cross the Thames there, seven of his arquebusiers fired at a boat from the Tower, and killed a waterman on board. The next morning, the Lieutenant of the Tower turning seven cannon on the steeples of St. Olave's and St. Mary Overie's, the people of Southwark begged Wyatt to withdraw, which he generously did.

In Elizabeth's reign the bridge was restored with great splendour. The City built a new gate and tower, three storeys high, at the Southwark end—a huge pile, full of square Tudor windows, with a covered way below. About the same time was also reared that wonder of London, Nonsuch House—a huge wooden pile, four storeys high, with cupolas and turrets at each corner, brought from Holland, and erected with wooden pegs instead of nails. It stood over the seventh and eighth arches, on the north side of the drawbridge. There were carved wooden galleries outside the long lines of transom-casements, and the panels between were richly carved and gilt. In the same reign, Peter Moris, a Dutchman, established water-works at the north end of London Bridge; and, long before this, corn-mills had been erected at the south end of the same overtaxed structure. The ghastly custom of displaying the heads of the victims of the scaffold continued for many years after, both here and at the Tower. In the next reign, after the discovery of the Gunpowder Plot, the head of Father Garnet (the account of whose execution in St. Paul's Churchyard we gave in a previous chapter) was added to the horrible collection on the bridge.

In 1632 forty-two houses on the north side of the bridge were destroyed by a fire, occasioned by a careless servant setting a tub of hot ashes under a staircase; and the Great Fire of 1666 laid low several houses on the same side of the bridge.

There are several old proverbs about London Bridge still extant. Two of these—"If London Bridge had fewer eyes it would see better," and "London Bridge was made for wise men to go over and fools to go under"—point to the danger of the old passage past the starlings.

The old bridge had by the beginning of the eighteenth century become perilously ruinous. Pennant speaks of remembering the street as dark, narrow, and dangerous; the houses overhung the road in such a terrific manner as almost to shut out the daylight, and arches of timber crossed the street to keep the shaky old tenements from falling on each other. Indeed, Providence alone kept together the long-toppling, dilapidated structure, that was perilous above and dangerous below. "Nothing but use," says that agreeable and vivacious writer, Pennant, "could preserve the repose of the inmates, who soon grew deaf to the noise of the falling waters, the clamour of watermen, and the frequent shrieks of drowning wretches." Though many booksellers and other tradesmen affected the great thoroughfare between Kent, Surrey, and Middlesex, the bridge houses were, in the reign of George II., chiefly tenanted by pin and needle makers; and

economical ladies were accustomed to drive there from the west end of the town to make cheap purchases.

Although the roadway had been widened in the reigns of James II. and William, the double lines of rickety houses were not removed till 1757–60 (George II.). During their removal three pots of Elizabethan money were dug up among the ruins.

In 1758, a temporary wooden bridge, built over the Thames while repairs of the old bridge were going on, was destroyed by fire, it was supposed by some footman in passing dropping his link among the woodwork. Messrs. Taylor and Dance, the repairers, chopped the old bridge in two, and built a new centre arch; but the join became so insecure that few persons would venture over it. The celebrated Smeaton was called in, in 1761, and he advised the Corporation to buy back the stone of the old City gates, pulled down and sold the year before, to at once strengthen the shaky starlings. This was done, but proved a mere makeshift, and in 1768 the starlings again became loose, and an incessant wail of fresh complaints arose. The repairs were calculated at £2,500 yearly; and it was rather unfeelingly computed that fifty watermen, bargemen, or seamen, valued at £20,000, were annually drowned in passing the dangerous bridge. In 1823, the City, in sheer desperation, resolved on a new bridge, 100 feet westward of the old, and in 1824 Mr. Rennie began the work by removing 182 houses. The earlier bridges had been eastward, and facing St. Botolph's. During the excavations coins were discovered of Augustus, Vespasian, and later Roman emperors, besides many Nuremberg and tradesmen's tokens. There were also dredged up brass rings, buckles, iron keys, silver spoons, a gilt dagger, an iron spear-head, some carved stones, a bronze lamp, with a head of Bacchus, and a silver effigy of Harpocrates, the god of silence. This figure, having attached to it a large gold ring, and a chain of pure gold, is supposed to have been a priest's amulet, to be worn at religious ceremonies. The bridge cost £506,000. The first stone was laid in June, 1825, by the Right Honourable John Garratt, Lord Mayor, the Duke of York being present.

Among the celebrated persons who have resided on London Bridge there may be mentioned, among the most eminent, Hans Holbein, the great painter of Henry VIII.'s court; Peter Monamy, the marine painter, apprenticed to a sign-painter on the bridge —he died in 1749; Jack Laguerre, the humorist, singer, player, and scene-painter, son of the Laguerre satirised by Pope; and Crispin Tucker, a waggish bookseller and author, who was intimate with Pope and Swift, and who lived under the southern gate, in a rickety bow-windowed shop, where Hogarth, when young, and engraving for old John Bowles, of the Black Horse, Cornhill, had once resided. This Bowles was the generous man who used to buy Hogarth's plates by weight, and who once offered an artist, who was going abroad on a sketching tour, clean sheets of copper for all the engravings he chose to send over.

The second edition of that curious anecdotic old book, "Cocker's Dictionary," the compilation of the celebrated penman and arithmetician, whose name has grown into a proverb, was "printed for T. Norris, at the Looking-Glass on London Bridge; C. Brown, at the Crown in Newgate Street; and A. Bettesworth, at the Red Lyon in Pater-noster-row. 1715."

One anecdote of the old bridge must not be forgotten. Mr. Baldwin, haberdasher, living in the house over the chapel, was ordered, when an old man of seventy-one, to go to Chislehurst for change of air. But the invalid found he could not sleep in the country for want of the accustomed sound of the roar

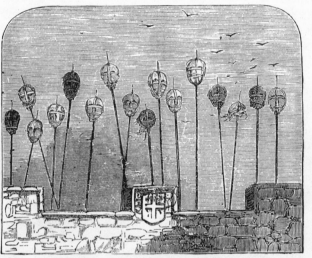

HEADS ON OLD LONDON BRIDGE.

and rush of the tide under the old ruinous arches. In 1798 the chapel was a paper warehouse. Within legal memory, says the *Morning Advertiser* of that date, "service has been performed there every Sabbath and saint's-day."

The English Jews still have a very curious tradition which associates London Bridge with the story of the expulsion from England of their persecuted forefathers in the reign of Edward I. Though few Jews have probably ever read Holinshed, the legend is there to be found, and runs thus :—"A sort of the richest of them," says Holinshed, "being shipped with their treasure in a mighty tall ship, which they had hired, when the same was under sail and got down the Thames, towards the mouth of the river, near Queenborough, the master-mariner bethought him of a wile, and caused his men to cast anchor, and so rode at the same, till the ship, by ebbing of the stream,

remained on the dry sands. The master herewith enticed the Jews to walk out with him on land for recreation ; and at length, when he understood the tide to be coming in, he got him back to the ship, whither he was drawn up by a cord.

"The Jews made not so much haste as he did, because they were not aware of the danger ; but when they perceived how the matter stood, they cried to him for help ; howbeit he told them that they ought to cry rather unto Moses, by whose conduct their fathers passed through the Red Sea, and therefore, if they would call to him for help, he was able enough to help them out of those raging floods, which now came in upon them. They cried, indeed, but no succour appeared, and so they were swallowed up in the water. The master returned with the ship, and told the king how he had used the matter, and had both thanks and reward, as some have written ; but others affirm (and more truly, as should seem) that divers of those mariners, which dealt so wickedly against the Jews, were hanged for their wicked practice, and so received a just reward of their fraudulent and mischievous dealing."

That this story of Holinshed is true there seems little doubt, as the modern English Jews have preserved it by tradition, but with an altered locality. Mr. Margoliouth, an Anglo-Jewish writer, says :— "The spot in the river Thames, where many of the poor exiles were drowned by the perfidy of a master-mariner, is under the influence of ceaseless rage ; and however calm and serene the river is elsewhere, that place is furiously boisterous. It is, moreover, affirmed that this relentless agitation is situated under London Bridge. There are, even at the present day, some old-fashioned Hebrew families who implicitly credit the outrageous fury of the Thames. A small boat is now and then observed by a Hebrew observer, filled with young and old credulous Jews, steering towards the supposed spot, in order to see and hear the noisy sympathy of the waters. There are many traditions on the subject."

An average day of four-and-twenty hours will

witness (it was computed some years ago) more than 168,000 persons passing across the present bridge from either side—107,000 on foot, and 61,000 in vehicles. These vehicles, during the same average day of twenty-four hours, number 20,498, including fifty-four horses that are led or ridden. Every day since then has increased the vast and tumultuous procession of human beings that momentarily pass in and out of London. In what congestion of all traffic this will end, or how soon that congestion will come to pass, it is quite impossible to say; while by what efforts of engineering genius London will eventually be rendered traversable, we are equally ignorant.

CHAPTER III.

UPPER THAMES STREET.

Noblemen's Mansions in Thames Street—Clarence's House—Queen's Pin Money—The old Legend of Queen Eleanor—The "Three Cranes" in the Vintry—Cromwell's Widow—Caxton's Patron—Vintners' Hall—Old Wines—Wine Patentees—The Vintners' Swans—The Duke of Buckingham's House on College Hill—Dryden's Zimri—George Villiers—The Mercers' School, College Hill—St. Michael's Church—Cleveland the Poet.

AMONG the great mansions and noblemen's palaces that once abounded in this narrow river-side street, we must first of all touch at Cold Harbour, the residence of many great merchants and princes of old time. It is first mentioned, as Stow tells us, in the 13th of Edward II., when Sir John Abel, Knight, let it to Henry Stow, a draper. It was then called Cold Harbrough, in the parish of All Saints ad Fœnum (All Hallows in the Hay), so named from an adjoining hay-wharf. Bequeathed to the Bigots, it was sold by them, in the reign of Edward III., to the well-known London merchant, Sir John Poultney, Draper, four times Mayor of London, and was then called Poultney's Inn. Sir John gave or let it to Humphrey de Bohun, Earl of Hereford and Essex, for one rose at Midsummer, to be given to him and his heirs for all services. In 1397 Richard II. dined there, with his half-brother John Holland, Earl of Huntingdon, who then lodged in Poultney's Inn, still accounted, as Stow says, "a right fair and stately house." The next year, Edmund, Earl of Cambridge, lodged in it. It still retained its old name in 1410, when Henry IV. granted the house to Prince Hal for the term of his life, starting the young reveller fairly by giving him a generous order on the collector of the customs for twenty casks and one pipe of red Gascony wine, free of duty. In 1472 the river-side mansion belonged to Henry Holland, Duke of Exeter. This duke was the unfortunate Lancastrian (great-grandson of John of Ghent) who, being severely wounded in the battle of Barnet, was conveyed by one of his faithful servants to the Sanctuary at Westminster. He remained in the custody of Edward IV., with the weekly dole of half a mark. The duke hoped to have obtained a pardon from the York party through the influence of his wife, Ann, who was the king's eldest sister. But flight and suffering had made both factions remorseless. This faithless wife obtaining a divorce, married Sir Thomas St. Leger; and not long after, the duke's dead body was found floating in the sea between Dover and Calais. He had either been murdered or drowned in trying to escape from England. Thus the Duke of Exeter's Inn suffered from the victory of Edward, as his neighbour's, the great Earl of Worcester's had paid the penalties of Henry's temporary restoration in 1470. Richard III., grateful to the Heralds for standing up for his strong-handed usurpation, gave Cold Harbour to the Heralds, who, however, were afterwards turned out by Cuthbert Tunstal, Bishop of Durham, whom Henry VIII. had forced out of Durham House in the Strand. In the reign of Edward VI., just before the death of that boy of promise, the ambitious Earl of Northumberland, wishing to win the chief nobles to his side, gave Cold Harbour to Francis, the fifth Earl of Shrewsbury, and its name was then changed to Shrewsbury House (1553), six days before the young king's death. The next earl (guardian for fifteen years of Mary Queen of Scots) took the house down, and built in its place a number of small tenements, and it then became the haunt of poverty, as we see by the following extracts from old writers :—

> "Or thence thy starvèd brother live and die,
> Within the Cold Coal-harbour sanctuary."
> *Bishop Hall's "Satires,"* b. v., s. 1.

"*Morose.* Your knighthood itself shall come on its knees, and it shall be rejected ; . . . or it (knighthood) shall do worse—take sanctuary in Cole-Harbour, and fast."—*Ben Jonson, "The Silent Woman,"* act ii., sc. 1.

"*Old Harding.* And though the beggar's brat—his wife, I mean—
Should, for the want of lodging, sleep on stalls,
Or lodge in stocks or cages, would your charities
Take her to better harbour?

"*John.* Unless to Cold Harbour, where, of twenty chimneys standing, you shall scarce, in a whole winter, see two smoking. We harbour her? Bridewell shall first."—*Heywood and Rowley, "Fortune by Land and Sea,"* 4to, 1655.

On the east side of Dowgate, near the church of St. Mary Bothaw, formerly stood a celebrated old house frequently mentioned by Stow and the old chroniclers, and called, we know not why, the Erber. Edward III. is known to have given it to one of the Scropes. The last Scrope, in the reign of Henry IV., gave it to his brother, Ralph Neville, Earl of Westmoreland, who married Joan, daughter of the Duke of Lancaster. This earl was the son

Clarence obtained, after the battle of Barnet, a grant of the house in right of his wife, Isabel, daughter of Warwick. After Clarence's murder in the Tower, his younger brother, Richard of Gloucester—the Crookback and monster usurper of Shakespeare—occupied the Thames Street house, repaired it, and called it "the King's Palace." Ralph Darnel, a yeoman of the Crown, kept the building for King Richard till that hot day at Bosworth Field rendered such matters indifferent to him; and Henry VII. then gave it back to Edward, son of the Duke of Clarence, who kept it till his attainder in 1500. It was rebuilt in 1584

NONSUCH HOUSE. (*See page* 15.)

of John, Lord Neville of Raby, the knightly companion of Edward III., and who had shared with his chivalrous monarch the glory won in France. From the earl it descended to the king-making Earl of Warwick, that great warrior, who looms like a giant through the red battle-fields of the Wars of the Roses, and who lodged his father, the Earl of Salisbury, and 500 men here in the congress of 1458, when there was a pretended reconciliation of the Houses of York and Lancaster, to be followed in two years by the battle of Northampton and the deposition of the weak king. The great earl himself lived in Warwick Lane, Newgate Street. After the death of this maker and unmaker of kings, the house passed to the "false, fleeting, perjured Clarence," who had fought on both sides, and, luckily for himself, at last on the victorious side.

by Sir Thomas Pullison (a Draper, ancestor of the Stanleys), Lord Mayor of London, and was afterwards honoured by being the residence of that great sea-king, Sir Francis Drake, who must have found it convenient for dropping down to Greenwich.

Mr. Jesse, in writing of the Neville family, dwells with much pathos on the fate of the family that once held the Erber. "When the granddaughter of John of Gaunt," he says, "sat in her domestic circle, watching complacently the childish sports and listening to the joyous laughter of her young progeny, how little could she have anticipated the strange fate which awaited them! Her husband perished on the bloody field of Wakefield; her first-born, afterwards Edward IV., followed in the ambitious footsteps of his father, and waded through bloodshed to a throne; her second son, Edmund,

Earl of Rutland, perished at the battle of Wakefield; her third son, 'false, fleeting, perjured Clarence,' died in the dungeons of the Tower; and her youngest son, Richard, succeeded to a throne and a bloody death. The career of her daughters was also remarkable. Ann, her eldest daughter, married Henry Holland, Duke of Exeter, whose splendid fortunes and mysterious fate are so well known. Elizabeth, the second daughter, became the wife of John de la Pole, Duke of Suffolk, and lived to see

Holy Trinity within Aldgate. King John is said to have given it to his mother, Eleanor, queen of Henry II. If two vessels came up the river together, one had to discharge at Billingsgate and one at Queenhithe; if three, two went to Queenhithe and one to Billingsgate. These tolls were, in fact, the Queen of England's pin-money. Vessels which brought corn from the Cinque Ports usually discharged their cargoes here. At the end of the fifteenth century, however, Fabian says the harbour

THE "THREE CRANES," THAMES STREET.   (*See page* 20.)

her son, the second duke, decapitated on Tower Hill for his attachment to the House of York. Lastly, her third daughter, Margaret, married Charles, Duke of Burgundy. This lady's persevering hostility to Henry VII., and open support of the claims of Perkin Warbeck, believing him to be the last male heir of the House of Plantagenet, have rendered her name conspicuous in history."

Queenhithe—or Queenhive, as it was corruptly called by the Elizabethan dramatists—was originally, according to Stow, called "Edred's Hythe," or bank, from some Saxon owner of that part of Thames Street. It was royal property as early as the reign of King Stephen, who bestowed it upon William de Ypres, who left it to the convent of the

dues at Queenhithe were worth only £15 a year. A century later (Stow's time) it was quite forsaken. In the curious old ballad quoted with such *naïveté* in Peele's chronicle-play of Edward I., Queen Eleanor (Eleanor of Castile, wife of Edward I.), having taken a false oath, sinks into the ground at Charing Cross and rises again at Queenhithe. The ballad-writer makes her say:—

"If that upon so vile a thing
    Her heart did ever think,
She wished the ground might open wide,
    And therein she might sink.

"With that at Charing Cross she sunk
    Into the ground alive,
And after rose to life again
    In London at Queenhithe."

It was at Queenhithe that the rash Essex, the favourite of Elizabeth, took boat after the affray in the City, when he was beginning to be hemmed in, and he rowed back from here to Essex House in the Strand, where he was soon after besieged. He might as well, poor fellow! have pulled straight to the Tower, and ordered the block to be got ready.

St. Nicholas Olave's stood on the west side of Bread Street Hill, in the ward of Queenhithe. That it is of great antiquity is evident from Gilbert Foliot, Bishop of London, having given the same to the Dean and Chapter of St. Paul's about the year 1172; and its name is supposed to be derived from Olave, or Olaus, King of Norway. The church sharing the common fate in the flames of 1666, was not rebuilt, and the parish was annexed to the church, of St. Nicholas Cole Abbey. The following epitaph relating to Blitheman, organist of the Queen's Chapel, and buried in St. Nicholas, has been preserved :—

> " Here Blitheman lies, a worthy wight,
>   Who feared God above ;
> A friend to all, a foe to none,
>   Whom rich and poore did love.
> Of Prince's Chapel, gentleman,
>   Unto his dying day,
> Whom all tooke great delight to heare
>   Him on the organs play ;
> Whose passing skill in musicke's art
>   A scholar left behind,
> *John Bull* (by name), his master's veine
>   Expressing in each kind.
> But nothing here continues long,
>   Nor resting-place can have :
> His soul departed hence to heaven,
>   His body here in grave.
> " He died on Whitsunday, Anno Domini 1591."

The "Three Cranes" was formerly a favourite London sign. Instead of the three cranes which in the Vintry used to lift the barrels of wine, three birds were represented. The "Three Cranes" in Thames Street was a famous tavern as early as the reign of James I. It was one of the taverns frequented by the wits in Ben Jonson's time. In one of his plays he says :—

> " A pox o' these pretenders to wit ! your 'Three Cranes,' ' Mitre,' and 'Mermaid' men! Not a corn of true salt, not a grain of right mustard amongst them all."—*Bartholomew Fair*, act i., sc. 1.

And in another of his plays we have :—

> " *Iniquity.* Nay, boy, I will bring thee to the sluts and the roysters,
> At Billingsgate, feasting with claret-wine and oysters ;
> From thence shoot the bridge, child, to the ' Cranes,' in the Vintry,
> And see there the gimblets how they make their entry.'
>   *Ben Jonson, "The Devil is an Ass,"* act i., sc. 1.

On the 23rd of January, 1661–2, Pepys suffered a bitter mortification of the flesh in having to dine at this tavern with some poor relations. The sufferings of the snobbish secretary must have been intense :—" By invitacion to my uncle Fenner's, where I found his new wife, a *pitiful, old, ugly, ill-bred woman* in a hatt, a midwife. Here were many of his, and as many of her relations, *sorry, mean people ;* and after choosing our gloves we all went over to the 'Three Crane' Taverne, and (though the best room of the house), in such a narrow dogg-hole we were crammed (and I believe we were near forty), that it made me loath my company and victuals, and a sorry poor dinner it was too."

The *Mercurius Politicus* of May 14th, 1660, says : " Information was given to the Council of State that several of His Majesty's goods were kept at a fruiterer's warehouse near the 'Three Cranes,' in Thames Street, for the use of Mistress Elizabeth Cromwell, wife to Oliver Cromwell, sometime called Protector ; and the Council ordered that persons be appointed to view them, and seventeen cart-loads of rich house stuff was taken from thence and brought to Whitehall, from whence they were stolen."

"New Queen Street," says Strype, " commonly called the 'Three Cranes,' in the Vintry, a good open street, especially that part next Cheapside, which is best built and inhabited. . . . At the low end of the street, next the Thames, is a pair of stairs, the usual place for the Lord Mayor and aldermen to take water at, to go to Westminster Hall, for the new Lord Mayor to be sworn before the Barons of the Exchequer. This place, with the 'Three Cranes,' is now of some account for the coster-mongers, where they have their warehouses for their fruit."

The church of St. Martin in the Vintry was sometimes, according to Stow, called by the name of St. Martin de Beremand. This church, destroyed in the Great Fire, was not rebuilt. A curious epitaph in it related to Robert Dalusse, barber in the reign of Edward IV. :—

> " As flowers in the field thus passeth life,
>   Naked, then clothed, feeble in the end ;
> It sheweth by Robert Dalusse, and Alison, his wife,
>   Christ them save from power of the Fiend."

A little to the west of Vintner's Hall once stood a most celebrated house, in Lower Thames Street, the residence of that learned nobleman, John Tiptoft, Earl of Worcester, and Lord High Treasurer of England (Edward IV.), but more distinguished to later generations as the generous patron of Caxton, our first great printer.

In the dedication of his " Cicero," Caxton says of the earl : " I mean the right virtuous and noble earl, the Earl of Worcester, which late piteously lost his life, whose soul I recommend unto your special prayers; and also in his time made many other virtuous works, which I have heard of. O good blessed Lord God, what great loss was it of that noble, virtuous, and well-disposed lord! when I remember and advertise his life, his science, and his virtue, me thinketh God displeased over the great loss of such a man, considering his estate and cunning; and also the exercise of the same, with the great labours of going on pilgrimage unto Jerusalem; visiting there the holy places that our blessed Lord Jesu Christ hallowed with his blessed presence; and shedding there his precious blood for our redemption, and from thence ascended unto his Father in heaven; and what worship had he at Rome in the presence of our Holy Father the Pope. And so in all other places unto his death, at which death every man that was there might learn to die and take his death patiently, wherein I hope, and doubt not, but that God received his soul into his everlasting bliss."

"The Earl of Worcester, while he resided in Italy, was a great collector of books. 'The Earl of Worcester,' says Laurentius Carbo, 'captivated by the charms of the Muses, hath remained three years in Italy, and now resides at Padua, for the sake of study, and detained by the civilities of the Venetians, who, being exceedingly fond of books, hath plundered, if I may so speak, our Italian libraries to enrich England.' After his return home the earl made a present of books to the University Library of Oxford, which had cost him 500 marks —a great sum in those times," &c. But this prosperity was not of long duration. A new revolution took place. Edward IV. was obliged to abandon his kingdom with great precipitation to save his life. The Earl of Worcester was not so fortunate as to escape; but, after he had concealed himself a few days, he was discovered on a high tree in the forest of Waybrig, conducted to London, condemned at Westminster, and beheaded on Tower Hill, October 15, 1470. He was accused of cruelty in the government of Ireland; but his greatest crime, and that for which he suffered, was his steady loyalty to his rightful sovereign and generous benefactor, Edward IV. "The axe," says Fuller, in his usually pithy way, "then did, at one blow, cut off more learning than was in the heads of all the surviving nobility." While the earl resided at Padua, which was about three years, during the heat of the civil wars in England, he visited Rome, and delivered an oration before Pope Pius II. (Æneas Silvius) and his cardinals, which drew tears of joy from His Holiness, and made him say aloud,

"Behold the only prince of our times who, for virtue and eloquence, may be compared to the most excellent emperors of Greece and Rome;" and yet so barbarous was the age, that this same learned man impaled forty Lancastrian prisoners at Southampton, put to death the infant children of the Irish chief Desmond, and acquired the nickname of "the Butcher of England."

Vintners' Hall—one of the most interesting buildings now existing in Thames Street, once so much inhabited by the rich and noble—stands on the river-side not far from Queenhithe.

According to worthy Stow, the Vintry, up till the 28th of Edward I., was the special spot where the Bordeaux merchants unloaded their lighters and sold their wines. Sir John Stodie, Vintner, gave the ground, in 1357 (Edward III.), to the Vintners, with all the neighbouring tenements, and there the Vintners built a fair hall, and thirteen almshouses for thirteen poor people.

The contentions between the citizens of London and the Gascon wine merchants, in the reign of Edward I., it has been remarked, would lead us to infer that the Vintners had long before that time acted as a fraternity, though not formally incorporated till the reign of Henry VI. Edward I. granted them Botolph Wharf, near Billingsgate, in the mayoralty of Henry de Valois, on their paying a silver penny annually at the feast of the Nativity of St. John the Baptist. Towards the French wars they contributed £23 6s. 8d., a greater sum than that given by the majority of the companies; and in 50 Edward III. they sent six members to the Common Council, which showed their wealth and importance.

The Saxons seem to have had vineyards. In the Norman times there was a vineyard in the Tower precincts. It is supposed this uncomfortable home-made wine was discarded when Gascony fell into our hands. Some writers who disbelieve in English wines declare that the Saxons used the English word "vineyard" for "orchard," and that wine was, after all, cider. Certain, however, it is that at Bath and other old towns there are old streets still called the Vineyard. The traffic in Bordeaux wines is said to have commenced about 1154, when Henry II. married Eleanor of Aquitaine.

"The Normans," says Herbert, "were the great carriers, and Guienne the place from whence most of our wines came." The wines enumerated are Muscadell, a rich wine; Malmsey, Rhenish; Dale wine, a sort of Rhenish; Stum, strong new wine; Gascony wine; Alicant, a Spanish wine, made of mulberries; Canary wine, or sweet Sack (the grape of which was brought from the Canaries); Sherry, the original sack, not sweet; Rumney, a sort of Spanish wine. Sack was a term loosely applied at first to all white wines. It was probably those species of wines that Fitzstephen, in the reign of Henry II., mentions to have been sold in the ships, and in wine-cellars near the public places of cookery on the Thames' bank.

There were four Vintner mayors in the reign of Edward III., and yet, says Stow, gravely, "Gascoyne wines were then sold at London not above 4d., nor Rhenish wine above 6d. the gallon." In this reign John Peeche, a fishmonger, was imprisoned and fined for having obtained a monopoly for the sale of sweet wines; and in the 6th of Henry VI., John Rainewell, Mayor of London, finding that the Lombard wine merchants adulterated their sweet wines, he, in his wrath, ordered 150 vessels to be staved in, "so that the liquor, running forth, passed through the cittie like a stream of rain-water in the sight of all the people, from whence there issued a most loathsome savour."

In 2 Henry VI. there was a petition to Parliament praying that the wine-casks from Gascony—tonnes, pipes and hogsheads—should be of full and true measure; and in 10 Henry VI. there was another petition against the adulteration of Gascon and Guienne wines, in which the writer says, "wines that formerly had been fine and fair were drinking for four or five lives."

The charter confirmed by Henry VI. forbids any but such as are enfranchised by the craft of Vintners to trade in wines from Gascony; and Gascoigners were forbidden to sell wine except in the tun or pipe. The right of search in taverns and the regulation of prices was given to four members of the Company, annually chosen. It also permitted merchant Vintners to buy cloth, and the merchants of Gascoigne to purchase dried fish in Cornwall and Devon, also herrings and cloth, in what other parts of the kingdom they please. All wines coming to London were to be unloaded above London Bridge, at the Vintry, so that the king's bottlers and gaugers might there take custom.

Charles I., always arbitrary and greedy, seems to have extorted 40s. a tun from the Vintners, and in return prohibited the wine coopers from exporting wines. Licences for retailing wine were at this time granted by the Vintners' Company for the king's benefit. He also forbade the sale of wines in bottles instead of measures.

The Vintners have six charters—Edward III., Henry VI. (two), Mary, Elizabeth, and their acting charter, 9 James I. The Vintners' arms, granted by Henry VI., are sable, a chevron cetu, three tuns argent, with a Bacchus and loving-cup for the crest.

Patents received their death-blow from the Parliament in 1641, when two patentees, Alderman Abell and Richard Kilvert, were severely fined for having obtained from Charles I. an exclusive patent for wine. The *Perfect Diurnall* of 5th February, 1641, thus notices the transaction:—"A bill was brought into the House of Commons concerning the wine business, by which it appeared that Alderman Abell and Mr. Kilvert had in their hands, which they deceived the King of, £57,000 upon the wine licence; the Vintners of London, £66,000; the wine merchants of Bristol, £1,051; all of which moneys were ordered to be immediately raised on their lands and estates, and to be employed to the public use."

A very scarce and satirical contemporaneous tract on the subject (says Herbert) gives, in a supposed dialogue between the two parties, a ludicrous exposure of this business of patent hunting. Abell and Kilvert, who in the tract are called "the two maine projectors for wine," accidentally meet, and the latter claiming acquaintance with the alderman, as one at whose house he had often been a guest, "when he kept the 'Ship' tavern behind Old Fish Street," Abell answers that he did indeed get a good estate there by retailing wines, but chiefly through finding hidden treasure in digging a vault near his cellar, or, as he terms it, "the cardinal's cellar," and without which, he adds, "I had never came to wear this gold chaine, with my thumbes under my girdle." Kilvert's proposal contains a fine piece of satire on the mode in which such patents were first obtained:—

"*Kilv.* Marry, thus: We must first pretend, both in the merchant and vintner, some gross abuses, and these no meane ones either. And that the merchant shall pay to the king forty shillings for every tun ere he shall vent it to the vintner; in lieu of which, that the vintner may be no looser, he shall rayse the price also of his wines—upon all French wines a penny in the quart, upon all Spanish wines two-pence the quart: it is no matter how the subject suffers, so we get and gaine by it. Now to cover this our craft (I will not say coinage), because all things of the like nature carry a pretence for the king's profit, so we will allow him a competent proportion of forty thousand pounds per annum; when, the power of the patent being punctually executed, will yield double at least, if not treble that sume, and returne it into the coffers of the undertakers.

"*Abell.* Mr. Kilvert, I honour thee before all the feasts in our hall. Nay, we are free Vintners and brothers of the guild, and are for the most part true Trojans, and know where to find the best butts of wine in the cellar, and will pierce them for thee; it shall be pure wine from the grape, not mixt and compounded, but real and brisk. You thinke there are no brewers but such as brew ale and beere; I tell you we do brew and cunger in our sellers, as much as any brewer of their ale. Yea, and without fire too; but so much for that. Methinkes I see myselfe in Cheapside, upon an horse richly caparisoned, and my two shrieves to attend me; and methinkes thee in thy caroch, drawn by four horses, when I shall call to thee and say, 'Friend Kilvert, give me thy hand.'

"*Kilv.* To which I shall answer, 'God bless your honour, my good Lord Maior!'"

The song we annex occurs at the end of the only printed pageant of the Vintners, and was sung in the hall. No subsequent City pageant was ever publicly performed since; that written for 1708 was not exhibited, owing to the death of Prince George of Denmark the day before. For that pageant no songs were written, so that this is the *last* song of the *last* City poet at the *last* City pageant, and a better specimen than usual of his powers :—

" Come, come, let us drink the Vintners' good health ;
'Tis the cask, not the coffer, that holds the true wealth ;
If to founders of blessings we pyramids raise,
The bowl, next the sceptre, deserves the best praise.
Then, next to the Queen, let the Vintners' fame shine ;
She gives us good laws, and they fill us good wine.

" Columbus and Cortez their sails they unfurl'd,
To discover the mines of an Indian world,
To find beds of gold so far they could roam ;
Fools ! fools ! when the wealth of the world lay at home.
The grape, the true treasure, much nearer it grew :
One Isle of Canary's worth all the Peru.

" Let misers in garrets lay up their gay store,
And keep their rich bags to live wretchedly poor ;
'Tis the cellar alone with true fame is renown'd :
Her treasure's diffusive, and cheers all around.
The gold and the gem's but the eye's gaudy toy,
But the Vintners' rich juice gives health, life, and joy."

Many of the documents of the Company kept at the first hall are supposed to have been lost in the Fire of London ; this is said to be the reason why some of the almshouse and other donations cannot be satisfactorily accounted for.

The New View of London (1708) describes Vintners' Hall as "situated on the south side of Thames Street, near Queen Street," and as "well built of brick, and large and commodious. The room," it adds, " called the Hall is paved with marble, and the walls richly wainscoted with right wainscot, enriched with fruit, leaves, &c., finely carved, as is more especially the noble screen at the east end, where the aperture into the Hall is adorned with columns, their entablature and pitched pediment ; and on acrosters are placed the figures of Bacchus between several Fames, and these between two panthers ; and there are other carved figures, as St. Martin, their patron, and the cripple, and pilasters ; there are also other embellishments of several coats of arms, &c."

Two of the London Companies—the Dyers' and the Vintners' Companies—are, with the Crown, the principal owners of swans in the Thames. These two companies have long enjoyed the privilege of keeping swans on the river, from the Metropolis to a considerable distance above Windsor. "The swans in the Thames," says Mr. Kempe, "are much less numerous than they used to be. In August, 1841, the following number of old and young swans belonged to Her Majesty and the two civic companies :—

	Old Swans.	Cygnets.	Total.
The Queen	185	47	232
The Vintners' Company.........	79	21	100
The Dyers' Company............	91	14	105
	355	82	437

At one period, however, the Vintners' Company alone possessed 500 birds.

"On the first Monday in August in every year, the swan-markers of the Crown and the two City companies go up the Thames for the purpose of inspecting and taking an account of the swans belonging to their respective employers, and marking the young birds. They proceed to the different parts of the river frequented by the swans for breeding, and other places where these birds are kept. They pay half-a-crown for each young bird to the fishermen who have made nests for the old birds, and two shillings per week to any person who during the winter has taken care of the swans by sheltering them in ponds, or otherwise protecting them from the severity of the weather. When, as it sometimes happens, the cob bird (male) of one owner mates with a pen bird (female) belonging to another, the brood are divided between the owners of the parent birds, the odd cygnet (except in Buckinghamshire) being allotted to the owner of the cob.

" The *marks* are made upon the upper mandible with a knife or other sharp instrument. The forms and devices greatly differ. Thus, the swan-mark of Eton College, which has the privilege of keeping swans on the Thames, is the armed point and feathered end of an arrow, and is represented by nail-heads on the door of one of the inner rooms of the college. The Dyers' and Vintners' marks date from the reign of Elizabeth, and anciently consisted of circles or amulets on the beak ; but the cutting of these being considered to inflict more severe pain on the birds than straight lines, the rings are now omitted, and the lines are doubled. The two nicks are probably intended for two half-lozenges, or a demi-lozengesee on each side. The V is perhaps a chevron reversed, the arms of the Company being sable, a chevron between three tuns argent ; for the true chevron could scarcely be cut on the beak of the bird without each lateral branch crossing its elongated and tender nostril ; and this, from a feeling of humanity, the marker would be disposed to avoid. That many of these swan-marks, besides being heraldic, have the adaptation of the initial letter of the word 'Vintner,' and form also the Roman numeral V, is supported by a custom at the feasts of the Vintners' Company, where one of the regular stand-up toasts of the day is, ' The Worshipful Company of Vintners with Five.' The royal swan-mark has been unchanged since the commencement of the reign of George III."

On College Hill, while intriguing with the City,

" In the first rank of these did Zimri stand;
A man so various that he seemed to be
Not one, but all mankind's epitome ;
Stiff in opinions, always in the wrong,
Was everything by starts and nothing long ;
But, in the course of one revolving moon,
Was chemist, fiddler, statesman, and buffoon ;
Then all for women, painting, rhyming, drinking,
Besides ten thousand freaks that died in thinking.
Blest madman, who could every hour employ,
With something new to wish, or to enjoy !
Railing and praising were his usual themes ;
And both, to show his judgment, in extremes :

COLD HARBOUR.   (*See page* 17.)

lived Dryden's " Zimri," the second Duke of Buckingham. In a pasquinade, preserved in the State Poems, entitled the " D. of B's. (Duke of Buckingham's) Litany," occur the following lines :—

" From damning whatever we don't understand,
From purchasing at *Dowgate* and selling in the Strand,
From calling streets by our name when we've sold the land,
          Libera nos, Domine.

" From borrowing our own house to feast scholars ill,
And then be un-chancellored against our will,
Nought left of a College but *College Hill*,
          Libera nos," &c.

Nor would our readers ever pardon us if we omitted Dryden's immortal portrait of the mercurial duke :—

So over-violent, or over-civil,
That every man with him was God or devil.
In squandering wealth was his peculiar art ;
Nothing went unrewarded but desert.
Beggar'd by fools, whom still he found too late,
He had his jest, and they had his estate.
He laughed himself from court ; then sought relief
By forming parties, but could ne'er be chief ;
For, spite of him, the weight of business fell
On Absalom and wise Achitophel."

Lord Clarendon, in his own biography, indeed, informs us that "the duke had many lodgings in several quarters of the City ; and though his Majesty had frequent intelligence where he was, yet when the serjeant-at-arms, and others, employed for his apprehension, came where he was known to have been but an hour before, he was gone from hence, or so concealed that he could not be found."

"Dryden's inimitable description," says Sir Walter Scott, who has himself nobly sketched the "Zimri" of the poet, "refers, as is well known, to the famous George Villiers, Duke of Buckingham, son of the favourite of Charles I., who was murdered by

famous administration called the Cabal, which first led Charles into unpopular and arbitrary measures, and laid the foundation for the troubles of his future reign. Buckingham changed sides about 1675, and becoming attached to the country party, made a most active figure in all proceedings which had relation to the Popish plot; intrigued deeply

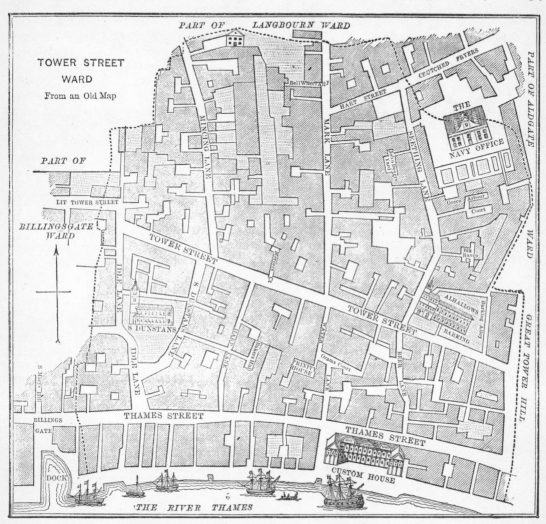

TOWER STREET WARD. (*From a Map made for Stow's Survey.*)

Felton. The Restoration put into the hands of the most lively, mercurial, ambitious, and licentious genius who ever lived, an estate of twenty thousand a year, to be squandered in every wild scheme which the lust of power, of pleasure, of licence, or of whim, could dictate to an unrestrained imagination. Being refused the situation of president of the North, he was suspected of having favoured the disaffected in that part of England, and was disgraced accordingly. But in 1666 he regained the favour of the king, and became a member of the

with Shaftesbury, and distinguished himself as a promoter of the Bill of Exclusion. Hence he stood an eminent mark for Dryden's satire, which, we may believe, was not the less poignant that the poet had sustained a personal affront, from being depicted by his grace under the character of Bayes in the *Rehearsal*. As Dryden owed the duke no favour, he has shown him none; yet, even here, the ridiculous rather than the infamous part of his character is touched upon; and the unprincipled libertine, who slew the Earl of Shrewsbury while his adulterous countess held his horse in the disguise of a page, and who boasted of caressing her before he changed the bloody clothes in which he had murdered her husband, is not exposed to hatred, while the spendthrift and castle-builder are held up to contempt."

The death of this butterfly Pope has drawn with terrible force :—

> " In the worst inn's worst room, with mat half hung,
> The floors of plaister, and the walls of dung ;
> On once a flock-bed, but repaired with straw,
> With tape-tied curtains, never meant to draw ;
> The George and Garter dangling from that bed,
> Where tawdry yellow strove with dirty red,
> Great Villiers lies ! alas, how changed from him
> That life of pleasure, and that soul of whim ;
> Gallant and gay, in Cliveden's proud alcove,
> The bower of wanton Shrewsbury and love ;
> Or just as gay at council, in a ring
> Of mimick'd statesmen, and a merry king ;
> No wit to flatter left of all his store,
> No fool to laugh at, which he valued more ;
> There, victor of his health, of fortune, friends,
> And fame, this lord of useless thousands ends."

It must, however, be allowed that the poet's shadows are too dark, for the duke died in the house of a respectable tenant in Yorkshire, from a fever caught out hunting.

The Mercers' School, College Hill, is one of the four ancient schools of London, of which number the Mercers' Company have the proud privilege of having given their generous patronage to two. It stood originally in the Old Jewry (west side), and formed part of a cemetery for strangers and a house of the Knights Hospitalers, founded during the reign of Henry II. by Thomas Fitz-Theobald de Helles, who married Agnes, a sister of the so-called martyr Thomas à Becket. The school was held in a chapel of St. Thomas of Acon (Acre). It was classed among the four City schools which received the sanction of Parliament in 1447 (Henry VI.), when "four grave clergymen and parsons" of City parishes, seeing the gross ignorance prevalent in London since Henry V. had seized many of the alien priories and religious houses in England, and so reduced the number of schools, humbly petitioned that they might be allowed to play a part in the advancement of learning. These worthy men were at once allowed to set up schools of their own founding in their respective parishes —i.e., Great Allhallows, St. Andrew's, Holborn, St. Peter's, Cornhill, and St. Mary Colechurch (St. Thomas Acons). When Henry VIII. laid his eager hands on the Abbot of St. Nicholas' princely revenues, and sold the hospital to the Mercers' Company, he expressly stipulated that the school, chapel, and cemetery should be retained. After

the Great Fire, in the Act for rebuilding the City (1676), it was expressly provided that there should be a plot of ground set apart on the west side of Old Jewry for Mercers' Chapel Grammar School. In 1787 the school was removed to No. 13, Budge Row, about thirty yards from Dowgate Hill. On the death of Mr. Waterhouse, the master, in 1804, the school was suspended for a time, and then removed to No. 20, Red Lion Court, Watling Street. There it remained till 1808, when it was removed to its present situation on College Hill. Up to 1804 it had been a free school with twenty-five scholars, the master being allowed to take private pupils. Greek and Latin were alone taught ; but after 1804 English and the modern sciences were also introduced. The school reopened with a single scholar, but soon began to take root ; and in 1805 the Company increased the number of scholars to thirty-five. There are two exhibitions of £70 each, founded by Mr. Thomas Rich, a master of the school, who died in 1672. The rules of 1804 require every boy to bring wax tapers for his use in winter. Mr. William Baxter, an eminent grammarian, who died in the year 1725, was master of this school for more than twenty years.

The list of eminent persons educated in the Mercers' school includes the wise and worthy Dean Colet, the friend of Erasmus and founder of St. Paul's School ; that great merchant, Sir Thomas Gresham ; William Fulke, master of Pembroke Hall, Cambridge, and a commentator on the Rheims Testament ; John Young, Bishop of Rochester (died 1605) ; Davenant, Bishop of Salisbury (died 1641) ; Sir Lionel Cranfield, afterwards Earl of Middlesex and Lord Treasurer to James I.; and Matthew Wren, Bishop of Ely (died 1667).

St. Michael's Paternoster Royal, College Hill, is mentioned as early as 1283, when Hugh de Derby was rector. It is interesting to us from having been rebuilt by the illustrious Richard Whittington, thrice Lord Mayor of London. Here, on the north side of the church, he built almshouses (now the site of the Mercers' School), some years since removed to Highgate ; and here, in great state, he was buried. Alas for human fame and human gratitude ! no memorial of the good man now exists at St. Michael's—not even a half-worn-out stone—not even a thin, trodden, defaced brass. The great sculptured marble tomb is gone to dust ; the banners have faded like the leaf. In the reign of Edward VI. one Mountain, an incumbent (may the earth lie heavy on him !), believing great riches of gold and jewels were buried with Whittington, dug up his remains, and, in his vexation, destroyed the tomb. In the reign of Mary the parishioners reopened the grave, to re-wrap the dishonoured body in lead. It is now beyond desecration, nor could it be sifted from the obscurer earth. In the old epitaph, which is in excellent rhyming Latin, Whittington is quaintly termed " Richardus Albificans villam."

> " Ut fragrans Nardus,
>   Fama fuit iste Richardus,
> Albificans villam,
>   Qui juste rexerat illam.
>
> *   *   *   *
>
> Pauperibus pater,
>   Et Major qui fuit urbis,
> Martins hunc vicit,
>   En ! Annos gens tibi dicit,
> Finiit ipse dies,
>   Sit sibi Christe quies.   Amen."

" This church," says Stow, " was made a College of St. Spirit and St. Mary by Richard Whittington, Mercer, four times maior, for a master, four fellows, Masters of Art, clerks, conducts, chorists, &c. ; and an almshouse, called God's house or hospital, for thirteen poor men, one of them to be tutor, and to have 16d. a week, the other twelve each of them to have 14d. the week for ever, with other necessary provision ; an hutch with three docks, a common seal, &c."

The original declaration of the executors begins thus : " The fervent desire and besy intention of a prudent, wyse, and devout man shal be to cast before and make seure the state and thende of the short liffe with dedys of mercy and pite ; and, namely, to provide for such pouer persons which grevous penuere and cruel fortune have oppressed, and be not of power to get their lyving either by craft or by any other bodily labour ; whereby that at the day of the last judgment he may take his part with them that shal be saved. This considering, the foresaid worthy and notable merchant, Richard Whyttington, the which while he lived had ryght liberal and large hands to the needy and poure people, charged streitly, in his death-bed, us his foresaid executors to ordeyne a house of almes, after his deth, for perpetual sustentacion of such poure people as is tofore rehersed ; and thereupon fully he declared his wyll unto us."

The laws of the college required that " every tutour and poor folk every day first when they rise fro their bedds, kneeling upon their knees, say a Pater Noster and an Ave Maria, with special and herty commendacion-making of the foresaid Richard Whyttington and Alice, to God and our blessed lady Maidyn Mary ; and other times of the day, when he may best and most commody have leisure thereto, for the staat of al the souls abovesaid, say two or three sauters of our Lady at the least—that is to say, threies seaven Ave Marias, with xv. Pater Nosters and three credes."

St. Michael's was destroyed in the Great Fire, and rebuilt under Wren's directions. The spire was erected in 1715. The parish of St. Martin Vintry is incorporated with that of St. Michael. In this church is Hilton's commendable picture of St. Mary Magdalene anointing the feet of Christ, presented by the directors of the British Institution in 1820. There is some good carving in the oak altar-piece below the picture. The marble font was the gift of Abraham Jordan in 1700. The monument to Sir Samuel Pennant (an ancestor of the London historian), who died in the year of his mayoralty (1750), is worthy of record, as is that of Marmaduke Langdale, a descendant of that Lord Langdale who commanded the left wing of King Charles's army in the battle of Naseby. The lower storey of the steeple is formed by eight projecting Ionic columns, bearing an entablature and vases, and the effect, though fantastic, is not unpicturesque.

In St. Michael's lies buried that brave young Cavalier poet, John Cleveland, as clever and as unfortunate a bard as his contemporary, poor Lovelace. Expelled from a Cambridge fellowship as a malignant, Cleveland mounted his horse and drew sword for King Charles, for whom he wrote or fought till his life's end. He was thrown into prison by Cromwell, who let him out on his telling him that he was too poor to purchase his release. The poet then took up his abode in Gray's Inn, close to Butler, the author of " Hudibras," and there they established a nightly Cavalier club. Cleveland died young, and his friend, good Bishop Pearson, preached his funeral sermon. Of the poet's quick, overstrained fancy, and of his bitter satire against the Scotch, who had betrayed King Charles for money, we give two examples :—

UPON PHILLIS WALKING IN A MORNING BEFORE SUNRISE.

> " The sluggish morn as yet undrest,
>   My Phillis broke from out her east,
>   As if she'd made a match to run
>   With Venus, usher to the sun.
>   The trees, like yeomen of the guard
>   (Serving her more for pomp than ward),
>   Ranked on each side, with loyal duty,
>   Weav'd branches to inclose her beauty.
>
> *   *   *   *   *
>
>   The winged choristers began
>   To chirp their matins, and the fan
>   Of whistling winds like organs played,
>   Until their voluntaries made
>   The wakened earth in odours rise
>   To be her morning sacrifice.

"   The flowers, call'd out of their beds,
      Start and raise up their drowsie heads;
      And he that for their colour seeks
      May see it vaulting to her cheeks,
      Where roses mix : no civil war
      Divides her York and Lancaster."

Against the Scotch our poet discharges not
merely bullets, but red-hot shot :—

" Come, keen iambicks, with your badgers' feet,
   And bite like badgers till your teeth do meet :
   Help ye tart satyrists to imp my rage
   With all the scorpions that should whip this age.
   Scots are like witches : do but whet your pen,
   Scratch till the blood come, they'll not hurt you then.

   *   *   *   *   *   *   *

   A land where one may pray with curst intent,
   Oh, may they never suffer banishment !
   Had Cain been Scot, God would have changed his doom,
   Not forc'd him wander, but confined him home.
   Like Jews they spread, and as infection fly,
   As if the devil had ubiquity.
   Hence 'tis they live as rovers, and defy
   This or that place—rags of geography.

      They're citizens o' th' world, they're all in all—
      Scotland's a nation epidemical.

   *   *   *   *   *   *   *

      A Scot, when from the gallows-tree got loose,
      Drops into Styx, and turns a Soland goose."

Some curious characteristic touches on Cromwell
are to be found in Cleveland's prose satires, as for
instance where he says : " But the diurnal is weary
of the arm of flesh, and now begins an hosanna to
Cromwel, one that hath beat up his drums clean
through the Old Testament : you may learn the
genealogy of our Saviour by the names in his regi-
ment : the muster-master uses no other list but the
first chapter of Matthew. This Cromwel is never
so valorous as when he is making speeches for the
association, which, nevertheless, he doth somewhat
ominously with his neck awry, holding up his ear
as if he expected Mahomet's pigeon to come and
prompt him. He should be a bird of prey, too,
by his bloody beak " (*i.e.*, poor Cromwell's red
nose, the result of ague).

CHAPTER IV.

UPPER THAMES STREET (*continued*).

Merchant Taylors' School—Old Mulcaster—Anecdote of Bishop Andrewes--Celebrated Men Educated at Merchant Taylors'—St. James's,
Garlick Hythe–Wat Tyler's Master—The Steel Yard—Holbein's Pictures—Mr. Ruskin on Holbein—The Romans in Thames Street—
Roman Walls—Thames Street Tributaries, North—St. Bennet, Paul's Wharf—St. Nicholas Cole Abbey—Fyefoot Lane—Painter-Stainers'
Hall—Pictures belonging to the Company—College Hill—Dowgate—The Skinners : their Origin and History—The Hall of the Skinners'
Company—Parish Church of St. Laurence Poultney—Curious Epitaphs—Allhallows the Great—Swan Stairs—Dyers' Hall—Joiners' Hall—
Calamy's Strange Adventure.

THE Merchant Taylors' School, so many years
situated in Suffolk Lane, demands a special notice.
The first intention of the Merchant Taylors' Company to found a grammar school, " for the better
education and bringing up of children in good
manners and literature," says Mr. Staunton, was
manifested in the spring of 1561. About this
period, a leading member of the fraternity, Mr.
Richard Hills, generously offered the sum of £500
(equivalent to about £3,000 at the present day)
towards the purchase of a part of the " Manor of
the Rose," in the parish of St. Laurence Poulteney.
The " Rose " was a spacious mansion, originally
built by Sir John Pulteney, Knight, five times
Lord Mayor of London, in the reign of Edward III.
Its fortunes had been various. After passing
through the hands of several noble families—the
Hollands, De la Poles, Staffords, and Courtenays—
their tenancies in too many instances terminating
by the tragical process of attainder, it was granted
to the Ratcliffe or Sussex family, who obtained
leave to part with it in a more business-like manner.
Shakespeare has rendered the " Manor of the Rose,"

or " Pulteney's Inn," as it was sometimes called, a
memorable spot to all time by his allusion to it
in *King Henry VIII.* In the first act of that
play, it will be remembered, Buckingham's surveyor
appears before the court to impeach his master,
and tells the king—

" Not long before your Highness sped to France,
   The Duke, being at the Rose, within the parish
   St. Laurence Poultney, did of me demand
   What was the speech among the Londoners
   Concerning the French journey."

The name of the street, Suffolk Lane, from which
it was entered, and of the parish, St. Laurence Poultney, or Pountney, in which it was situated, still recalls
its former occupants. Ducksfoot Lane, in the
vicinity, was the *Duke's Foot-lane*, or private pathway from his garden, which lay to the east of the
mansion, towards the river ; while the upper part of
St. Laurence Pounteney Hill was, until the last few
years, called " Green Lettuce Lane," a corruption
of *Green-Lattice Lane*, so named from the lattice
gate which opened into what is now named Cannon
Street.

The Merchant Taylors' Company purchased, for a school, in 1561, part of Sussex House, including a gate-house, a long court, a winding stair leading to the leads over the chapel, two galleries at the south end of the court, and part of the chapel. The remainder of the mansion, and the site of the garden, which lay to the east of it, were acquired by the Company about 1860, for £20,000, in order to enlarge the school. In 1873 they expended the sum of £90,000 in purchasing a large portion of the Charterhouse, and thither the school was removed in 1874. By the original statutes of 1561 it was ordained that the high master should be "a man in body whole, sober, discrete, honest, vertuous, and learned in good and cleane Latin literature, and also in Greeke, yf such may be gotten." He might be either wedded or single, or a priest that had no benefice. He must have three ushers. The number of scholars was limited to 250, "of all nations and countries indifferently." The children of Jews were afterwards ungenerously excluded. There was, lastly, to be every year an examination of the scholars.

The first head master was that famed old pedagogue, Richard Mulcaster, who wielded the ferule, and pretty sharply too, for many years. He was a Cumberland man, brought up at Eton, and renowned for his critical knowledge of Greek, Latin, and Oriental literature. A veritable old Tartar he seems to have been, according to Fuller, who says of him, that he was a severe disciplinarian, but beloved by his pupils when they came to the age of maturity, and reflected on the benefit they had derived from his care.

Mulcaster was great at Latin plays, and they were often acted at Hampton Court and elsewhere, before Queen Elizabeth. Many of his boys who went to St. John's, Oxford, became renowned as actors in Latin plays before Elizabeth and James. Mulcaster also wrote mythological verses, which were recited before long-suffering Queen Bess, and two educational treatises, dry but sound. The worthy old pedant had frequent quarrels with the Merchant Taylors, and eventually left them in 1586, and became upper master of St. Paul's School. To the Company, who would have detained him, he replied scornfully, "Fidelis servus est perpetuus asinus." He boldly resisted an attempt to tax teachers in 1581–2, was successful in preserving the immunities of the school granted after the Reformation, and died in 1610.

In 1566 the school made a tremendous stride. Sir Thomas White, a princely Merchant Taylor, founded St. John's College, Oxford, and munificently appropriated no less than forty-three fellowships in the college to the scholars of Merchant Taylors' School. Much quarrelling eventually took place between the Company and the President and Fellows of St. John's, who delayed, for inadequate reasons, the election of scholars, and declared that their funds were inadequate to support the expenses of coming to London every year to the St. Barnabas' Day examinations.

The school soon rising to eminence, several rich and benevolent citizens gave exhibitions to poor and struggling scholars, a very noble way of spending money. The most eminent of these were Walter Ffysshe, John Vernon, and Thomas Wheatenhole. The school was destroyed in the Great Fire, when only the books in the library were preserved; and ten years elapsed before the new building was completed. The new school, erected in 1675, consisted of a long school-room, supported on the east side by a number of stone pillars, forming a sort of cloister, the only playground. The library was formerly the ducal chapel.

The list of eminent men educated at the Merchant Taylors' is a proud one. It boasts of William Juxon, Bishop of London, and, after the Restoration, Archbishop of Canterbury, who faithfully attended Charles I. on the scaffold; William Dawes and John Gilbert, Archbishops of York; and Hugh Boulter, Archbishop of Armagh.

Among these bishops was that eminent scholar and divine, Bishop Andrewes, before whom even James I. dared not indulge in ribaldry. He defended King James's "Defence of the Rights of Kings" against Cardinal Bellarmine, and in return obtained the see of Ely.

There is a pleasant story told of Andrewes while he was Bishop of Winchester. Waller the poet, going to see the king at dinner, overheard an extraordinary conversation between his Majesty and two prelates, Andrewes and Neale (Bishop of Durham), who were standing behind the royal chair. "My lords," asked the king, "cannot I take my subjects' money when I want it without all this formality in Parliament?" The Bishop of Durham readily answered, "God forbid, sir, but you should: you are the breath of our nostrils." Whereupon the king turned and said to the Bishop of Winchester, "Well, my lord, what say you?" "Sir," replied he, "I have no skill to judge of parliamentary cases." The king quickly rejoined, "No put-offs, my lord; answer me at once." "Then, sir," said he, "I think it quite lawful for you to take my brother Neale's money, for he offers it." Waller reports that the company were well pleased with the answer, and the wit of it seemed to affect the king.

The list of Merchant Taylor bishops also includes Thomas Dove, Bishop of Peterborough, chaplain to Queen Elizabeth, who, from his flowing white locks, called him the "Dove with silver wings;" Matthew Wren, Bishop of Ely, Sir Christopher's uncle, who accompanied Prince Charles to Spain, and was imprisoned in the Tower eighteen years, refusing to come out on Cromwell's offer; John Buckridge, also Bishop of Ely; Giles Thompson, Bishop of Gloucester; and Peter Mews, Bishop of and-thirty children." Other pupils of the school were Thomas Lodge, the physician and dramatist, who wrote a novel, "Rosalynde," on which Shakespeare founded his *As You Like It;* James Shirley, the author of thirty-seven plays, who died of grief at being ruined by the Great Fire; Edmund Gayton; Sir Edwin Sandys, traveller, and author of "Europæ Speculum;" William Sherard, founder of the Oxford professorship of botany which bears his name; Peter le Neve, Norroy King-at-Arms,

THE MERCHANT TAYLORS' SCHOOL, SUFFOLK LANE (1874).

Winchester, who, expelled Oxford by the Puritans, entered the army, and served under the Duke of York in Flanders.

Of the other professions, Sir James Whitelocke, Justice of the Common Pleas and of the King's Bench; Bulstrode Whitelocke, his son, the author of the "Memorials of English Affairs, from the Beginning of the Reign of Charles II. to the Restoration," were Merchant Taylors' scholars. Whitelocke, the son, a but half-and-half Cromwellian, began life by supporting Hampden in his resistance to ship-money, and afterwards served Cromwell with more or less fidelity. At the Restoration Charles II. dismissed him to go into the country, and "take care of his wife and one- an eminent genealogist, and one of the earliest presidents of the Antiquarian Society; Samuel Harris, first professor of modern history at Cambridge; Daniel Neale, who wrote the "History of the Puritans;" Henry Woodward, the famous actor; John Byrom; James Townley, afterwards head master of the school; Robert, the first Lord Clive; John Latham, author of the "History of Birds;" Vicesimus Knox, who wrote the well-known book called "Knox's Essays;" Joshua Brookes, the most eminent anatomist of his time; Charles Mathews the elder, and likewise his son, Charles James Mathews, the popular comedians; Charles Young, the favourite tragedian; Sir Henry Ellis, formerly librarian to the British Museum; Henry Cline, the

THE STEEL YARD AND NEIGHBOURHOOD IN 1540. (*From Van Wyngard's Plan, taken for Philip II. of Spain.*)

great surgeon at St. Thomas's Hospital; Dixon Denham, the African traveller; Philip Bliss, editor of Wood's "Athenæ Oxon.;" John Gough Nichols, the antiquary; Sir Samuel Shepherd, Lord Chief Baron of Scotland (1828); Sir R. B. Comyn, Lord Chief Justice of Madras; Right Hon. Sir John Dodson, Judge of the Prerogative Court; Edward Bond, Chief Keeper of Manuscripts in the British Museum; Samuel Birch, Keeper of the Antiquities at the British Museum; Dr. Woodford, Bishop of Ely; and the late Albert Smith.

St. James's, Garlick Hythe, was rebuilt by Richard Rothing, Sheriff, in 1326. Weever, that "Old Mortality" of his times, gives the epitaph of Richard Lions, a wine merchant and lapidary, who was beheaded by Wat Tyler's men, and buried here. According to Grafton the chronicler, Wat Tyler had been once servant to this merchant, who had beaten him, and this was the Kentish rebel's revenge. Stow says of this monument of Richard II.'s time—"Richard Lions, a famous merchant of wines and a lapidary, some time one of the sheriffs, beheaded in Cheap by Wat Tyler and other rebels, in the year 1381: his picture on his grave-stone, very fair and large, is with his hair rounded by his ears and curled, a little beard forked; a gown, girt to him down to his feet, of branched damask, wrought with the likeness of flowers; a large purse on his right side, hanging in a belt from his left shoulder; a plain hood about his neck, covering his shoulders, and hanging back behind him."

Destroyed in the Great Fire, this church was rebuilt by Wren at an expense of £5,357 12s. 10d. The coarse altar-piece of the Ascension was painted by A. Geddes, and given to the church in 1815 by the rector, the Rev. T. Burnet, brother of the eminent engraver. The organ was built by the celebrated Father Smith in 1697. On the dial, which projects from the face of the church, is a carved figure of St. James. In a vault beneath the church lies the corpse of a man in a singular state of preservation. Four or five mediæval lord mayors are buried in this church.

In the *Spectator* (No. 147) there is an interesting notice of St. James's, Garlick Hythe. Steele, speaking of the beautiful service of the Church of England, remarks—"Until Sunday was se'nnight, I never discovered, to so great a degree, the excellency of the Common Prayer. Being at St. James's Church, Garlick Hill, I heard the service read so distinctly, so emphatically, and so fervently, that it was next to an impossibility to be inattentive. My eyes and my thoughts could not wander as usual, but were confined to my prayers. . . The Confession was read with such a resigned humility, the Absolution with such a comfortable authority, the Thanksgiving with such a religious joy, as made me feel those affections of the mind in a manner I never did before." The rector of the parish at this period was the Rev. Philip Stubbs, afterwards Archdeacon of St. Albans, whose fine voice and impressive delivery are said to have been long remembered by his old parishioners.

The Steel Yard, on the river-side, near Cousin Lane (now Iron Wharf), was the old residence of the Hanse Town, German, and Flemish merchants, who obtained a settlement in London as early as 1250. Henry III., in 1259, at the request of his brother Richard, Earl of Cornwall and King of the Romans, granted them very valuable privileges, renewed and confirmed by Edward I. The City also conceded them many privileges, on condition of their maintaining Bishopsgate in repair (they rebuilt it once), and sustaining a third of the charges in money and men to defend it when need was. In spite of English jealousy, the Steel Yard merchants flourished till the reign of Edward VI., when the Merchant Adventurers complained of them, and they were held, like all "other strangers," to have forfeited their liberties. In vain Hamburg and Lubeck sent ambassadors to intercede for their countrymen. Their monopoly was gone, but the Steel Yard men still throve, and continued to export English cloth. Elizabeth, however, was rougher with them, and finally expelled them the country in 1597–8.

"Their hall," says Stow, "is large, built of stone, with three arched gates towards the street, the middlemost whereof is far bigger than the others, and is seldom opened; the other two be secured up. The same is now called the old hall. The merchants of Almaine used to bring hither as well wheat, rye, and other grain, as cables, ropes, masts, pitch, tar, flax, hemp, linen cloth, wainscots, wax, steel, and other profitable merchandise."

In the Privy Council Register of the year 1597–8, Mr. Peter Cunningham discovered an entry appointing the Steel Yard as a house "for the better bestowing and safe custody of divers provisions of the navy (naval stores)."

"In the hall of this Company," says Pennant, "were the two famous pictures, painted in distemper by Holbein, representing the triumphs of Riches and Poverty. They were lost, being supposed to have been carried into Flanders, on the destruction of the Company, and from thence into France. I am to learn where they are at present, unless in the cabinet of M. Fleischman, at Hesse-Darmstadt. The celebrated Christian a Mechel, of Basil, has lately published two engravings of these pictures, either from the originals, or the drawings of Zucchero, for 'Frid. Zucchero, 1574,' is at one corner of each print. Drawings of these pictures were found in England by Vertue, ascribed to Holbein, and the verses over them to Sir Thomas More. It appears that Zucchero copied them at the Steel Yard; so probably these copies, in process of time, might have fallen into the hands of M. Fleischman.

"In the triumph of Riches, Plutus is represented in a golden car, and Fortune sitting before him, flinging money into the laps of people holding up their garments to receive her favours. Ventidius is wrote under one, Gadareus under another, and Themistocles under a man kneeling beside the car; Crœsus, Midas, and Tantalus follow; Narcissus holds the horse of the first; over their heads, in the clouds, is Nemesis. There are various allegorical figures I shall not attempt to explain. By the side of the horses walk dropsical and other diseased figures, the too frequent accompaniment of riches.

"Poverty appears in another car, mean and shattered, half naked, squalid, and meagre. Behind her sits Misfortune; before her, Memory, Experience, Industry, and Hope. The car is drawn by a pair of oxen and a pair of asses; Diligence drives the ass, and Solicitude, with a face of care, goads the ox. By the sides of the car walks Labour, represented by lusty workmen with their tools, with cheerful looks; and behind them, Misery and Beggary, in ragged weeds, and with countenances replete with wretchedness and discontent."

According to Mr. Wornum (a most competent authority), in his excellent "Life of Holbein," these two pictures were presented, in 1617, by the representatives of the Steel Yard merchants to Henry Prince of Wales, a well-known lover of art. They afterwards passed into the possession of Charles I., and are said to have perished in the fire at Whitehall, 1698. Felibien, however, in 1661, describes having seen them in Paris; and it is more probable they were among the art-treasures sold and dispersed in Cromwell's time. Sandrart mentions having seen the pictures, or drawings of them, in the Long Gallery at Arundel House. Zucchero copied them in 1574, and Vosterman Junior engraved them. Vertue describes drawings of them at Buckingham House in black and white chalk, with coloured skies, which he supposes to be Vosterman's copies. Horace Walpole, however, who purchased them, considered one drawing only to be Vosterman's, and the other to be Zucchero's. The British Museum possesses copies of these pictures by Bischop, a Dutch artist, and a sketch of the "Riches," done by Holbein himself, drawn with the pen and washed with Indian ink. On the "Riches" of Bischop are written two lines on the penalties of wealth, attributed to Sir Thomas More—

"Aurum blanditiae pater est natusque doloris,
Qui caret hoc moeret, qui tenet hoc metuit."

These lines were originally inscribed over the entrance of the Steel Yard.

On a tablet suspended to a tree, in the picture representing "Poverty," is a Latin line, also attributed to More, as the reward of poverty—

"Qui pauper est, nihil timet, nihil potest perdere."

Holbein, on his return to London from Basel, in 1531, seems to have painted many portraits of his fellow-countrymen in the Steel Yard. Mr. Wornum especially mentions a nameless member of the Stahlhof in the Windsor collection. It represents a young man with a brown beard, clad in a black cap and furred surtout, who, seated at a table, is about to open a letter by cutting the string that fastens it with a knife. The letter is inscribed "Stahlhof." But the most celebrated picture of this class is the "George Gyze," in the Berlin gallery. He is also about to open a letter inscribed "To the Honourable George Gyze, in London, in England, my brother, to be delivered into his hands." Mr. Ruskin has adorned this picture with the rich enamel of his well-chosen words. "Every accessory," he says, "in the portrait of the Kauffmann George Gyzen is perfect with a fine perfection; the carnations in the glass vase by his side; the ball of gold, chased with blue enamel, suspended on the wall; the books, the steelyard, the papers on the table, the seal-ring, with its quartered bearings, all intensely there, and there in beauty of which no one could have dreamed that even flowers or gold were capable, far less parchment or steel. But every change of shade is felt, every rich and rubied line of petal followed, every subdued gleam in the soft blue of the enamel, and bending of the gold, touched with a hand whose patience of regard creates rather than paints. The jewel itself was not so precious as the rays of enduring light which form it, beneath that errorless hand. The man himself, what he was—not more; but to all conceivable proof of sight—in all aspect of life or thought—not less. He sits alone in his accustomed room, his common work laid out before him; he is conscious of no presence, assumes no dignity, bears no sudden or superficial look of care or interest, lives only as he lived—but for ever.

"It is inexhaustible. Every detail of it wins, retains, rewards the attention, with a continually increasing sense of wonderfulness. It is also wholly true. So far as it reaches, it contains the absolute facts of colour, form, and character, rendered with an unaccusable faithfulness. . . . What of this man and his house were visible to Holbein are visible to us; . . . if we care to know anything concerning them, great or small, so much as may by the eye be known, is for ever knowable, reliable, indisputable."

The original toll of the Steel Yard merchants was, at Christmas and Easter, two grey cloths and one brown one, with ten pounds of pepper, five pairs of gloves, and two vessels of vinegar. They had a special alderman for their judge, and they were to be free from all subsidies to the king.

According to Mr. Hudson Turner, the Steel Yard derived its name not from the steel imported by the Hanse merchants, but from the king's steel yard here erected, to weigh the tonnage of all goods imported into London, the tonnage-office being afterwards transferred to the City. The king's beam was moved, first to Cornhill, and then to Weigh House Yard, Little Eastcheap.

"At this time," says Pennant (in 1790), "the Steel Yard is the great repository of the imported iron which furnishes our metropolis with that necessary material. The quantity of bars that fill the yards and warehouses of this quarter strike with astonishment the most indifferent beholder. Next to the water-side are two eagles with imperial crowns round their necks, placed on two columns."

In few streets of London have more Roman remains been found than in Thames Street. In 1839, in excavating the ground for rebuilding Dyers' Hall, in College Street, Dowgate Hill, at thirteen feet eight inches below the level of the street, and just above the gravel, the remains were found of a Roman pavement, formed of small pieces of tiles about an inch square, bedded apparently on fine concrete; two thin earthen jars or bottles were also found near the same spot; and two coins, nearly obliterated. The lower part of the ground in which the above were discovered, for four feet six inches in thickness, appeared to be the sediment or earthy matter from water, probably from the ancient Walbrook; and in it, scattered over the surface, was a large quantity— twenty hundred weight—of animal bones.

A fibula or brooch was found in April (1831), in an excavation in Thames Street, at the foot of Dowgate Hill. The circular enamelled work in the centre was of a very peculiar description; the outlines of the features of a portrait, and those of the mantle and tunic on the bust (together with the nimbus or crown round the head) were executed in gold, into which enamel appeared to

have been worked when in a fluid or soft state. The colours of the enamel were yellow, blue, purple, red, and white. This work was surrounded by a rich filagree border of gold, beautifully worked, in which were inserted, at equal distances, four large pearls. Nothing has hitherto been found that could be compared to this jewel; the gold-work interwoven with the enamel was new to every one. The general character, design, and ornamental goldwork, seemed Byzantine, and somewhat assimilated to the style of art of the time of Charlemagne; so that perhaps we should not be far wrong in assigning its date to the ninth or tenth century.

As to the old river-side ramparts in Thames Street, Mr. Roach Smith, one of the best-informed antiquaries on Roman London, writing in 1841, says—

"The line of the wall on the land side is well ascertained; of that portion which Fitzstephens informs us bounded the City on the banks of the Thames, many persons have hitherto been in doubt, though without reason. At the same time what Fitzstephens adds relative to this wall on the water-side being overturned and destroyed by the water, seems altogether erroneous and improbable, as the Roman masonry is well known to be impervious to the action of that element. The present Thames Street follows the line of the Roman wall.

"In 1840 some valuable contributions to our scanty topographical materials were furnished, which confirm the account given us of the line of the wall by the before-mentioned author. The excavations for sewerage, which led to the discovery I am about to detail, commenced at Blackfriars. The workmen having advanced without impediment to the foot of Lambeth Hill, were there checked by a wall of extraordinary strength, which formed an angle with the Hill and Thames Street. Upon this wall the contractor for the sewers was obliged to open his course to the depth of about twenty feet; so that the greater portion of the structure had to be overthrown, to the great consumption of time and labour. The delay occasioned by the solidity and thickness of this wall gave us an opportunity of making careful notes as to its construction and courses.

"It extends (as far as I had the means of observing) from Lambeth Hill to Queenhithe, with occasional breaks. In thickness it measured from eight to ten feet. The height from the bottom of the sewer was about eight feet, in some places, more or less; it reached to within about nine feet from the present street, and three from that which indicates the period of the Fire of London, in this district easily recognised. In some places the ground-work of the houses destroyed by the Fire of 1666 abut on the wall.

"The foundation was made in the following manner:—Oaken piles were first used; upon these was laid a stratum of chalk and stones, and then a course of hewn sandstones, from three to four feet by two and two and a-half, firmly cemented with the well-known compound of quick-lime, sand, and pounded tile. Upon this solid substructure was built the wall, composed of rag and flint, with layers of red and yellow, plain and curved-edged tiles. The mortar throughout was quite equal in strength to the tiles, from which it could not be separated by force.

"One of the most remarkable features of this wall is the evidence it affords of the existence of an anterior building, which, from some cause or other, must have been destroyed. Many of the large stones above mentioned are sculptured and ornamented with mouldings, which denote their prior use in a frieze or entablature of an edifice, the magnitude of which may be conceived from the fact of these stones weighing, in many instances, half a ton. Whatever might have been the nature of this structure, its site, or cause of its overthrow, we have no means of determining. The probability of its destruction having been effected by the insurgent Britons under Boadicea suggests itself. I observed also that fragments of sculptured marble had been worked into the wall, and also a portion of a stone carved with an elegant ornament of the trellis-work pattern, the compartments being filled alternately with leaves and fruit. This has apparently belonged to an altar. In Thames Street, opposite Queen Street, about two years since, a wall precisely similar in general character was met with, and there is but little doubt of its having originally formed part of the same.

"In the middle of Pudding Lane, running to the bottom, and, as the workmen told me, even across Thames Street, is a strong wall formed of layers of red and yellow tiles and rag-stones, which appeared to have appertained to a building of considerable extent. The hypocaust belonging thereto was partly laid open.

"In Queen Street, near Thames Street, several walls crossed the street; among them were found two thin bands of pure gold, apparently used for armlets; and midway, opposite Well Court, at the depth of thirteen feet, was a flooring of red tesseræ, fourteen feet square. Three or four feet above ran chalk walls, such as are met with throughout London, which, of course, are subsequent to the Roman epoch.

"Advancing up Bush Lane, several walls of con-siderable thickness were crossed, which, together with abundance of fresco-paintings, portions of tessellated pavements and tiles, betokened the former appropriation of the site for dwelling-houses. But opposite Scot's Yard a formidable wall of extra-ordinary thickness was found to cross the street diagonally. It measured in width twenty feet. It was built of flints and rags, with occasional masses of tiles. On the north side, however, there was such a preponderance of flints, and on the south such a marked excess of ragstone, as to justify raising a question as to whether one half might not have been constructed at a period subsequent to the other, though the reason for an addition to a ten-foot wall is not apparent. So firmly had time solidified the mortar and ripened its power, that the labourers, in despair of being able to demolish the wall, were compelled literally to drill a tunnel through it to admit the sewer. Whatever might have been the original destination of this wall, whether it formed part of a public building or a citadel, it must have been perverted from its primary destination at some period during the Roman dynasty. The excavation was carried to the depth of fifteen feet, the remains of the wall appearing six feet below the street level. Adjoining the north side of the wall, and running absolutely upon it, was a pavement of white tesseræ, together with a flooring of lime and pounded tiles, supporting the tiles of a hypocaust, in rows of about one dozen, two feet apart.

"In Scot's Yard, opposite the great wall, at the depth of eight feet, was another wall, eight feet thick, composed entirely of the oblong tiles and mortar. It descended to the depth of thirteen feet, where, alongside, were pavements of lime and gravel, such, in fact, as are used as substrata for tessellæ, and are still, in many parts of the country, employed for the floorings of barns."

Having now visited the chief spots of interest in Upper Thames Street, let us note the chief tributaries north, for those south are, for the most part, alleys leading to wharves. The first, Addle Hill, like the street before mentioned by us in Alder-manbury, bears a Saxon name, either referring to King Athelstan or to the nobles who once dwelt there.

St. Bennet, Paul's Wharf, is a small church rebuilt by Wren after the Great Fire. Stow mentions the burial here of Edmund Denny, Baron of the Exchequer, whose learned son, Anthony, was gentleman of the bedchamber to Henry VIII. By his will the Baron desired twenty-eight trentals of masses to be said for his soul and the souls of his father, mother, and three wives. In this quiet and unpretending river-side church lies buried Inigo Jones, the architect of the adjoining St. Paul's (1655). His monument, for which he left £100, was destroyed in the Great Fire, which also destroyed his work at St. Paul's. Many of the hair-splitting advocates of Doctors' Commons, and laborious heralds from Heralds' College, are also interred in this tranquil spot. We may mention Sir William Le Neve (Clarencieux), a friend of Ashmole; John Philpott (Somerset Herald), who spent many dusty

ford about 1234. There was a Bishop of Hereford buried here, as well as one in the church of St. Mary Somerset, also now removed. People living close by have already forgotten the very names of the churches.

Concerning one of the Fish Street Hill churches, St. Mary Magdalen, Stow records nothing of interest, except that near it was a lane called Dolittle Lane, and another called Sermon or Shiremoniars Lane, from the Black Loft where, in the time of Edward I.,

CHAPEL OF MERCHANT TAYLORS' SCHOOL (1874).

days over "Camden's Remaines;" and, in the north aisle, William Oldys (Norroy), the herald whose eccentricities and love of humming ale we have described in a former chapter. The living is a rectory, in the gift of the Dean and Chapter of St. Paul's.

Boss Alley is so called, says Stow, from a small boss or conduit there placed by the executor of Whittington, who is buried hard by.

In Lambeth Hill is a warehouse once the Blacksmiths' Hall. The church of St. Mary Mounthaw, which stood close by, and of which the tower alone remains, was originally a chapel of the Mounthaws, an old Norfolk family, who lived on Old Fish Street Hill, and sold their house to the Bishops of Here-

the king's minters melted silver. Old Fish Street Hill and its antecedents we have already glanced at in our chapter on the Fishmongers' Company. It was the early fish market of London before Billingsgate. The stalls, says Stow, first grew to shops, then gradually to tall houses. The change of garden stalls into shops may be very well seen in our suburban roads. Sir William Davenant, the author of "Gondibert," describes the odours of Fish Street Hill with much unction.

St. Nicholas Cole Abbey, situate on the south side of Old Fish Street, in the ward of Queenhithe, was named from *Cole Abbey*, from *Golden Abbey*, or from *Cold-Abbey* or *Cold-by*, from its cold or bleak situation. John Brand was rector before the year

1383. In 1560 Queen Elizabeth granted the patronage thereof to Thomas Reeve and George Evelyn, and their heirs in soccage, who conveying it to others, it came at last to the family of the Hackers; one whereof was Colonel Francis Hacker, commander of the guard that guarded Charles I. to and from his trial, and at last to the scaffold; for which, after the Restoration, he was executed. This church was destroyed in 1666, and handsomely rebuilt, and the parish of St. Nicholas Olave there-

guild or fraternity prior to 1581, in which year Queen Elizabeth granted the charter of incorporation which they now possess. According to Horace Walpole, the first charter of the Company of Painter-Stainers, in which they are styled "Peyntours," was granted in the sixth year of Edward IV.; but they had existed as a fraternity in the time of Edward III. They were called Painter-Stainers because a picture on canvas was formerly called a "stained cloth," as one on panel

DYERS' HALL, 1850 (*see page* 41).

unto united. The following is among the monumental inscriptions :—

> "Leonard Smith, fishmonger, ended his days,
> He feared the Lord and walked in his wayes.
> His body here in earth doth rest,
> His soul with Christ in heaven is blest.
> The 14th day of May, Anno Dom. 1601."

The next turning eastward, Fyefoot Lane, should be written Five-foot Lane, as the lane was once only five feet wide at one end. Little Trinity Lane, the next turning eastward, derives its name from a church of the Holy Trinity, destroyed in the Great Fire, and not rebuilt (a Lutheran Church afterwards occupied its site); and here we come on Painter-Stainers' Hall, No. 9, which existed as a

was called a "table," probably from the French *tableau*. In the inventory of pictures of Henry VIII. they are always so distinguished, as "ITEM, *a table with the picture of the Lady Elizabeth, her Grace.*" "ITEM, *a stained cloth with the picture of Charles the Emperor.*"

The Company must have attained some importance in the sixteenth century, for Strype tells us that they were charged with the setting forth of twelve soldiers and all their furniture, though they had neither lands nor revenues, nor any riches to discharge the same; but the amount was levied among the brethren, every man according to his ability. The charter of Elizabeth was confirmed by a fresh charter granted by James II.

From an early period down to the middle of the last century, when the Royal Academy of Arts was founded, the Painters' Company included the principal artists of England. The present hall, built after the Great Fire of London, stands on the site of the old Painters' Hall, once the residence of Sir John Browne, "Sergeant Paynter" to Henry VIII., by whose will, dated 1532, he conveyed to his "brother Paynter-Stainers" his house in Little Trinity Lane, which has from that time continued to be the site of the hall of the Company. The hall contains several pictures, the gifts of artists, former liverymen of the Company, which serve to illustrate how intimately this ancient guild was associated with artists in the olden time.

Although the Painter-Stainers' Company receive and pay away large sums annually, they have very limited corporate funds. They were, however, the first of the City Companies to open an exhibition of works of decorative art.

In the barbarous days of the culinary art, when whales and dolphins were eaten, and our queens quaffed strong ale for breakfast, garlic was a great article of kitchen consumption, and according to Stow, was then sold on Garlick Hill.

Queen Street, which leads from Cheapside (in a line with King Street) right down to Southwark Bridge, was one of the improvements after the Great Fire. It opened out of Soper Lane, and was intended to furnish a direct road to the water-side from the Guildhall, as it still does. College Hill was so called from the College of St. Spirit and St. Mary, founded by Whittington, and described by us in a previous part of the chapter. The Duke of Buckingham's house stood near the top, on the east side. The second and last Duke used to come here and intrigue with the City men of the Puritan party.

Dowgate Hill leads to one of the old water-gates of London, and gives its name to one of the twenty-six wards of the City. Stow enumerates two churches and five halls of companies in this ward—All Hallows the More and the Less ; Tallow Chandlers' Hall, Skinners' Hall, Maltsters' Hall, Joyners' Hall, and Dyers' Hall. The Steel Yard, or depôt of the Hanse Town merchants, already noticed, is in this ward. Dowgate, or Down-gate, from its rapid descent, was famous in Strype's time for its flooding discharge during heavy rains : Stow mentions a boy losing his footing, and being carried down the stream, in spite of men trying to stop him with staves, till he struck against a cart-wheel, and was picked up dead. Ben Jonson, speaks of

"Dowgate torrents falling into Thames."

Pennant says that Dowgate (from Dwr, Celtic,

water) was one of the old Roman gates of London, where passengers went across by ferry to a continuation of the military way towards Dover. It was a water wharf in the reigns of Henry III. and Edward III. Customs were paid for ships resting here, in the same manner as if they were at Queenhithe.

The Erber (already described) stood near Dowgate.

In College Street, between College Hill and Dowgate, stands a venerable-looking edifice of red brick, the Innholders' Hall.

In Laurence Poultney Hill many eminent persons seem to have lived towards the end of the seventeenth century. Daniel and Eliab Harvey, brothers of Dr. William Harvey, Charles I.'s physician, and the great discoverer of the circulation of the blood, were rich merchants on this hill.

The Skinners, whose hall is situated in Dowgate, were incorporated in the first year of Edward III. (1327), and made a brotherhood in the eighteenth of Richard II. Their original title is " Master and Wardens, Brothers and Sisters of the Guild or Fraternity of the Skinners of London, to the Honour of God, and the precious Body of our Lord Jesus Christ."

Furs, though known to the Saxons, were brought into more general use by the Normans. A statute of Edward III. restricts the wearing of furs to the royal family, prelates, earls, barons, knights, ladies, and rich priests. A charter of Henry VII. enumerates ermine, sables, minever, badger, and many other furs then used to trim coats and gowns. Rabbit skin was also much worn, even by nobles and gentlemen.

The Skinners had a hall as early as the reign of Henry III., and they were among the first of the guilds chartered by Edward III. In this reign they ranked so high as to venture to dispute precedence with the powerful Fishmongers. This led, in 1339, to the celebrated fray, when prisoners were rescued, and one of the Mayor's officers wounded. The end of this was the rapid execution of two of the ringleaders in Cheapside. In the offerings for the French war (37 Edward III.) the Skinners contributed £40, which was double even the Goldsmiths' subsidy.

In 1395, the Skinners, who had previously been divided into two brotherhoods, one at St. Mary Spital, and the other at St. Mary Bethlehem, were united by Richard II. They then resided in St. Mary Axe, and in Strype's time they removed to Budge Row and Walbrook. In the Great Watch, on the vigil of St. Peter and St. Paul (6 Edward IV.), the Skinners rank as sixth among the twelve great companies, and sent twenty men to attend. In Richard III.'s time they had stood as seventh of the thirteen mysteries. They then sent twenty-four members, in murry-coloured coats, to meet the usurper on entering London, the five great companies alone sending thirty; and at Richard's coronation John Pasmer, "pellipar" (Skinner), was in the deputation from the twelve companies, who attended the Lord Mayor as chief butler.

In the reign of Elizabeth, though the richer furs were less worn, the Skinners were still numerous. They employed "tawyers," or poor workmen, to dress the coney and other English furs, which pedlars collected from the country people. To restrict merchants from forestalling them in the purchase of furs, the Skinners petitioned Elizabeth for the exclusive monopoly, but were opposed by the Lord Mayor and the Eastland merchants.

The ordinances of the Skinners in the reign of Edward II. prescribe regulations for importing and manufacturing skins into furs, fixing the number of skins in a package, and forbidding the sale of second-hand furs for new.

One of the great ceremonials of the Skinners' Company was the annual procession on Corpus Christi Day. They had then borne before them more than 200 painted and gilded wax torches, "burning bright," says Stow; then came above 200 chanters and priests, in surplices and copes, singing. After them came the sheriffs' officers, the clerks of the City prisons, the sheriffs' chaplains, mayor's serjeants, the counsel of the City, the mayor and aldermen in scarlet, and lastly the Skinners in their best livery. The guests returned to dinner in the Company's Hall. On the following Sunday they again went in procession to church, heard a mass of requiem solemnised for their deceased members, and made offerings. The bead-roll of the dead was then called, and the Company repeated their orisons. The priests then said a general prayer for all the surviving members of the fraternity, mentioning each by name. They afterwards returned to their hall, paid their quarterage, and any balances of livery money, and enjoyed themselves in a comfortable but unpretentious dinner, for which they had duly and thriftly paid in advance. Oh, simple life of quiet enjoyment !

The election ceremonies of the Company are highly curious. " The principals of the Company being assembled," says Mr. Herbert, " on the day of annual election, ten Christchurch scholars, or 'Blue-coat Boys,' with the Company's almsmen and trumpeters, enter the hall in procession, to the flourish of trumpets. Three large silver cocks, or fowls so named, are then brought in and de-livered to the master and wardens. On unscrewing these pieces of plate they are found to form drinking-cups, filled with wine, and from which they drink. Three caps of maintenance are then brought in ; the first of these the old master tries on, and finds it will not fit him, on which he gives it to be tried on to several next him. Being tried by two or three whom it will not fit, it is then given to the intended new master, whom fitting, of course, he is then announced with flourish and acclamation as the master elect. The like ceremonies are afterwards repeated with the two other caps, on behalf of the wardens to be elected, who succeed in a similar manner, and are announced with the like honours when the healths of the whole are drank by the company."

The arms of the Company are—Ermine, on a chief gules, three crowns or, with caps of the first. Crest—A leopard proper, gorged with a chaplet of bays or. Supporters—A lucern (lynx) and a wolf, both proper. Motto—"To God only be all glory." Hatton, in his " New View of London," boasts of the Company having enrolled, in its time, six kings, five queens, one prince, nine dukes, two earls, and a baron.

Strype says the hall in Dowgate was built after the Fire of London at an expense of above £1,800. The original hall, " Coped Hall," had been purchased by the Company as early as the reign of Henry III. It was afterwards alienated, and passed into the hands of Sir Ralph de Cobham, who made Edward III. his heir. In the later hall the mayors sometimes held their mayoralty, and the new East India Company held its general courts before its incorporation with the old Company. The hall is described in 1708 as a noble structure, built with fine bricks, and richly furnished, the great parlour being lined with odoriferous cedar. The hall was altered by Mr. Jupp at the end of the last century. It is an Ionic building, with a rusticated basement. Six pilasters, sustaining an entablature and pointed pediment, divide a double tier of six windows. In the tympanum of the pediment the architect has shown a noble disregard to heraldry by doubling up the supporters of the Company's arms, to fit into the space. The frieze is ornamented with festoons and leopards' heads. A small paved court separates the front from the more ancient building, which is of brick. The hall, a light and elegant apartment, has a stained-glass window. The court-room is no longer wainscoted with odoriferous cedar. The staircase displays some of the massy and rich ornaments in fashion in the reign of Charles II.

" The parish church of St. Laurence Poultney was increased, with a chapel of Jesus, by Thomas

Cole, for a master and chaplain; the which chapel and church were made a college of Jesus, and of Corpus Christi, for a master and seven chaplains, by John Poultney, mayor, and was confirmed by Edward III., the twentieth of his reign. Of him was this church called St. Laurence Poultney in Candlewick Street. The college was surrendered in the reign of Edward VI., who granted and sold it to John Cheke, his schoolmaster, and Walter Moyle." The following is one of the curious old epitaphs preserved by Strype :—

> " Every Christian heart
>   Seeketh to extoll
> The glory of the Lord,
>   Our onely Redeemer;
> Wherefore Dame Fame
>   Must needs inroll
> Paul Withypoll his childe,
>   By Love and Nature,
> Elizabeth, the wife
>   Of Emanuel Lucar,
> In whom was declared
>   The goodnesse of the Lord,
> With many high vertues,
>   Which truely I will record.
>
> She wrought all needle-workes
>   That women exercise,
> With Pen, Frame, or Stoole,
>   All pictures artificiall,
> Curious Knots or Trailes,
>   What fancy would devise,
> Beasts, Birds, or Flowers,
>   Even as things naturall.
> Three manner hands could she
>   Write, them faire all.
> To speak of Alegorisme,
>   Or accounts, in every fashion,
> Of women, few like
>   (I thinke) in all this nation.
>
>   *   *   *   *
>
> Latine and Spanish,
>   And also Italian,
> She spake, writ, and read,
>   With perfect utterance ;
> And for the English,
>   She the Garland wan.
> In Dame Prudence Schoole,
>   By Graces' purveyance,
> Which cloathed her with vertues
>   From naked ignorance ;
> Reading the Scriptures,
>   To judge light from darke,
> Directing her faith to Christ,
>   The onely marke."

A monument at the upper end of the north aisle bore this inscription :—

> " Hoc est nescire, sine Christo
>   plurima scire ;
> Si Christum bene scis,
>   satis est, si cætera nescis."

"St. Laurence Poultney Church," says Aubrey, "was the only London church that could then boast of a leaden steeple, except St. Dunstan in the East." Richard Glover, the author of that tenth-rate epic, "Leonidas," was also a merchant on this hill. "Leonidas," an epic in twelve books, praised by Fielding, and written to vex Sir Robert Walpole by covert patriotic allusions, had its day. By many people of his time Glover was generally believed to have written the "Letters of Junius," but Junius has more of the old nobleman about him than the Hamburg merchant. Sir Patience Ward, that great City politician, was living in 1677 on Laurence Poultney Hill; and in the same year also lived there William Vanderbergh, the father, as Mr. Peter Cunningham thinks, of the wit and dramatist, Sir John Vanbrugh, the architect of Blenheim. Thomas Creede, the great play-printer of Queen Elizabeth's time, lived in this parish. The register records the marriage, in 1632-3, of Anne Clarges to Thomas Radford, farrier, of the parish of St. Martin's-in-the-Fields. This lady (a laundress) afterwards married General Monk, the restorer of Charles II.

"On the south side of Thames Street," says Mr. Jesse, "close to where the Steel Yard formerly stood, is the church of All Hallows the Great, anciently called All Hallows the More, and sometimes All Hallows in the Ropery, from its being situated in a district chiefly inhabited by rope-makers. It was founded in 1361 by the Despencer family, from whom the presentation passed by marriage to the Beauchamps, Earls of Warwick, and subsequently to the Crown. The present uninteresting church was built by Sir Christopher Wren, shortly after the destruction of the old edifice by fire in 1666. Stow informs us that there was a statue of Queen Elizabeth in the old church, to which the following verses were attached :—

> " If Royal virtue ever crowned a crown ;
>   If ever mildness shined in majesty ;
> If ever honour honoured true renown ;
>   If ever courage dwelt with clemency ;
>
> " If ever Princess put all princes down,
>   For temperance, prowess, prudence, equity ;
> This, this was she, that, in despite of death,
>   Lives still admired, adored, Elizabeth !"

"The only object of any interest in the interior of the church is a handsome oak screen, said to have been manufactured in Hamburg, which was presented to the church by the Hanse merchants, in grateful memory of their connection with the parish."

The Swan Stairs, a little "above bridge," was the place where people coming by boat used to land, to walk to the other side of Old London Bridge, when the current was swift and narrow between the starlings, and "shooting the bridge" was rather like going down the rapids.   Citizens usually took boat again at Billingsgate, as we find Johnson and Boswell once doing, on their way to Greenwich, in 1763.

Dyers' Hall, Dowgate Hill, was rebuilt about 1857.   The Company was incorporated as early as 1472, and the ancient hall, on the site of Dyers' Hall Wharf, was destroyed in the Great Fire.   The Innholders' Hall, in the same street, was also built after the Great Fire.   The Company was incorporated in 1515.   Joiners' Hall, Joiners' Hall Buildings, has a carved screen and entrance doorway, and the piers are surmounted with the Company's crest—a demi-savage, life-size, wreathed about the head and waist with oak-leaves.   The Joiners were incorporated about 1567.   The Plumbers' Hall, in Great Bush Lane, is a modern brick building.   The Company was incorporated by James I. in 1611.

The celebrated Calamy gives a curious account of an adventure he met with at Trigg stairs, in this district.   "As I was going," he says, "one day, from Westminster into the City, designing to dine with Sir Richard Levet, I landed at Trigg Stairs. Walking up from the water-side towards Maiden Lane, where he lived, I was overtaken by a woman who had seen me pass by, and ran very eagerly after me, till she was almost out of breath.   She seemed greatly frightened, and caught hold of me, begging me, for God's sake, to go back with her.   I asked her what the matter was, and what she had to say to me.   She told me there was a man had just hanged himself in a cellar, and was cut down, and she ran up and saw me go by, and was overjoyed at my coming so seasonably, and begged of me, for the Lord's sake, that I would go back with her and pity the poor man.   I asked her what she expected from me, and whether she thought I could bring a dead man to life.   She told me the man was not dead, but was cut down alive, and come to himself, and she hoped if, at such a season as this, he was seriously talked with, it might do him good.   Though I was an utter stranger to this woman, I was yet prevailed with by her earnestness and tears, which were observed by all that passed, to go back with her.   She carried me up-stairs into a handsome dining-room.   I found a grave, elderly woman sitting in one corner; a younger woman in another; a down-looking man, that had discontent in his countenance, and seemed to be between thirty and forty years of age, in a third corner; and a chair standing in a fourth, as if set for me, and upon that I placed myself."   After reasoning with the man, and endeavouring to restore peace in the family, the good man left.

CHAPTER V.

LOWER THAMES STREET.

Septem Cameræ—A Legend about Billingsgate—Hogarth visits it—Henry Mayhew's Description of it—Billingsgate Dock in King Ethelred's Time—The Price of Fish as regulated by Edward I.—Billingsgate constituted a Free and Open Market by Act of Parliament—Fish Monopolists and their Evil Practices—The Habitual Frequenters of Billingsgate—The Market at its Height—Oyster Street—Fishing in the Thames a Long Time ago—A Sad Falling-off—A Curious Billingsgate Custom—A Thieves' College—The Coal Exchange—Discovery of Roman Remains on its Site—The Waterman's Hall—Thames Watermen and Wherrymen—Fellowship Porters' Hall—The Custom House—Growth of the Revenue—The New Building—Customs Officials—Curious Stories of the Customs—Cowper and his Intended Suicide—The System of Business in the Custom House—Custom House Sales—"Passing" Baggage.

IN St. Mary-at-Hill Lane, Thames Street, is the fair parish church of St. Mary, called "on the Hill," because of the ascent from Billingsgate.   "In this parish there was a place," says Stow, "called 'Septem Cameræ,' which was either one house, or else so many rooms or chambers, which formerly belonged to some chantry, the rent whereof went towards the maintaining of a priest to pray superstitiously for the soul of the deceased, who left those septem cameræ for that use."

Stow has preserved the following epitaph from a tomb in the chancel of St. Mary's:—

"Here lyeth a knight, in London borne,
    Sir Thomas Blanke by name,
Of honest birth, of merchant's trade,
    A man of worthy fame.
Religious was his life to God,
    To men his dealing just ;
The poor and hospitals can tell
    That wealth was not his trust.
With gentle heart, and spirit milde,
    And nature full of pitie,
Both sheriffe, lord maior, and alderman,
    He ruled in this citie.
The 'Good Knight' was his common name,
    So called of many men ;
He lived long, and dyed of yeeres
    Twice seven, and six times ten."

Billingsgate, though a rough and unromantic place at the present day, has an ancient legend of its own, that associates it with royal names and venerable folk.　Geoffrey of Monmouth deposes that about 400 years before Christ's nativity, Belin, a king of the Britons, built this gate and gave it its name, and that when he was dead the royal body was burnt, and the ashes set over the gate in a vessel of brass, upon a high pinnacle of stone. Stow, more prosaic, on the other hand, is quite satisfied that one Biling once owned the wharf, and troubles himself no further.

the aspect of Billingsgate.　Formerly, passengers embarked here for Gravesend and other places down the river, and a great many sailors mingled with the salesmen and fishermen.　The boats sailed only when the tide served, and the necessity of being ready at the strangest hours rendered many taverns necessary for the accommodation of travellers.　"The market formerly opened two hours earlier than at present," says Mr. Platt, writing in 1842, "and the result was demoralising

THE CHURCH OF ALLHALLOWS THE GREAT IN 1784 (*see page* 40).

In Hogarth's memorable tour (1732) he stopped at Billingsgate for the purpose of sketching.　His poetical chronicler says—

" Our march we with a song begin.
　　Our hearts were light, our breeches thin.
　　We meet with nothing of adventure
　　Till Billingsgate's dark house we enter ;
　　Where we diverted were, while baiting,
　　With ribaldry not worth relating
　　(Quite suited to the dirty place) ;
　　But what most pleased us was his Grace
　　Of Puddle Dock, a porter grim,
　　Whose portrait Hogarth, in a whim,
　　Presented him, in caricature,
　　He pasted on the cellar door."

The introduction of steamboats has much altered

and exhausting.　Drink led to ribald language and fighting, but the refreshment now taken is chiefly coffee, and the general language and behaviour was improved."　The fish-fags of Ned Ward's time have disappeared, and the business is done smarter and quicker.　As late as 1842 coaches would sometimes arrive at Billingsgate from Dover or Hastings, and so affect the market.　The old circle from which dealers in their carts attended the market, included Windsor, St. Albans, Hertford, Romford, and other places within twenty-five miles.　Railways have now enlarged the area of purchasers to an indefinite degree.　In the Dutch auction system used at Billingsgate, the prices asked sink till they reach the level of the purchaser.　The cheap fish-sellers practise many tricks, blowing the cod-fish larger with pipes, and mixing dead eels with live ones. Railways have made fish a main article of food with the London poor, so that, according to Mr. Mayhew, the London costermongers sell one-third of the entire quantity of fish sent to Billings-

begins. Many of the costers that usually deal in vegetables buy a little fish on the Friday. It is the fast-day of the Irish, and the mechanics' wives run short of money at the end of the week, and so make up their dinners with fish : for this reason the attendance of costers' barrows at Billingsgate on a

HALL OF THE SKINNERS' COMPANY.

gate. The salesmen divide all fish into two classes, "red" and "white." The "red" fish is salmon, all other descriptions are known as "white."

To see this market in its busiest costermonger time, says Mr. Mayhew, the visitor should be there about seven o'clock on a Friday morning. The market opens at four, but for the first two or three hours it is attended solely by the regular fishmongers and "bummarees," who have the pick of the best there. As soon as these are gone the costers' sale

Friday morning is always very great. As soon as you reach the Monument you see a line of them, with one or two tall fishmongers' carts breaking the uniformity, and the din of the cries and commotion of the distant market begin to break on the ear like the buzzing of a hornet's nest. The whole neighbourhood is covered with hand-barrows, some laden with baskets, others with sacks. The air is filled with a kind of sea-weedy odour, reminding one of the sea-shore; and on entering the market, the smell of whelks, red herrings, sprats, and a hundred other sorts of fish, is almost overpowering. The wooden barn-looking square where the fish is sold is, soon after six o'clock, crowded with shiny cord jackets and greasy caps. Everybody comes to Billingsgate in his worst clothes; and no one knows the length of time a coat can be worn until they have been to a fish-sale. Through the bright opening at the end are seen the tangled rigging of the oyster-boats, and the red-worsted caps of the sailors. Over the hum of voices is heard the shouts of the salesmen, who, with their white aprons, peering above the heads of the mob, stand on their tables roaring out their prices. All are bawling together—salesmen and hucksters of provisions, capes, hardware, and newspapers—till the place is a perfect Babel of competition.

"Ha-a-andsome cod! the best in the market! All alive! alive! alive, oh!"—"Ye-o-o! ye-o-o! Here's your fine Yarmouth bloaters! Who's the buyer?"—"Here you are, governor; splendid whiting! some of the right sort!"—"Turbot! turbot! All alive, turbot!"—"Glass of nice peppermint, this cold morning? Halfpenny a glass!" —"Here you are, at your own price! Fine soles, oh!"—"Oy! oy! oy! Now's your time! Fine grizzling sprats! all large, and no small!"— "Hullo! hullo, here! Beautiful lobsters! good and cheap. Fine cock crabs, all alive, oh!"—"Five brill and one turbot—have that lot for a pound! Come and look at 'em, governor; you won't see a better lot in the market."—"Here! this way; this way, for splendid skate! Skate, oh! skate, oh!"—"Had-had-had-had-haddock! All fresh and good!"—"Currant and meat puddings! a ha'penny each!"—"Now, you mussel-buyers, come along! come along! come along! Now's your time for fine fat mussels!"—"Here's food for the belly, and clothes for the back; but I sell food for the mind!" shouts the newsvendor.—"Here's smelt, oh!"— "Here ye are, fine Finney haddick!"—"Hot soup! nice pea-soup! a-all hot! hot!"—"Ahoy! ahoy, here! Live plaice! all alive, oh!"—"Now or never! Whelk! whelk! whelk!"—"Who'll buy brill, oh! brill, oh?"—"Capes! waterproof capes! Sure to keep the wet out! A shilling apiece!"— "Eels, oh! eels, oh! Alive, oh! alive, oh!"— "Fine flounders, a shilling a lot! Who'll have this prime lot of flounders?"—"Shrimps! shrimps! fine shrimps!"—"Wink! wink! wink!"—"Hi! hi-i! here you are; just eight eels left—only eight!"— "O ho! O ho! this way—this way—this way! Fish alive! alive! alive, oh!"

Billingsgate Dock is mentioned as an important quay in Brompton's Chronicle (Edward III.), under the date 976, when King Ethelred, being then at Wantage, in Berkshire, made laws for regulating the customs on ships at Blynesgate, or Billingsgate, then the only wharf in London. 1. Small vessels were to pay one halfpenny; 2. Larger ones, with sails, one penny; 3. Keeles, or hulks, still larger, fourpence. 4. Ships laden with wood, one piece for toll. 5. *Boats with fish*, according to size, a halfpenny and a penny; 6. Men of Rouen, who came with wine or peas, and men of Flanders and Liege, were to pay toll before they began to sell, but the Emperor's men (Germans of the Steel Yard) paid an annual toll. 7. Bread was tolled three times a week, cattle were paid for in kind, and butter and cheese were paid more for before Christmas than after.

By King Stephen's time, according to Becket's friend and biographer, Fitzstephen, the different foreign merchants had drafted off to their respective quays—Germans and Dutch to the Steel Yard, in Upper Thames Street; the French wine merchants to the Vintry. In the reign of Edward I., a great regulator of the price of provisions, the price of fish was fixed at the following scale:—

	s.	d.
A dozen of best soles . . .	0	3
Best haddock . . .	0	2
Best mullett . . .	0	2
Best John Dory . . .	0	5
Best whitings, four for . .	0	1
Best fresh oysters, a gallon . .	0	2
Best Thames or Severn lamprey .	0	4
Best turbot	0	6
Best porpoise . . 6d. to	0	8
Best fresh salmon (after Easter), four for .	5	0
Best roach . . .	0	1
Best pike . . . 6d. to	0	8
(Probably brought from abroad, pickled).		
Best eels, a strike, or quarter of a hundred .	0	2
Best conger	1	0

Seal, sturgeon, ling, and dolphin were also eaten.

Edward III. fixed the Billingsgate dues at 2d. for large ships, 1d. for smaller, and one halfpenny for boats or battles. For corn one farthing was paid for two quarters; one farthing for two measured quarters of sea-coal. Every tun of ale exported was taxed at 4d.; and every 1,000 herrings, one farthing.

In May, 1699, an Act of Parliament constituted Billingsgate a free and open market for the sale of fish six days in the week, and on Sundays (before Divine service) for mackerel; and any fishmonger who bought, except for his own sale, was to be sentenced to a fine of £20 for every offence. Several fishery-laws were passed in 1710, to restrain abuses, and the selfish greediness of fishermen. Eel-spears were forbidden, and it was made unlawful to use a flue, trammel, hooped net, or double-walled net, or to destroy the fry of fish. No draw-nets were to be shot before sunrise or after sunset. No fisherman was to try for flounders between London Bridge and Westminster more than two casts at low and two at high water. No flounders were to be taken under the size of six inches. No one was to angle within the limits of London Bridge with more than two hooks upon his line ; no one was to drag for salmon in the Thames with nets under six inches in the mesh ; and all unlawful nets were to be destroyed.

An Act of the 33rd year of George II. was passed, to regulate the sale of fish at Billingsgate, and prevent a monopoly of the market. It was found that the London fishmongers bought up the fishing-boats, and kept the fish down at Gravesend, supplying the market with only boat-loads at a time, so as to keep up the price. An attempt had been made, in the year 1749, to establish a fish-market at Westminster, and fishing-boats were bought by subscription ; but the fishmongers prevented any supply of fish reaching the new depôt. The Act of Parliament above referred to (33 Geo. II.) was intended to remedy these evils. The master of every fishing-vessel arriving at the Nore with fish had to report the time of his arrival, and the cargo he brought, to the clerk of the coast-office, under penalty of £20 ; and for any marketable fish he destroyed he was to be sentenced to not less than one month's hard labour. No fish was to be placed in well-boats or store-boats, unless to go straight to Billingsgate, under a penalty of £20. No one by the same Act was allowed to sell fish-spawn, or unsizable fish, or any smelt less than five inches long from nose to tail.

Stow (Elizabeth) describes Billingsgate as a port or harborough for ships and boats bringing fish, fresh and salt, shell-fish, oranges, onions, fruit, roots, wheat, rye, and other grain. It had become more frequented after the decline of Queenhithe. Steam-vessels, of late years, have superseded the old hoys and sailing-boats that once visited Billingsgate stairs. Steamers are not, of course, dependent on the state of the tide, and the old summons for their departure (under penalty) at the ringing of the bell, which announced high water at London Bridge, is no longer an observance.

Addison, who glanced at nearly every kind of London life, with his quiet kindly philosophy, and large toleration for folly, did not forget to visit Billingsgate, and refers, in his delightful way, to the debates which frequently arose among "the ladies of the British fishery." Tom Brown gives a ribald sketch of the fish-fag ; and coarse-tongued Ned Ward, that observant publican of Defoe's time, painted a gross Dutch picture of the shrill-voiced, bloated Moll Flagons of the Dark House, scolding and chattering among their heaps of fish, ready enough to knock down the auctioneer who did not knock down a lot to them.

In Bailey's English Dictionary (1736) a Billingsgate is described as meaning "a scolding, impudent slut," and Munden, incomparable as Sir Abel Handy, in Morton's excellent comedy of *Speed the Plough*, when asked about the temper and manners of his wife, replies, in the true Socratic mode, by the query, "Were you ever at Billingsgate in the sprat season ?"

Mr. Henry Mayhew, writing in 1861, calculates that every year in Billingsgate there are sold 406,000 salmon, 400,000 live cod, 97,520,000 soles, 17,920,000 whiting, 2,470,000 haddocks, 23,520,000 mackerel, 4,000,000 lbs. of sprats, 1,050,000,000 fresh herrings, in bulk, 9,797,760 eels, 147,000,000 bloaters, 19,500,000 dried haddocks, 495,896,000 oysters, 1,200,000 lobsters, 600,000 crabs, and 498,428,648 shrimps. Of this vast salvage from the seas the 4,000 London fish costermongers sell 263,281,000 pounds' weight. Mr. Mayhew calculated that the sprat costermongers sell 3,000,000 pounds' weight annually, and realise £12,000.

The forestallers or middlemen at Billingsgate are called "bummarees," probably a word of Dutch origin. They buy residues, and sell again in lots, at a considerable profit, to the fishmongers and costermongers. They are said to derive their name from the bumboat-men, who used to purchase of the wind-bound smacks at Gravesend or the Nore, and send the fish rapidly up to market in light carts.

The costermongers are important people at Billingsgate market. Sprat-selling in the streets generally commences about the 9th of November (Lord Mayor's Day), which is accordingly by costermongers sometimes called "Sprat Day." Sprats continue in about ten weeks. They are sold at Billingsgate by the "toss" or "chuck," which is about half a bushel, and weighs from forty to fifty pounds. The price varies from 1s. to 5s. A street sprat-seller can make from 1s. 6d. to 2s. 6d. a day, and often more. About 1,000 "tosses" of sprats are sold daily in London streets during the season. The real costermonger thinks sprat-selling *infra dig.* A street shell-fish-seller will make his 15s. a week, chiefly by periwinkles and mussels. The London costermongers, in Mr. Mayhew's time, sold about 770,000 pints of shrimps annually, which, at 2d. a pint, a low calculation, amounts to £6,400 yearly. The costermongers sell about 124,000,000 oysters a year, which, at four a penny, the price some years ago, would realise £129,650. The periwinkles sold in London Mr. Mayhew calculated from good data to be 3,600,000 pints, which, at a penny a pint, gives the large sum of £15,000. The sellers of "Wink, wink, winketty, wink, wink," make, on an average, 12s. a week clear profit in the summer season. Taking fresh, salt, and shell-fish together, Mr. Mayhew calculated that £1,460,850 was spent annually on fish by London street purchasers.

In the days before railways, when the coaches were stopped by snow, or the river by ice, fish used sometimes to command great prices at Billingsgate. In March, 1802, a cod-fish of eight pounds was sold to a Bond Street fishmonger for £1 8s. In February, 1809, a salmon of nineteen pounds went for a guinea a pound. In March, 1824, three lobsters sold for a guinea each; and Mr. Timbs mentions two epicures dividing the only lobster in the market for sauce, and paying two guineas each for the luxury. On the other hand, the prolific sea furnishes sometimes great gluts of fish. Sixty tons of periwinkles at a time have been sent from Glasgow; and in two days from ninety to a hundred tons of plaice, soles, and sprats have been landed at Billingsgate. Perhaps we may live to see the time when the better sorts of fish will grow scarce as oysters, and cod-fish will have to be bred at the Dogger Bank, and encouraged in its reproduction.

All fish is sold at Billingsgate by tale, except salmon, which go by weight, and sprats, oysters, and shell-fish, which are sold by measure. In Knight's "London" (1842), the number of boxes of salmon sent to Billingsgate is said to begin in February at about thirty boxes a day, and to increase in July to 1,000 boxes a day. In 1842 probably not less than 2,500 tons of salmon reached Billingsgate. In 1770 salmon was sent to London in panniers on horseback; after that, it was packed in straw in light carts. After April it was impossible to send the fish to market. About the year 1785, Mr. Alexander Dalrymple, a servant of the East India Company, told a Mr. George Dempster, at the East India House, the Chinese fishermen's mode of conveying fresh fish great distances packed up in snow. Dempster instantly wrote off to a Scotch friend, who had already tried the plan of sending salmon, packed in ice, to London from Aberdeen and Inverness. In 1852 there were about sixty fish-salesmen in London, and fifty of these had stalls in Billingsgate.

The old water-gate of Beling, the friend of Brennus the Gaul, was long ago a mere collection of dirty pent-houses, scaly sheds, and ill-savoured benches, with flaring oil-lamps in winter, daybreak disclosing a screaming, fighting, and rather tipsy crowd; but since the extension of the market in 1849, and the disappearance of the fishermen, there is less drinking, and more sober and strenuous business.

Mr. Henry Mayhew has painted a minute yet vivid picture of this great market. "In the darkness of the shed," he says, "the white bellies of the turbots, strung up bow-fashion, shine like mother-of-pearl, while the lobsters, lying upon them, look intensely scarlet from the contrast. Brown baskets piled upon one another, and with the herring-scales glittering like spangles all over them, block up the narrow paths. Men in coarse canvas jackets, and bending under huge hampers, push past, shouting, 'Move on! move on, there!' and women, with the long limp tails of cod-fish dangling from their aprons, elbow their way through the crowd. Round the auction-tables stand groups of men, turning over the piles of soles, and throwing them down till they slide about in their slime; some are smelling them, while others are counting the lots. 'There, that lot of soles are worth your money,' cries the salesman to one of the crowd, as he moves on leisurely; 'none better in the market. You shall have 'em for a pound and half-a-crown.' 'Oh!' shouts another salesman, 'it's no use to bother him; he's no go.' Presently a tall porter, with a black oyster-bag, staggers past, trembling under the weight of his load, his back and shoulders wet with the drippings from the sack. 'Shove on one side,' he mutters from between his clenched teeth, as he forces his way through the mob. Here is a tray of reddish-brown shrimps piled up high, and the owner busy shifting his little fish into another stand, while a doubtful customer stands in front, tasting the flavour of the stock, and consulting with his companion in speculation. Little girls carrying matting-bags, that they have brought from Spitalfields, come up, and ask you in a begging voice to buy their baskets; and women, with bundles of twigs for stringing herrings, cry out, 'Halfpenny a bunch!' from all sides. Then there are blue-black piles of small live lobsters, moving about their bound-up claws and long 'feelers,' one of them occasionally being taken up by a looker-on, and dashed down again like a stone. Everywhere every one is asking, 'What's the price, master?' while shouts of laughter, from round the stalls of the salesmen, bantering each other, burst out occasionally over the murmuring noise of the crowd. The transparent smelts on the marble slabs, and the bright herrings, with the lump of transparent ice magnifying their eyes like a lens, are seldom looked at until the market is over, though the hampers and piles of huge maids, dropping slime from the counter, are eagerly examined and bartered for.

"The costermongers have nicknamed the long row of oyster-boats moored close alongside the wharf 'Oyster Street.' On looking down the line of tangled ropes and masts, it seems as though the little boats would sink with the crowds of men and women thronged together on their decks. It is as busy a scene as one can well behold. Each boat has its black sign-board, and salesman in his white apron walking up and down 'his shop,' and on each deck is a bright pewter pot and tin-covered plate, the remains of the salesman's breakfast. 'Who's for Baker's?' 'Who's for Archer's?' 'Who'll have Alston's?' shout the oyster-merchants; and the red cap of the man in the hold bobs up and down as he rattles the shells about with his spade. These holds are filled with oysters—a grey mass of sand and shell—on which is a bushel-measure well piled up in the centre, while some of them have a blue muddy heap of mussels divided off from the 'natives.' The sailors, in their striped guernseys, sit on the boat-sides smoking their morning's pipe, allowing themselves to be tempted by the Jew boys with cloth caps, old shoes, and silk handkerchiefs."

Mr. Mayhew has also sketched, with curious photographic realism, the Dutch eel-boats, with their bulging polished oak sides, half hidden in the river mist. They are surrounded by skiffs full of traders from the Surrey and Middlesex shores. You see wooden sabots and china pipes on the ledges of the boats, and the men wear tall fur caps, red shirts, and canvas kilts. The holds of the vessels are tanks, and floating at the stern are coffin-shaped barges pierced with holes, with eel-baskets hanging over the sides. In the centre of the boats stand the scales, tall and heavy, with, on one side, the conical net-bag for the eels; on the other, the weights and pieces of stone to make up for the water that clings to the fish. The captain, when purchasers arrive, lays down his constant friend, his black pipe, and dives into the tank a long-handled landing-net, and scoops from the tank a writhing knot of eels. Some of the purchasers wear blue serge aprons; others are ragged women, with their straw pads on their crushed bonnets. They are busy sorting their purchases, or sanding them till they are yellow.

In old times the Thames fish half supplied London. Old Stow says of the Thames in his day, "What should I speak of the fat and sweet salmons daily taken in this stream, and that in such plenty (after the time of the smelt is past) as no river in Europe is able to exceed it? But what store also of barbels, trouts, chevens, perches, smelts, breams, roaches, daces, gudgeons, flounders, shrimps, eels, &c., are commonly to be had therein, I refer me to them that know by experience better than I, by reason of their daily trade of fishing in the same. And albeit it seemeth from time to time to be, as it were, defrauded in sundry wise of these, her large commodities, by the insatiable avarice of fishermen; yet this famous river complaineth commonly of no want, but the more it loseth at onetime it gaineth at another."

Stow also tells us that, before 1569, the City ditch, without the wall of the City, which then lay open, "contained great store of very good fish, of divers sorts, as many yet living know, who have taken and tasted them, can well witness, but now (he says) no such matter." Sir John Hawkins, in his edition of Walton's "Angler" (1760), mentions that, about thirty years before, the City anglers were accustomed to enjoy their sport by the starlings of old London Bridge. "In the memory of a person not long since living, a waterman that plied at Essex Stairs, his name John Reeves, got a comfortable living by attending anglers with his boat. His method was to watch when the shoals of roach came down from the country, and, when he had found them, to go round to his customers and give them notice. Sometimes they (the fish) settled opposite the Temple; at others, at Blackfriars or Queenhithe; but most frequently about the chalk hills (the deposit of chalk rubble) near London Bridge. His hire was two shillings a tide. A certain number of persons who were accustomed thus to employ him raised a sum sufficient to buy him a waterman's coat and silver badge, the impress whereof was 'Himself, with an angler in his boat;' and he had annually a new coat to the time of his death, which might be about the year 1730." Mr. Goldham, the clerk or yeoman of Billingsgate Market, stated before a Parliamentary Committee that, in 1798, 400 fishermen, each of whom was the owner of a boat, and employed a boy, obtained a good livelihood by the exercise of their craft between Deptford and London, above and below bridge, taking roach, plaice, smelts, flounders, salmon, shad, eels, gudgeon, dace, dabs, &c. Mr. Goldham said that about 1810 he had known instances of as many as ten salmon and 3,000 smelts being taken at one haul up the river towards Wandsworth, and 50,000 smelts were brought daily to Billingsgate, and not fewer than 3,000 Thames salmon in the season. Some of the boats earned £6 a week, and salmon was sold at 3s. and 4s. a pound. The fishery was nearly destroyed at the time when this evidence was given, in 1828. The masters of the Dutch eel-ships stated before the same committee that, a few years before, they could bring their live eels in "wells" as far as Gallion's Reach, below Woolwich; but now (1828) they were obliged to stop at Erith, and they had sustained serious losses from the deleterious quality of the water, which killed the fish. The increase of gas-works and of manufactories of various kinds, and of filth disgorged by the sewers, will sufficiently account for this circumstance. The number of Dutch eel-vessels which bring supplies to Billings-

would climb up bundles of weeds for a moment's fresh air.

Bagford, the old antiquary, mentions a curious custom that once prevailed at Billingsgate. "This," he says, speaking of an old custom referred to in "Hudibras," "brings to my mind another ancient custom that hath been omitted of late years. It seems that in former times the porters that plyd at Billingsgate used civilly to entreat and desire every man that passed that way to salute a post that

BILLINGSGATE.   (*From a View taken in* 1820.)

gate varied, in 1842, from sixty to eighty annually. They brought about fifteen hundredweight of fish each, and paid a duty of £13. Mr. Butcher, an agent for Dutch fishermen, stated before the committee above mentioned that, in 1827, eight Dutch vessels arrived with full cargoes of healthy eels, about 14,000 pounds each, and the average loss was 4,000 pounds. Twelve years before, when the Thames was purer, the loss was only thirty pounds of eels a night; and the witness deposed that an hour after high water he had had 3,000 pounds of eels die in an hour. (How singularly this accounts for the cheap eel-pie!) The river had been getting worse yearly. Fish were often seen trying to save themselves on floating pieces of wood, and flounders

stood there in a vacant place. If he refused to do this, they forthwith laid hold of him, and by main force bouped him against the post; but if he quietly submitted to kiss the same, and paid down sixpence, they gave him a name, and chose some one of the gang for a godfather. I believe this was done in memory of some old image that formerly stood there, perhaps of Belus or Belin."

Adjoining Billingsgate, on the east side, stood Smart's Quay or Wharf, which we find noticed in the reign of Queen Elizabeth as containing an ingenious seminary for the instruction of young thieves. The following extract of a letter, addressed to Lord Burleigh, in July, 1585, by Fleetwood, the Recorder of London, evinces that the "art and mystery" of picking pockets was brought to considerable perfection in the sixteenth century :—

"Amongst our travels this one matter tumbled out by the way. One Wotton, a gentleman born, and some time a merchant of good credit, having

and over the top did hang a little scaring-bell ; and he that could take out a counter without any noise, was allowed to be a *public hoyster ;* and he that could take a piece of silver out of the purse without the noise of any of the bells, he was adjudged *a judicial nipper.* N. B.—That a *hoyster* is a pick-

THE OLD COAL EXCHANGE (*see page* 50).

fallen by time into decay, kept an ale-house at Smart's Key, near Billingsgate ; and after, for some misdemeanour, being put down, he reared up a new trade of life, and in the same house he procured all the cut-purses about this city to repair to his said house. There was a school-house set up to learn young boys to cut purses. There were hung up two devices ; the one was a pocket, the other was a purse. The pocket had in it certain counters, and was hung about with hawks' bells,

pocket, and a *nipper* is termed a pick-purse, or a cut-purse."

The Coal Exchange faces the site of Smart's Quay, Billingsgate. English coal is first mentioned in the reign of Henry III., who granted a charter to the people of Newcastle, empowering them to dig it. Soon afterwards, dyers, brewers, &c., began to use coal in their trade, and the nobles and gentry complaining of the smoke, a severe proclamation was passed against the use of sea-coal, though wood was yearly growing scarcer and dearer. Edward I. also issued a proclamation against the use of coal. Nevertheless, a charter of Edward II. shows Derbyshire coal to have been then used in London. In 1590 (Elizabeth) the owners of the Newcastle coal-pits, combining, raised the price of coals from 4s. to 9s. per chaldron ; and the following year the Lord High Admiral claimed the coal metage in the port of London. The mayor and citizens disputed and overthrew this claim, and, by the influence of Lord Treasurer Burleigh, obtained the Queen's confirmation of the City's right to the office. At one period in Elizabeth's reign it was prohibited to burn stone-coal during the session of Parliament for fear the health of the members (country gentlemen accustomed to their wood-fires) should be injured. Shakespeare speaks in a cozy way " of the latter end of a sea-coal fire ;" but others of the dramatists abuse coals ; and the sea-coal smoke was supposed to have much injured the stone of old St. Paul's. In 1655 (Commonwealth) the price of coal in London was usually above 20s. a chaldron ; and there were 320 "keels" at Newcastle, each of which carried 800 chaldrons, Newcastle measure ; and 136 of these made 217 chaldrons, London measure. A duty of only 1s. a chaldron was paid on coals in London, yet the great Protector generously granted the Corporation a licence to import 400 chaldrons every year for the poor citizens, duty free. The coal-carts numbered 420, and were placed under the regulation of the President and Governors of Christ's Hospital ; and all coal-sacks and measures were illegal unless sealed at Guildhall. It was also at this same period generously provided that the City companies should lay up stores of coal in summer (from 675 chaldrons to three, according to their ability), to be retailed in the winter in small quantities. To prevent extortion, conspiracy, and monopoly, retail dealers, by the same Act, were prohibited under penalties from contracting for coals, or meeting the coal-vessels before they arrived in the port of London.

By statute 16 and 17 Charles II., all sea-coal brought into the river Thames was to be sold by the chaldron, containing thirty-six bushels ; and all other coals sold by weight were to be sold after the proportion of 112 pounds to the hundred avoirdupois. By the 12th Queen Anne, the coal measure was ordered to be made round, and to contain one Winchester bushel and one quart of water ; the sack to hold three such bushels ; the bushel to be sealed or stamped at the Exchequer Office or the Guildhall, under penalty of £50.

In 1713 the master-meters of the Coal Office were only allowed to employ or dismiss the deputies sanctioned by the Lord Mayor and Aldermen. An Act of George II. required the ancient custom to be kept up of giving one chaldron in addition to every score purchased on board ship, under penalty of £100. This bonus was called *ingrain*, and constituted good Pool measure. By a later Act any lighterman receiving any gratuity from owners or fitters for preference in the quality in lading ships was fined £500. All bargains for coals at Billingsgate had to be entered on the factor's book, signed by buyer and seller, and witnessed by the factor, who gave a copy of the contract to each. Masters of ships were fined for delaying their cargoes at Gravesend.

The old Coal Exchange, erected in 1805, for the use of the black-diamond merchants, was a quaint and picturesque building, with a receding portico, supported by small Doric pillars, and with some stone steps, that led into a quadrangle. The narrow windows lit the upper storeys. The present Coal Exchange was opened by Prince Albert in 1849, and Mr. J. B. Bunning was the architect. The design was thought original yet simple. The fronts in Thames Street and St. Mary-at-Hill are 112 feet wide and 61 feet high. The entrance vestibule is in a circular tower 109 feet high. The lowest storey is Roman-Doric ; the first storey Ionic. The inner rotunda is crowned by a dome 74 feet high, which rests on eight piers. About 300 tons of iron were used in the building. The Raphaelesque decorations were designed by Mr. Sang. Above emblematical figures of the collier rivers are figures of the Virtues, and over these are groups of shells, snakes, and lizards. In some of the arabesques the leading features are views of the Wallsend, Percy, Pitt Main, and other celebrated collieries, adorned with groups of flowers and fossil plants.

While digging for the foundation of the new building, on the site of the old "Dog" tavern, the workmen came on a Roman sweating-bath, with tiled floors and several rooms. This hypocaust is still shown.

The floor of the rotunda is composed of inlaid woods, disposed in form of a mariner's compass, within a border of Greek fret. The flooring consists of upwards of 4,000 pieces of wood, of various kinds. The varieties of wood employed comprise black ebony, black oak, common and red English oak, wainscot, white holly, mahogany, American elm, red and white walnut, and mulberry. The appearance of this floor is beautiful in the extreme. The whole of these materials were prepared by Messrs. Davison and Symington's patent process of seasoning woods. The same desiccating process has been applied to the wood-work throughout the building. The black oak introduced is part of an old tree which was discovered in the river Tyne, where it had unquestionably lain between four and five centuries. The mulberry-wood, of which the blade of the dagger in the shield of the City Arms is composed, is a piece of a tree planted by Peter the Great, when he worked as a shipwright in Deptford Dockyard.

"The coloured decorations of this Exchange have been most admirably imagined and successfully carried out. They are extremely characteristic, and on this point deserve praise. The entrance vestibule is peculiarly rich and picturesque in its embellishments; terminal figures, vases with fruit, arabesque foliage, &c., all of the richest and most glowing colours, fill up the vault of the ceiling; and, looking up through an opening in the ceiling, a figure of Plenty scattering riches, and surrounded by *figurini*, is seen painted in the ceiling of the lantern. Over the entrance doorway, within a sunk panel, is painted the City Arms."

The Hall of the Watermen's Company was originally situated at Coldharbour, near the "Three Cranes," in the Vintry, and is referred to in the statute of 1 James I., 1603. It was burnt, with many of the Company's old records, in the Great Fire of 1666, but was again rebuilt in the old place. It was rebuilt once more in 1722, and in 1776 the Company removed to St. Mary-at-Hill, Billingsgate, where it now remains, Calvert's brewery occupying the old site. In 1555 an Act was passed, directing that the Court should consist of eight watermen, to be called overseers and rulers, to be annually appointed by the Court of Lord Mayor and Aldermen. In 1641 an order was made by the Court of Lord Mayor, that fifty-five persons at the different stairs should select twenty of their number to choose the eight rulers to carry out the laws. These fifty-five persons assumed the title of "assistants."

In 1700 the lightermen of the City were incorporated with the watermen (called Watermen and Lightermen's Company). Three lightermen were to be appointed as additional overseers and rulers, and a court of forty assistants. In 1729 an Act was passed which reduced the number of assistants to thirty. In 1827 a new Act was passed, re-incorporating the Company, to consist of a master, four wardens, and twenty-one assistants. In case of vacancy in court, the court were to select three qualified persons, for the Court of Lord Mayor, &c., to choose one to fill the vacancy. In 1859 an Act was passed, by which the court were empowered to fill up vacancies, without reference to the Court of Lord Mayor, &c.

The various Acts passed from the time of Henry VIII. gave power to the Company to hold general courts, courts of binding, and courts for hearing and determining complaints, and to punish offenders by fine and imprisonment; power to license passenger-boats, register craft, and to appoint Sunday ferries, the rent of which has always been applied to the relief of the poor of the Company, and to make bye-laws for the regulation of boats, barges, and steam-boats on the river, and the men navigating the same. There are about 350 apprentices bound annually, and about 250 complaints are investigated during the year. The introduction of steam greatly reduced the watermen, but the lightermen and barges have been annually increasing. There are now about 6,000 freemen of the Company, and 2,000 apprentices. The court distribute about £1,600 per annum, out of their ferry-rents, in pensions to 400 poor freemen and widows. Forty almshouses have been established at Penge, supported by the voluntary contributions of the public.

The fares of the Thames watermen and wherrymen were regulated by Henry VIII. in 1514. Taylor, the water-poet, *temp.* Elizabeth, states the watermen between Windsor and Gravesend at 40,000. A third statute regulates the dimensions of the boats and wherries, then dangerously "shallow and tickle;" the Lord Mayor and Aldermen to limit the watermen's fares, if confirmed by the Privy Council. Strype was told by one of the Company that there were 40,000 watermen upon their rolls; that they could furnish 20,000 men for the fleet, and that 8,000 were then in the service. Taylor, the water-poet, with his fellow-watermen, violently opposed the introduction of coaches as trade-spoilers. The Company (says Mr. Timbs) condemned the building of Westminster and Blackfriars bridges, as an injury to the ferries between Vauxhall and the Temple, the profits of which were given to the poor, aged, decayed, and maimed watermen and their widows; and in both cases the Company were compensated for their losses. The substitution of steam-boats for wherries has, however, been as fatal to the watermen as railways to stage-coachmen.

The Lord High Admiral, or the Commissioners of the Admiralty, used to have power to demand a certain number of watermen to serve in the Royal Navy, by an Act of William and Mary; and in 1796 nearly 4,000 watermen were thus enrolled. The ribald banter of the Thames watermen was formerly proverbial, and is mentioned by Ned Ward, and nearly all the essayists. Dr. Johnson, Boswell says, was particularly proud of having silenced some watermen who tried to ridicule him. By an order of the Company in 1761, this foul kind of extemporaneous satire was forbidden by the rulers and auditors of the Company; and any waterman or apprentice convicted of using indecent language was fined 2s. 6d. for each offence; the fines to go to the use of the "poor, aged, decayed, and maimed members of the Company, their widows and children."

All wherries were formerly required to be 12½ feet long and 4½ broad in the midships, under pain of forfeiture; and all wherries and boats were to be entered and numbered. Extortion and abuse was punishable by fine and imprisonment. A statute (34 George III.) placed the watermen more immediately under the mayor's jurisdiction; and the highest penalty was fixed at £3.

Before the time of steamboats, a bell used to ring at Gravesend at high water, as a warning to hurry off the London watermen. A report of the Dock Committee in 1796 shows that there were then 12,283 watermen, 8,283 freemen, 2,000 non-free-men, and 2,000 apprentices; the annual number of apprentices being from 200 to 300. In 1828 there were above 3,000 wherries on the Thames.

When the opening of Blackfriars Bridge destroyed the landing ferry there, established for the benefit of the Waterman's Poor Fund, the bridge committee gave £13,650 Consolidated Three per Cents to the rulers of the Company, as a recompense, and the interest is now appropriated to the same purpose as the ferry-fund used to be.

Close to Waterman's Hall is the Fellowship Porters' Hall. This brotherhood was incorporated as early as 1155 (Henry II.), and re-incorporated in 1613 (James I.). The business of the Fellowship Porters, which is now less strictly defined than in old times, is to carry or house corn, salt, coals, fish,

and fruit of all descriptions. There were formerly about 3,000 Fellowship Porters; there are now about 1,500. The Ticket Porters and Tackle Porters have no hall. The fraternity of Fellowship Porters had the power, by an Act of Council of 1646, to choose twelve rulers, the Lord Mayor and Aldermen reserving the right to appoint one of the number. There are now six rulers. The governor, deputy-governor, and deputy of the ward act as superintendents of the Company. The Company has no livery or arms, and ranks the nineteenth in the order of precedence.

In accordance with a pretty old custom, every Sunday before Midsummer Day a sermon is preached to the Fellowship Porters in the church of St. Mary-at-Hill. They overnight furnish the merchants and families above Billingsgate with nosegays, and in the morning proceed from the hall to the church, two and two, carrying nosegays. They walk up the middle aisle to the communion-table, and each places an offering in one of the two basins

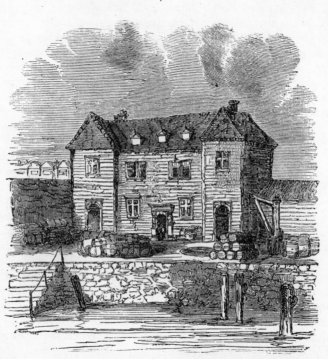

THE CUSTOM HOUSE—TIME OF ELIZABETH.

on the communion-rails, for the relief of the Company's poor; and after they have prayed, the deputy, the merchants, their wives, children, and servants walk in order from their seats, and perform the same solemnity. The annual cost of the nosegays amounts to nearly £20.

And now we come to that great Government toll-bar, the Customs House. The first building of this kind in London was rebuilt by John Churchman, Sheriff of London, in 1385 (Richard II.), and it stood on the site of the present buildings. Another and larger edifice, erected in the reign of Elizabeth, was destroyed by the Great Fire. A new Custom House, built by Wren, was destroyed by fire in 1715, and its successor, the design by Ripley, was burnt down February 12, 1814.

In Elizabeth's time, the farmers of the Customs

made immense fortunes. A chronicler of her reign says: "About this time (1590) the commodity of the Custom House amounted to an unexpected value; for the Queen, being made acquainted, by means of a subtle fellow, named Caerwardine, with the mystery of their gains, so enhanced the rate, that Sir Thomas Smith, Master of the Custom House, who heretofore farmed it of the Queen for £14,000 yearly, was now augmented to £42,000, and afterwards to £50,000, which, notwithstanding, was valued but as an ordinary sum for such oppressing gaine. The Lord Treasurer, the Earls of Leicester and Walsingham, much opposed themselves against this Caerwardine, denying him entrance into the Privy Chamber, insomuch that, expostulating with the Queen they traduced her harkening to such a fellow's information, to the disparagement of the judgment of her Council, and the discredit of their case. But the Queen answered them, that all princes ought to be, if not as favourable, yet as just, to the lowest as the highest, deciding that they who falsely accuse her Privy Council of sloth or indiscretion should be severely punished; but that they who justly accused them should be heard. That she was Queen as well to the poorest as to the proudest, and that, therefore, she would never be deaf to their just complaints. Likewise, that she would not suffer that those toll-takers, like horse-leeches, should glut themselves with the riches of the realm, and starve her exchequer; which, as she will not bear it to be *docked*, so hateth she to enrich it with the poverty of the people."

The revenue has grown like the green bay-tree of the Psalmist. In the first year of Elizabeth, the Customs realised £73,846; in her fifth year, £57,436; in her tenth, £74,875. The average of sixteen years, before the Restoration, was £316,402. In Elizabeth's time the Custom House establishment consisted of eight principal officers, each of whom had from two to six men under him; but the principal waiter had as many as sixteen subordinates. From 1671 to 1688, says D'Avenant, the first inspector-general of imports and exports, the revenue derived from the English Customs averaged £555,752 a year. From 1700 to 1714, the Customs averaged £1,352,764. At the close of the century they exceeded £6,000,000. They now exceed £20,000,000.

The Custom House built after the Great Fire was said to have cost £10,000. The new Custom House of 1718 had better-arranged apartments and accommodation for a greater number of clerks. The new building was 189 feet long, and the centre 29 feet deep. It was built of brick and stone, and

the wings had a passage colonnade of the Tuscan order, towards the river, the upper storey being relieved by Ionic pilasters and pediments. The great feature of the building was the "Long Room," which, extending the whole length of the centre, was 127 feet long, 29 wide, and 24 high. Here several commissioners superintended personally the numerous officers and clerks of various departments.

This building, already too small for the ever-growing commerce of London, was destroyed, as before mentioned, in 1814, by a fire, which also destroyed ten houses on the north side of Thames Street. Cellars and warehouses full of valuable property, and stores of documents and records, were also lost. But, several years before this catastrophe, the enlargement of the Custom House had been planned. It had been at first proposed to build an additional wing, but on a survey the old building was found too much decayed and dilapidated to warrant much expenditure on its renovation. The Lords of the Treasury selected Mr. Laing's design. Between the old Custom House and Billingsgate there had been eight quays, equal to 479 feet; but the site now selected was immediately east of Billingsgate, with only a landing-stair between. It had been suggested to place the Custom House on the north side of Thames Street, so as to save the expense of embankment; but this would have necessitated the widening of many narrow and crooked streets, and the formation of two docks, one east and one west of the quay. The estimate for the new building was £165,000, exclusive of the formation of the foundation-ground and some other contingencies. The owners of private property claimed £84,478, and were paid £41,700. The materials of the old building were sold for £12,400. The first necessity was to test the substratum. The soil was bored with huge augers that screwed down eighteen to twenty feet. A substratum of close gravel, at first promising well, proved to be artificial. The whole ground, from the level of the river to the south side of Thames Street, proved to have once been part of the bed of the river. Rushes were found mixed with mussel-shells and the chrysalids of water insects. The workmen also came on three distinct lines of wooden embankments at the distances of 58, 86, and 103 feet within the range of the existing wharves; and about fifty from the campshot, or under edge of the wharf wall, a wall built of chalk and rubble, and faced with Purbeck stone, was discovered, running east and west. This was, no doubt, the river rampart of London, mentioned by Fitzstephen. It was so strongly built that it could scarcely be broken even by iron wedges. Many coins and other Roman antiquities were found. Rows of piles, twenty-eight and thirty feet long, were then sunk, and on these were placed sleepers of beech fitted in with brickwork.

The first stone of the new building was laid in 1813, by Lord Liverpool, then First Lord of the Treasury, and was opened for business, May 12, 1817. The north side, fronting Thames Street, was plain, but on the south front, towards the

cheaply or too quickly, and the foundation gave way. This was bitterly complained of in a Parliamentary Committee of 1828, when it was stated that this failure had led to a charge of nearly £180,000, in addition to the original expenditure of £225,000. The Long Room eventually had to be taken down by Mr. Laing, the architect, the foundations relaid, and the allegorical figures removed.

THE PRESENT COAL EXCHANGE.

river, the central compartment projected, and the wings had a hexastyle detached Ionic colonnade. The central attic, comprising the exterior of the celebrated Long Room, was decorated with alto and basso relievos, representing in allegorical groups the Arts, Sciences, Commerce, Industry, and types of the nations who are our principal commercial allies. The dial-plate, nine feet in diameter, was supported by colossal figures of Industry and Plenty, while the royal arms were sustained by figures of Ocean and Commerce. The Long Room was 196 feet by 66.

Unfortunately, however, the work was done too

The quay is too narrow to afford a good view, but there is a simple grandeur about the design, when seen from the bridge or river. The water front, says Mr. Platt, is 488 feet, 90 feet longer than the old Post Office, and 30 feet longer than the National Gallery.

The number of officers and clerks in this great public office is over 600, out and in. The out-door *employés* are about 300. The inspectors-general superintend the tide-surveyors, tide-waiters, and watermen, and appoint them their daily duty, each inspector attending in rotation at Gravesend. The tide-surveyors visit ships reported inwards or out-

THE OLD CUSTOM HOUSE. *(From a View by Maur r, published in 1753.)*

wards, to see that the tide-waiters put on board discharge their duty properly. The tide-waiters, if the vessel is coming in, remain on board, unless the vessel be in the docks, like men in possession, till the cargo is discharged. The landing-officers, under the superintendence of the surveyors, attend the quays and docks, and take a note of goods as they are craned on shore, and on the receipt of warrants showing that the duties are paid, permit the delivery of goods for home consumption. The officers of the coast department attend to vessels arriving and departing between London and the out-ports, and give permits for landing their cargoes, and take bonds for the delivery at their destination of goods sent coastwise. They appoint the coast-waiters, who attend the shipping, and discharge all coastwise goods. The searchers see to all goods shipped for abroad, the entries of which, after passing the Long Room, are placed in their hands, and they examine the packages, to see that they duly correspond. As the amount of work fluctuates, and when a special wind blows, flocks of vessels arrive together, the number of supernumeraries employed at the Custom House is very large. There are sometimes, says a good authority, as many as 2,000 persons a day working at Custom House business between Gravesend and London Bridge.

The Long Room is the department where most of the documents required by the Customs' Laws are received by officials. The first thing necessary upon the arrival of a vessel from a foreign country is the report of the ship, that is, the master must, within twenty-four hours of entering the port, deliver at the Report Office in the Long Room an account of her cargo. Then, before any goods are delivered out of charge by the officers of the out-door department, who board and watch vessels on their arrival, entries of the goods passed also in the Long Room must have reached the officers. These entries are documents giving particulars of the goods in greater detail than is required in the master's report, and are delivered in the Long Room by the consignees of the cargo, or by their representatives. A single entry may suffice for an entire cargo, if it be all of one kind of goods and be the property of one person, or any number of entries may be necessary if the cargo be varied in nature. The report and the entries—that is, the account of the cargo rendered by the master and that supplied by the consignees—are compared, and delivery of goods not mentioned in the report, though correctly entered, is refused until the omission has been satisfactorily explained. In the case of goods liable to duty, the entries are not suffered to leave the

Long Room until it is ascertained that the payment has been made. The entry for such goods, when signed by the Long Room officers, in testimony of its having been passed by them, vouches for the payment of the duty, and constitutes the warrant authorising the officers at the waterside to deliver the goods. Such is the general course of routine applicable to vessels arriving from foreign ports. The officers of the Long Room sit at their desks along the four sides. The visitors are chiefly weather-beaten sea-captains, shipowners, and ship-owners' clerks, who come and report arrivals or obtain clearances, and wholesale merchants, who have goods to import or export, or goods to place in bond.

A correct account is also required of the cargoes of vessels sailing from this country, and the documents by which this is obtained are presented in the Searcher's Office in the Long Room either by the shippers of the goods or by the master of the vessel. The operation performed in the Long Room by the master of an outward-bound ship, which corresponds to the reporting of an arriving vessel, is termed "clearing" or "obtaining clearance."

The documents required from the masters of vessels engaged in trade from one port of the United Kingdom to another, termed "coasting trade," are less elaborate.

From the particulars obtained by the various papers thus delivered in the Long Room, are prepared the monthly returns of trade and navigation, published by the Board of Trade, and the collection and arrangement of the information so obtained occupies a large staff of clerks in the Statistical Department of the Custom House.

At each outport the room where the business described above is transacted bears the name of the Long Room, although in most cases it is neither long nor in any other way extensive.

The establishment of docks surrounded by high walls, from which goods can be removed only through gateways easily guarded, has made it possible to provide for the security of the duties upon importations with a far less numerous staff of officers than would be necessary if every vessel discharged in the river or at open quays. And the gradual reduction which has taken place in the number of articles in the tariff liable to duty during the last thirty years renders a less rigid examination of goods necessary than was previously requisite. These and other causes enable the present reduced staff to deal efficiently with an amount of business to which under former circumstances it would have been wholly inadequate.

The warehousing system, which consisted in permitting the payment of duties upon goods deposited under Crown locks in warehouses duly approved for the purpose by the Board of Customs, to be deferred until the goods are wanted for consumption, offers great facilities to trade, and is largely availed of. This system involves the keeping of very elaborate accounts, which form the duty of the warehousing departments.

Of the 170 or so distinct apartments in the Custom House, all classified and combined to unite order and contiguity, the king is the Long Room, 190 feet long, 66 wide, and between 40 and 50 feet high. The eye cannot take in at once its breadth and its length, but it is not so handsome as the room that fell in, to the dismay of Mr. Peto. The floor is plank. The cellars in the basement form a groined fireproof crypt.

The rooms are perfectly plain, all but the Board Room, which is slightly decorated, and contains portraits of George III. and George IV., the latter by Sir Thomas Lawrence. The Queen's Warehouse is on the ground floor. The entrance to the Custom House is on the north front. On the southern side there is an entrance from the quay and river.

Nearly one-half of the Customs of the United Kingdom, says a writer on the subject, are collected in the port of London. In 1840, while the London Customs were £11,116,685, the total of the United Kingdom were only £23,341,813. In the same year the only place approaching London was Liverpool, where the Customs amounted to £4,607,326. In 1849 the London Customs were £11,070,176. The same year the declared value of the exports from Liverpool amounted to no less than £33,341,918, or nearly three times the value of the exports from London, for in foreign trade London is surpassed by Liverpool. Mr. M'Culloch estimates, including the home and foreign markets, the total value of produce conveyed into and from London annually at £65,000,000 sterling.

The number of foreign vessels that entered the port of London in the year 1841 was estimated at 8,167, and the number of coasters at 21,122. The expense of collecting the Customs in Great Britain alone is calculated at over a million sterling. The Board of Commissioners, that sits at the Custom House, has all the outports of the United Kingdom under its superintendence. It receives reports from them, and issues instructions from the central Board. The recording of the business of the great national firm, now performed by the Statistical Office in the Custom House, was attempted in the reign of Charles II., and urged on the Commissioners of Customs by the bewildered Privy Council

for Trade; but it was declared, after many trials, to be impossible. It was first really begun in the business-like reign of William III., when the broad arrow was first used to check thefts of Government property, and when the office of Inspector-General of Imports and Exports was established, and the Custom House ledger, to record their value, first started. The Act of 1694 required all goods exported and imported to be entered in the Custom House books, with the prices affixed. Cotton, therefore, was taxed at this the official value, till 1798. In this year the Government imposed a convoy duty of four per cent., *ad valorem*, upon all exports; and to do this equitably, every shipper of goods was compelled to make a declaration of their then actual value. This was what is called "the declared or real value." A daily publication, called the "Bill of Entry," is issued at the Custom House, to report the imports and exports and the arrival and clearance of vessels.

Prior to the year 1825, says a writer in Knight's "London," the statutes relating to the Customs had accumulated, from the reign of Edward I., to 1,500, and were naturally as confusing and entangled as they were contradictory. Mr. Huskisson, Mr. J. D. Hume, and eventually the slow-moving Board of Trade, at last revised the statutes, and consolidated them into eleven acts. They were still further simplified in 1833, and again consolidated in 1853. One of the Acts passed in 1833 enumerates not fewer than 1,150 different rates of duty chargeable on imported articles, while the main source of revenue is derived from a very small number of articles. "For example," says a writer on the subject, "the duty on seventeen articles produced, in 1839, about $94\frac{1}{2}$ per cent. of the total revenue of Customs, the duties on other articles being not only comparatively unproductive, but vexatious and a hindrance to the merchants, shipowners, and others. In the above year, forty-six articles were productive of $98\frac{2}{3}$ per cent. of the total Customs' revenue.

"The occasional importation of articles which are not enumerated in the tariff of duties is often productive of amusing perplexity. Mr. Huskisson mentioned a case of this nature when he brought forward the plans of consolidation already mentioned. A gentleman had imported a mummy from Egypt, and the officers of Customs were not a little puzzled by this non-enumerated article. These remains of mortality, muscles and sinews, pickled and preserved three thousand years ago, could not be deemed a raw material, and therefore, upon deliberation, it was determined to tax them as a manufactured article. The importer, anxious that his mummy should not be seized, stated its value at £400; and the declaration cost him £200, being at the rate of £50 per cent. on the manufactured merchandise which he was about to import. Mr. Huskisson reduced the duties on non-enumerated manufactured articles from £50 to £20 per cent., and of non-enumerated unmanufactured articles from £20 to £10 per cent." A somewhat similar case, relating to an importation of ice from Norway, was mentioned in a debate in the House of Lords in 1842. A doubt was started what duty it ought to pay, and the point was referred from the Custom House to the Treasury, and from the Treasury to the Board of Trade; and it was ultimately decided that the ice might be introduced on the payment of the duty on dry goods; but as one of the speakers remarked, "The ice was dissolved before the question was solved."

In the time of Charles I. the Customs were farmed, and we find Garrard writing to Lord Stafford, January 11th, 1634, mentioning that the farmers of the Customs (rejoicing over their good bargains, no doubt), had been unusually liberal in their new year's gifts to the king, having sent him, besides the usual 2,000 pieces, £5,000 in pieces, and an unset diamond that had cost them £5,000. Yet what a small affair the Customs must have been compared to now, when sugar, tea, tobacco, wine, and brandy produce each of them more than a million a year!

Defoe says, "In the Long Room it's a pretty pleasure to see the multitude of payments that are made there in a morning. I heard Count Tallard say that nothing gave him so true and great an idea of the richness and grandeur of this nation as this, when he saw it after the Peace of Ryswick."

Mr. Platt's account of the working of the Custom House system of thirty years ago shows a remarkable contrast with that of the present day. Writing in the year 1853, he says, "The progress of an article of foreign merchandise through the Customs to the warehouse or shop of the dealer is as follows :—First, on the arrival of the ship at Gravesend, tide-waiters are put on board and remain until she reaches the appointed landing-place. The goods are reported and entered at the Custom House, and a warrant is transmitted to the landing-waiters, who superintend the unloading of the cargo. A landing-waiter is specially appointed to each ship; officers under him, some of whom are gaugers, examine, weigh, and ascertain the contents of the several packages, and enter an account of them. These operations are subject to the daily inspection of superior officers. When warehoused, the goods are in charge of a locker, who is under the warehouse-keeper. When goods are delivered for home consumption, the locker receives a warrant from the Custom House certifying that the goods had been paid; he then looks out the goods, and the warehouse-keeper signs the warrant. When foreign or colonial goods are exported, the process is more complicated. The warehouse-keeper makes out a 're-weighing slip;' a landing-waiter examines the goods, which continue in the charge of the locker, and a cocket, with a certificate from the proper officers at the Custom House, as his authority for their delivery. The warehouse-keeper signs this document, and a counterpart of the cocket, called a 'shipping bill,' is prepared by the exporting merchant. The goods pass from the warehouse-keeper into the hands of the searcher, who directs a tide-waiter to receive them at the water-side and to attend their shipment, taking an account of the articles; and he remains on board until the vessel reaches Gravesend, when she is visited by a searcher stationed there; the tide-waiter is discharged, and the vessel proceeds. But before her final clearance the master delivers to the searcher a document called 'a content,' being a list of the goods on board, and which is compared with the cocket. It is then only that the cargo can be fairly said to be out of the hands of the Custom House officers."

Tide-waiters are not now specially appointed to each ship on arrival. There are no export duties now and no *ad valorem* duties. Cockets have been abolished.

The following statement from the "Statesman's Year Book" is valuable as a comparison :—

Ports.	1870.	1871.	Increase.	Decrease.
	£	£	£	£
London	10,017,682	10,023,573	5,891	—
Liverpool ...	2,723,217	2,875,584	152,367	—
Other ports of England	3,131,902	2,991,888	—	140,014
Scotland......	2,577,826	2,502,127	—	75,699
Ireland	1,919,072	1,942,721	23,649	—
Total	20,369,699	20,335,893	181,907	215,713
Decrease......	—	—	—	33,806

It will be seen that the amount of Customs receipts collected in London in each of the years 1870 and 1871 was more than that of all the other ports of Great Britain taken together, and five times that of the whole of Ireland. Besides London and Liverpool, there is only one port in England, Bristol, the Customs receipts of which average a million a year, and one more, Hull, where they are above a quarter of a million. It is to be observed that there has been a great reduction of Customs duties of late years. During the sixteen years from 1857 to 1872 the actual diminution of Customs has been no less than £14,255,855.

The annual summary as to trade in the port of London for the year 1872 shows a steady increase in the number of vessels arriving, and a trifling decrease in the departures. A total of 11,518 vessels arrived during the year, 7,054 of which were sailing and 4,464 steam-ships, thus indicating a total increase of 113 as compared with the previous year. The vessels which cleared outwards were 8,730, both kinds, 6,041 of which were with cargo, and 2,689 in ballast, or a total decrease of 339 as compared with the departures in 1871. A considerable increase arose in London in the total number of seizures of tobacco, cigars, and spirits, as compared with the year 1871, 293 cases having occurred in 1872. The total quantity of tobacco and cigars seized in London was 2,369 lbs., being an increase of 947 lbs. as compared with that seized in 1871, while the total quantity of spirits seized was 63 gallons only, being a decrease of 66 gallons.

The Custom House Quay fronts the Thames. Here Cowper, the poet, came, intending to make away with himself. "Not knowing," he says, "where to poison myself, I resolved upon drowning. For that purpose I took a coach, and ordered the man to drive to Tower Wharf, intending to throw myself into the river from the Custom House Quay. I left the coach upon the Tower Wharf, intending never to return to it; but upon coming to the quay I found the water low, and a porter seated upon some goods there, as if on purpose to prevent me. This passage to the bottomless pit being mercifully shut against me, I returned back to the coach."

A modern essayist has drawn a living picture of the Custom House sales:—"The Queen's Warehouse is situated on the ground-floor of the Custom House. The Queen's Warehouse is not an imposing apartment, either in its decorations or extent; it is simply a large, square room, lighted by an average number of windows, and consisting of four bare walls, upon which there is not the most distant approach to decoration. Counters are placed in different directions, with no regard to order of effect. Here and there masses of drapery for sale are hung suspended from cords, or to all appearance nailed against the wall. Across one corner of the room, in the immediate vicinity of a very handsome inlaid cabinet, two rows of dilapidated Bath chaps are slung upon a rope. Close under these delicacies stands a rosewood piano, on which a foreign lady, supported by a foreign gentleman, is playing a showy fantasia. . . .

"Eighty-nine opera-glasses; three dozen 'companions'—more numerous than select, perhaps; forty dozen black brooches—ornamental mourning, sent over probably by some foreign manufacturer, relying in the helplessness of our Woods-and-Forest-ridden Board of Health, and in the death-dealing fogs and stinks of our metropolis; seventeen dozen daguerreotype plates, to receive as many pretty and happy faces; eighty dozen brooches; nineteen dozen pairs of ear-rings; forty-two dozen finger-rings; twenty-one dozen pairs of bracelets. The quantities and varieties are bewildering, and the ladies cluster about in a state of breathless excitement, or give way to regrets that the authorities will not sell less than ten dozen tiaras, or half-a-dozen clocks. The French popular notion, that every Englishman has an exhaustless store of riches, seems to hold as firmly as ever; for here we find about three hundred dozen portemonnaies, and countless purses, evidently of French manufacture. Presently we are shown what Mr. Carlyle would call 'a gigantic system of shams,' in five hundred and thirty-eight gross of imitation turquoises. . .

"On the particular occasion to which we have been all along referring three hundred gross of lucifer-matches figured in the bazaar, besides several acres of East India matting, forty-nine gallons of Chutney sauce; eighteen gallons of curry-paste; thirty millions of splints; seventy-seven hundredweight of slate-pencils, sixty-eight gallons of rosewater, one package of visiting cards, one ship's long-boat, and 'four pounds' of books in the English language."

One of Mr. Dickens's staff has bitterly described the delay in passing baggage through the Custom House. "A fine view of the river," he says, "seen through one of the open windows, was being calmly enjoyed by a portly person, evidently of considerable official pretensions. A clerk, writing the reverse of a running hand, sat at a desk; another (who seemed, by the jaunty style in which he wore his hat, to be a dropper-in from some other department of the Customs) leaned lazily against the desk, enjoying the proceedings of the baffled, heated ladies and gentlemen who had escaped from the crowd, and who were anxiously threading the confused maze of passengers' effects strewed on the floor, to find their own. The scene was made complete by two or three porters, whose deliberate mode of opening carpet-bags, boxes, and trunks, showed that it was not their fate to be hurried, in their passage through this life."

All these inconveniences have now been removed, and much civility and promptitude is shown by the Custom House official.

ROMAN REMAINS FOUND IN BILLINGSGATE (*see page* 50).

CHAPTER VI.

THE TOWER.

Cæsar's Tower—Bishop Gundulfus—Henry III.'s Buildings—The White Tower—Free Access to the Tower claimed by London Citizens—
Flambard's Escape—Prince Griffin—Thomas de Beauchamp—Charles of Orleans—Lord Cobham—Wyatt and his Cat—Murder of the Young
Princes—The Earl of Surrey—Pilgrims of Grace—Lady Jane Grey—Sir Thomas Wyat—The "White Rose of York."

THE Tower has been the background of all the
darkest scenes of English history. Its claims to
Roman descent we have before noticed. There
can be little doubt that the Roman wall that ran
along Thames Street terminated in this fort, within
which bars of silver stamped with the name of
Honorius have been discovered. Our Saxon
chapter showed that Alfred unquestionably built a
river-side stronghold on the same site. Alfred has
been long forgotten within the Tower walls, but the
name of Cæsar's Tower Shakespeare has, by a few
words, kept alive for ever. This castle—for centuries a palace, for centuries a prison, and now a
barrack, a show-place, a mere fossil of the sterner
ages—was commenced, in its present form, by
Gundulf, the Bishop of Rochester, for that stern
represser of Saxon discontent, William the Conqueror. This Benedictine friar, who had visited
the East, built the White Tower, the first St. Peter's

Church, and the Hall (or Jewel) Tower. He lived
to the age of eighty, and saw the Tower completed.

The next great builder at the Tower was Henry
III., who erected Corfe, Conway, and Beaumaris
Castles. He added to the tall square White Tower
the Water Gate, the great wharf, the Cradle Tower,
the Lantern (where his bedroom and private closet
were), the Galleyman Tower, and the first wall of
the *enceinte*. He adorned the St. John's Chapel,
in the White Tower, with frescoes, and gave bells
to St. Peter's Church on Tower Green. In the
Hall Tower, from which a passage led through the
Great Hall into the Lantern, he built that small
private chapel before whose cross, says Mr. Dixon,
Henry VI. was afterwards stabbed.

The embankment and wharf which the Water
Gate commanded was Henry's greatest work. The
land recovered from the river, and much exposed
to the sweep of the tide, was protected by piles,

CAPTIVITY OF THE DUKE OF ORLEANS IN THE TOWER.   (*Fr m an Illumination in the Royal MS.*)

enclosed by a front of stone. The London citizens rejoiced when, in 1240, the Water Gate and wall both fell, under the action of high spring-tides.

The next year the Barbican fell again, and people said that the spirit of St. Thomas à Becket had appeared, and, indignant at the infringement of public rights, had struck down the walls with a blow of his crucifix. After wasting more than 12,000 marks, the king at last secured a firm foundation, and reared the Water Gate as it now stands. The saints obnoxious to the walls raised against London citizens were propitiated by an oratory called the Confessor's Chapel, the martyr giving his name to the gate itself.

The whole wharf, 1,200 feet long, lay open to the Thames, except a patch of ground at the lower end, near the Iron Gate, which led to the Hospital of St. Catherine the Virgin, where sheds and magazines were built (now the docks). To the river-front there were three stairs. The Queen's Stairs, where royalty landed, lay beneath the Byeward Gate and the Belfry, with a passage by bridge and postern through the Byeward Tower into Water Lane. The Water-way passed under St. Thomas's Tower to the flight of steps in Water Lane, and was generally known as Traitor's Gate, the entrance for prisoners. The Galleyman Stairs (seldom used) lay under the Cradle Tower, by which there was a private entrance to the royal quarters.

Under the Plantagenet kings, says Mr. Dixon, the Tower warden claimed a right, very obnoxious to the London citizens, of putting "kiddles" or weirs filled with nets in front of the Tower Wharf, and, indeed, in any part of the Thames. For sums of money any one could buy licences of the Tower wardens to set kiddles in the Thames, Lea, and Medway with nets that stopped even the smallest fish. Ceaseless were the complaints of this intolerable injustice, till Richard I. surrendered the Tower rights on religious grounds, for the salvation of his soul and those of his ruthless ancestors; but the warden soon reasserted his privileges.

By Magna Charta all kiddles were to be removed from the Thames. The warden still disregarding these claims of the citizens, the Sheriff of London, on one occasion, made a raid, and by force of arms destroyed all the obnoxious nets. In the reign of Henry III. this quarrel assumed a more serious aspect. Enraged at the kiddles placed in the Medway, Jordan de Coventry and a body of armed men proceeded to Yantlet Creek, near Rochester, carried off thirty kiddles, and made prisoners of five men of Rochester, seven men of Strood, and three men of Cliff, with nine other malefactors, and threw them into Newgate. The Rochester men resolved to bring the case before the king, and it was tried at his palace at Kennington. The justiciar who attended for the Crown was a collateral ancestor of Sir Walter Raleigh. The mayor's defence for putting the Kentish men into gaol was that they were infringing the rights of the

City, lessening the dignity of the Crown, and, according to an express clause of Magna Charta, incurring the ban of excommunication. The judges agreed with the mayor, and the prisoners were each fined £10, and the captured nets were burnt with rejoicings in Westcheap.

The White Tower, says its latest chronicler, is ninety feet high, and from twelve to fifteen feet thick. It is built in four tiers—the vaults, the main floor, the banqueting-floor, and the state floor. Each tier contains three rooms, not counting the stairs, corridors, and small chambers sunk in the solid wall. In each storey there is a large west room running north and south the whole length of the tower, an east room lying parallel to the first, and a cross chamber at the south-west corner. The rooms are parted by walls never less than ten feet thick. On each angle of the tower is a turret, one of which is round. The vaults have no stairs or doors of their own. Loopholes in the wall let in the damp river air, but little light. The cross-chamber vault, or Little Ease, is darker and damper than its two brethren. There is some ground for belief, says Mr. Dixon, that Little Ease was the lodging of Guy Fawkes. On the walls of the vaults are many inscriptions; amongst them is one of Fisher, a Jesuit priest mixed up in the Powder Plot. It runs—

" Sacris vestibus indutus,
Dum sacra mysteria
Servans, captus et in
Hoc angusto carcere
Inclusus.—I. FISHER."

That is, "While clad in the sacred vestments, and administering the sacred mysteries, taken, and in this narrow dungeon immured."

Out of the north-east vault a door opens into a secret hole built in the dividing wall. This place has neither air nor light, and is known as Walter Raleigh's cell. Absurd legend!

The main floor consists of two large rooms and the crypt. One of the rooms was a guard-room. The crypt, a lofty room, was used as a prison for three of the Kentish men taken with Sir Thomas Wyat, in Mary's reign. There are two niches in the solid wall, and the largest of these is also called Raleigh's cell, though he was never confined there. Mr. Dixon suggests that it may have been "the secret jewel-room in the White Tower," often mentioned in old records. The long room on the banqueting-floor was a banqueting-hall, and is the only room in the keep which boasts a fireplace. The cross-chamber, the chapel of St. John the Evangelist, occupied two tiers of the Keep. On this tier Bishop Flambard, Prince Griffin, John Baliol, and Prince Charles d'Orleans were confined.

On the state-room floor were the great council-chamber, a lesser hall where the justiciaries sat, and the galleries of St. John's Chapel, from which there was a passage into the royal apartments. The roof is flat, and strong enough to bear the carronades of later times. The largest of the four turrets, built for a watch-tower, was the prison of poor Maud Fitzwalter, King John's victim, and was afterwards used as an observatory by Flamstead, Newton's contemporary.

The Keep, though a palace, was also a fortress, and security, rather than comfort, was what its builder had in view. It had originally only one narrow door, that a single man could defend. One well-stair alone connected the vaults with the upper floors. The main floor had no way up or down, except by the same staircase, which could only be approached through a passage built in the wall. The upper tiers had other stairs for free communication with the council-chamber and the parapets. Thus we still have existing in the White Tower the clearest and most indelible proofs, better than any historian can give, of the dangers that surrounded the Conqueror, and the little real trust he had in the fidelity of those surrounding him.

The second church of St. Peter was built by Edward I. The bills for clearing the ground are still preserved in the Record Office in Fetter Lane. The cost of pulling down the old chapel was forty-six shillings and eight pence.

The Tower, says Mr. H. Dixon, was divided into two parts, the inner and the outer ward. The inner ward, or royal quarter, was bounded by a wall crowned by twelve towers. The points of defence were the Beauchamp Tower, the Belfry, the Garden Tower (now called the Bloody Tower), the Hall Tower, the Lantern, the Salt Tower, the Broad Arrow Tower, the Constable Tower, the Martin Tower, the Brick Tower, the Flint Tower, the Bowyer Tower, and the Devilin Tower. The inner ward contained the Keep, the Royal Galleries and Rooms, the Mint, the Jewel-house, the Wardrobe, the Queen's Garden, St. Peter's Church, the open Green, and in later days the Lieutenant's house. In the Brick Tower the master of the ordnance resided; in the Lantern turret lights were kept burning at night as river signals.

The outer ward contained some lanes and streets below the wall and works which overlooked the wharf. In this ward stood the Middle Tower, the Byeward Tower, the Water Gate, the Cradle Tower, the Well Tower, the Galleyman Tower, the Iron-gate Tower, Brass Mount, Legge Mount, and the covered ways. Into it opened the Hall Tower, afterwards called the Record Tower, and now the Jewel-house. Close by the Hall Tower stood the Great Hall, the doors of which opened into this outer court. Spanning the ditch on the Thames side was the Water Gate, or St. Thomas's Tower, and under the building was the wide arch so often depicted by painters, and called Traitor's Gate.

Into the outer ward, says Mr. Dixon, the Commons had always claimed a free access. On stated occasions the right of public entry to all citizens was insisted on with much ceremonial. The aldermen and commoners met in Barking Church on Tower Hill, and chose six sage persons to go as a deputation to the Tower, and ask leave to see the king, and demand free access for all people to the courts of law held within the Tower. They were also to beg that no guard would close the gates or keep watch over them while the citizens were coming or going, it being against their freedom for any but their own guard to keep watch during that period. On the king granting their request the six messengers returned to Barking Church, reported progress, and sent the citizen guard to keep the ground. The Commons then elected three men of standing to act as spokesmen and presenters. Great care was taken that no person should go into the royal presence who had sore eyes or weak legs, or was in rags or shoeless. Every one was to have his hair cut close and his face newly shaved. Mayor, aldermen, sheriff, cryer, beadles, were all to be clean and neat, and every one was to lay aside his cape and cloak, and put on his coat and surcoat.

The exact site of the two courts of justice Mr. Dixon has clearly made out. The King's Bench was held in the Lesser Hall, under the east turret of the Keep. The Common Pleas were held in the Great Hall by the river—a hall long since gone, but which stood near the Hall Tower, to which it gave a name. It seems to have been a Gothic edifice in the style of Henry III. After Henry VI.'s death, the Hall Tower was turned into a Record Office.

One of the first prisoners ever lodged in the Tower that Gundulf built for William the Conqueror was Ralph Flambard, Bishop of Durham, the great treasurer and justiciar who had helped by his cruel greediness to collect the very money by which it was built. On the death of William Rufus, this prelate was seized by the Commons and thrown into the Tower, with the consent of Henry I. He was not kept very close, and one night, plying the Norman soldiers who guarded him with wine, Flambard, who had had ready a coil of rope sent to him in a wine-jar, let himself down from a window sixty-five feet from the ground, and escaped safe to France.

In the north-east turret of the White Tower King

John imprisoned Maud, the beautiful daughter of Robert Fitzwalter, Lord of Baynard's Castle, whose untimely fate we have noticed in a former chapter. In the banqueting hall, Edward I. lodged John de Baliol, whom he had stripped of his crown at the battle of Dunbar. It was from this campaign that Edward returned with the coronation-stone of Scotland, on which our own monarchs have ever since been crowned. Baliol, according to existing records, seems to have lived in state in the White Tower, having his chaplain, tailor, pantler, barber, clerk of the chapel, chamberlain, esquires, and laundress in attendance; and his dogs and horses in the stables waiting his commands, at the cost of seventeen shillings a day. He remained a prisoner 189 days, after which he was given up to the Papal nuncio, John de Pontissera, on condition of residing abroad. Fifty years after another royal Scotchman, David, son of the brave Robert Bruce, was taken prisoner by Queen Philippa, at the battle of Neville's Cross, and brought here, while Edward was away chastising France.

Every new effort to widen England brought fresh prisoners to the Tower; and next came to Flambard's old room, Griffin, Prince of Wales, whom his brother David had surrendered to the English king. Resolved to escape, he tore up his bed-clothes, knotted them into a rope, and dropped ninety feet from the leads of the White Tower. Being a heavy man, however, the rope unluckily snapped, and he was killed in the fall. His son remained a prisoner, but was afterwards released, returned to Wales, and fought against Edward I. Slain in battle, his head was brought to London, and fixed on the turret of his old prison.

Edward II. and his cruel queen, Isabella, kept court in the Tower; and here the Prince Joanna de la Tour was born. John de Cromwell, the Constable, was dismissed from office for having let the royal bed-chamber become so ruinous that the rain penetrated through the roof. Here, in Edward's absence, Isabella fell in love with Roger Mortimer, a Welsh chief, who was then in prison in the Tower. By the connivance, no doubt, of the guilty wife, Mortimer escaped by the kitchen chimney, and down the river, to France. His death and the king's barbarous murder at Berkeley Castle were the result of these fatal days of dalliance in the White Tower.

The Beauchamp Tower, on the west wall of the fortress, derives its name from Thomas de Beauchamp, Earl of Warwick, son of the earl who fought at Crecy and Poictiers. He was appointed by the House of Commons governor to the young king, Richard II., and his first act, in company with Gloucester, Arundel, and other great barons, was to march on London, and seize and put to death the young king's mischievous favourite, Sir Simon de Burley, whose greediness and insolence had rendered him hateful to the nation. This act of stern justice Richard never forgave; and directly he came of age the earl was banished to his own Warwick Castle, where he built Guy's Tower. The king resolved on obtaining despotic power. The earl was invited to dine with the king, and was seized as he was leaving the royal table, where he had been welcomed with special and treacherous hospitality. The king's uncle, the good Duke of Gloucester, was decoyed from his castle of Pleshey by the king himself, then hurried over to Calais, and suffocated by his guards. Lord Arundel, another obnoxious lord, was also executed by this royal murderer. Beauchamp, in his trial before the House of Peers, pleaded a pardon he had obtained under the Great Seal for all offences. The Chief Justice declared the pardon had been repealed by the king. Ultimately the earl's castles, manors, and estates were all forfeited, and he was sentenced to be hung, drawn, and quartered. The king, however, afraid to put to death so popular a man, banished him to the Isle of Man, and then recalled him to his old prison in the Tower. Two years later, on the accession of Henry IV., the earl was released. He was buried in the nave of St. Mary's Church, Warwick, which he had built.

The next captive in the banqueting-hall of the White Tower was that poet-warrior, Charles of Orleans, grandson of Charles V. of France, and father of Louis XII., a gay knight, whom Shakespeare has glanced at in the play of *Henry V.* He had been a rival of Henry, when Prince of Wales, for the hand of Isabella of Valois, the widow of Richard II. She had married him, and died a year after in childbirth. The young prince shortly after, for reasons of state, was induced to marry a second wife, Bona, daughter of Bernard, Count of Armagnac. At Agincourt Charles was found sorely wounded among the dead, and carried to England: he was placed in the White Tower, where a ransom of 300,000 crowns was placed upon his head; for the knights of those days, however chivalrous, drove hard bargains with their prisoners. Orleans was twenty-four years old then, and he remained in the Tower five-and-twenty years. He had a daughter by Queen Isabella, and it was to Henry's interest, as he had married a French princess, and claimed the throne of France, that Orleans should die without having a son. Charles spent the long years of his imprisonment looking out on the Thames and the hills of Surrey, and writing admirable French and English verses, which still exist. After Henry's death, and when Joan of Arc had recovered nearly the whole of France, the ransom was raked together, and Charles was released. He then married a third wife, Mary of Cleves, and by her had the son who afterwards became the invader of Italy, Louis XII.

The reign that saw Charles of Orleans enter the White Tower also saw Sir John Oldcastle, "the good Lord Cobham," brought to the Beauchamp Tower. This Kentish nobleman, who had fought bravely in France and in Wales, was a favourer of the Lollard reformers, and a despiser of the monks. He accepted Wycliffe's doctrines, denied the real presence, read the Bible openly, and sheltered Lollard preachers. The great enemy of this bold man was Thomas Arundel, Archbishop of Canterbury, who had introduced from Spain the savage custom of burning contumacious heretics. Disobeying a citation of the primate, Lord Cobham was sent to the Tower. Before a synod Oldcastle boldly asserted the new doctrines, and was sentenced to be burnt to death. "Ye judge the body," said the old soldier to the synod, "which is but a wretched thing, yet am I certain and sure that ye can do no harm to my soul. He who created that will of His own mercy and promise save it. As to these articles, I will stand to them even to the very death, by the grace of my eternal God."

In the Beauchamp Tower, when the monks spread reports that Cobham had recanted, he issued a bold denial that he had changed his view of "the sacrament of the altar," of which St. Paul had said to the Corinthians, "The bread which we break is it not the communion of the body of Christ?"

The people were deeply agitated, and one October night, four weeks after, a band of citizens broke into the Beauchamp Tower (with or without the connivance of the guards), released Cobham, and carried him safely to his own house in Smithfield. There, defying the primate and the monks, Cobham remained for three months. The Lollards at last, probably urged forward by the primate's spies, agreed to meet, 100,000 strong, in St. Giles's Fields, and choose Lord Cobham as their general. The king, enraged at this, collected his barons, closed the City gates, put a white crusader's cross on his royal banner, rode with his spears into St. Giles's Fields, and dispersed the Lollard party, who were waiting for the good lord. For four years Cobham wandered through Wales and England, with 1,000 marks set on his head. Fisher, a skinner, the leader of the band that released Oldcastle from the Tower, was tried at Newgate, and afterwards hung at Tyburn, and his head stuck on London Bridge.

Eventually, after a hard fight, Oldcastle was betrayed in Wales by a Welsh adherent named Powis. He was brought to London, and without further trial, he was burnt in front of his own house, in Smithfield, the first man there burnt for religion.

In the old monastic plays this brave and consistent man was always represented as a coward and buffoon. Shakespeare himself, following the convention, named his Falstaff at first Oldcastle; then, probably having his attention drawn by some better-read friend to the injustice done to the memory of a good man and true Protestant, he changed it to Falstaff, unfortunately, another brave soldier of Cobham's period, whom tradition had unjustly slandered. It is a singular fact that a "Boar's Head" in the Borough, not that in Eastcheap, had belonged to the great Falstaff of the French wars. The man who wrote in the epilogue to the *Second Part of King Henry the Fourth*, the words "Oldcastle died a martyr," says Mr. Hepworth Dixon, "was a Puritan in faith." This dictum we hold, nevertheless, to be extremely doubtful, as nearly all the religious passages in Shakespeare's plays point to a great reverence for Roman Catholic traditions; and surely an honest writer can free a good man from slander without necessarily believing in his doctrines. Moreover, Lord Cobham was a Protestant, but by no means a Puritan, and probably as far apart in belief from the later martyrs of Smithfield as the Lollards were from John Wesley.

There is a pretty tradition connected with the Tower in the time of the Wars of the Roses. Sir Henry Wyatt, of Allington Castle, in Kent, father of the poet, and grandfather of the unfortunate rebel, was imprisoned in the Tower for being a resolute Lancastrian. He was thrown into a cold and narrow tower, where he had neither bed to lie on, sufficient clothes to warm him, nor enough food to eat. One day a cat came into his dungeon, and he laid her in his bosom to warm him, "and by making much of her won her love." After this the cat would come several times a day, and sometimes bring him a pigeon. The gaoler dressed these pigeons, without inquiring where they came from. Sir Henry Wyatt after this retained an affection for cats, and was always painted with one by his side. One day, when Wyatt was being tortured with the barnacles, Richard III., who was present, exclaimed with regret, "Wyatt, why art thou such a fool? Thou servest for moonshine in water. Thy master," meaning Henry of Richmond, "is a beggarly fugitive: forsake him and become mine. Cannot I reward thee?" To which Wyatt replied, "If I had first chosen you for my master, thus faithful would

I have been to you if you should have needed it. But the earl, poor and unhappy though he be, is my master; and no discouragement, no allurement, shall ever drive me from him, by God's grace."

And now came, in due sequence, Gloucester's murder of the two princes, his nephews, usually said to have been in the Bloody Tower, but the locality of the crime is still uncertain. Bayley, the fullest and best historian of the Tower, thinks it highly unlikely that Gloucester would have sent the two young princes to such a mere porter's lodge as the Bloody Tower—a tower, moreover, which, in an official survey of the reign of Henry VIII., is called the Garden Tower, showing that the popular name is of later date. When sent to what was to be their tomb, Edward V. was twelve, and Richard, Duke of York, was eight. They stood between the Crookback and the crown, but not for long. Their mother was in sanctuary at Westminster. The Protector had already thrown out rumours that the children were illegitimate, and a bishop had been base enough, it is said, to have sworn to a previous secret marriage of the licentious Edward. Lord Hastings, under an accusation of witchcraft, had just been dragged from the council-chamber, and beheaded on a block of timber on Tower Green. Murder followed murder fast, and the word soon went forth for the children's death. Brackenbury, the Governor of the Tower, receiving the order, when on his knees in St. John's Chapel, refused to obey or to understand it. Gloucester, told of this at midnight in Warwick Castle, instantly rose from his bed, and sent Sir James Tyrrell, his Master of Horse, to London, with power to use the keys and pass-words of the Tower for one night. Two dogged ruffians, John Dighton and Miles Forrest, rode at Tyrrell's heels. It is said that one boy had his throat cut, and the other was smothered with a pillow. Tyrrell stood near the gate while the deed was doing, and saw the bodies of the poor children when all was over, then rode back to York to tell Richard. The two murderers, helped by an obsequious Tower priest, carried down the bodies, dug a hole near the gateway wall, and threw them in. They were afterwards re-interred, in a fit of superstition, by Richard, behind a staircase in the Keep. In Charles II.'s time the bones were found under the steps, and removed to a royal tomb in Henry VII.'s Chapel, Westminster Abbey. The last-named king had tried hard to find the bodies, and prove that Perkin Warbeck was not the son of Edward IV.; but the priest who had removed them was dead, and the search was unsuccessful. Sir Thomas More and Lord Bacon both agree that the children were murdered by Richard's command.

The pride and cruelty of Henry VIII., his theologic doubts, and his Bluebeard habit of getting rid of his wives, sent many victims to the Tower. One of the most venerable of these was John Fisher, Bishop of Rochester, a determined opponent of the king's marriage with a Protestant beauty. He was imprisoned in the Belfry Tower, on the ground floor of which lived the Lieutenant. Fisher had professed belief in an hysterical Kentish girl, subject to fits, whom the monks had persuaded to utter rhyming prophecies against the divorce of Queen Catherine. The poor maid of Kent, urged forward by the priests, at last went too far, declaring that, if Henry put away his Spanish wife, he would die in seven months, and his daughter Mary would ascend the throne. Such prophecies, when spread among fanatics, are apt to produce their own fulfilment. Henry gave the signal, and in a very short time the monks who instigated the nun, and the nun herself, were in a cart bound for Tyburn. Fisher himself was soon arrested, and browbeaten by Cromwell, who told him he believed the prophecies true because he wished them to be true. Fisher was eighty years old, and might have been spared, had not Paul III. at that very time, unfortunately, and against the king's express command, sent him a cardinal's hat. "'Fore God," said Henry, with brutal humour, "if he wear it, he shall wear it on his shoulders." The death-warrant was at once signed. They brought the old man the news that he seemed to have expected, at five a.m. He slept till seven, then rose and donned his bravest suit, for what he called his marriage-day. He passed to the scaffold with the New Testament in his feeble hands. When he opened the book, he read the passage, "This is life eternal, to know Thee, the only true God, and Jesus Christ, whom Thou hast sent." A few hours after the old grey head fell on Tower Hill it was spiked upon London Bridge. The room over Coldharbour Gateway, says Mr. Dixon, where the Maid of Kent was imprisoned, was long known as the Nun's Bower.

The poet Earl of Surrey was another of Henry's victims, and he passed from the Tower to die on the block for blazoning the Confessor's arms upon his shield. His father, too, the third Duke of Norfolk, had a narrow escape from the same block, though he was a near relation of Henry, and the uncle of two queens. He was charged £22 18s. 8d. a month, and yet complained of having no exercise and wanting sheets enough for his bed. Luckily for him, Henry expired the very night the warrant for his execution was signed, and he escaped.

The Beauchamp Tower bears on its walls records of earlier prisoners than the duke—abettors of that

THE TOWER OF LONDON. (*From a View published about* 1700.)

very Pilgrimage of Grace which he had helped to put down. This last great struggle of English Popery against the Reformation brought many of the old North country families to this place of durance.

The royal decree for putting down monastic houses had, in 1536, set all Yorkshire in a ferment. A vast rabble had armed and threatened to march on London, hang Cromwell, weed the Court of evil councillors, restore Queen Catherine, and revive the religious houses. The pilgrims fastened on their breasts scrolls displaying the five wounds of Christ. Near Appleby a band of these fanatics stopped a lawyer named Aske, who was returning to London from a Yorkshire hunting party, and chose him as their general. Aske determined to make Henry Percy, sixth Earl of Northumberland, the commander-in-chief. Percy, who had been a lover of Anne Boleyn, was the Warden of the East and Middle Marches. The earl was afraid to join them; but the pilgrims demanded the earl's brothers, Thomas and Ingram, in spite of the tears and remonstrances of their mother. York at once surrendered to the 30,000 pilgrims. At Pomfret Castle they enrolled Lord Darcy among their band. At Doncaster Bridge, however, the Duke of Norfolk met the wild rout, and by proffered pardon and promises of the changes they desired, soon broke up the host.

In the meantime lesser rebellions of the same kind prospered for a while. Foremost among the leaders of these were the Bulmers, one of whom had had the command of Norham Castle. Sir John Bulmer brought with him to the camp a dangerous and fanatical woman, named Margaret Cheyne, his paramour, and a bastard daughter of the Duke of Buckingham, whom Henry VIII. had beheaded. When the first pilgrimage failed, and the news came that Cromwell was not disgraced, that no parliament was to be held at York, and that the king would place garrisons in Newcastle, Scarborough, and Hull, the Bulmers, urged on by this wild woman and Adam Sedburgh, Abbot of Jervaulx, and the Abbot of Fountains, resolved on a new pilgrimage. Thomas and Ingram Percy had been deprived of their command in the North by Earl Henry, and were ready for any desperate effort. They defied the king's new lieutenant, and prepared for a fresh outbreak. As Norfolk's army approached, the rebels seized Beverley, and Sir Francis Bigod prepared to fight for the old order of things; but Yorkshire was afraid of the king's power, and a vain attempt on Chillingham Castle, and another on Hull, led to total ruin. A few days more, and the ringleaders were all arrested and packed in the Tower. Aske, Darcy, Bigod, Sir Thomas Percy, the Abbot of Jervaulx, Sir John Bulmer, all perished at Tyburn, and Margaret Cheyne was burnt in Smithfield.

The next prisoners of importance who came to the Beauchamp Tower, the Garden Tower, and the Nun's Bower, were Lady Jane Grey, her young husband, and the ambitious nobles who forced on her the fatal crown to which she was indifferent. The nine days' reign of poor Lady Jane Grey filled the Tower prisons with the Dudleys, who had driven the mild, tender-hearted girl to usurp the crown on the death of Edward VI. With the Queen came Dudley, the Duke of Northumberland; John, the young Earl of Warwick; Lord Robert, already married to luckless Amy Robsart; Lord Ambrose Dudley, a mere lad; Lord Guildford, the weak youth who had married Lady Jane to gratify his father's ambition; and Lord Henry Guildford, his brother. The duke was shut in the Gate House, Lord Ambrose and Lord Henry in the Nun's Bower, Jane herself in the house of the Deputy-Lieutenant, Lord Robert in the lower tier of the Beauchamp Tower, Lord Guildford in the middle tier. In two places, on the north side of his prison, and, in one instance, just above the name of the Abbot of Jervaulx, Guildford carved his wife's name, "Jane."

Lady Jane Grey's claim to the throne arose in this way. Mary, the sister of Henry VIII., on the death of her husband, Louis XII. of France, married her stalwart lover, Charles Brandon, afterwards Duke of Suffolk. She had issue, two princesses, Frances and Eleanor. Frances married Henry Grey, Marquis of Dorset, and Lady Jane was the eldest of her three daughters. When King Edward, that precocious boy, died—as some still think, of poison—at Greenwich Palace, Dudley kept his death secret for a whole day, and then sent for the Lord Mayor and the richest aldermen and merchants of London, and showed them forged letters-patent giving the crown to Lady Jane, who had already married his son. The duke's first effort was to seize the Princess Mary, but here he failed; faithful friends had instantly warned her of her danger, and she had already taken flight, to rouse her adherents to arms. Lady Jane was then, against her will, proclaimed queen. She was taken to the Tower from Sion House, and was received as a monarch by crowds of kneeling citizens, her husband walking by her side, cap in hand. She refused, however, to let Guildford be proclaimed king, and the lad cried petulantly at her firmness. Mary's friends fast rising in Norfolk, Dudley was sent against them, with a train of guns and 600 men. As they rode along Shoreditch, the distrusted duke said to

Lord Grey, "The people press to see us, but no man cries 'God speed you!'" In London all went wrong. Ridley, Bishop of London, denounced Mary and Popery, but the crowd was evidently for the rightful heiress.

The rebellion was soon over. Dudley could do nothing in Norfolk without more men. The great nobles were faithless to the Queen of Nine Days. The tenth day Mary was proclaimed in Cheap, and in St. Paul's Churchyard. The archers came to the Tower and demanded the keys, which were given up. Grey rushed into his daughter's room, and found Lady Jane sitting, unconscious of her fate, beneath a royal canopy. "Come down, my child," said the miserable duke; "this is no place for you." From a throne the poor girl passed quickly to a prison.

In the middle room of the Beauchamp Tower, where Warwick and his brother Guildford were confined, Lord Warwick, in the dreary hours, carved an emblematic cipher of the family names, which has never yet been accurately read. Two bears and a ragged staff stand in a frame of emblems —roses, acorns, geraniums, honeysuckles—which some folks, Mr. Dixon says, fancy to indicate the initial letters of his kinsmen's names—the rose, Ambrose; the geranium, Guildford; the oak, Robert. Lord Robert (reserved for future greatness) carved in the lower room the plain words, "Robert Dudley." When sent to the upper room (probably after Guildford's death), he carved on the wall his emblem, an oak-branch, and the letters " R. D."

Lady Jane, with her two gentlewomen by her side, spent her time at Deputy Brydges' house, securely guarded, reading the Greek Testament, and mourning for her father's inevitable fate. Norfolk, released from prison, presided in Westminster Hall at the trial of his enemy, Dudley. The Duke, Warwick, and Northampton were condemned to death. Dudley and his son turned Roman Catholics, but failed to avert their doom. Wyat's mad rebellion brought Lady Jane and her foolish husband to the block. On the scaffold she declared her acts against the Queen were unlawful; "but touching the procurement and desire thereof, by me or on my behalf," she said, "I wash my hands thereof in innocency before God, and in the face of you, good Christian people, this day." She refused the executioner's help, drew the white kerchief over her own eyes, and said to the kneeling executioner, "I pray you dispatch me quickly." Kneeling before the block, she felt for it with inquiring hands. As she laid down her fair young head, she exclaimed, "Lord, into thy hands I commend my spirit!" and the heavy axe fell.

It was while Lady Jane and the Princess Elizabeth were prisoners in the Tower that Wyat's mad rebellion was crushed, and the reckless man himself was locked up in the middle chamber of the Beauchamp Tower. On the slant of the window looking towards the Green can still be seen carved the name of "Thomas Cobham, 1555" (the cousin of the leader of the rebels). The final break-down of Wyat, in his attempt to stop the Spanish match, we have already described in our chapter on Ludgate Hill, where the last throws of the game were played, and we need not recur to it here. The last moments of Wyat are still to be reviewed. Wyat is described as wearing, when taken prisoner, a coat of mail with rich sleeves, a velvet cassock covered with yellow lace, high boots and spurs, and a laced velvet hat. As he entered the Tower wicket, Sir John Brydges, the Lieutenant, threatened him, and said, "Oh, thou villain—traitor; if it were not that the law must pass upon thee, I would stick thee through with my dagger." "It is no mastery, now," said Wyat, contemptuously, and strode on.

In the Tower, out of the moonshine of vanity and display, Wyat for a time faltered. He made a charge against Courtenay, son of the Marquis of Exeter, and a descendant of Edward IV.; and even raised a suspicion against the Princess Elizabeth, which Renard, the Spanish Ambassador, used with dangerous effect. Chandos, the Keeper of the Tower, had planned a scene, as Wyat was led to execution, that should draw from him an open accusation of Elizabeth and Courtenay. On his way to death he was taken into the Garden Tower, where Courtenay lay. The Lord Mayor and the Privy Council were there, Courtenay himself was brought in, but Wyat had nothing to allege. On the scaffold Wyat told the people that he had never accused either the Princess or Courtenay of a knowledge of the plot; and a priest, eager for fresh victims, reminded him that he had said differently at the Council. "That which I then said, I said," replied Wyat; "that which I now say is true." And the axe fell.

The Courtenay mentioned above was nearly all his life a prisoner in the Tower. His father was executed for treason by Henry VIII. On Mary's accession he was released, and seemed for a time to have persuaded himself that she would accept him as a husband. He was made Earl of Devon, and was called by his friends "the White Rose of York." As the Spanish marriage drew near, people began to mention Courtenay as a fine husband for Elizabeth, who seems to have really had some youthful liking for the weak, handsome aspirant. On the outbreak of Wyat's rebellion he was again thrown into the Tower. After Mary's marriage, however, he was released and sent abroad. He died suddenly at Padua. On Courtenay's death the house of York was represented by the descendants of the Duke of Clarence, Edmund and Arthur, nephews of the Cardinal Pole. For some vague suspicion of encouraging the claim of Mary Queen of Scots to the English throne they were imprisoned for life in the Tower. In the Beauchamp Tower inscriptions by both brothers are still to be seen. Arthur has written, among other inscriptions—

"A passage perilous maketh a port pleasant."

Among the residents of the Tower, in Mary's brief reign, were Cranmer, Latimer, and Ridley.

Cranmer, who had refused to fly when Mary marched to London, proved but faint of heart when thrown into the Garden Tower. He had resolved to stay to own his share in the changes which had been made in the days of Edward VI., but the fireless cell soon brought down his courage, and he trembled for his life. There was more of Peter than of Paul about him. The Tower's solitude led the way to his miserable recantation at Oxford. But he revived when Latimer and Ridley came to share his prison, and they searched the Scriptures together for arguments against Feckenham, the Queen's confessor, whom they met daily at the Lieutenant's, where they dined, and whose last argument was the Smithfield fire.

CHAPTER VII.

THE TOWER (*continued*).

Queen Elizabeth's Prisoners in the Tower—The Bishop of Ross at work again—Charles Bailly—Philip Howard—Earl of Essex—Sir Walter Raleigh in the Tower—James I. and the Gunpowder Plot—Guy Fawkes—Father Garnet—Percy—Arabella Stuart—Murder of Sir Thomas Overbury—Felton—Prynne—Strafford and Laud—A Long Roll of Notable Tower Prisoners—The Spa Fields Riots—The Cato Street Conspirators.

AND now we come to Elizabeth's prisoners, the Roman Catholic plotters against her throne and life. In a room of the Belfry Tower are the names of the Countess of Lennox and her five attendants. This countess was first cousin to Elizabeth, and married by Henry to the fourth Earl of Lennox. While Elizabeth was proposing Lord Robert Dudley to Mary as a husband, offering, as the condition of her accepting a Protestant husband, to at once appoint Mary heir to the throne, the Countess of Lennox was proposing her son Darnley, a Catholic. Immediately before the latter marriage taking place the countess was sent to the Tower, not to be released till Darnley's miserable death. Lennox himself was assassinated, and the countess, released from the Tower, died poor, and was buried in Westminster Abbey at the Queen's expense.

Of other victims of Mary Queen of Scots the Tower bears traces. One of these was a young Fleming, named Charles Bailly, who was employed by the ambassador in London, John Leslie, the intriguing Bishop of Ross, to carry dangerous letters to Brussels and Madrid, respecting the plots of the Duke of Norfolk. In vain Elizabeth had said to the duke, "Take care, my lord, on what pillow you lay your head." He plotted on till he blundered into the Tower. The Earl of Northumberland collected 10,000 men, in hope to rescue Mary and restore the Catholic religion, and in a few days was a hunted fugitive. Norfolk was released after many lying promises. The Bishop of Ross at once determined on a new effort. A Papal bull was to be launched, deposing the Queen; the Catholic lords were to seize the Tower; Norfolk was to march to Tutbury, rescue Queen Mary, and bring her to London to be crowned. In the meantime he wrote a treasonable book, which was printed at Liége, entitled "A Defence of the Honour of Mary, Queen of Scotland." Bailly, on his return with the book and some dangerous letters referring to Norfolk, was arrested at Dover. The Cobham already mentioned as one of Wyat's adherents, having charge of the prisoner and the letters, and being a Catholic, resolved to befriend the bishop. He therefore sent him the letters to change for others of a more harmless character. Burleigh, however, by a Catholic spy, discovered the truth, and put Charles Bailly to the rack. The plot disclosed led to the instant arrest of the Duke of Norfolk and the Bishop of Ross. In the good Lord Cobham's room Bailly has inscribed the following words :—

"I.H.S. 1571. Die 10 Aprilis. Wise men ought circumspectly to see what they do, to examine before they speak, to prove before they take in hand, to beware whose company they use, and, above all things, to whom they trust.—CHARLES BAILLY."

In a prison in the Tower the Bishop of Ross confessed the Norfolk and Northumberland plots, and declared Mary's privity to the death of Darnley. He has left his name carved in the Bloody Tower, with a long Latin inscription, now half erased.

Eventually, squeezed dry of all secrets, and full of cramps and agues, he was contemptuously released and sent abroad. Norfolk died denouncing his religion, and begging pardon of the Queen. He was the first political offender who suffered in Elizabeth's reign. Northumberland was executed at York, and left his title to his brother Henry, who perished in the Tower. The new earl soon fell into treason. Misled by Jesuit intriguers, he was waiting for the landing of the Duke of Guise and a Catholic crusade against Elizabeth, when he was thrown into the Tower, where he remained a whole year in the Bloody Tower untried. On Sunday, June 21, 1585, he shot himself as he lay in bed, to prevent the confiscation of his estates. An absurd rumour was spread by the Catholics that the earl was murdered by order of Hatton and Raleigh. Cecil and Raleigh's other rivals did their best to perpetuate such a calumny. A modern historian, in the face of all evidence, has given affected credence to the report.

Another Roman Catholic martyr of this reign was Philip Howard, a son of the Duke of Norfolk and Mary the daughter of the Earl of Arundel, a weak intriguing man. He has left in the large room of the Beauchamp Tower this inscription, carved in an Italian hand :—

" The more suffering for Christ in this world, so much the more glory with Christ in the life to come.—ARUNDELL. June 22, 1587."

Arundel was a convert, and had been captured while on his way to join the army of Philip of Spain. Having lost favour with Elizabeth for having gone over to the Church of Rome, Arundel had despaired of further progress at Court, and had fled to Spain on the very eve of the Armada. By means of bribes paid by his wife, Arundel contrived to have mass celebrated in his cell. For this offence he was condemned to death ; but the Queen pardoned the poor man, and he lingered in prison for ten years, at the end of which he died—poisoned, as the Jesuits said ; but more probably from the injury he had done his health by repeated fasts.

Of that wilful and unfortunate favourite of Elizabeth, the Earl of Essex, we shall say little here. His story belongs more naturally to another part of our work—the chapter on the Strand, where he lived. His rash revolt we have already glanced at. At the age of thirty-five he laid down his head on the block on Tower Green. He was attended by three divines, to whom he expressed deep penitence for his "great sin, bloody sin, crying and infectious sin," and begged pardon of God and his sovereign. He never mentioned his wife, children, or friends ; took leave of no one, not even of those present ;

and when he knelt down to pray, exhibited considerable agitation of mind.

On James's accession, that great man, yet not without many a stain, Sir Walter Raleigh, became a tenant of the Bloody Tower. He had been imprisoned before by Elizabeth in the Brick Tower, for having seduced Elizabeth Throgmorton, one of her maids of honour.

"A very great part of the second and long imprisonment of the founder of Virginia," says Mr. Dixon, "was spent in the Bloody Tower and the adjoining Garden House, writing at this grated window, working in the little garden on which it opened, pacing the terrace on this wall, which was afterwards famous as Raleigh's Walk. Hither came to him the wits and poets, the scholars and inventors of his time—Jonson and Burrell, Hariot and Pett— to crack light jokes, to discuss rabbinical lore, to sound the depths of philosophy, to map out Virginia, to study the shipbuilder's art. In the Garden House he distilled essences and spirits, compounded his great cordial, discovered a method (afterwards lost) of turning salt water into sweet, received the visits of Prince Henry, wrote his political tracts, invented the modern war-ship, wrote his 'History of the World.'"

Raleigh was several times in the Tower; but many vaults and cells pointed out by the warders in absurd places—such as the hole in Little Ease, a recess in the crypt, a cell in the Martin Tower, and one in the Beauchamp Tower—were never occupied by him. After the seduction of his future wife, Raleigh was placed in the Brick Tower, the residence of Sir George Carew, Master of the Ordnance, and his own cousin, and was released upon his marriage. As a first step towards peace with Spain, James I., on his accession, imprisoned Raleigh in the Bloody Tower. The pretext for his seizure was his aiding Lord Cobham, the brother-in-law of Cecil, in a plot to raise Arabella Stuart to the throne. Cobham, clinging to life with the baseness of Claudio, in *Measure for Measure*, accused Raleigh of complicity, and then retracted. A report was spread that Raleigh had tried to stab himself while sitting at the Lieutenant's table. He remained a prisoner for fourteen years. His wife and son were allowed to live at the Tower, where her husband and his three poor servants lived on five pounds a week. He was at last, from poverty, obliged to part with his faithful friend, Thomas Hariot, whom he had sent to Virginia in 1584, and whose mathematical discoveries Descartes is said to have stolen.

During this long imprisonment, Raleigh was allowed to use a hen-roost in the garden near the

Bloody Tower as a place for distilling and for chemical experiments. There he made balsams and cordials, and occupied himself with many scientific inquiries. When increased suspicions fell on Raleigh, he was deprived of this still-room, and his wife and two children (for a second son had been born since his imprisonment) were sent from the Tower. He then became so ill from the chill of the cell that he was allowed to live in the Garden House, which had been the still-room where he studied. Here he discovered a cordial still used by doctors; here he discoursed of naval battles with Prince Henry, who, after one of these visits, cried out to his attendants, "No man but my

written by King James, to record the discovery of the Gunpowder Plot; for in this chamber Guy Fawkes was first examined by Cecil, Nottingham, Mountjoy, and Northampton. Two of the inscriptions run thus :—

"James the Great, King of Great Britain, illustrious for piety, justice, foresight, learning, hardihood, clemency, and the other regal virtues; champion and patron of the Christian faith, of the public safety, and of universal peace; author most subtle, most august, and most auspicious :

"Queen Anne, the most serene daughter of Frederick the Second, invincible King of the Danes :

"Prince Henry, ornament of nature, strengthened with learning, blest with grace, born and given to us from God :

"Charles, Duke of York, divinely disposed to every virtue :

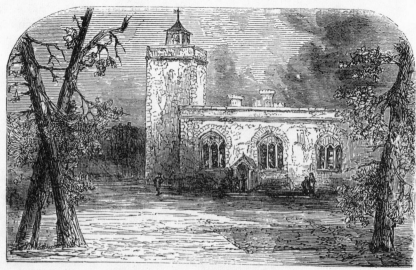

THE CHURCH OF ST. PETER ON TOWER GREEN.

father would keep such a bird in a cage." Here he finished the first volume of his "History of the World," assisted, it is said, by Ben Jonson and other scholars. Here, bit by bit, King James stripped him of houses and lands, including Durham House and Sherborne Castle.

After his release and unsuccessful voyage to seek for gold in Guiana, Raleigh returned to the Tower, and was placed in a poor upper room of the Brick Tower. He had at first pleasant rooms in the Wardrobe Tower. But Spain had now resolved on his death, and James was ready to consent. His enemies urged him in vain to suicide. The morning he died, Peter, his barber, complained, as he dressed his master to go to the scaffold, that his head had not been curled that morning. "Let them comb it that shall have it," answered Raleigh.

In a chamber of the house of the Lieutenant of the Tower, looking out on the Thames, several oak panels bear inscriptions, some of them probably

"Elizabeth, full sister of both, most worthy of her parents :

"Do Thou, all-seeing, protect these as the apple of the eye, and guard them without fear from wicked men beneath the shadow of Thy wings."

"To Almighty God, the guardian, arrester, and avenger, who has punished this great and incredible conspiracy against our most merciful Lord the King, our most serene Lady the Queen, our divinely disposed Prince, and the rest of our Royal House; and against all persons of quality, our ancient nobility, our soldiers, prelates, and judges; the authors and advocates of which conspiracy, Romanised Jesuits, of perfidious, Catholic, and serpent-like ungodliness, with others equally criminal and insane, were moved by the furious desire of destroying the true Christian religion, and by the treasonous hope of overthrowing the kingdom, root and branch; and which was suddenly, wonderfully, and divinely detected, at the very moment when the ruin was impending, on the 5th day of November, in the year of grace 1605—William Waad, whom the King has appointed his Lieutenant of the Tower, returns, on the ninth of October, in the sixth year of the reign of James the First, 1608, his great and everlasting thanks."

Fawkes was confined in a dungeon of the Keep. He would not at first disclose his accomplices, but, after thirty minutes of the rack, he confessed all. It is not known who first proposed the mode of destruction by powder, but Fawkes, a pervert, who had been a soldier, was selected as a fitting worker-out of the plan. To the last Fawkes affirmed that when the conspirators took oath in his lodgings in Butcher's Row, Strand, Father Gerard, who administered the sacrament, was ignorant of the purpose of their oath. Fawkes, with Keyes, Rookwood, and Thomas Winter, were drawn on hurdles to Palace Yard, and there hung and disembowelled. Digby, Robert Winter, Grant, and Bates were hung near Paul's Cross.

Another Tower prisoner in this reign was the Earl of Northumberland, a patron of science. His kinsman, Thomas Percy, had been deep in the plot, and was the man who hired the cellar where the barrels of powder were laid. He was allotted a house in the Martin Tower, at the north-east angle of the fortress, afterwards the Jewel House, where Colonel Blood made his impudent dash on the regalia. There he remained for sixteen years, pacing daily on the terrace which connected his rooms with the Brick Tower and the Constable's Tower, and which still bears his name. A sun-dial fixed for him on the south face of the Martin Tower,

GUY FAWKES AND THE CONSPIRATORS. (*From a Contemporary Print.*)

Father Garnet was found hiding at Hindlip Hall, in Worcestershire. He was at first confined in the Keep, then in a chamber on the lower tier of the Bloody Tower. When it was said to him, " You shall have no place in the calendar," " I am not worthy of it," he replied, "but I hope to have a place in heaven." In the Tower, Garnet was persuaded by a spy to converse with another priest in an adjoining cell, and their conversations were noted down by spies. He confessed that in Elizabeth's time he had declared a powder plot to be lawful, but wished to save as many as he could. Garnet's servant, Little John, in fear of the rack, stabbed himself in his cell. On the scaffold before St. Paul's, Garnet asserted the virtue of Anne Vaux, with whom it is stated he had carried on an intrigue, and hoped the Catholics in England would fare no worse for his sake.

by the famous astronomer Hariot, is still to be seen there. Accused of wishing to put himself at the head of the English Catholics, he was fined £30,000, deprived of all his appointments, and sentenced to imprisonment for life. He spent his time in mathematical studies, and kept Hariot by his side. He was a friend of Raleigh, and was visited by men of science. He was at last released by the intercession of his beautiful daughter Lucy, who had married Hay, a Court favourite, afterwards Earl of Carlisle.

Nor must we forget that fair prisoner, Arabella Stuart, a kinswoman of James, who was sent to the Tower for daring to marry her relation, William Seymour, who was also of royal descent. Seymour escaped to France, but she remained five years in the Tower, in neglect and penury, and died at last, worn out with pining for freedom, her mind a wreck.

The murder of Sir Thomas Overbury in the Tower is one of the darkest of the many dark pages in the reign of James I. It was the last great crime committed in the blood-stained building where so many good and wise men had pined away half their lives. Overbury, a poet and statesman of genius, was the friend of the king's young Scotch favourite, Carr. When a handsome boy he had been injured in a tilt, and had attracted the king's attention. James, eager to load his young Ganymede with favours, wedded him to the divorced wife of Lord Essex, a beautiful but infamous woman, whose first marriage had been conducted at Whitehall with great splendour, Inigo Jones supplying the scenery, and Ben Jonson, in beautiful verse, eulogising the handsome couple in fallacious prophecies. Carr ruled the king, and Overbury ruled Carr. All went well between the two friends, who had begun life together, till Overbury had exerted himself to prevent Carr's marriage with the divorced Lady Essex. The lady then resolved on his death. She tried to bribe assassins and poisoners, and, all these plans failing, the king was persuaded to send him as an envoy to Moscow. Overbury refusing to go, was thrown into the Bloody Tower. Here Lady Essex exerted all her arts to take away his life. An infamous man, named Sir Gervaise Helwyss, was appointed Lieutenant of the Tower, and a servant of Mrs. Turner, the infamous poisoner (mentioned in our chapter on Paternoster Row), placed as keeper in the Bloody Tower. Poisoned jellies and tarts were frequently sent to Overbury by Lady Essex in the name of Carr, and poisons were mixed in almost everything he took. Yet so strong was the poet's constitution, that he still bore up, till a French apothecary was sent to him, who administered medicines that soon produced death. The marriage of Lady Essex and Carr, now made an earl, soon took place, and was celebrated with great splendour at Whitehall. The Earl of Northampton, who had aided Lady Essex in this crime, died a few months afterwards, and all was for a time hushed up. In the meantime Overbury's friends had printed his fine poem of "The Wife" (the model of virtue held out for his friend's example), and five editions of the poem had roused public attention. Just at this time, a boy employed in the Tower by the French apothecary who gave Overbury his *coup de grâce*, fell sick in Flanders, and confessed his crime to the English resident. Gradually the murder came out. The Lieutenant of the Tower half confessed, and the criminals were soon under arrest. Hands were also laid on Carr and his wife, Mrs. Turner, Weston, the man placed in charge of Overbury, and an apothecary, Franklin. The nation was infuriated and cried for vengeance. There were even rumours that the same wretches had poisoned Prince Henry, the heir to James's throne. Helwyss was hung in chains on Tower Hill; Mrs. Turner at Tyburn; Franklin and Weston were contemptuously put to death. The trial of the greater culprits followed. The countess pleaded guilty, and was condemned to death; and in Carr's case the chief evidence was suppressed. Eventually the earl and countess were pardoned. They left the Bloody Tower and the Garden House, and lived in seclusion and disgrace. The only child of these murderers was the mother of that excellent Lord William Russell who was afterwards beheaded.

Mention of every State prisoner whom the Tower has housed would in itself fill a volume. We must therefore confine ourselves to brief notices of the greater names. Nor must his innocence prevent our mentioning, after the murderers of Overbury, that patriarch of English philosophy, Lord Bacon, who, on his sudden fall from greatness, when Buckingham threw him as a sop to appease the people, was confined here for a period which, though short, must have been one of extreme mental agony. He was only imprisoned one day in the Lieutenant's house. "To die in this disgraceful place, and before the time of His Majesty's grace, is even the worst that could be," said the great man, whose improvidence and whose rapacious servants had led him to too freely accept presents which his enemies called "bribes."

But we must hasten on to the reign of Charles, when Felton struck that deadly blow in the doorway at Portsmouth, and Charles's hated favourite, the Duke of Buckingham, fell dead. Felton, an officer whose claims had been disregarded, had stabbed the duke, believing him to be a public enemy. He was lodged in the Bloody Tower, and as he passed to his prison the people cried, "The Lord bless thee!" The Parliament Remonstrance against the duke, which Felton had read in the "Windmill" Tavern, in Shoe Lane, had first roused him to the deed. The turning-point of Charles's fate was the committal of the nine members— Holles, Eliot, Selden, Hobart, Hayman, Coryton, Valentine, Strode, and Long—to the Tower. They had carried resolutions against the tax by tonnage and poundage proposed by the king. These men, so active against Laud and despotic power, were lodged in the Lieutenant's House. Two were at once pardoned; the others were heavily fined. The ringleader, Eliot, refused to retract, died in confinement, resolute to the last, and he was buried in the Tower.

Then came to the Tower that tough, obstinate lawyer, Prynne, who, for an attack on theatres, was put in the pillory, fined £5,000, and had both his ears shorn off. After four years' imprisonment Prynne again attacked Archbishop Laud's Popish practices, and was again punished. But the tide was now turning. Presently through the Tower gates passed Thomas Wentworth, Earl of Strafford, that dark bold spirit that had resolved to brave it out for despotism, and in the attempt was trodden under foot. Charles gave him up to the people, in one of his feeble and vain attempts to conciliate those whom he had wronged. When there was fear that Strafford might be torn to pieces on his way to the scaffold, he said, "I care not how I die, by the executioner or by the people." He stopped under Laud's window for his blessing, but Laud, in the act of blessing, swooned. Four years after Laud was impeached of high treason, and committed to the Tower. The Commons, however, changed the impeachment into an ordinance for his execution. He was accordingly sentenced to death, and perished on Tower Hill in January, 1640–1. As he went to the scaffold, says his last historian, his face turned from purple to ghastly white.

The Tower prisoners of Charles II.'s time were men of less mark and of less interest. The first offender was James Harrington, the author of that political romance, "Oceania," the publication of which Cromwell had been too magnanimous to resent. He eventually became insane, and after several changes of prison, died and was buried next Raleigh, in St. Margaret's, Westminster. In the same foolish revelling reign the Duke of Richmond got shut up in the Tower for three weeks, being compromised for proposing marriage to Frances Terese, one of the king's mistresses, the "Britannia" of our English halfpence. The Duke eventually eloped with her, but he survived the marriage only a few years. In 1665 Lord Morley was sent to the Tower for stabbing a gentleman named Hastings in a street fight, with the help of a duellist named Captain Bromwich. He pleaded benefit of clergy, and peers being, at that period of our history, allowed to murder without punishment, he was acquitted.

The half-mad Duke of Buckingham seems to have been fond of the Tower, for he was no less than five times imprisoned there. The first time (before the Restoration), Cromwell had imprisoned him for marrying the daughter of Fairfax. The last time, he accompanied Shaftesbury, Salisbury, and Wharton, for opposing the Courtier Parliament. Penn, the eminent Quaker, was also imprisoned in the Tower in Charles's reign, nominally for writing a Unitarian pamphlet, but really to vex his father, the Admiral, who had indirectly accused the Duke of York of cowardice at sea, on the eve of a great engagement with the Dutch. Stillingfleet at last argued the inflexible prisoner into Christianity, and he was released.

When, on the discovery of the Rye House Plot, Lord William Russell was arrested, he was sent to the Tower first, and then to Newgate. "Arbitrary government cannot be set up in England," he said to his chaplain, "without wading through my blood." The very day Russell was removed from his prison, and Charles II. and James visited the place, the Earl of Essex, in a fit of despair at being mixed up in the Rye House Plot, or from fears at his own guilt, killed himself with a razor. He was imprisoned at the time in lodgings between the Lieutenant's house and the Beauchamp Tower.

Lord Stafford, one of the victims of Titus Oates and his sham Popish Plot, was imprisoned in the Tower, and perished under the axe on Tower Hill. When the rabble insulted him, Stafford appealed to the officials present. Sheriff Bethel brutally replied, "Sir, we have orders to stop nobody's breath but yours."

Another victim of this reign was the famous Algernon Sidney, a stern opponent of Charles, but no plotter against his person. The wretch Jeffreys hounded on the jury to a verdict. Sidney's last words in court were a prayer that the guilt of his death might not be imputed to London. On his way to Tower Hill, he said, "I know that my Redeemer liveth, and I die for the old cause."

Another turn of Fortune's wheel, and James, Duke of Monmouth, the fugitive from Sedgemoor, was found half-starved in a ditch, and was brought to his prison lodgings at the Lieutenant's house. He proved a mere craven, offered to turn Catholic to save his life, and talked only of his mistress. Tenison, the Vicar of St. Martin's Church, refused him the sacrament, and the last words of the prelates in attendance were, as the axe fell, "God accept your imperfect repentance."

James fled, and the next State prisoner was that cruel and brutal myrmidon of his, Judge Jeffreys. Detected in the disguise of a sailor, he was taken, and with difficulty saved from the enraged mob. He was discovered at a low ale-house in Wapping by a man whom he had once bullied and frightened in court. He spent his time in the Bloody Tower drinking, of which he at last died. He was at first buried near the Duke of Monmouth, then removed to St. Mary Aldermary. Our readers will remember the cruel jest played upon Jeffreys in the Tower, by a man who sent him a barrel, apparently full of Colchester oysters, but which when opened proved to contain only a halter.

In 1697, when Sir John Fenwick was in the Tower for a plot to assassinate King William, his friends, afraid he would "squeak," interceded that he should be beheaded. It was certainly very unlike a gentleman to swing, but he was so proud of being beheaded, that he grew quite tractable when the request was granted.

The Scotch Jacobite lords were the next visitors to the Tower. When the white cockade was trodden into the mire, the leaders of the chevalier's followers soon found their way there. The Earl of Derwentwater, about whom so many north-country ballads exist, and Lord Kenmure, the grandson of Charles II., perished on Tower Hill. Derwentwater's last words were, "I die a Roman Catholic. I am in perfect charity with all the world; I thank God for it. I hope to be forgiven the trespasses of my youth by the Father of infinite mercy, into whose hands I commend my soul." Kenmure, who had expected a pardon, came on the scaffold in a gay suit. "God bless King James," he cried, as he knelt to the block. Lord Winton filed the bars of his window, and escaped.

Lord Nithsdale also escaped, thanks to his brave wife. His escape is one of the prettiest romances connected with the Tower. Failing to obtain mercy from George I., who shook her from him, she struck out, in her love and despair, a stratagem worthy of a noble wife. With the help of some female friends and a useful Welsh servant girl, she disguised her husband as her maid, and with painted cheeks, hood, and muffler, he contrived to pass the sentries and escape to the house of the Venetian agent. The next morning the earl would have perished with his comrades.

In 1722, Pope's friend Atterbury, the Jacobite Bishop of Rochester, was thrown into the Tower, and, with ferocious drollery, it was advised that he should be thrown to the Tower lions. Layer, a barrister, one of his fellow-conspirators, was chained in the Tower and soon after executed. The unlucky '45 brought more Scottish lords to the Tower; the Earl of Cromartie, the Earl of Kilmarnock, Derwentwater's younger brother, Lord Balmerino, and that hoary old rascal, Simon, Lord Lovat, whom Hogarth sketched on his way to London, as he was jotting off the number of the rebel clans on his mischievous old fingers. Cromartie was spared: of the rest, Kilmarnock died first; then the scaffold was strewn with fresh sawdust, the block new covered, a new axe brought, and the executioner re-clad, by the time old Balmerino appeared, calm and careless, as with the air

of an old soldier he stopped to read the inscription upon his own coffin. At Lovat's execution, in 1747, a scaffold fell with some of the spectators, and the doomed man chuckled and said, "The mair mischief, the mair sport." "Dulce et decorum est pro patria mori," said the greatest rascal of his day; and then declaring himself a true Catholic, Lovat died, the last State criminal beheaded on Tower Hill. A stone with three rude circles in St. Peter's Church marks the grave of the three Scotch Jacobites.

Of Wilkes's imprisonment in the Tower we shall have occasion to speak elsewhere.

Then came other days, when Pitt frightened England with rumours of revolutionary conspiracies. The leaders of the London Corresponding Society, and the Society for Constitutional Information, were seized in 1794—the Habeas Corpus Act being most tyrannically suspended. Among the reformers then tried on a charge of constructive treason were Horne Tooke, the adversary of Junius, Thelwall, and Hardy, a shoemaker, secretary of the Corresponding Society. Erskine defended Hardy, who was acquitted; as also were Horne Tooke and Thelwall, to the delight of all lovers of progress.

Sir Francis Burdett's story will come more naturally into our Piccadilly chapter, but a few facts about his imprisonment in the Tower will not be out of place. In 1810 he was committed by a Tory House of Commons for a bold letter which he had written to his constituents on the case of John Gale Jones, a delegate of the Corresponding Society, who had been lodged in Newgate for a libel on the House. Burdett denied the power of the House to order imprisonment, or to keep men in prison untried.

The year 1816 brought some less noble prisoners than Sir Francis to the Tower. The Spa Fields riots were followed by the arrest of Watson, a bankrupt surgeon, Preston, a cordwainer, and Hoope a labourer, all of whom were members of certain socialist clubs.

The desperate but foolish Cato Street conspirators of 1820 were the last State prisoners lodged in the Tower, which Mr. Dixon seems to think was thus robbed of all its dignity. The cells that have held Ings, the butcher, and Davidson, the negro, can never be perfumed sufficiently to hold noble traitors or villains of mediæval magnitude. Thistlewood, that low Cataline, who had served in the army, was lodged in the Bloody Tower, as the place of honour, Brunt in the Byeward Tower, Ings and Davidson in the Water Gate, and Tidd in the Seven-Gun Battery.

CHAPTER VIII.

THE TOWER (*continued*).

The Jewels of the Tower—The Imperial State Crown—St. Edward's Crown—Prince of Wales's Crown—Ancient Queen's Crown—The Queen's Diadem or Circlet of Gold—The Orb—St. Edward's Staff—The King's Sceptres—The Queen's Sceptre—The Queen's Ivory Rod—The Ampulla—The Curtana, or Sword of Mercy—Bracelets—The Royal Spurs—The Saltcellar of State—Blood's Desperate Attempt to Steal the Regalia—The Tower Armouries—Absurd Errors in their Arrangement—Chain Mail—German Fluted Armour—Henry VIII.'s Suit of Armour—Horse Armour—Tilting Suit of the Earl of Leicester—A Series of Strange Blunders—Curiosities of the Armoury—Naval Relics—Antiquities.

THE present Jewel House at the Tower is the old Record Tower, formerly called the Hall Tower. The regalia were originally kept in a small building at the south side of the White Tower, but in the reign of Charles I. they were transferred to a strong chamber in the Martin Tower, afterwards called the Jewel Tower, which being damaged in the great fire of 1841, the warders removed the regalia to the governor's house. The new Jewel House was erected the same year, and is more commodious than the old room.

Here you see the types of power and sovereignty. The collection is surmounted by the imperial State crown of Her Majesty Queen Victoria. This crown, says Professor Tennant, "was made by Messrs. Rundell and Bridge, in the year 1838, with jewels taken from old crowns, and others furnished by command of Her Majesty. It consists of diamonds, pearls, rubies, sapphires, and emeralds, set in silver and gold ; it has a crimson velvet cap with ermine border, and is lined with white silk. Its gross weight is 39 oz. 5 dwt. troy. The lower part of the band, above the ermine border, consists of a row of 129 pearls, and the upper part of the band a row of 112 pearls, between which, in front of the crown, is a large sapphire, partly drilled, purchased for the crown by His Majesty George IV. At the back is a sapphire of smaller size, and six other sapphires, three on each side, between which are eight emeralds.

"Above and below the seven sapphires are fourteen diamonds, and around the eight emeralds 128 diamonds. Between the emeralds and sapphires are sixteen trefoil ornaments, containing 160 diamonds. Above the band are eight sapphires, surmounted by eight diamonds, between which are eight festoons, consisting of 148 diamonds.

"In the front of the crown, and in the centre of a diamond Maltese cross, is the famous ruby, said to have been given to Edward, Prince of Wales, son of Edward III., called the Black Prince, by Don Pedro, King of Castile, after the battle of Najera, near Vittoria, A.D. 1367. This ruby was worn in the helmet of Henry V. at the battle of Agincourt, A.D. 1415. It is pierced quite through, after the Eastern custom, the upper part of the piercing being filled up by a small ruby. Around this ruby, to form the cross, are seventy-five brilliant diamonds. Three other Maltese crosses, forming the two sides and back of the crown, have emerald centres, and contain respectively 132, 124, and 130 brilliant diamonds.

"Between the four Maltese crosses are four ornaments in the form of the French fleur-de-lis, with four rubies in the centres, and surrounded by rose diamonds, containing respectively eighty-five, eighty-six, eighty-six, and eighty-seven rose diamonds.

"From the Maltese crosses issue four imperial arches, composed of oak-leaves and acorns ; the leaves containing 728 rose, table, and brilliant diamonds ; thirty-two pearls forming the acorns, set in cups containing fifty-four rose diamonds and one table diamond. The total number of diamonds in the arches and acorns is 108 brilliant, 116 table, and 559 rose diamonds.

"From the upper part of the arches are suspended four large pendant pear-shaped pearls, with rose diamond caps, containing twelve rose diamonds, and stems containing twenty-four very small rose diamonds. Above the arch stands the mound, containing in the lower hemisphere 304 brilliants, and in the upper 244 brilliants ; the zone and arc being composed of thirty-three rose diamonds. The cross on the summit has a rose-cut sapphire in the centre, surrounded by four large brilliants, and 108 smaller brilliants."

The next crown to be mentioned is known as *St. Edward's.** It is the imperial crown with which the kings of England have been crowned. It was made for the coronation of Charles II., to replace the one broken up and sold during the civil wars. It is embellished with pearls, diamonds, rubies, emeralds, and sapphires, with a mound of gold on the top, enriched with a band or fillet of gold, garnished also with precious stones, and three very large oval pearls, one at the top, and

---

* It derives its name from the ancient crown, supposed to have been worn by King Edward the Confessor, and which was preserved in Westminster Abbey till the rebellion in the reign of Charles I., when it was sacrilegiously taken away, together with many other articles belonging to the regalia.

the others pendant to the ends of the cross. This crown is formed of four crosses, and as many fleurs-de-lis of gold, rising from a rim or circlet, also of gold, and set with precious stones; and the cap within is made of purple velvet, lined with taffeta, and turned up with ermine.

The Prince of Wales's Crown. This is formed of pure gold, and is unadorned by jewels. On occasions of State it is placed before the seat in the House of Lords which is occupied by the heir apparent.

hand at his coronation, and is borne in his left on his return to Westminster Hall, is a ball of gold six inches in diameter, encompassed with a band or fillet of gold, embellished with roses of diamonds encircling other precious stones, and edged with pearls. On the top is an extraordinary fine amethyst, of an oval shape, nearly an inch and a half in height, which forms the foot or pedestal of a cross of gold three inches and a quarter high, set very thick with diamonds, and adorned with a sapphire, an emerald, and several large pearls.

THE JEWEL ROOM AT THE TOWER.

The Ancient Queen's Crown, being that used at coronations for the queen consort, is a very rich crown of gold, set with diamonds of great value, intermixed with other precious stones and pearls; the cap being similar to the preceding.

The Queen's Diadem or Circlet of Gold. This was worn by Queen Mary, consort of James II., in proceeding to her coronation. It is a rim or circle of gold, richly adorned with large diamonds, curiously set, and around the upper edge a string of pearls; the cap is of purple velvet, lined with white taffeta, and turned up with ermine, richly powdered. It cost, according to Sandford, £111,000.

The Orb, which rests in the sovereign's right

St. Edward's Staff, which is carried before the sovereign at the coronation, is a staff or sceptre of beaten gold, four feet seven inches and a half in length and about three quarters of an inch in diameter, with a pike or foot of steel four inches and a quarter long, and a mound and cross at the top.

The *King's Sceptre with the Cross*, or *Sceptre Royal*, likewise of gold, is two feet nine inches in length, and of the same size as that with the dove; the handle is plain, but the upper part is wreathed, and the pommel at the bottom set with rubies, emeralds, and small diamonds. On the top is a mound, and on the mound is a cross adorned with precious stones. This sceptre is placed in the

THE TOWER · OF LONDON

WHITE TOWER

MIDDLE TOWER

BYWARD TOWER

STAIRCASE WHITE TOWER

PASSAGE IN BLOODY TOWER

ST JOHN'S CHAPEL

JANE

BLOODY TOWER

BELL TOWER

BOWYER TOWER

W. H. PRIOR del.

TRAITOR'S GATE

BYWARD TOWER.

right hand of the sovereign at the coronation by the Archbishop of Canterbury.

The *King's Sceptre with the Dove* is gold, in length three feet seven inches, and about three inches in circumference. It is set with diamonds and other precious stones, and upon the mound at the top, which is enriched with a band or fillet of rose diamonds, is a small cross, whereon is fixed a dove with wings expanded, as the emblem of mercy.

The *Queen's Sceptre with the Cross* is also of gold, adorned with diamonds and other precious stones, and in most parts is very like the king's, but not wreathed, nor quite so large.

The *Queen's Ivory Rod*, which was made for Queen Mary, consort of James II., is a sceptre of white ivory three feet one inch and a half in length, with a pommel, mound, and cross of gold, and a dove on the top.

Besides these there is another very rich and elegant sceptre with a dove, which was discovered in 1814 behind a part of the old wainscot of the Jewel House, where it seems to have lain unobserved for a great number of years. This nearly assimilates to the king's sceptre with the dove, and there is every probability that it was made for Queen Mary, consort of William III., with whom she was jointly invested with the exercise of the royal authority.

The *Ampulla*, or *Eagle of Gold*, which contains the holy oil at the ceremony of the coronation, is in the form of an eagle, with wings expanded, standing on a pedestal, all of pure gold finely chased. The head screws off about the middle of the neck, for the convenience of putting in the oil, which is poured out through the beak into a spoon called the anointing-spoon, which is likewise of pure gold, with four pearls in the broadest part of the handle. These are considered to be of great antiquity.

Curtana, or the *Sword of Mercy*, which is borne naked before the king, between the two swords of justice, at the coronation, is of plain steel, gilded. The blade is thirty-two inches in length, and nearly two in breadth; the handle is covered with fine gold wire, and the point flat. The *Swords of Justice* are the spiritual and temporal, which are borne, the former on the right hand and the latter on the left, before the king or queen at their coronation. The point of the spiritual sword is somewhat obtuse, but that of the temporal sword is sharp. Their blades are about forty inches long, the handles cased with fine gold wire, and the scabbards of all three are alike, covered with a rich brocaded cloth of tissue, with a fine ferule, hook, and chape.

Armillæ, or *Bracelets*, which are ornaments for the king's wrist, worn at coronations, are of solid fine gold, an inch and a half in breadth, and edged with rows of pearl. They open by means of a hinge, for the purpose of being put on the arm, and are chased with the rose, thistle, fleur-de-lis, and harp.

The *Royal Spurs* are also made of fine gold, curiously wrought, and are carried in the procession at coronations by the Lords Grey of Ruthyn, a service which they claim by descent from the family of Hastings, Earls of Huntingdon.

The *Saltcellar of State*, which is said to be a model in gold of the White Tower, a grand silver font, double gilt, generally used at the baptisms of the royal family, and a large silver fountain, presented to Charles II. by the town of Plymouth, are likewise worthy of notice; and there is also deposited in the Jewel House a magnificent service of communion-plate belonging to the Tower Chapel; it is of silver, double gilt, superbly wrought, the principal piece containing a beautiful representation of the Lord's Supper.

The summary of jewels comprised in the crown is as follows:—1 large ruby, irregularly polished; 1 large broad-spread sapphire; 16 sapphires; 11 emeralds; 4 rubies; 1,363 brilliant diamonds; 1,273 rose diamonds; 147 table diamonds; 4 drop-shaped pearls; and 273 pearls.

A curious fact in connection with the regalia is related by Haydon the painter. The crown, he says, at George IV.'s coronation, "was not bought, but borrowed. Rundell's price was £70,000; and Lord Liverpool told the king he could not sanction such an expenditure. Rundell charged £7,000 for the loan, and as some time elapsed before it was decided whether the crown should be bought or not, Rundell charged £3,000 or £4,000 more for the interval."

The crown jewels have been exhibited for a fee since the restoration of King Charles II. They had been before that period kept sometimes in the Tower, in the treasury of the Temple or other religious house, and in the treasury at Westminster. The royal jewels have on several occasions been pledged to provide for the exigencies of our monarchs, by Henry III., Edward III., Henry V., Henry VI.; and Richard II. offered them to the merchants of London as a guarantee for a loan. The office of Keeper of the Regalia, conferred by the king's letters patent, became, in the reign of the Tudors, a post of great emolument and dignity, and "The Master of the Jewel-House" took rank as the first knight bachelor of England; the office was some time held by Cromwell, afterwards Earl of Essex. During the civil war under Charles I. the regalia were sold and destroyed. On the restoration of Charles II. new regalia were made, for which the king's goldsmith, Sir Robert Vyner, was paid £21,978 9s. 11d.

At the great fire of 1841 the grating was broken open and the jewels removed for safety. Mr. G. Cruikshank made a clever drawing of this scene.

The history of the regalia would be incomplete without some short mention of Blood's desperate and impudent attempt to steal the crown, globe, and sceptre, in the reign of Charles II. This villain, Blood, had been a lieutenant in Cromwell's army, and had turned Government spy. He had joined in a plan to seize Dublin Castle and kill the Lord Lieutenant. He had actually stopped the Duke of Ormond's coach in Piccadilly, carried off the duke, and tried to hang him at Tyburn, a plan which had all but succeeded; and the Duke of Buckingham was suspected by the Ormond family of having encouraged the attempt. In the attempt on the regalia Blood had four accomplices. Blood, disguised as a country parson, in band and gown, began the campaign by going to see the crown with a woman who passed for his wife. This woman, while seeing the jewels, pretended to be taken ill, and was shown into the private rooms of Talbot Edwards, the old Deputy Keeper of the Crown Jewels, a man eighty years of age. Blood then observed the loneliness of the Tower, and the scanty means of defence. He called four days later with a present of gloves for Mrs. Edwards, and repeated his visits, till he at last proposed that his nephew, a young man, as he said, with £200 or £300 a year, should marry the old man's daughter. He finally fixed a day when the young bridegroom should present himself for approval. On the appointed day he arrived at the outside of the Iron Gate with four companions, all being on horseback. The plan for action was fully matured. Hunt, Blood's son-in-law, was to hold the horses, and keep them ready at St. Katharine's Gate. Parrot, an old Roundhead trooper and now a Government spy, was to steal the globe while Blood carried off the crown, and a third accomplice was to file the sceptre into pieces and slip them into a bag. A fourth rogue represented the lover. The five men were each armed with sword-canes, sharp poignards, and a brace of pistols. While pretending to wait for the arrival of his wife, Blood asked Edwards to show his friends the jewels. The moment the door was locked inside, according to Tower custom, the ruffians muffled and gagged the old man, and then felled him to the ground and beat him till he was nearly dead. Unluckily for the rascals, young Edwards at that moment returned from Flanders, and ran upstairs to see where his

mother and sisters were. Blood and Parrot made off at once with the globe and crown. The sceptre they could not break. The old man freeing himself from the gag, screamed and roused the family. Blood wounded a sentinel and fired at another, but was eventually overpowered. The crown fell in the dirt, a pearl was picked up by a sweeper, a diamond by an apprentice, and several stones were lost. Parrot was captured and the globe found in his pocket; one fine ruby had broken loose. Hunt was thrown from his horse and taken. But none of these culprits were punished. Blood betrayed pretended plots, or in some way obtained power over the king. He was received at court, and £500 a year was given him.

From the Jewel House we pass to the Armouries. The Armouries in the Tower were established by our earliest kings. We find Henry III. issuing a mandate to the Archdeacon of Durham to transmit to the arsenal twenty-six suits of armour, five iron cuirasses, one iron collar, three pairs of fetters, and nine iron helmets. In 1339 (Edward III.) John de Flete, keeper of the arms in the Tower, was commanded to bring as many "espringals, quarrells, hauberks, lances, arbalasts, bows and arrows," as were necessary for the defence of the Castle of Southampton. Two years afterwards the Sheriff of Gloucester was ordered to purchase and transmit to the Tower 1,000 bows, and 300 sheaves of arrows; 250 of the bows to be painted, the rest to be white or plain.

A curious inventory of Tower armour in the reign of Edward VI. enumerates:—"Brigandines complete, having sleeves covered with crimson; ditto, with sleeves covered with cloth of gold; ditto, with sleeves covered with blue satin; millars' coats covered with fustian and white cloth; and brigandines covered with linen cloth with long taces." The inventory also enumerates targets covered with steel, and having pistols in the centre; a target with twenty pistols; a target "of the shell of Tortys;" steel horse-trappings; poleaxes with pistols at the end; gilt poleaxes, the staves covered with crimson velvet and fringed with silk of gold: holy water sprinklers, or Danish clubs, with spiked balls fastened to a chain. Some of these arms still remain in the Tower, especially a "holy water sprinkler with 3 guns," which the warders used to call "King Harry the Eighth's Walking-Staff."

In the reign of Elizabeth the Tower armouries were described by Hentzner, a German traveller, in 1598, and our readers will see, by the following extract, that many of the chief curiosities now shown were even then on view:—

"We were," says Hentzner, "next led to the

Armoury, in which were these peculiarities. Spears out of which you may shoot; shields that will give fire four times; a great many rich halberds, commonly called partisans, with which the guard defend the royal person in battle; some lances covered with red and green velvet; and the suit of armour of Henry VIII.; many and very beautiful arms, as well for men as for horse-fights; the lance of Charles Brandon, Duke of Suffolk, three spans thick; two pieces of cannon, the one fires three, the other seven balls at a time; two others, made of wood, which the English had at the siege of Boulogne, in France, and by this stratagem, without which they could not have succeeded, they struck a terror as at the appearance of artillery, and the town was surrendered upon articles; nineteen cannons of a thicker make than ordinary, and, in a room apart, thirty-six of a smaller; other cannons for chain-shot and balls, proper to bring down masts of ships; cross-bows, bows and arrows, of which to this day the English make great use in their exercises. But who can relate all that is to be seen here? Eight or nine men, employed by the year, are scarce sufficient to keep all the arms bright."

Hewitt, in his account of the Tower, argues very shrewdly, from Hentzner's silence about the spoils of the Armada still exhibited, and, in fact, about the "Spanish Armoury" altogether, that those pretended trophies were never trophies at all. The Spanish "coller of torment" is an undoubted relic of the Armada; the rest, Mr. Hewitt decides, were taken from a collection of Spanish arms, chosen for their excellent quality, and of a far earlier date than 1588. Hentzner visited England soon after the Armada. As a German he would be interested in all relics of the defeated Spanish invasion. He visited the Spanish Armoury, and had he been shown there any relics of Philip's armament, would be sure to have mentioned it.

The first mention of a Spanish weapon-house is in a survey of 1675, which enumerates targets with pistols, Spanish pikes, partisans, Spanish boar-spears, Spanish poleaxes, and Spanish halberts. Some later exhibitors, says Mr. Hewitt, finding a room called the Spanish Weapon-house, immediately set it down, with true showman's instinct, as a room of Armada spoils, and so the error has been perpetuated.

During the Commonwealth the Tower collection of armour lay in abeyance, but at the Restoration, William Legg, Master of the Armouries, made a survey of the stores, and in it enumerates Brandon's huge lance, the Spanish collar of torture, and the ancient head-piece with rams'-horns and spectacles still named after William Somers, the Jester of Henry VIII. Some of the suits are noted as

having come from the Green Gallery, at Greenwich. These last included both suits of Prince Henry and suits of Henry V., Henry VIII., Edward III., Edward IV., Henry VI., the Earl of Leicester, and Charles Brandon. There is also mentioned a gilt and graven suit for "his late majesty, of ever blessed memory, Charles I.;" a suit of Charles II., when a boy; and a suit sent to Charles II. by the Great Mogul.

On the Restoration, says Meyrick, the armour which had been formerly in the Green Gallery at Greenwich, placed on horseback and dignified with the name of some of our kings, gave the hint for an exhibition at the Tower of the same sort. The Tudors and Stuarts were added; and in 1686, the year after the death of Charles II., his figure and that of his father were added, their horses and faces carved by Grinling Gibbons.

Towards the close of the seventeenth century armour fell into disuse, and was sent by various regiments to the Tower stores. A survey in 1697 enumerates thousands of back and breast pieces, pots, and head-pieces. The equestrian figures, when fitted out from these and from various gifts, increased from ten to twenty-seven.

Among the confused suits Meyrick found both William the Conqueror and William III. clad in plate armour of the age of Edward VI. The suit of Henry V. was composed from parts of three others, of which the upper portion was of the time of Charles I., while the legs—which were not fellows!—were of the age of Henry VII. Henry VIII. also had the misfortune to have odd legs. George I. and George II. were armed cap-à-pie in suits of Henry VIII.'s time, and mounted on Turkish saddles, gilt and ornamented with the globe, crescent, and star. John of Gaunt was a knight of Henry VIII.'s reign, and De Courcy a demi-lancer of Edward VI.'s. The helmet of Queen Elizabeth was of the period of Edward VI.; the armour for her arms, of that of Charles I.; her breastplate went as far back as Henry VIII.; and the garde de reins of that monarch covered Her Majesty's "abdomen." A big suit of Henry VIII., rough from the hammer, had first been described by the warders as "made for the king at the age of eighteen," and then "as much too small for him."

The absurd inventions of the Tower warders were endless. A "Guide to the Tower of London and its Curiosities" (says Mr. Planché), published in the reign of George III., mentions a breastplate desperately damaged by shot, which was shown as having been worn by a man, part of whose body, including some of the intestines, was carried away by a cannon-ball, notwithstanding which, being put under the care of a skilful surgeon, the man recovered, and lived for ten years afterwards. "This story," adds the Guide, "the old warder constantly told to all strangers, till H.R.H. Prince Frederick, father of the present king, being told the accustomed tale, said, with a smile, 'And what, friend, is there so extraordinary in all this? I remember myself to have read in a book of a soldier who had his head cleft in two so dextrously by the stroke of a scimitar, that one half of it fell on one shoulder, and the other half of it on the other shoulder; and yet, on his comrade's clapping the two sides nicely together again, and binding them close with his handkerchief, the man did well, drank his pot of ale at night, and scarcely recollected that he had ever been hurt." The writer goes on to say that the old warder was "so dashed," that he never had the courage to tell his story again; but, though he might not, it was handed down by his successors, by several of whom, Mr. Planché says, he heard it repeated in his boyhood, fifty years after the death of Frederick Prince of Wales. The old battered breastplate is still in the collection, and has not been "sold as old iron," being thoroughly unworthy of preservation.

In the year 1825 Dr. (afterwards Sir) Samuel Rush Meyrick received the royal commands to re-arrange the Horse and Spanish Armouries, a task for which that antiquary's taste and knowledge eminently qualified him. This task he executed, but, unfortunately, was compelled by ignorant officials to appropriate every suit (right or wrong) to some great personage of the period, distinguishing the few that could actually be identified by stars on the flags above them. The storekeeper then resumed his care, and everything went wrong: forgeries were bought and carefully preserved under glass, and valuable pieces of armour, which had been actually stolen or sold from the armoury, were often offered for sale to the authorities and rejected by them. In 1859, Mr. Planché, an eminent authority on armour, drew the attention of the Right Hon. Sidney Herbert to the confusion of the whole collection, and to the fact that the armoury produced an annual revenue of £2,000 and odd, being, therefore, self-supporting. The same public-spirited gentleman also pointed out that the Horse Armoury admitted the rain, and had an inflammable wooden shed at one end. In 1869, to the great satisfaction of all true antiquaries, Mr. Planché was commissioned to arrange the armour in the Tower in strict chronological order. In his "Recollections and Reflections," he suggests that a fine gallery could be made out of the row of carpenters' shops on the east side of the White Tower.

The negligence of the Government led, Mr. Planché says, in his own time, to many blunders. One of the bargains missed by the Keeper of the Armouries was the complete suit in which Sir Philip Sidney was killed at the battle of Zutphen, the embossed figures on which were of solid gold. This national and magnificent relic was at Strawberry Hill, and is now at St. Petersburg. Another relic lost to the Tower was a heaume of the time of King John, now at Warwick Castle. A third was the gauntlets of a fine suit made for Henry VIII., now in the Tower, imperfect from their absence. They had found their way out of the Tower, and, on being brought back, were ignored and refused by the authorities, and bought by Lord Londesborough. A fourth was a most singular quaint helmet, probably as early as the time of Stephen, if not actually the helmet of that monarch, or of his son, now in the Musée d'Artillerie at Paris. Two other helmets, one *temp.* Henry III., the other of the fifteenth century, with part of the crest remaining, were also rejected. At the very same time a helmet newly made at Vienna, for theatrical purposes, was purchased at the price of £50, and is now in one of the glass cases at the Tower. The only armour at Alton Towers that could possibly have belonged to the great Talbot was suffered by some gentleman sent down by the Tower to pass into the hands of dealers. The back-plate, a most elegant specimen, sold for £10, and is now in the collection of Lord Londesborough.

The present Horse Armoury, at the south-west corner of the White Tower, was completed in 1826, when Meyrick re-arranged the collection. This is a single apartment, about 150 feet long by 34 wide. A row of pillars supporting pointed arches runs the whole length of the interior. The space in front of the columns is occupied by figures, some equestrian and some on foot, clothed in armour from the reign of Henry VI. to that of James II. Several military trophies and emblems adorn the walls and ceilings of the apartment, and the space devoted to the armed figures is divided into several compartments by stands containing weapons of the various periods.

The visitor can pass here from the simple mail of early days by easy steps to the engraved and ornamented armour of Elizabeth's reign.

The Crusaders of Henry III.'s reign brought chain-mail from the East. Mixed plate and chain suits were introduced in the reign of Edward II. In the reign of Richard II. the visors were peaked, and projected from the face like birds' beaks. With Henry IV. armour became all plate, and the steel monster was now fully hatched. With Henry V. came two-handed swords, to hew to pieces the said armour. In Edward IV.'s days came all sorts of novelties in armour—tuilles to cover the hips, pauldrons for the shoulders, grande-gardes, or extra half-breastplates, to cover the left breast. In the time of Richard III., say most authorities, armour attained its highest perfection

The Henry VIII. suit, the first suit in the collection, really belonged to the king whose effigy it covers. The armour is damasked, and the stirrups are curious, from their great size. But one of the finest suits in the world, and belonging to this same burly king, is in the central recess of the south wall.

THE TOWER HORSE ARMOURY.

of form and arrangement. The shoes have long, pointed toes. The Richard III. suit at the Tower was brought from Spain, and was worn by the Marquis of Waterford at the fantastic Eglinton Tournament in 1839.

In the reign of Henry VII. came in the beautiful German fluted armour. The helmets worn were the round Burgundian, and the shoes were round and large at the toes. The horse-armour, too, is splendid.

"This," says Hewitt, "is one of the most curious suits of armour in the world, having been made to commemorate the union of Henry VIII. and Katharine of Arragon. The badges of this king and queen, the rose and pomegranate, are engraved on various parts of the armour. On the fans of the genouillères is the sheaf of arrows, the device adopted by Ferdinand, the father of Katharine, on his conquest of Granada. Henry's badges, the portcullis, the fleur-de-lis, and the red dragon, also appear ; and on the edge of the lamboys, or skirts, are the initials of the royal pair, 'H. K.,' united by a true lovers' knot. The same letters, similarly united by a knot, which includes also a curious love-badge, formed of a half rose and half pomegranate, are engraved on the croupière of the horse.

"But the most remarkable part of the embellishment of this suit consists in the saintly legends which are engraved upon it. These consist of ten beneath which a fire is blazing, to boil the oil within ; a female saint suffering decapitation; while in the background is predicted the retribution that awaits the persecutor ; another saint about to suffer decapitation ; St. Agatha led to be scourged; and St. Agatha being built up in prison.

"Round the lower edge of the horse-armour, many times repeated, is the motto, 'Dieu et mon Droit,' while numerous other decorations—human figures, heraldic badges, arabesque work, and

THE TOWER MENAGERIE ABOUT 1820.

subjects, full of curious costume, and indicating curious manners.

"On the breastplate is the figure of St. George on foot, encountering the dragon. On the backplate appears St. Barbara, with her usual emblems. On the front of the poitrail St. George, on horseback, is dispatching the dragon ; the armour of his horse is embellished with the rose and pomegranate. Also, on the poitrail, St. George accused before Diocletian ; and another subject, representing some lady of rank, attended by her maids, directing the fortifications of a town or fortress. On the croupière, St. George, stretched on the rack ; a saint receiving martyrdom, by being enclosed as high as the waist in the brazen figure of an ox, grotesque devices of fabulous and other animals— are continued over the whole suit, both of man and horse. Among these engravings is one of a female figure, bearing on the front of her bodice the German word 'Glück'—good luck, health, prosperity. From this, it has been suggested by Sir S. Meyrick, we may infer that the suit before us was presented by the Emperor Maximilian to Henry, in honour of his marriage with Katharine of Arragon. We own this inference seems rather a bold one.

"The armour is doubtless of German manufacture, and one of the finest of the period. It was formerly gilt, and when new must have had a most gorgeous appearance. From its discoloration by time, the elaborate decorations of its surface are almost entirely lost, but might easily be restored by a judicious renewal of the gilding."

"We find another splendid suit of armour, of the reign of Edward VI. It is of the kind called *russet*, which was produced by oxidising the metal, and then smoothing its surface. By this means the gold-work with which it was afterwards damasquined looked much richer than if inlaid on a ground of polished steel, or *white* armour, as it was technically called. The suit before us is covered with the most beautiful filagree-work. The helmet especially is most elaborately ornamented; embossed lions' heads adorn the pauldrons, elbow-pieces, gauntlets, breastplate, genouillères, and sollerets; and the whole is in the finest preservation. The helmet, which is a burgonet, is also embellished with a lion's head. In the right hand is a mace, terminating in a spear. This figure was formerly exhibited as Edward the Black Prince.

"The horse-armour, which is a complete suit, is embossed and embellished with the combined badges of Burgundy and Granada. The probabilities are that it belonged to Philip of Flanders, surnamed 'the Fair.' He was the son of the Emperor Maximilian, by Mary, daughter and heiress of Charles the Bold, last Sovereign-Duke of Burgundy, and consequently, in right of his mother, Duke of Burgundy and Count of Flanders. He married Joanna, second daughter of Ferdinand and Isabella, and sister of Katharine of Arragon, queen of Henry VIII.

"The badge of the pomegranate was borne by all the children of Isabella and Ferdinand the conqueror of Granada. Philip and Joanna, on the death of Isabella, in 1504, became sovereigns of Castile and Arragon, and in 1506, on a voyage to Spain, were obliged by a violent tempest to take shelter in England, where they were detained upwards of three months in a sort of honourable captivity by Henry VII. The armour might have been left behind, in England, on the departure of the royal travellers, or presented by Philip to Henry."

The tilting-suit of the Earl of Leicester is still shown. "That the armour before us was worn by Leicester," says Mr. Hewitt, "there is not the slightest doubt. His initials, ' R. D.,' are engraved on the genouillères. His cognizance of the bear and ragged staff appears on the chanfron of the horse, encircled by the collar of the Garter; and the ragged staff is repeated on every part of the suit. The suit was originally gilt, and 'was kept,' says Sir S. Meyrick, 'in the tilt-yard, where it was exhibited on particular days.' It afterwards

figured in the old horse armoury as that of King James I."

The suit of Sir Henry Lee, champion of Queen Elizabeth, was formerly exhibited as that of William the Conqueror. The fine engraved and gilt suit of the Earl of Essex (1581) was worn by the king's champion at the coronation of George II. The figure of James I. was formerly shown as Henry IV. The suit of Charles I. was given him by the Armourers' Company. It is richly gilt and arabesqued. The suit is specially interesting as being the identical one laid on the coffin of the Duke of Marlborough at his public funeral. The head of the effigy of James II. was carved by Grinling Gibbons as a portrait of Charles II.

The suit long called John of Gaunt's turned out to be an engraved suit for a man-at-arms of the reign of Henry VIII., and the Norman Crusader to have come from the Mogul country. There is a fine suit of Italian armour here, date 1620, once worn by Count Oddi, of Padua. It is ornamented with the imperial eagle, the badge of his house. The devices, formed of swords, pistols, and bayonets, are very ingenious. The large pavois shield (*temp.* James I.) should be noticed. The russet and gold armour is Venetian, of the sixteenth century; and the six pieces of a puffed and engraved suit of the time of Henry VIII. are extremely curious and rare. The ancient German saddle of bone inlaid with figures is of uncertain date. The inscription is—

> " I hope the best to you may happen ;
>   May God help you well in Saint George's name."

The fantastic helmet with horns, made for mock tournaments, is said to have belonged to Henry VIII.'s jester. The crossbows are of all ages. Firearms can here be traced, from the earliest hand-gun of 1430. One flint-lock rifle, of Austrian make (1750), could be fired eighteen times in a minute. Here we see the steel mace combined with the pistol, *temp.* Edward VI. The padded Chinese armour, too, is curious; and there is a curious suit of the Great Mogul, sent to Charles II., made partly of plates and partly of small iron tubes bound in rows. The Elizabethan Armoury contains a goodly store of glaives, black-bills, Lochaber axes, and boar-spears. The great curiosity here is the block on which Lords Balmerino, Kilmarnock, and Lovat laid down their heads; the old heading-axe, said to have taken off the head of Essex; the iron torture-cravat, called in the Tower, "Skeffington's Daughter," from the name of the inventor; the bilboes; the thumbscrews; the Spanish collar of torture, from the Armada; two yew-bows, from the wreck of the *Mary Rose*, sunk off Spithead in the reign of Henry VIII. ; and a breech-loading match-lock petronel, that belonged to Henry VIII. The relics of Tippoo Sahib have also a special interest.

The grand storehouse for the royal train of artillery, and the small-arms armoury for 150,000 stand of arms, destroyed by fire October 30, 1841, were built in the reign of James II. or William III., since which the Tower has been remodelled, many small dwelling-houses cleared away, and several towers and defences rebuilt. The houses of Petty Wales and the outworks have been removed, as well as the menagerie buildings near the west entrance. In the great fire of 1841 only 4,000 stand of arms were saved out of about 100,000, and the loss was computed at about £250,000. But for the height of the tide and the fulness of the ditch, the whole Tower would have been destroyed. In 1830 the store of arms in the Tower had amounted to 600,000. Among the curiosities destroyed was one of the state swords carried before the Pretender when he was proclaimed in Scotland, in 1715, and a curious wooden gun.

The Train Room contained some interesting naval relics ; among others, the steering-wheel of Lord Nelson's *Victory*, trophies of William III. and General Wolfe, and relics of Waterloo. The earliest guns were of the reigns of Henry VI. and Edward IV.—hooped guns, with movable chambers. There was also a great treasure which fortunately escaped the fire—a large iron chamber-gun, recovered from the wreck of the *Mary Rose* (Henry VIII.). The Great Harry, which is of brass, weighs five tons (*temp*. Henry VIII.). It has the date 1542, and the English rose engraved upon it is surmounted by the crown of France. There were guns, too, from Ramillies, and relics of the *Royal George*. One old brass German gun, date 1581, had the spirited motto—

> " I sing and spring,
> My foe transfixing."

One of the finest guns preserved was a brass gun taken from the French. It had formerly belonged to the Knights of Malta. The date is 1773. It is covered with exquisite figures in alto-relievo. In one part is a medallion portrait of the artist, Philip Lattarellus, and in another the portrait of the Grand Master of Malta, supported by two genii. The carriage also is very curious ; its trails are formed of the intertwined figures of two furies holding torches, and grasping a huge snake. The centre of the wheel represents the sun, the spokes forming its rays. There was also saved a small brass gun, presented to the Duke of Gloucester, the son of Queen Anne.

In other parts of the Armoury are ancient British flint axes, Saxon weapons, a suit of Greek armour, found in a tomb at Cumæ ; kettle-drums from Blenheim ; the cloak in which General Wolfe died ; the sword-sash of that popular Commander-in-Chief, the Duke of York ; Saracenic, Indian, Moorish, New Zealand, and Kaffrarian arms, and even a door-mat suit from the South Seas. In 1854, 2,000 stand of Russian arms, taken at Bomarsund, the first trophies of the war against the Emperor Nicholas, were placed in the Tower. There are also ten small brass cannon to be seen, presented by the brass-founders of London to Charles II. when a boy. Hatton, in 1708, mentions among the curiosities of the Tower the sword which Lord Kinsale took from an officer of the French body-guard, for which deed he and his posterity have the right of remaining covered in the king's presence. A tablet on the staircase marks the spot where the bones of the two murdered princes were discovered.

From the above account it will be seen that the Tower contains as many interesting historical relics as any museum in England. Here the intelligent visitor can trace the progress of weapons from the rude flint axe of the early Briton to the latest rifle that science has invented. Here he can see all the changes of armour, from the rude suits worn at Hastings to the time when the Italians turned the coat of steel into a work of the finest art, and lavished upon it years of anxious and refined labour. There are breastplates in the Tower on which Montfort's spear has splintered, and cuirasses on which English swords struck fire at Waterloo. There are trophies of all our wars, from Cressy and Poictiers to Blenheim and Inkermann, spoils of the Armada, relics of the early Crusade wars, muskets that were discharged at Minden, swords of Marlborough's troopers, shields carried at Agincourt, suits of steel that Elizabeth's champions wore at Cadiz, flags that have been scorched by Napoleon's powder, blades that have shared in struggles with Dane and Indian, Spaniard and Russian. Thanks to Mr. Planché, the Tower Armoury can now be studied in sequence, and with intellectual advantage. The blunders of former days have been rectified, and order once more prevails, where formerly all was confusion and jumble. Thanks to the imperishability of steel, the old war-costumes of England remain for us to study, and with the smallest imagination one can see Harry of Monmouth, in the very arms he wore, ride forth against the French spears, all blazoned with heraldic splendour, and, shouting "God and St. George for merry England," scatter the French, as he did when he won his crowning victory.

CHAPTER IX.

THE TOWER (*continued*).

The Tower of London Officials—Locking-up the Tower—The Tower Menagerie—The Moat—The Church of St. Peter ad Vincula—Early Sufferers for State Errors—Gerald Fitzgerald—Fisher—Lord Seymour of Dudley—The Protector Somerset—The Earl of Essex—Sir Thomas Overbury—Anne Boleyn—The Monuments in St. Peter ad Vincula—A Blood-stained Spot—Historical Treasure Trove—The Waterloo Barracks—The Royal Mint—Nooks and Corners of the Tower—Its Terrible Cells—The Tower Ghost.

THE Constable of the Tower was anciently called "the Constable of London," "the Constable of the Sea," and "the Constable of the Honour of the Tower." William I. chose as the first Constable of his new fortress Geoffrey de Mandeville, who had fought well at Hastings. The Constable *temp.* Edward II. received a dole of twopence from each person going and returning by the Thames on a pilgrimage to St. James of Compostella. In the reign of Richard II. he received £100 a year, with fees from prisoners for the "suite of his irons" —for a duke, £20; for an earl, twenty marks; for a baron, £10; for a knight, 100 shillings. Later, he had wine-tolls, which were taken from passing ships by his officers. Taylor the Water-poet farmed this office, and naïvely confesses that he could make no profit of it till he cheated. The Constable's salary is at present about £1,000 a year. The Duke of Wellington was Constable from 1820 till his death, in 1852, and he was succeeded by that brave old veteran, Viscount Combermere. The Lieutenant of the Tower ranks next to the Constable, and then follow the Tower Major and the Master Gunner. The warders' old dress was obtained for them by the Duke of Somerset, after his release from prison in the reign of Edward VI.

"There are two officers," says Bayley, "who are now joined in the command and custody of the Tower, with the denomination of Deputy-Lieutenant and Major, both of whom are appointed by commission from the Crown, though the patronage is virtually in the Constable, who exercises the power of recommending." These officers, however, were of very modern date, having both sprung up in the course of the last century. The earliest mention we find of a Deputy-Lieutenant is in the time of Queen Anne, and that of a Major not till many years afterwards. The office of Deputy-Lieutenant has been abolished. The civil establishment of the Tower also consists of a chaplain, whose appointment is in the Crown exclusively; the chief bailiff, who has his office by letters patent, at the recommendation of the Constable; a surgeon, who is appointed by Royal Commission at the recommendation of the Constable; the keeper of the regalia, the steward or coroner, the yeoman-gaoler, the yeoman-porter, and forty yeoman-warders, all of whom have their places by warrant of the Constable.

Locking-up the Tower is an ancient, curious, and stately ceremony. A few minutes before the clock strikes the hour of eleven—on Tuesdays and Fridays, twelve—the head warder (yeoman-porter), clothed in a long red cloak, bearing a huge bunch of keys, and attended by a brother warder carrying a lantern, appears in front of the main guardhouse, and loudly calls out, "Escort keys!" The sergeant of the guard, with five or six men, then turns out and follows him to the "Spur," or outer gate, each sentry challenging as they pass his post, "Who goes there?" "Keys." The gates being carefully locked and barred, the procession returns, the sentries exacting the same explanation, and receiving the same answer as before. Arrived once more in front of the main guardhouse, the sentry there gives a loud stamp with his foot, and asks, "Who goes there?" "Keys." "Whose keys?" "Queen Victoria's keys." "Advance, Queen Victoria's keys, and all's well." The yeoman-porter then exclaims, "God bless Queen Victoria!" The main guard respond, "Amen!" The officer on duty gives the word, "Present arms!" The firelocks rattle, the officer kisses the hilt of his sword, the escort fall in among their companions, and the yeoman-porter marches across the parade alone, to deposit the keys in the Lieutenant's lodgings. The ceremony over, not only is all egress and ingress totally precluded, but even within the walls no one can stir without being furnished with the countersign.

The Tower has a separate coroner, and the public have access to the fortress only by sufferance. When Horwood made his survey of London, 1799, he was denied admission to the Tower, and the refusal is thus recorded upon the map: "The Tower; the internal parts not distinguished, being refused permission to take the survey." The Tower is now open free to the public on Mondays and Saturdays.

Nor must we forget the now extinct menagerie in the Tower. The first royal menagerie in England was at Woodstock, where Henry I. kept some lions and leopards to amuse his ladies and courtiers.

Henry III. having three leopards sent him by the Emperor Frederick II., moved his wild beasts to the Tower, and thus commenced the menagerie which existed there till 1834. Among the national records many orders exist to the sheriffs of London, Bedfordshire, and Buckinghamshire to provide for the animals and their keepers. Thus in 1252 (Henry III.) the London sheriffs were ordered to pay fourpence a day for the maintenance of a white bear, and to provide a muzzle and chain to hold him while fishing or washing himself in the river Thames. In the same reign they are again desired to build a house in the Tower for an elephant, sent to the king by Louis of France—the first ever seen in England since the Roman period. In the reigns of Edward I., Edward II., and Edward III., the lions and leopards were paid for at the rate of sixpence a day, while the keepers received only three-halfpence. At later periods the keeper of the Tower lions was a person of quality, who received sixpence a day, and the same sum for every animal under his charge. Henry VI. gave the post to his marshal, Robert Mansfield, and afterwards to Thomas Rookes, his dapifer.

The post was often held by the Lieutenant or Constable of the Tower, on condition of his providing a sufficient deputy. Our ancient kings had in their household an official called "the Master of the King's Bears and Apes." In a semi-circular enclosure round the Lion Tower, James I. and his court used to come to see lions and bears baited by dogs. In Howel's time there were six lions in the Tower, and probably no other animals. In 1708 Strype enumerates eleven lions, two leopards or tigers (the worthy historian, it seems, knows not which), three eagles, two owls, two cats of the mountain, and a jackal. In 1754 Maitland gives a much larger catalogue. By 1822, however, the Tower menagerie had sunk to a grizzly bear, an elephant, and a few birds. By the diligence of Mr. Cops, the keeper, the collection had increased, in 1829, to the following :—Bengal lion, lioness and cubs, Cape lion, Barbary lioness, tiger, leopard, jaguar, puma, ocelot, caracal, chetah or hunting leopard, striped hyæna, hyæna dog, spotted hyæna, African bloodhound, wolf, clouded black wolf, jackal, civet or musk cat, Javanese civet, grey ichneumon, paradoxurus, brown coati, racoon, American black bear, and grizzly bear.

A century ago, says Cunningham, the lions in the Tower were named after the reigning kings, and it was long a vulgar belief, "that when a king dies, the lion of that name dies after him." Addison alludes to this popular error in his own inimitable way :—"Our first visit," he says in the *Freeholder*, "was to the lions. My friend (the Tory Foxhunter), who had a great deal of talk with their keeper, inquired very much after their health, and whether none of them had fallen sick upon the taking of Perth and the flight of the Pretender? And hearing they were never better in their lives, I found he was extremely startled ; for he had learned from his cradle that the lions in the Tower were the best judges of the title of our British kings, and always sympathised with our sovereigns."

The Bengal lion of 1829, "George," as the keepers called him, after the reigning king, had been captured when a cub by General Watson, who shot the parents. The general made a goat foster the two cubs during the voyage to England. They were at first allowed to walk in the open yard, the visitors playing with them with impunity. They used to be fed once a day only, on a piece of beef of eight or nine pounds weight. The lioness was perfectly tame till she bore cubs. One of the keepers on one occasion finding her at large, drove her back into her den, though he was only armed with a stick, and evaded the three springs she made at him. The menagerie declining, and the damp position and restricted room being found injurious to the animals, they were transferred to the Zoological Gardens, Regent's Park, in 1834. The refreshment room and ticket office occupy part of the site of the Lion Tower, but the buildings were not entirely removed until 1853. The "washing the Tower lions" on the 1st of April used to be an old London hoax.

The Tower Moat, long an offensive and useless nuisance, was finally drained in 1843, and then filled up and turfed as a small *campus martius* for the garrison. Evergreens are planted on the banks, and on the north-east is a shrubbery garden.

In draining the moat the workmen found several stone shot, supposed to be missiles directed at the fortress during the siege of 1460, when Lord Scales held the Tower for Henry VI., and the Yorkists cannonaded the fortress from a battery in Southwark. Our readers will remember two occasions when the Tower fired on the City : first, when the Bastard Falconbridge attacked the bridge under pretence of aiding the king ; and again on Evil May Day, in the reign of Henry VIII., when the Constable of the Tower, enraged at the tumult, discharged his cannon on Cheapside way. In 1792, when there was much popular discontent, several hundred men were employed to repair the Tower fortifications, opening the embrasures, and mounting cannon ; and on the west side of the fortress, a strong barricade was formed of old casks, filled with earth and rubble. The gates were closed at an early hour, and no one but soldiers allowed upon the ramparts. In 1830, when the Duke of Wellington, the Constable, filled the Tower Ditch with water, and cleansed and deepened it, the Radicals declared he was putting the fortress into order against the Reformers, as very likely was the case.

with shrines and sculpture. A letter still existing, and quoted by Strype, from Henry III. (that great builder), desires the keeper of the Tower works to plaster the chancel of St. Peter, and to colour anew the shrine and figure of Mary, and the images of St. Peter, St. Nicholas, St. Katharine, the beam

THE TOWER MOAT. (*From a View taken about* 1820.)

The church of St. Peter ad Vincula, situated near to the north-west of the White Tower, was built, or rebuilt, by Edward III.; the private or royal chapel, in the upper part of the keep, having till then been the chief ecclesiastical building within the fortress where so many prisoners have groaned. The earlier church of St. Peter seems to have been large and spacious, fitted up with stalls for the king and queen, and with two chancels, adorned

beyond the altar of St. Peter, and the little cross with its figures, and to erect a painted image of the giant St. Christopher carrying Jesus. There were also to be made two tables, painted with the stories of the blessed St. Nicholas and St. Katharine, before the altars of the said saints. The king also ordered two fair cherubims, with cheerful and joyful countenances, to be made, and erected on the right and left of the great cross in the said

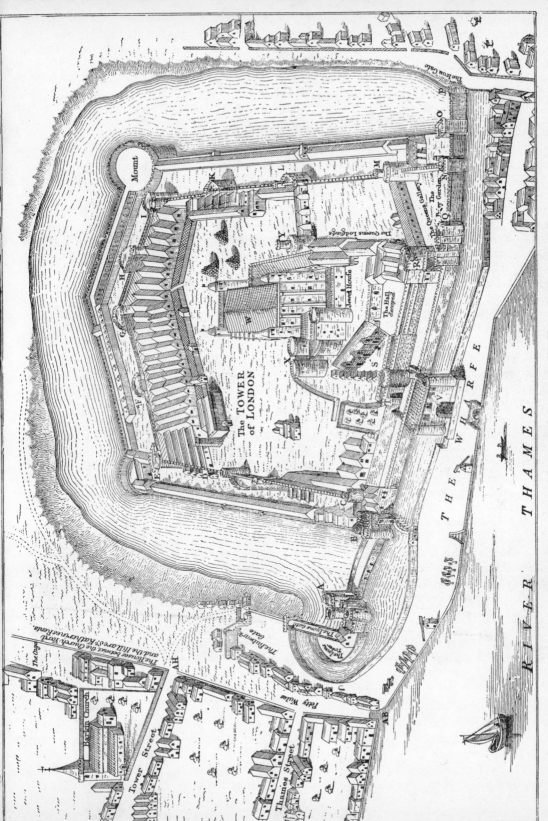

THE TOWER. (From a Survey made in 1597 by W. Haiward and J. Gascoyne.)

A Middle Tower. B. Tower at the Gate. C. Bell Tower. D. Beauchamp Tower. E. Devilin Tower. F. Flint Tower. G. Bowyer Tower. H. Brick Tower. I. Martin Tower. K. Constable Tower. L. Broad Arrow Tower. M. Salt Tower. N Well Tower. O. Tower leading to Iron Gate. P. Tower above Iron Gate. Q. Cradle Tower. R. Lantern Tower. S. Hall Tower. T. Bloody Tower. V. St. Thomas's Tower. W. Cæsar's, or White Tower. X. Wardrobe Tower. Y. Cole Harbour. A B. House at Water Gate, called the Ram's Head. A H. End of Tower Street.

church, and also a marble font with pillars, well and handsomely wrought; "and the cost for this you shall be at, by the view and witness of liege men, shall be reckoned to you at the Exchequer."

The interesting old church has been modernised by degrees into a small mean building, with five cinquefoil windows of late Gothic, a rude wooden porch, and a small square bell-turret at the west end. In a bird's-eye view of the Tower Liberties, made in 1597, the church is represented as having battlements, and two of the five windows are bricked up. They continued in that state till after 1739. It is supposed the old windows were destroyed by fire in the reign of Henry VIII. In the reign of Henry III. there was a small cell or hermitage for a male or female recluse behind the church, the inmate daily receiving a penny of the king's charity. The church now consists of a nave, chancel, and north aisle, the nave and aisle being separated by five low pointed arches.

In this building lie many great persons whose heads paid forfeit for their ambition or their crimes. There are innocent men and women, too, among them—victims of cruelty and treachery. Many who lie here headless suffered merely from being unfortunately too nearly allied to deposed royalty. In this little Golgotha are interred mighty secrets now never to be solved; for half the crimes of our English monarchs were wrought out on the little plot outside the church-door of St. Peter ad Vincula.

One of the earliest of the sufferers for state errors who lie in St. Peter's is Gerald Fitzgerald, Earl of Kildare and Lord Deputy of Ireland, who, committed to the Tower for treasonable practices, died there of a broken heart in 1534. Of the Tower prisoners already mentioned by us there here rest—Fisher, Bishop of Rochester, for vexing Henry VIII. by refusing to deny the Papal supremacy. By his own request he was buried near Sir Thomas More. The next year the body of poor Anne Boleyn was tossed into an old arrow-chest, and hurriedly buried here. Katharine Howard, a really guilty queen, though more deserving contempt than death, came next. In the same reign other graves were filled by Cromwell, Earl of Essex, the king's deposed favourite, and Margaret, Countess of Salisbury, mother of Cardinal Pole. The executioner chased this old countess, who refused to lay her head on the block as a traitor, round the scaffold, and killed her at last after many hasty blows.

The reign of Edward VI. brought some really evil men to the same burying-place. One by one they came, after days of greatness and of sorrow. First, Thomas Lord Seymour of Dudley, the Lord Admiral, beheaded by order of his brother, the Protector Somerset; then the bad and ambitious Protector himself.

In the reign of Mary were buried here, after execution, that poor unoffending young wife, Lady Jane, the victim of her selfish kinsman's ambition; and then the kinsman himself, John Dudley, Earl of Warwick and Duke of Northumberland. In Elizabeth's mild reign only the Earl of Essex, who so well deserved death, is to be added to the list.

In James's shameless reign the murdered Sir Thomas Overbury was interred here; and in the reign of Charles I. his victim, the great-hearted Sir John Eliot. His son begged to be allowed to convey his father's body to Cornwall, to lie among his ancestors; but Charles, cold and unrelenting, wrote at the foot of the petition, "Let Sir John Eliot's body be buried in the church of that parish where he died." After the Restoration, Okey, the regicide, was buried in the same place. The weak Duke of Monmouth lies beneath the communion-table, and beneath the west gallery are the bodies of Lords Kilmarnock, Balmerino, and of Simon Fraser, Lord Lovat. The Dukes of Somerset and Northumberland, Anne Boleyn, and Katharine Howard were buried before the high altar.

The monuments in the church are interesting, because the church of St. Peter escaped the Great Fire. At the west end of the north aisle is a fine enriched table-tomb, to the memory of Sir Richard Cholmondeley, who was for some years Lieutenant of the Tower, and his wife, Lady Elizabeth, both of whom died early in the reign of Henry VIII. The knight's recumbent effigy is in plate-armour, with collar and pendant round his neck. His hands are joined in prayer. His lady wears a pointed head-dress, and the tomb has small twisted columns at the angles, and is divided at the sides into square panels, enclosing blank shields and lozenges. The monument formerly stood in the body of the church. In the chancel stands also a stately Elizabethan monument, to the memory of Sir Richard Blount, and Michael his son, both Lieutenants of the Tower. "Sir Richard, who died in 1560," says Bayley, "is represented on one side, in armour, with his two sons, kneeling; and opposite his wife and two daughters, who are shown, in the dress of the times, on the other. Sir Michael is represented in armour attended by his three sons, his wife and daughter, all in the attitude of prayer." There is also a monument in the chancel to Sir Allan Apsley, a Lieutenant of the Tower, who died in 1630. He was the father of that noble woman, Mrs. Lucy Hutchinson, whose husband was afterwards confined in the Bloody Tower. On the floor of the nave is a small and humble slab, to the memory of Talbot Edwards, gentleman, who died in 1674, aged eighty years. This was the brave old guardian of the regalia, whom Blood and his ruffians nearly killed, and who had at last to sell his long-deferred annuity of £200 for £100 ready money. There is also a monument to Colonel Gurwood, that brave soldier who led the storming party at Ciudad Rodrigo, who edited the " Wellington Despatches," and who died by his own hand, from insanity produced by his wounds. Other officers of the Tower are buried here, and amongst them George Holmes, the first Vice-President of the Society of Antiquaries, and Deputy Keeper of the Records in the Tower (died 1748). On the outside of the church is a monument to the memory of William Bridges, Surveyor-General of the Ordnance under Queen Anne.

The blood-stained spot where the private executions formerly took place, nearly opposite the door of St. Peter's Church, is denoted by a large oval of dark flints. Here Anne Boleyn, Lady Jane Grey, and Essex perished. It was an old slander against Raleigh that at the execution of Essex he stood at a window opposite, and puffed out tobacco in disdain of him. But in his speech at the scaffold Raleigh declared, with all the solemnity due to such a moment, " My lord of Essex did not see my face at the time of his death, for I had retired far off into the armoury, where I indeed saw him, and shed tears for him, but he saw not me."

Archbishop Laud, in his very minute " Diary," records with the utmost horror the fact, that in the lieutenancy of Alderman Pennington, the regicide Lord Mayor of London, one Kem, vicar of Low Leyton, in Essex, preached in this very St. Peter's in a gown over a buff coat and scarf.

In the reigns of Henry III. and Edward I. the chaplains of St. Peter's received 50s. per annum from the Exchequer. Afterwards the chaplain was turned into a rector, and paid 60s. a year. In 1354 Edward III., however, converted the chapel into a sort of collegiate church, and appointed three chaplains to help the rector, granting them, besides the 60s., a rent of 31s. 8d. from tenements in Tower Hill and Petty Wales. Petty Wales was an old house in Thames Street, near the Custom House, supposed to be where the Princes of Wales used to reside when they came to the City. The chaplains also received a rent of 5s. from the Hospital of St. Katharine, and certain tributes from Thames fishing-boats, together with ten marks from the Exchequer, 20s. from the Constable of the Tower, 10s. from the clerk of the Mint, 13s. 4d. from the

Master of the Mint, and 1d. per week from the wages of each workman or teller of coins at the Mint. The church was exempt from episcopal authority till the time of Edward VI.

Several interesting discoveries of Roman antiquities within the Tower precincts encourage us to the belief in the old tradition that the Romans built a fortress here. In 1777, workmen digging the foundations of a new office for the Board of Ordnance, after breaking through foundations of ancient buildings, found below the level of the present river-bed a double wedge of silver, four inches long, and in the broadest part nearly three inches broad. In the centre was the inscription, " Ex officinâ Honorii." This ingot is supposed to have been cast in the reign of the Emperor Honorius, A.D. 393, the Roman emperor who, harassed by the Goths, in A.D. 410 surrendered Britain to its own people, and finally withdrew the Roman troops. The unhappy Britons, then overwhelmed by the Picts and Scots, applied for assistance to the Saxons, who soon conquered the people they had come to assist. With this silver ingot were found also three gold coins, one of Honorius, and two of his brother Arcadius. The coins of Arcadius were probably struck at Constantinople, the capital of the Eastern empire. On these coins (reverse) there is a soldier treading a captive under foot. In his left hand the soldier holds the labarum ; in the right, a small figure of Victory. In the same spot was also found a square stone, dedicated to the manes of Titus Licinius, and a small glass crown.

In the year 1772 an elegant little open jewelled crown was found near the east side of the White Tower, leading from Cold Harbour. It seems to have been the crown of some image, and was set with emeralds, rubies, and pearls.

The Waterloo Barracks, a large modern Gothic building, that will hold 1,000 men, used as a barrack and armoury, and loopholed for musketry, was completed in 1849, on the site of the Grand Storehouse, burned down in 1841. The first stone was laid in 1845 by the Duke of Wellington, a stone statue of whom, by Milnes, stands near the spot. North-east of the White Tower is another modern castellated range of buildings, for the officers of the garrison. South-eastward are the Ordnance Office and storehouses. The area of the Tower within the walls is twelve acres and five poles, and the circuit outside the ditch is 1,050 yards. The portcullis of the Bloody Tower is one of the last complete relics of feudalism, being the only perfect and usable portcullis in England.

The Royal Mint had its offices in the Tower till 1811, when the present building on Tower Hill was completed. Stow speaks of the Tower as a citadel to defend or command the City, a royal palace for assemblies or treaties, a state prison for dangerous offenders, the only place for coining in England in his time, an armoury for warlike provisions, the treasury of the jewels of the crown, and the storehouse of the records of the king's courts of justice at Westminster. Many of our poets have specially mentioned the Tower. Of these, Shakespeare stands pre-eminent. In the tragedy of *Richard III.* he shows us the two princes' instinctive horror of the place in which their cruel uncle, the Crookback, wished them to spend the few days before the coronation of the young Edward :—

> " *Prince.* I do not like the Tower, of any place.
> Did Julius Cæsar build that place, my lord ?
> *Buck.* He did, my gracious lord, begin that place,
> Which since succeeding ages have re-edified.
> *Prince.* Is it upon record, or else reported
> Successively from age to age, he built it ?
> *Buck.* Upon record, my gracious lord."

And in another passage, in *Richard II.*, the poet seems to hint at a similar association :—

> " This is the way
> To Julius Cæsar's ill-erected Tower."

Gray, in his " Bard," apostrophises the building thus :—

> " Ye towers of Julius, London's lasting shame,
> With many a foul and midnight murder fed."

Before tearing ourselves from the Tower, we may mention a few nooks and corners of interest not generally known to visitors. In the north-eastern turret of the White Tower was the observatory of that great astronomical rival of Newton, John Flamstead. Here often he " outwatched the bear." The Ordnance Office gave him £100 a year. The roof of this tower was a promenade for prisoners. In 1708 there were 3,000 barrels of gunpowder stored close to the White Tower. The Record Tower, or Hall Tower, was formerly called the Wakefield Tower, from the Yorkist prisoners confined there after that great battle of the Roses.

The most terrible cells of the fortress, such as those over which Mr. Harrison Ainsworth threw a blue fire, are in the Bowyer Tower, where there is a ghastly hole with a trap-door, opening upon a flight of steps. In the lower chambers of the Devereux Tower are subterranean passages, leading to St. Peter's Church. In the Beauchamp Tower a secret passage has been discovered in the masonry, where spies could cower, and listen to the conversations and soliloquies of poor unsuspecting prisoners. One torture-chamber was called, says

Mr. Hewitt, " Little Ease," because it was so small that a prisoner could not stand erect, or even lie down at full length. Other cells are said to have been full of rats, which at high water were driven up in shoals from the Thames. Hatton, in 1708, describes the Tower guns as sixty-two in number ; they were on the wharf, and were discharged on all occasions of victories, coronations, festival days, days of thanksgiving, and triumphs. They are now fired from a salutation-battery facing Tower Hill. The prisoners' walks in the Tower, spots of many a mournful hour of regret and contemplation, are specially interesting. There is one—a passage on the leads between the (alarm) Bell Tower and the Beauchamp Tower. The walls are carved with names. In the Garden Tower are also leads where prisoners used to pace; and on Pepys visiting the Tower, March 11, 1669, in order to see Sir W. Coventry, he visited what was then called " My Lord of Northumberland's Walk ;" at the end of it there was a piece of iron upon the wall with his arms upon it, and holes to put in a peg for every turn made upon the walk. Mrs. Hutchinson especially mentions that her husband was confined in the room of the Bloody Tower where it was said the two princes were murdered. The room that led to it was that in which, it is popularly believed, the Duke of Clarence was drowned. " It was a dark, great room," says the amiable and faithful wife, " with no window in it, and the portcullis of a gate was drawn up within it, and below there sat every night a court of guard."

The council-chamber of the Lieutenant's lodgings, where Guy Fawkes was examined, and perhaps tortured, is said to be haunted, and the soldiers of the Tower have a firm belief that a ghost, in some ambiguous and never clearly-defined shape, appeared on one occasion to a drunken sentry near the Martin Tower, the old Jewel House. It is said that upwards of 1,000 prisoners have been groaning together at one time in the Tower. The person who believes in the Tower ghost can swallow this too. Bayley mentions that the bones of an old ape, which had hidden itself and died in an unoccupied turret, were set down in his time as those of the two murdered princes.

During the Spa Fields riot some of the rioters, including Thistlewood, afterwards the desperate leader of the Cato Street conspirators, came to the Tower walls and tried to persuade the soldiers to join them, offering them £100 each, but failed to win over even a single recruit. In the year 1851 the population of the Tower, including the garrison, was 1,488.

In old times, says Mr. Dixon, in his book on

London Prisons, whenever it was found necessary to carry a prisoner through the streets, the sheriffs received him from the king's lieutenants at the entrance to the City, gave a receipt for him, and took another on delivering him up at the gates of the Tower. The receipt of the Governor of the Tower for the body of the Duke of Monmouth—his living body—is still extant.

CHAPTER X.

THE NEIGHBOURHOOD OF THE TOWER.

Tower Hill—Some of its Ghastly Associations—A Great Whig Downfall—Perambulating the "Bounds" of the Tower Liberties—Famous Residents on Tower Hill—Lady Raleigh—William Penn—Otway and the Story of his Death—Felton's Knife—Old Houses—Spenser—Great Tower Street and Peter the Great—Bakers' Hall—Thomson the Poet—A Strange Corruption of a Name—Seething Lane—The Old Navy Office.

Of Tower Hill, that historical and blood-stained ground to the north-west of the Tower, old Stow says :—" Tower Hill, sometime a large plot of ground, now greatly straitened by encroachments (unlawfully made and suffered) for gardens and houses. Upon this hill is always readily prepared, at the charges of the City, a large scaffold and gallows of timber, for the execution of such traitors or transgressors as are delivered out of the Tower, or otherwise, to the Sheriffs of London, by writ, there to be executed."

Hatton, in 1708 (Queen Anne) mentions Tower Hill as "a spacious place extending round the west and north parts of the Tower, where there are many good new buildings, mostly inhabited by gentry and merchants." The tide of fashion and wealth had not yet set in strongly westward. An old plan of the Tower in 1563 shows us the posts of the scaffold for state criminals, a good deal north of Tower Street and a little northward of Legge Mount, the great north-west corner of the Tower fortifications. In the reign of Edward IV. the scaffold was erected at the charge of the king's officers, and many controversies arose at various times, about the respective boundaries, between the City and the Lieutenant of the Tower.

On the Tower Hill scaffold perished nearly all the prisoners whose wrongs and sorrows and crimes we have glanced at in a previous chapter ; the great Sir Thomas More, the wise servant of a corrupt king ; the unhappy old Countess of Salisbury, who was chopped down here as she ran bleeding round the scaffold ; Bishop Fisher, a staunch adherent to the old faith ; that great subverter of the monks, Cromwell, Earl of Essex ; and the poet Earl of Surrey—all victims of the same bad monarch.

Then in the reigns of Edward VI. and Mary, in ghastly procession after the masked headsman, paced Lord Seymour ; in due course followed the brother who put him to death, the proud Protector Somerset ; then that poor weak young noble, Lady Jane Grey's husband, Lord Guildford Dudley ; and Sir Thomas Wyat, the rash objector to a Spanish marriage.

The victims of Charles's folly followed in due time—the dark and arrogant Strafford, who came like a crowned conqueror to his death ; then his sworn ally, the narrow-browed, fanatical Laud. The Restoration Cavaliers took their vengeance next, and to Tower Hill passed those true patriots, Stafford, insisting on his innocence to the very last, and Algernon Sydney. The unlucky Duke of Monmouth was the next to lay his misguided head on the block.

Blood ceased to flow on Tower Hill after this execution till the Pretender's fruitless rebellions of 1715 and 1745 brought Derwentwater, "the pride of the North," Kilmarnock, Balmerino, and wily old Lovat to the same ghastly bourne. In 1746 Lord Derwentwater's brother and successor was executed here. He had been a prisoner in the Tower for his share in the rebellion of 1715, but succeeded in escaping. He was identified by the barber, who thirty-one years before had shaved him when in prison.

Chamberlain Clarke, who died in 1831, aged ninety-two (a worthy old City authority, who has been mentioned by us in a previous chapter), well remembered (says Mr. Timbs), as a child, seeing the executioner's axe flash in the sunshine as it fell upon the neck of Derwentwater. At the last execution which took place on Tower Hill, that of Lord Lovat, April 9, 1747, a scaffolding, built near Barking Alley, fell, with nearly 1,000 persons on it, and twelve of them were killed. Lovat, in spite of his awful situation, seemed to enjoy the downfall of so many Whigs.

There is a passage in *Henry VIII.*—a play considered by many persons to be not Shakespeare's writing at all, and by some others only partly his work—that has much puzzled those wise persons, the commentators. The author of the play, which is certainly not quite in the best Shakespearian manner, makes a door-porter say, talking of a mob, "These are the youths that thunder at a play-house and fight for bitten apples: that no audience but the tribulation of Tower Hill or the

formed upon the parade, including a headsman, bearing the axe of execution; a painter, to mark the bounds; yeomen, warders, with halberds; the Deputy Lieutenant and other officers of the Tower, &c. The boundary-stations are painted with a red "broad arrow" upon a white ground, while

LORD LOVAT. (*From Hogarth's Portrait.*) *See page* 95.

limbs of Limehouse are able to endure." This passage seems to imply that there were low theatres in Shakespeare's time near Tower Hill and Lime-house: or did he refer to the crowd at a Tower Hill execution, and to the mob of sailors at the second locality?

A curious old custom is still perpetuated in this neighbourhood. The "bounds" of the Tower Liberties are perambulated triennially, when, after service in the church of St. Peter, a procession is

the chaplain of St. Peter's repeats, "Cursed be he who removeth his neighbour's landmark." Another old custom of lighting a bonfire on Tower Hill, on the 5th of November, was suppressed in the year 1854.

The traditions of Tower Hill, apart from the crimson block and the glittering axe, are few, but what there are, are interesting. Poor suffering Lady Raleigh, when driven from the side of her imprisoned husband, as James began to drive him faster towards death, lodged on Tower Hill with her son who had been born in the Tower.

William Penn, the founder of Pennsylvania, was born on Tower Hill, October 14, 1644. The house of his father, the Admiral, was "on the east side, within a court adjoining to London Wall." Penn, ever, already been deeply impressed by the preaching of a Quaker. In old age this good and wise man fell into difficulties, and actually had to mortgage the province of Pennsylvania for £6,600. He died at Beaconsfield, in Buckinghamshire, in 1718.

That tender-hearted poet, Thomas Otway, the

AN OLD HOUSE ON LITTLE TOWER HILL.   (*From a Drawing by Smith made in* 1792.)

in one of his works, states that "the Lord first appeared to him about the twelfth year of his age, and that between that and the fifteenth the Lord visited him and gave him divine impressions of himself." It was when he was at school at Chigwell, in Essex, that one day, alone in his chamber, he was suddenly "surprised with an inward comfort, and surrounded by a visible external glory, that convinced the youth's excited imagination that he had obtained the seal of immortality. He had, how-

friend of Shadwell—whose poverty and wretchedness Rochester cruelly sneered at in his "Session of the Poets," and whose nature and pathos Dryden praised, though somewhat reluctantly—died, as it is generally thought, of starvation, at the "Bull" public-house on Tower Hill. He was only thirty-four when he died. The stories of his untimely death differ. Dr. Johnson's version is that, being naked and in a rage of hunger, he went to a neighbouring coffee-house, and asked a gentleman for a shilling. The gentleman generously gave the starving poet a guinea, on which Otway rushed into the nearest baker's, bought a roll, and, eating with ravenous haste, was choked with the first mouthful. But Spence was told by Dennis, the well-known critic, and the great enemy of Pope, that an intimate friend of Otway's being shot by an assassin, who escaped to Dover, *en route* for France, Otway pursued him. In the excitement he drank cold water, and brought on a fever, which carried him off. Goldsmith, in the "Bee," tells a story of Otway having about him when he died a copy of a tragedy which he had sold to Bentley the bookseller for a mere trifle. It was never recovered, but in 1719 a spurious forgery of it appeared.

It was at a cutler's shop on Tower Hill that Felton, that grim fanatic, who believed himself an instrument of Heaven, bought the broad, sharp, ten-penny hunting-knife with which he gave the heavy and sure blow at Portsmouth, that ended the ambition and plots of the first Duke of Buckingham, the mischievous favourite of Charles I.

That admirable antiquarian artist, Smith, has engraved a view of a curious old house on Tower Hill, enriched with medallions evidently of the time of Henry VIII. (probably terra cotta), like those, says Peter Cunningham, at old Whitehall and Hampton Court. It was not unusual, when coins were found upon a particular spot whereon a house was to be erected, to cause such coins to be represented in plaster on the house. A reproduction of this engraving will be found on the previous page.

In Postern Row, the site of the old postern gate at the south-eastern end of the City wall, used, says Timbs, to be the old rendezvous for enlisting soldiers and sailors, and for arranging the iniquitous press-gangs to scour Wapping and Ratcliff Highway. The shops here are hung with waterproof coats, sou'-westers, and other articles of dress; and the windows are full of revolvers, quadrants, compasses, ship's biscuits, &c., to attract sailors.

At the south-west corner of Tower Hill is Tower Dock, where luckless Sir Walter Raleigh, in disguise, after his escape from the Tower in 1618, took boat for Tilbury. That most poetical of all our poets, Edmund Spenser, was born near Tower Hill, in 1552. Very little is known of his parentage, but though poor, it must have been respectable, as he was sent at sixteen to Pembroke College, Cambridge, as a humble student or sizar. He dedicated one of his early poems to Sir Philip Sidney, that star of Elizabethan knighthood, and began his career by going to Ireland (a country whose wild

people he often sketches in his "Fairy Queen"), as secretary to Lord Grey of Wilton, the viceroy. He is said to have there commenced his "Fairy Queen," urged on by Sir Walter Raleigh. He seems to have spent about seventeen years in that Patmos, and returned to London poor and heart-broken, having had his castle burnt down, and his infant child destroyed in the fire. He was buried in Westminster Abbey, at the expense of the Earl of Essex. The poems of Spenser furnished many suggestions to Shakespeare, who probably derived from them the story of *King Lear*, and some of the most beautiful of his heroine's names. Spenser himself drew his inspiration from the Italian poets.

The second Duke of Buckingham used often to visit in disguise, in his days of political intrigue, a poor astrologer, who drew horoscopes, near Tower Hill. Science was then making great advances, thanks to the inductive system introduced by Bacon; but even Newton practised alchemy, and witches were still burnt to death.

The parishes and liberties now called the Tower Hamlets, and since 1832 returning two members to the House of Commons, included Hackney, Norton Folgate, Shoreditch, Spitalfields, Whitechapel, East Smithfield, St. Katharine's, Wapping, Ratcliff, Shadwell, Limehouse, Poplar, Blackwall, Bromley, Old Ford, Mile End, Bethnal Green, &c. An alteration was effected by the Reform Bill of 1867, when Hackney was made a separate electoral district, returning two members to Parliament.

Great Tower Street has not many traditions to boast of, though sailors and Tower warders have haunted it for centuries. Its two main antiquarian heroes are the Earl of Rochester and that royal savage, Peter the Great. One of this mad earl's maddest freaks brought him to Tower Street. While in disgrace at court, we believe for his bitter satire on Charles II., called the "History of the Insipids," he robed and bearded himself as an Italian quack or mountebank physician, and under the name of Alexander Bendo, set up at a goldsmith's house, next door to the "Black Swan," in Tower Street, where he advertised that he was sure to be seen "from three of the clock in the afternoon till eight at night." His biographer, Bishop Burnet, mentions this; and it is said that the earl surprised his patients by the knowledge of court secrets he displayed.

The second story of Great Tower Street relates to the true founder of the Russian Empire. This extraordinary man, whose strong shoulder helped his country out of the slough of ignorance and obscurity, was born in 1672, and visited Holland in 1698, to learn the art of shipbuilding, having resolved to establish a Russian navy. Having worked among the Dutch as a common labourer, he finally came to England for four months, to visit our dockyards and perfect himself in ship-building. While in England he lived alternately in Buckingham Street, Strand, as we shall see hereafter, and at John Evelyn's house at Deptford. After a hard day's work with adze and saw, the young Czar, who drank like a boatswain, used to resort to a public-house in Great Tower Street, and smoke and drink ale and brandy, almost enough to float the vessel he had been helping to construct. "The landlord," says Barrow, Peter's biographer, "had the Czar of Muscovy's head painted and put up for his sign, which continued till the year 1808, when a person of the name of Waxel took a fancy to the old sign, and offered the then occupier of the house to paint him a new one for it. A copy was accordingly made from the original, which maintains its station to the present day as the sign of the 'Czar of Muscovy.' The house has since been rebuilt, and the sign removed, but the name remains. Peter was recalled from his pitch-pots and adzes by the news of an insurrection in Russia, headed by his sister. A year after, he declared war on that 'madman of the North,' Charles XII. of Sweden."

Bakers' Hall hides itself with humility in Harp Lane, Great Tower Street. The "neat, plain building," as Mr. Peter Cunningham calls it, repaired by Mr. James Elmes, the author of the "Life of Wren," was, says Stow, some time the dwelling-house of Alderman Chicheley, Chamberlain of London, who was related to the celebrated Chicheley, Archbishop of Canterbury, ambassador from Henry IV. to the Pope. He accompanied Henry V. to the French war. His life was spent in a two-handed warfare—against the Pope and against the Wickliffites. This generous prelate improved Canterbury Cathedral and Lambeth Palace, and founded All Souls' College at Oxford. The London bakers were originally divided into "white" and "brown" bakers. The chief supply of bread (says Strype) came from Stratford-le-Bow. By a somewhat tyrannical edict of the City, the Stratford loaves were required to be heavier in weight than the London loaves.

In the uncongenial atmosphere of Little Tower Street, that fat, lazy, and good-natured poet, James Thomson, wrote his fine poem of "Summer," published in 1727. In a letter to Aaron Hill, dated May 24, 1726, he says, "I go on Saturday next to reside at Mr. Watts's academy, in Little Tower Street, in quality of tutor to a young gentleman there." Thomson was the son of a Roxburgh-shire clergyman, and was educated for the Church —a profession which, however, he never entered. He came to London in 1725, and published his "Winter," a poem whose broadly-painted landscapes remind us of those of Wilson and contemporaneous painters, just as Byron's poems remind us of Turner. In 1730 Thomson went abroad, as travelling tutor, with the son of Lord Chancellor Talbot. There was no return to dingy Little Tower Street for the epicurean poet, who soon after obtained some Government sinecures, among others the post of Surveyor-General to the Leeward Islands, and became patronised by the Prince of Wales. Thomson's poem of the "Seasons" did much to foster our national love of Nature, but the poet's *chef-d'œuvre* is, after all, his "Castle of Indolence," a poem full of the poet's idiosyncrasy.

One of the strangest corruptions of the names of London streets occurs in the Tower precincts. A place once called "Hangman's Gains," as if built with the fees of some Tower executioner, should really have been "Ham and Guienne," for here (says Strype) poor refugees from "Hammes and Guynes" were allowed to lodge in Queen Mary's reign, after Calais and its vicinity had been recovered from our strong grip by the French.

Seething Lane, Tower Street, running northward to Crutched Friars, was originally (says Stow) called Sidon Lane, and in his time there were fair and large houses there. The old chronicler of London mentions among its distinguished residents the wily Sir Francis Walsingham, Elizabeth's principal secretary. This great counter-plotter against the Jesuits in Spain died April 5, 1590, and the next night, at ten o'clock, was quietly buried in Paul's Church. Walsingham's name occurs perpetually in Elizabethan annals, and no one by darker or more secret means fought better for Elizabeth against the dangerous artifices of Mary Queen of Scots.

The garrulous, gallant, and inimitable Pepys was living in this lane, to be near his work at the Navy Office, the very year in which the Great Fire broke out. He describes putting his head out of window at the first alarm, and going quietly to sleep again, on the 6th of September, about two of the morning, when his handsome wife called him up and told him of new cries of fire, it being come to Barking Church (Allhallows, Barking), "which is at the bottom of our lane." In Strype's time Seething Lane had become "a place of no great account," but there were still merchants living there.

The old Navy Office in Seething or Sidon Lane had its chief entrance in Crutched Friars, and a smaller one in the lane. It stood, says

Cunningham, on the site of a chapel and college attached to the church of Allhallows, Barking, which had been suppressed and pulled down in the year 1548 (Edward VI.). The consecrated ground remained a garden-plot during the troubles of Edward's reign, the rebellions of Mary's reign, and the glorious days of Elizabeth, till at length Sir William Winter, surveyor of Elizabeth's ships, built

on it a great timber and brick storehouse for merchants' goods, which grew into a Navy Office. Cunningham found among the Audit Office enrolments an entry that in July, 1788, the purchase-money of the old Navy Office, £11,500, was handed over to Sir William Chambers, the architect of the Government offices in the new Somerset House.

CHAPTER XI.

NEIGHBOURHOOD OF THE TOWER.—THE MINT.

The Mint at the Tower—The First Silver Penny—Dishonest Minters—The First English Gold Coinage—Curious Anecdote respecting the Silver Groats of Henry IV.—First Appearance of the Sovereign and the Shilling—Debasement of the Coin in the Reigns of Henry VIII. and Edward VI.—Ecclesiastical Comptrollers of the Mint—Guineas and Copper Coins—Queen Anne's Farthings—The Sources from which the English Mint has been supplied with Bullion—Alchemists encouraged —The Mint as it is.

THAT the Romans had a mint in London is certain, and probably on the site of the present Tower. In the Saxon times London and Winchester were the chief places for coining money; but while the "White City," as Winchester was called, had only six "moneyers," or minters, London boasted eight. The chief mint of England was in the Tower, at all events from the Conquest till 1811, when, at an outlay of more than a quarter of a million of money, Sir Robert Smirke erected the present quiet and grave building which stands on the east side of Tower Hill. From those portals has since flowed forth that rich Niagara of gold which English wealth has yielded to the ceaseless cravings of national expenditure.

Letting alone the old Celtic ring-money of the ancient Britons, and the rude Roman-British coins of Cunobelin and Boadicea, we may commence a brief notice of English coinage with the silver penny mentioned in the laws of Ina, king of the West Saxons (689—726), the value of which, says Mr. J. Saunders, would be, in current coin, 2¾d. The silver penny of King Alfred is the earliest authentic Saxon coin, says that eminent authority, Mr. Ruding, which can be traced with certainty to the London Mint. The penny sank by slow degrees, through the reigns of many adulterating monarchs, from the weight of 22½ grains to about 7 grains. The great object of our monarchs seems to have been to depreciate as far as possible the real value of the coin, and at the same time to keep up its current value. We find, in fact, even such a great and chivalrous king as Edward III. shamelessly trying to give false weight, and busy in passing spurious money.

With this perpetual tampering with the coin,

which pretended to a value it never possessed, clippers and coiners of course abounded. They were given to the crows by hundreds, while the royal forgers escaped scot-free. Justice, so called, like a spider, let the wasps escape, but was down swift upon the smaller fry. Law was red-handed in the Middle Ages, and swift and terrible in its revenges on the poor and the unprivileged. In the reign of Edgar, the penny having lost half its weight, St. Dunstan (himself an amateur goldsmith) refused one Whitsun-day to celebrate mass till three of the unjust moneyers had had their guilty right hands struck off.

In the reign of Henry I., when the dealers refused to take the current money in the public markets, the hot-tempered monarch sent over a swift and angry message from Normandy, to summon all the moneyers of England to appear at Winchester against Christmas Day. Three honest men alone, out of ninety-four of the minters, escaped mutilation and banishment. In 1212, when Pandulph, the Pope's legate, excommunicated King John at Northampton, the king, who was making quick work with a batch of prisoners (being, no doubt, not in the best of tempers), ordered a priest, who had coined base money, to be immediately hung. Pandulph at once threatened with "bell, book, and candle" any one who should dare touch the Lord's anointed; and on King John at last surrendering the priest, the legate at once set the holy rogue free, in contempt of the royal laws. As for the Jews, who had always an "itching palm" for gold and silver, and filed and "sweated" every bezant they could rake together, Edward I., in an irresistible outburst of business-like indignation and religious zeal, on one occasion hung a batch of 280 of them. But the prudent king did more than this, for he confirmed the privileges of the Moneyers' Company, and entrusted them with the whole coinage of the country. In the following reign a Comptroller of the Mint was appointed, who was to send in his accounts distinct from those of the Warden and Master. The Company consisted of seven senior and junior members, and a provost, who undertook the whole coinage at fixed charges.

With Henry III. English money, says a good authority, began to improve in appearance, and to exhibit more variety. The gold penny of this monarch passed current for twenty pence. This was the first English gold coinage. In the reign of Edward I. silver halfpennies and farthings were for the first time made round, instead of square. About this coinage there is the following story. An old prophecy of Merlin had declared that whenever English money should become round, a Welsh prince would be crowned in London. When Llewellyn, the last Welsh prince, was slain by Edward, his head, probably in ridicule of this prophecy, was crowned with willows and sent to the Tower for exhibition.

Edward III., as national wealth increased national wants, introduced several fresh coins : a gold florin, with its divisions, a gold noble, a groat, and a half-groat. The gold florin, which passed for six shillings (now worth nineteen), soon gave place, says Saunders, to the gold noble or rose-noble, as it was sometimes called, of the value of 6s. 8d., or half a mark. On one side of this coin Edward stands in a tall turreted galley in complete armour, in reference probably to his great naval victory over the French at Sluys, when he made an end of nearly 15,000 of the enemy. The reverse bears a cross fleury, and the mysterious legend, " Jesus autem transiens per medium illorum ibat" (Jesus, however, passing over, went through the midst of them) ; an inscription which was traditionally supposed to allude to the fact of the gold used for the coin having been made by the famous alchemist Lully, who worked for that purpose in the Tower. In the reign of Henry VI. the rose-noble was called the rial, and promoted to the value of 10s.

The silver groat, says an authority on coins, derived its name from the French word *gros*, as being the largest silver coin then known.

Of the silver groats of Henry V.'s reign, Leake, in his "History of English Money," relates a curious anecdote from Speed. The coin has on one side a cross (so that the coin could be broken into four bits), and on the other a head of the young king, the crown set with three fleurs-de-lis, and the hair flowing as Absalom's. On each side of the niche

are two small circlets, said to be intended for eyelet holes, and to refer to the following story. Towards the close of his reign Henry IV. grew shaken in his mind, and alarmed at his son's loose and unworthy excesses with the Falstaffs of those days, began to fear some violence from his abandoned and undutiful son : "which when," says Speed, " Prince Henry heard of by some that favoured him of the King's Council, in a strange disguise he repaired to his court, accompanied with many lords and noblemen's sons. His garment was a gown of blue satin, wrought full of eyelet holes, and at every eyelet the needle left hanging by the silk it was wrought with. About his arm he wore a dog's collar, set full of SS of gold, the tirets thereof being most fine gold. Thus coming to Westminster and the court of his father, having commanded his followers to advance no farther than the fire in the hall, himself, accompanied with some of the king's household, passed on to his presence, and after his duty and obeisance done, offered to make known the cause of his coming. The king, weak then with sickness, and supposing the worst, commanded himself to be borne into a withdrawing chamber, some of his lords attending upon him, before whose feet Prince Henry fell, and with all reverent obeisance spake to him as followeth: ' Most gracious sovereign and renowned father, the suspicion of disloyalty and divulged reports of my dangerous intendments towards your royal person and crown hath enforced at this time and in this manner to present myself and life at your Majesty's dispose. Some faults and misspent time (with blushes I may speak it) my youth hath committed, yet those made much more by such fleering pick-thanks that blow them stronger into your unwilling and distasteful ears. The name of sovereign ties allegiance to all ; but of a father, to a further feeling of nature's obedience ; so that my sins were double if such suggestions possessed my heart ; for the law of God ordaineth that he which doth presumptuously against the ruler of his people shall not live, and the child that smiteth his father shall die the death. So far, therefore, am I from any disloyal attempts against the person of you, my father, and the Lord's anointed, that if I knew any of whom you stood in the least danger or fear, my hand, according to duty, should be the first to free your suspicion. Yea, I will most gladly suffer death to ease your perplexed heart ; and to that end I have this day prepared myself, both by confession of my offences past and receiving the blessed sacrament. Wherefore I humbly beseech your grace to free your suspicion from all fear conceived against me with this dagger, the stab whereof I will willingly receive here at your Majesty's hand; and so doing, in the presence of these lords, and before God at the day of judgment, I clearly forgive my death.' But the king, melting into tears, cast down the naked dagger (which the prince delivered him), and raising his prostrate son, embraced and kissed him, confessing his ears to have been over-credulous that way, and promising never to open them against him. But the prince, unsatisfied, instantly desired that at

sovereign, double sovereign, and half-sovereign, of gold, and the testoon, or shilling, of silver. The Saxons had used the word "shilling," but it now first became a current coin. The testoon borrowed its name from the French word, *teste*, " a head," the royal portrait, for the first time presented in profile.

Henry VIII., to his affectionate character as a husband, and his other virtues, pointed out so ably by Mr. Froude, added to them all the merit of being pre-eminent even among English monarchs

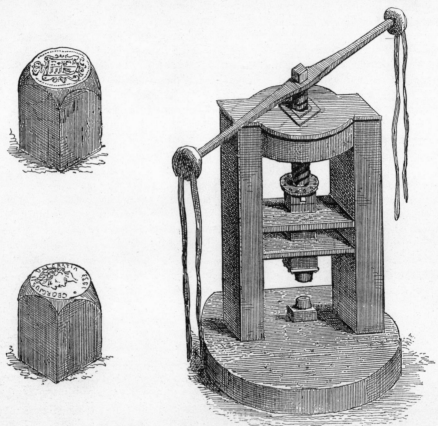

PRESS AND DIES FORMERLY USED IN THE MINT. (GEORGE II.)

least his accusers might be produced, and, if convicted, to receive punishment, though not to the full of their demerits; to which request the king replied that, as the offence was capital, so should it be examined by the peers, and therefore willed him to rest contented until the next Parliament. Thus by his great wisdom he satisfied his father from further suspicion, and recovered his love that nearly was lost."

The gold angel (with St. Michael striking the dragon) and the half-angel were first struck by Edward IV., and, although inferior in value to the noble and half-noble, were intended to pass in their room. Henry VII. originated many new coins—the

for debasing the coinage. Some of the earlier coins of this reign bear the portrait of Henry VII. One coin struck by Henry VIII. was the George noble, so called from the effigy of St. George and the Dragon, well known to all lovers of their sovereign, stamped on the reverse. Henry VIII. also coined a silver crown-piece, which was, however, issued by his son Edward, with the half-crown, sixpence, and threepence. In Edward's reign the debasement of coin grew more shameless than ever. There were now only three ounces of silver left in the pound of coinage metal. In one of his plain-spoken Saxon sermons, old Latimer denounced the custom of having ecclesiastics among the comptrollers of the

their common base. Thus Lully worked in the Tower for Edward I. Edward III., Henry VI., and Edward IV. also seem to have been deluded by impostors or fanatics to the same belief. which Chaucer ridiculed so admirably.

A modern essayist has graphically described the present method of coining money. "'The first place," he says, "that I was conducted to was the Central Office, where the ingots of gold are weighed when they come in from the Bank of England, or from other sources, and where a small piece is cut off each slab for the Mint assayer to test the whole by. A nugget of gold may be of any shape, and is generally an irregular dead yellow lump, that looks like pale ginger-bread ; but an ingot of gold is a small brick. After the precious metals have been scrupulously weighed in the Central Office, they are sent to the Melting House down an iron tramway. All the account books in the Mint are balanced by weight, so that even where there is so much money there is no use made of the three columns bearing the familiar headings of £ s. d. The Melting House is an old-fashioned structure, having what I may call the gold kitchen on one side, and the silver kitchen on the other, with just such a counting-house between the two—well provided with clean weights, scales, well-bound books, and well-framed almanacks—as George Barnwell may have worked in with his uncle before he became gay. The counting-house commands a view of both melting kitchens, that the superintendents may overlook the men at their work. Although the Mint contains nearly a hundred persons resident within its walls—forming a little colony, with peculiar habits, tastes, and class feelings of its own —a great many of the workpeople are drawn from the outer world. Dinner is provided for them all within the building ; and when they pass in to their day's work, between the one soldier and the two policemen at the entrance gate, they are not allowed to depart until their labour is finished, and the books of their department are balanced, to see that nothing is missing. If all is found right, a properly signed certificate is given to each man, and he is then permitted to go his way.

"The gold kitchen and the silver kitchen are never in operation on the same day, and the first melting process that I was invited to attend was the one in the latter department. The presiding cook, well protected with leather apron and thick coarse gloves, was driving four ingot bricks of solid silver into a thick plumbago crucible, by the aid of a crowbar. When these four pieces were closely jammed down to a level with the surface of the melting-pot, he seasoned it with a sprinkling of base coin, by way of alloy ; placing the crucible in one of the circular recesses over the fiery ovens to boil. The operations in the gold kitchen are similar to this, except that they are on a much smaller scale. A crucible is there made to boil three or four ingots, worth from four to five thousand pounds sterling ; and where machinery is employed in the silver kitchen, much of the work is done in the gold kitchen with long iron tongs that are held in the hand.

"When the solid metal has become fluid, a revolving crane is turned over the copper, and the glowing, red-hot crucible is drawn from its fiery recess, casting its heated breath all over the apartment, and is safely landed in a rest. This rest is placed over a number of steel moulds, that are made up, when cool, like pieces of a puzzle, and which look like a large metal mouth-organ standing on end, except that the tubes there present are square in shape and all of the same length. The crucible rest is acted upon by the presiding cook and another man, through the machinery in which it is placed, and is made to tilt up at certain stages, according to regulated degrees. When the molten metal, looking like greasy milk, has poured out of the crucible till it has filled the first tube of the metal mouth-organ, sounding several octaves of fluid notes, like the tone of bottle-emptying, the framework of moulds is moved on one stage by the same machinery, so as to bring the second tube under the mouth of the crucible, which is then tilted up another degree. This double action is repeated until the whole blinking, white-heated interior of the crucible is presented to my view, and nothing remains within it but a few lumps of red-hot charcoal.

"The next step is to knock asunder the framework of moulds, to take out the silver, now hardened into long dirty-white bars, and to place these bars first in a cold-water bath, and then upon a metal counter to cool. These bars are all cast according to a size which experience has taught to be exceedingly eligible for conversion into coin.

"From the silver-melting process, I was taken to the gold-coining department, the first stage in dealing with the precious metals being, as I have before stated, the same. Passing from bars of silver to bars of gold, I entered the Great Rolling Room, and began my first actual experience in the manufacture of a sovereign.

"The bars of gold, worth about twelve hundred pounds sterling, that are taken into the Great Rolling Room are about twenty-one inches long, one and three-eighths of an inch broad, and an inch thick. As they lie upon the heavy truck, before they are subjected to the action of the ponderous machinery in this department, they look like cakes of very bright yellow soap.

" An engine of thirty horse-power sets in motion the machinery of this room, whose duty it is to flatten the bars until they come out in ribands of an eighth of an inch thick, and considerably increased in length. This process, not unlike mangling, is performed by powerful rollers, and is repeated until the ribands are reduced to the proper gauged thickness, after which they are divided and cut into the proper gauged lengths. Having undergone one or two annealings in brick ovens attached to this department, these fillets may be considered ready for another process, which takes place, after twelve hours' delay, in a place that is called the Drawing Room.

" In this department the coarser work of the Rolling Room is examined and perfected. The fillets or ribands of gold, after being subjected to another rolling process, the chief object of which has been to thin both ends, are taken to a machine called a draw-bench, where their thickness is perfectly equalised from end to end. The thin end of the golden riband is passed between two finely-polished fixed steel cylinders into the mouth of a part of the concrete machine, which is called a 'dog.' This dog is a small iron carriage, travelling upon wheels over a bench, under which revolves an endless chain. In length and appearance this dog is like a seal, with a round, thick head, containing two large eyes that are formed of screws, and having a short-handled inverted metal mallet for a hat. Its mouth is large and acts like a vice, and when it has gripped the thin end of the golden riband in its teeth, its tail is affixed to the endless chain, which causes it to move slowly along the bench, dragging the riband through the fixed cylinders. When the riband has passed through its whole length, the thin end at its other extremity coming more quickly through the narrow space between the cylinders causes it to release itself with a sudden jerk, and this motion partly raises the mallet cap of the backing dog, which opens its broad mouth, and drops its hold of the metal badger which it has completely drawn. A workman now takes the fillet, and punches out a circular piece the exact size of a sovereign, and weighs it. If the golden dump or blank, as it is called, is heavy, the dog and the cylinders are put in requisition once more to draw the riband thinner; but if the weight is accurate (and perfect accuracy at this stage is indispensable), the smooth, dull, impressionless counter, looking like the brass button of an Irishman's best blue coat, is trans-

ferred to another department, called the Press Cutting Room.

" In this room twelve cutting-presses, arranged on a circular platform, about two feet in height, surround an upright shaft and a horizontal revolving fly-wheel; and at the will of twelve boys, who attend and feed the presses, the punches attached to the presses are made to rise and fall at the rate of a stroke a second. The ribands, cut into handy lengths, are given to the boys, who push them under the descending punches as sliding-frames are pushed under table microscopes. The blanks fall into boxes, handily placed to receive them, and the waste—like all the slips and cuttings, trial dumps, failures, &c., in every department—is weighed back to the melting kitchen for the next cooking day.

"From the Weighing Room I followed the dumps that were declared to be in perfect condition to a department called the Marking Room, where they received their first surface impression. This room contains eight machines, whose duty it is to raise a plain rim, or protecting edge, round the surface circumference of the golden blanks. This is done by dropping them down a tube, which conducts them horizontally to a bed prepared for them, where they are pushed backwards and forwards between two grooved 'cheeks' made of steel, which raise the necessary rim by pressure.

" From this department I am taken by my guide to a long bakehouse structure, called the Annealing Room. Here I find several men-cooks very busy with the golden-rimmed blanks, making them into pies of three thousand each, in cast-iron pans with wrought-iron lids, and closed up with moist Beckenham clay. These costly pies are placed in large ovens, where they are baked in intense heat for an hour, and then each batch is drawn as its time expires, and is not opened before the pan becomes cool. The grey plastic loam which was placed round the dish is baked to a red crisp cinder, and the golden contents of the pie are warranted not to tarnish after this fiery ordeal by coming in contact with the atmosphere.

" I next follow the golden annealed blanks to the Blanching Room, where they are put into a cold-water bath to render them cool; after which they are washed in a hot weak solution of sulphuric acid and water to remove all traces of surface impurity. Finally, after another wash in pure water, they are conveyed to a drying-stove, where they are first agitated violently in a heated tub, then turned into a sieve, and tossed about out of sight, amongst a heap of beechwood sawdust, kept hot upon an oven. After this playful process, they are sifted into the upper world once more, and then transferred to trays, like butchers' trays, which are conveyed to the Stamping Room.

"The Coining-press Room contains eight screw presses, worked from above by invisible machinery. Below, there is a cast-iron platform; and above, huge fly-arms, full six feet long, and weighty at their ends, which travel noisily to and fro, carrying with them the vertical screw, and raising and depressing the upper die. In front of each press, when the machinery is in motion, a boy is sitting to fill the feeding-tube with the bright plain dumps of gold that have come from the sawdust in the Blanching Room. On the bed of the press is fixed one of Mr. Wyon's head-dies, a perfect work of art, that is manufactured in the building; and the self-acting feeding apparatus—a slide moving backwards and forwards, much the same as in the delicate weighing-machines — places the golden dumps one by one on the die. The boy in attendance now starts some atmospheric pressure machinery, by pulling a starting-line; the press and upper die are brought down upon the piece of unstamped gold that is lying on the lower die, along with a collar that is milled on its inner circumference, and which closes upon the coin with a spring, preventing its undue expansion, and at one forcible but well-directed blow, the blank dump has received its top, bottom, and side impression, and has become a perfect coin of the realm. The feeder advances with steady regularity, and while it conveys another dump to the die, it chips the perfect sovereign down an inclined plane; the upper machinery comes down again; the dump is covered out of sight, to appear in an instant as a coin; other dumps advance, are stamped, are pushed away, and their places immediately taken. Some sovereigns roll on one side instead of going over to the inclined plane, others lie upon the edge of the machinery, or under the butcher's tray that holds the dumps, and the boys take even less notice of them than if they were so many peppermint drops.

"The metal has passed no locked doorway in its progress without being weighed out of one department into another; and it undergoes yet one more weighing before it is placed into bags for delivery to the Bank of England or private bullion-holders, and consigned to a stone and iron strong-room, containing half a million of coined money, until the hour of its liberation draws nigh."

CHAPTER XII.

NEIGHBOURHOOD OF THE TOWER (continued).

The Jewry—Allhallows Church—Terrible Gunpowder Accident near the Church—Famous Men buried at Allhallows—Monumental Brasses—St. Olave's Church—Dr. W. Turner—Sir John Minnes—A Well-known Couplet—Pepys' Wife—"Poor Tom"—Sir J. Radcliffe—Antiquities of the Church—Pepys on Allhallows—St. Dunstan's-in-the-East—Wren's Repairs—The Register Books—Old Roman Tower—The Trinity House and its Corporation—The Present Building—Decorations and Portraits—Famous Masters—A Bit of Old Wall.

STOW describes a Jewish quarter near the Tower. "There was," he says, "a place within the liberties of the Tower called the Jewry, because it was inhabited by Jews, and where there happened, 22nd Henry III., a robbery and a murther to be committed by William Fitz Bernard, and Richard his servant; who came to the house of Joce, a Jew, and there slew him and his wife Henna. The said William was taken at St. Saviour's for a certain silver cup, and was hanged. Richard was called for, and was outlawed. One Miles le Espicer, who was with them, was wounded, and fled to a church, and died in it. No attachment was made by the sheriffs, because it happened in the Jewry, and so belonged not to the sheriffs, but to the Constable of the Tower."

The churches near Tower Hill demand a brief notice. That of Allhallows, Barking, and Our Lady, in Tower Street, Stow mentions as having, in the early ages, a "faire chapel" of Our Lady on the north side, founded by Richard I., whose lion heart, as the erroneous tradition went, was buried there, under the high altar. Edward I. gave the chapel a statue of the Virgin. Edward IV. permitted his cousin, John Earl of Worcester, to form a brotherhood there, and gave them the advowson of Streatham and part of a Wiltshire priory for maintenance. Richard III. rebuilt the chapel, and founded a college of priests, consisting of a dean and six canons, and made Edmund Chaderton, a great favourite of his own, the dean. The college was suppressed and pulled down under Edward VI. The ground remained a garden plot till the reign of Elizabeth, when merchants' warehouses were built there by Sir William Winter, whose wife was buried in the church.

The church derives its name of Barking from the vicarage having originally belonged to the abbey and convent of Barking, in Essex. The church was much injured in 1649 by an accidental explosion of twenty-seven barrels of gunpowder at a ship-chandler's near the churchyard. A Mr. Leyborn, quoted by Strype, gives the following account of this calamity :—

"Over against the wall of Barking churchyard," says Leyborn, "a sad and lamentable accident befell by gunpowder, in this manner. One of the houses in this place was a ship-chandler's, who, upon

will instance two, the one a dead, the other a living monument. In the digging, as I said before, they found the mistress of the house of the Rose Tavern, sitting in her bar, and one of the drawers standing by the bar's side with a pot in his hand, only stifled with dust and smoke ; their bodies being preserved whole by means of great timbers falling cross one upon another : this is one. Another is this : the next morning there was found upon the upper leads of Barking Church a young child lying in a cradle,

THE CHURCH OF ALLHALLOWS, BARKING, IN 1750.

the 4th of January, 1649, about seven of the clock at night, being busy in his shop about barrelling up of gunpowder, it took fire, and in the twinkling of an eye blew up not only that, but all the houses thereabouts, to the number (towards the street and in back alleys) of fifty or sixty. The number of persons destroyed by this blow could never be known, for the next house but one was the Rose Tavern, a house never at that time of night but full of company ; and that day the parish dinner was in that house. And in three or four days after, digging, they continually found heads, arms, legs, and half bodies, miserably torn and scorched, besides many whole bodies, not so much as their clothes singed. In the course of this accident I

as newly laid in bed, neither the child nor cradle having the least sign of any fire or other hurt. It was never known whose child it was, so that one of the parish kept it for a memorial ; for in the year 1666 I saw the child, grown to be then a proper maiden, and came to the man that had kept her all that time, where he was drinking at a tavern with some other company then present, and he told us she was the child that was so found in the cradle upon the church leads as aforesaid."

Allhallows, from its vicinity to the Tower, was the burial-place of several State criminals, and many minor Court officials ; the poet Earl of Surrey, Bishop Fisher, and the arbitrary Laud, were buried there, but have been since removed. The six or seven brasses preserved here are, says an authority, among the best in London. The finest is a Flemish brass, to Andrew Evyngar, a salter, and his wife, *circa* 1535. There is also an injured brass of William Thynne, Clerk of the Green Cloth, Clerk of the Kitchen, and afterwards "Master of the and two other reformed preachers, to preach thirty sermons (two a week) at Allhallows, which, he said, would do more good than having masses said for his soul. He also forbad at his funeral the superstitious use of candles, the singing of dirges, and the tolling of bells. In the chancel Strype

ST. DUNSTAN'S-IN-THE-EAST.

Honourable Household of King Henry VIII., our Sovereign Lord." This worthy man published the first edition of the entire works of Chaucer, in 1532. Strype mentions the monument of Humfry Monmouth, a draper and sheriff, who protected Tindal, and encouraged him in his translation of the Testament, for which he was thrown into the Tower by Sir Thomas More. In his will he appointed Bishop Latimer, Dr. Barnes (the "Hot Gospeller"),

mentions the monument of Dr. Kettlewell, a famous controversial divine, who wrote "Measures of Christian Obedience," and refused to take the oaths on the accession of William of Orange.

In the pavement of the south aisle, near the chancel, is a large brass to the memory of John Rulche, who died in 1498. There is another, with small figures of a man and his two wives, with the date 1500. From the mouths of the figures rise labels (as in old caricatures), with pious invocations of "Libera nos," and "Salva nos." Another brass of a nameless knight and his lady is dated 1546; and in the north aisle there is an ecclesiastic and a lady, date probably, says Mr. Godwin, 1437. On a pillar in the south aisle is a brass plate, with doggerel verses to the memory of Armac Aymer, Governor of the Pages of Honour, or Master of the Henchmen, to Henry VIII., Edward VI., Mary, and Elizabeth, having served in the royal household fifty-six years. At the north side of the chancel stands a panelled altar tomb, of carved granite, crowned with strawberry leaves. Under a canopy are two groups of figures—the father and three sons, the mother and four daughters. Strype seems to erroneously connect this tomb with that of Thomas Pilke, who founded a chantry here in 1392 (Richard II.). Pilke's is more likely the canopied one on the opposite side of the church, with a plate of brass, on which is represented the resurrection of Christ.

The earliest legend connected with this very old church is one relating to Edward I. That warlike king had a vision, which commanded him to erect an image of the Virgin at Allhallows Barking, promising that, if he did so, visited it five times every year, and kept the chapel in repair, he should be victorious over all nations, should be King of England when his father died, and conqueror of Wales and Scotland. To the truth of this vision Edward swore before the Pope, and obtained a dispensation of forty days' penance for all true penitents who should contribute towards the lights, ornaments, and repairs of the chapel, and should pray for the soul of King Richard, whose heart was, as it is said, buried before the high altar. The pilgrims and worshippers of Our Lady of Barking continued numerous till the Reformation came and broke up these associations.

In 1639 the Puritan House of Commons proceeded against Dr. Layfield, the vicar of Allhallows, who had introduced various "Popish" innovations. The parishioners complained that he had altered the position of the communion-table, set up various images, had erected a cross over the font, placed the letters I.H.S. in forty-one various places, and also that he had bowed several times during the administration of the sacrament. The vicar, however, contrived to escape punishment. At the Great Fire this interesting church had a narrow escape, the vicarage being burned down. The present brick steeple was built in 1659, when the churchwardens put over the clock, which projects from the front of the church, the figure of an angel sounding a trumpet. In 1675 the succeeding churchwardens removed this figure, and placed it over the altar; but the clergyman being seen to perform genuflexions before it, the churchwardens were indicted, and compelled to burn the image.

The church, from an architectural point of view, is well worth a visit. The round massive pillars and sharp-pointed arches of the west end date from the beginning of the thirteenth century, while the eastern portion of the church is Perpendicular and Late Decorated. There is a clerestory, containing seven windows, and the windows of the north and south aisles are of different periods. It is said that many years ago the basement of a wall was found running across the building near the pulpit, showing vestiges of an earlier structure. The roof and ceiling were constructed in 1814, at a cost of £7,000. The marble font has a carved wooden cover (attributed, of course, to Gibbons), which represents three angels plucking flowers and fruit. On the south side of the building is an old staircase turret, which formerly led to the roof, but is now stopped up. In the porch, on the same side, is a good Tudor doorway.

Dr. Hickes, the great scholar who wrote the "Thesaurus," was vicar of Allhallows for six years (1680–6). Hickes, a Yorkshireman, born in 1642, was chaplain, in 1676, to the Duke of Lauderdale, the mischievous High Commissioner of Scotland, and was sent to Charles's court, with Bishop Burnet, to report the discontent of the Scotch. He was presented to the living of Allhallows by Archbishop Sancroft. At the Restoration of 1688, Dr. Hickes refused to take the oath of allegiance, and afterwards went over to France, to see King James, on the dangerous mission of arranging the consecration of fresh bishops. Hickes was very learned in the Fathers and in the old northern languages, and wrote much for Divine right.

Another church of interest in this neighbourhood is St. Olave's, Hart Street, at the corner of Seething Lane. This saint was the warlike King of Norway who helped Ethelred against the Danes. There was a church on this spot at least as long ago as 1319, for we find in that year the prior and brethren of the Holy Cross paying two marks and a half per annum to the rector, and his successors for ever, for any damage that might accrue to them by the building of the priory. The patronage was first vested in the Nevil family, then in that of Lord Windsor; but in 1651 it was bequeathed to the parish by Sir Andrew Riccard, who was Sheriff of London in 1651. Maitland mentions, in the middle aisle, a brass of "a King of Arms, in his coat and crown," date 1427. The most ancient brass now to be found is apparently that to the memory of John Orgene and Ellyne his wife, date 1584. Near this is a fine monument to that first of our English herbalists, Dr. William Turner, who died in 1614. This deep student was a violent Reformer, whom Bishop Gardiner threw into prison. On his release he went to live abroad, and at Basle became the friend of Gesner, the great naturalist. In the reign of Edward VI. he was made Dean of Wells and chaplain to the Protector Somerset, in which former dignity Elizabeth reinstated him.

On the south side of the communion-table there was, according to Strype, a monument to that brave and witty man, Sir John Mennes, or Minnes, vice-admiral to Charles I., and, after the Restoration, Governor of Dover Castle, and Chief Comptroller of the Navy. Born in the year 1598, and holding a place in the Navy Office in the reign of James I., Minnes, after many years of honest and loyal service, died in 1670, at the Navy Office in Seething Lane, where he must have spent half his long-shore life. He is generally spoken of as a brave, honest, generous fellow, and the best of all good company. Some of his poems are contained in a volume entitled "The Muses' Recreation," 1656, and he was the author of a clever scoffing ballad on his brother poet, Sir John Suckling's, foolish vaunts and miserable failure. In "The Muses' Recreation" we find the celebrated lines, so often quoted, and which are almost universally attributed to Butler, whose Hudibrastic manner they so exactly resemble—

"For he that fights and runs away,
May live to fight another day."

In the chancel, near the monument of Paul Bayning, mentioned by one of Stow's commentators as then hung with coat of arms and streamers, is a monument to the wife of Samuel Pepys, the Secretary to the Navy, who wrote the delightful gossiping "Diary" which we have so often quoted. Who that has read it can forget the portrait of that buxom beauty who was so jealous of pretty Mrs. Knipp, the actress? or how Pepys took her, Jan. 10, 1660, to the great wedding of a Dutch merchant, at Goring House, where there was "great state, cost, and a noble company? But among all the beauties there," says the uxorious husband, "my wife was thought the greatest." Does he not record how she took to wearing black patches, and how she began to study dancing and limning? Mrs. Pepys was the daughter of a French Huguenot gentleman, who had been gentleman carver to Queen Henrietta, and was dismissed for striking one of

the queen's friars, who had rebuked him for not attending mass. Mrs. Pepys had been brought up in a Ursuline convent in France, and this fact was probably remembered when the Titus Oates party endeavoured to connect poor Pepys with the (supposed) murder of Sir Edmundbury Godfrey. In this same church was also buried Thomas Pepys, brother of the diary-keeper, whose funeral Pepys records with a curious mixture of grief, thrift, and want of feeling. The entry notes some curious customs of the period :—

"18th March, 1664. Up betimes, and walked to my brother's, where a great while putting things in order against anon; and so to Wotton, my shoemaker, and there got a pair of shoes blacked on the soles against anon for me; so to my brother's. To church, and, with the grave-maker, chose a place for my brother to lie in, just under my mother's pew. But to see how a man's tombes are at the mercy of such a fellow, that for sixpence he would, as his own words were, 'I will justle them together but I will make room for him,' speaking of the fulness of the middle aisle, where he was to lie ; and that he would, for my father's sake, do my brother, that is dead, all the civility he can ; which was to disturb other corps that are not quite rotten, to make room for him ; and methought his manner of speaking it was very remarkable, as of a thing that now was in his power to do a man a courtesy or not. I dressed myself, and so did my servant Besse ; and so to my brother's again ; whither, though invited, as the custom is, at one or two o'clock, they come not till four or five. But, at last, one after another they come, many more than I bid ; and my reckoning that I bid was 120, but I believe there was nearer 150. Their service was six biscuits apiece, and what they pleased of burnt claret. My cousin, Joyce Norton, kept the wine and cakes above, and did give out to them that served, who had white gloves given them. But, above all, I am beholden to Mrs. Holden, who was most kind, and did take mighty pains, not only in getting the house and everything else ready, but this day in going up and down to see the house filled and served, in order to mine and their great content, I think ; the men sitting by themselves in some rooms, and the women by themselves in others, very close, but yet room enough. Anon to church, walking out into the street to the conduit, and so across the street ; and had a very good company along with the corps. And being come to the grave as above, Dr. Pierson, the minister of the parish, did read the service for buriall ; and so I saw my poor brother laid into the grave ; and so all broke up ; and I and my wife, and Madam

Turner and her family, to her brother's, and by-and-by fell to a barrell of oysters, cake, and cheese, of Mr. Honiwood's, with him, in his chamber and below, being too merry for so late a sad work. But, Lord! to see how the world makes nothing of the memory of a man an hour after he is dead! And, indeed, I must blame myself, for though at the sight of him dead, and dying, I had real grief for a while, while he was in my sight, yet, presently after, and ever since, I have had very little grief indeed for him."

Last of all of the Pepys family, to St. Olave's came the rich Secretary of the Navy, that pleasant *bon vivant* and musician, who was interred, June 4, 1703, in a vault of his own making, by the side of his wife and brother. The burial service was read at nine at night, by Dr. Hickes, author of the "Thesaurus."

Under the organ gallery, at the west end of the church, is a sculptured marble figure, set up by the Turkey Company, to Sir Andrew Riccard, the great benefactor of the parish, and a potent man after the Restoration, being chairman of both the East India Company and the Turkey Company. At the foot of the statue, which formerly stood in one of the aisles, is the following inscription :—

"Sacred be the statue here raised by gratitude and respect to eternize the memory of Sir Andrew Riccard, knight, a citizen, and opulent merchant of London ; whose active piety, inflexible integrity, and extensive abilities, alike distinguished and exalted him in the opinion of the wise and good. Adverse to his wish, he was frequently chosen chairman of the Honourable East India Company, and filled, with equal credit, for eighteen successive years, the same eminent station in the Turkey Company. Among many instances of his love to God and liberal spirit towards man, one, as it demands peculiar praise, deserves to be distinctly recorded. He nobly left the perpetual advowson of this parish in trust to five of its senior inhabitants. He died 6th Sept., in the year of our Lord, 1672, of his age, 68.

"Manet post funera virtus."

To one of the walls of the church is affixed part of a sculptured figure in armour, representing Sir John Radcliffe, one of the Sussex family, who died in the year of our Lord 1568 (Elizabeth). Stow describes this figure as recumbent on an altar-tomb, with a figure of his wife kneeling beside it. A figure something resembling that of his wife is still preserved in the church. Under the north gallery is a full-sized figure in armour kneeling beneath a canopy, inscribed to Peter Chapponius, and dated 1582. There is also a brass plate at the east end of the north aisle commemorating Mr. Thomas Morley, Clerk of the Household of Queen Katharine of Arragon; and Strype mentions one to Philip van Wyllender, musician, and one of the Privy

Chamber to Henry VIII. and Edward VI. The Baynings' monument, before mentioned, presents their painted and well-sculptured effigies under alcoves. Beneath the figure of Paul Bayning, who died in 1616, are some lame and doggrel verses, the concluding lines of which are :—

"The happy sum and end of their affaires,
　Provided well both for their soules and heires."

The registers of St. Olave's, which are well preserved and perfect from the year 1563 to the present time, contain a long list of names with the fatal letter P. (Plague) appended. The first entry of this kind is July 24, 1665—"Mary, daughter of William Ramsay, one of the Drapers' almsmen." Singularly enough, there was at the time of Mr. Godwin's writing, in 1839, a tradition in the parish that the Plague first broke out in this parish in the Drapers' Almshouses, Cooper's Row, which were founded by Sir John Milborn in the year 1535.

The ancient portions of this interesting church are the large east window (with stained glass of the year 1823), the sharp-pointed window at the end of the north aisle, the west window, and the columns and arches of the nave. The other windows are flatter at the top, and the ceilings of the aisles are studded with small stars. The corbels on the north side are formed of angels, holding shields. There was formerly a gallery on the south side of the church, for the august officers of the Navy Office. Here Samuel Pepys must have often dozed solemnly. This gallery was approached by a small quaint staircase on the outside of the church, as shown by an old engraving, published in 1726, by West and Toms. The churchyard gate is adorned with five skulls, in the true pagan churchwarden taste of the last century.

Pepys frequently mentions this church, where all the dresses he was so proud of—even his new lace band, the effect of which made him resolve to make lace bands his chief expense—were displayed to the admiring world of Seething Lane. He and Sir John Minnes were attendants here ; and it is specially mentioned on June 6, 1666, when Pepys says:—"To our church, it being the Common Fast-day, and it was just before sermon ; but, Lord! how all the people in the church stare upon me, to see me whisper 'the news of the victory over the Dutch' to Sir John Minnes and my Lady Pen! Anon I saw people stirring and whispering below ; and by-and-by comes up the sexton from my Lady Ford, to tell me the news which I had brought, being now sent into the church by Sir W. Batten, in writing, and passed from pew to pew." This battle was Monk's decisive victory over De Ruyter. And again, January 30, 1665–6. This day, the day after Pepys had discoursed of the vanity and vices of the court to Mr. Evelyn, who had proposed a hospital for sailors, and whom he found "a most worthy person," the chronicler writes :—"Home, finding the town keeping the day solemnly, it being the day of the king's murther; and they being at church, I presently into the church. This is the first time I have been in the church since I left London for the Plague; and it frighted me indeed to go through the church, more than I thought it could have done, to see so many graves lie so high upon the churchyard where people have been buried of the plague. I was much troubled at it, and do not think to go through it again a good while."

The register of St. Olave's shows that in this parish, from July 4 to December 5, 1665, there were buried 326 people. On the 31st of January Pepys notices his hope that the churchyard of St. Olave's will be covered with lime; and on February 4, when he slinks to church reluctantly, to hear a sermon from the vicar, who had been the first to fly and the last to return, he is cheered at finding snow covering the dreaded graves.

St. Dunstan's in the East, another church of this district, Stow describes as "a fair, large church, of an ancient building, and within a large churchyard," and speaks of the parish as full of rich merchants, Salters and Ironmongers. Newcourt's list of St. Dunstan rectors commences in 1312, and Stow records the burial of John Kennington, parson in 1372, the earliest date he gives in connection with the church. Strype mentions as a "remarkable passage" concerning this building, that in the Middle Ages, according to Archbishop Chichely's register, Lord l'Estrange and his wife did public penance from St. Paul's to this church, "because they gave a cause of murder in this same church, and polluted it." The old churchwarden's books, which begin in the fifteenth century, specify sums paid for playing "at organs" and "blowing of the organs," and money spent in garlands, and by priests in drinking, on St. Dunstan's Eve.

The church being seriously damaged in the Great Fire, Wren was employed to repair it. The lofty spire mentioned by Newcourt had gone, and Wren erected the present curious one, supported on four arched ribs—an idea taken from the church of St. Nicholas, at Newcastle-upon-Tyne, a fine Gothic building of the fifteenth century.

Mr. Godwin complains that though this church was one of Wren's best works in the Pointed style, yet still the mouldings of the tower are too Italian, the clock-case out of character, and the sunk panels on the pinnacles very shallow and tame.

Another critic calls the old St. Dunstan's a mole-hill compared to the Newcastle "Mountain," the latter tower being twenty feet less in width, much higher, and with two storeys more. Nevertheless, Wren was proud of this church; and being told one morning that a hurricane had damaged many London spires, he remarked, "Not St. Dunstan's, I am quite sure." There is a vulgar tradition about the shape of this steeple, which cannot be given here.

In digging the foundations for the present church the workmen found immense walls of chalk and rubble stretching in all directions, especially northwards, where the monks are supposed to have dwelt. Opposite there was a bricked-up porch, which had been used as a bonehouse. The old Purbeck marble floor was worn away several inches by the monks' sandals, and there were in the same porch some side benches of stone, and a curious window with four columns. Glazed tiles of the old church-floor were found two feet below the pavement, and at the east end fragments of a large mullioned window.

In the interior Wren washed his hands of the Gothic, using Doric and Corinthian columns, and circular-headed windows with key-stones. In 1810 the church became ruinous, the roof of the nave thrusting out the wall seven inches. Mr. Laing then prepared plans for a new church, which was begun in 1817, and opened in 1821. This modern Gothic building cost about £36,000. The east-end window is of the florid Perpendicular style, and is said to be an exact copy of the one discovered in pulling down the old building. The roof of the centre aisle is remarkable for some elegant fan-groining, and the side aisles have flat panelled ceilings in the corrupt Gothic style of George IV.'s reign.

The register-books of St. Dunstan's, which date back as far as 1558, escaped the Great Fire, and are in a fine state of preservation. The church contains many tablets of the seventeenth century, and one large monument on the south side of the church to Sir William Russel, a charitable London alderman, who died in 1705. The worthy man, in flowing Queen Anne wig, shoes, and buckles, lies on his left side, regretting the thirteen shillings he left to the sexton of St. Dunstan's for ever, to keep his monument clean. Strype mentions the tomb of Alderman James, who, before the Reformation, left large sums to this church for his funeral, and for chantry priests. At his interment ten men of the brotherhood of Jesus in this church were to carry six-pound torches of wax, and six shillings and eightpence was given to every priest and clerk for singing dirge and mass of requiem, till "his month's mind were finished."

That excellent man and delightful writer, Fuller, mentions St. Dunstan's-in-the-East when talking of his singular gift of memory. It is said that Fuller could "repeat five hundred strange words after twice hearing them, and could make use of a sermon *verbatim*, if he once heard it." Still further, it is said that he undertook, in passing from Temple Bar to the extremity of Cheapside, to tell, at his return, every sign as it stood in order on both sides

me in the vestry before credible people, that he, in Sidney College, had taught me the *art of memory*. I returned unto him, *That it was not so*, for I could not remember *that I had ever seen him before!* which, I conceive, was a real refutation."

At the lower end of a street now no longer existing, named the Vineyard, in the neighbourhood of the Tower, there used to be the basis of a Roman tower, about eight feet high, supporting a building of three storeys, in the wall of which was fixed a large stone, with the following inscription :—

ROMAN WALL ON TOWER HILL.

of the way (repeating them either backwards or forwards), and that he performed the task exactly. This is pretty well, considering that in that day every shop had its sign. That many, however, of the reports respecting his extraordinary memory were false or exaggerated, may be gathered from an amusing anecdote recorded by himself. " None alive," says he, " ever heard me pretend to the *art* of memory, who in my book (' Holy State') have decried it as a trick, no art ; and, indeed, is more of fancy than memory. I confess, some years since, when I came out of the pulpit of St. Dunstan's East, one (who since wrote a book thereof) told

" Glory be to God on high, who was graciously pleased to preserve the lives of all the people in this house, twelve in number, when the ould wall of the bulwark fell down three stories high, and so broad as three carts might enter a breast, and yet without any harm to anie of their persones. The Lord sanctify this his great providence unto them. Amen and Amen.

"It was Tuesday, the 23rd September, 1651."

One of the most interesting places on Tower Hill, next to the Mint (on whose site, by-the-bye, once stood a tobacco warehouse), is Trinity House, a corporation for the increase and encouragement of navigation, the examination of pilots, the regulation of lighthouses and buoys, and, indeed, all naval matters not under the express jurisdiction of the Admiralty.

The old Trinity House stood in Water Lane, Lower Thames Street, a little north-west of the Custom House; the spot is now Trinity Chambers. Hatton, in 1708, describes the second house, built after the Great Fire, as "a stately building of brick and stone (adorned with ten bustos), built anno down in 1787, was situated at Deptford. In 1680 its first lighthouse was erected, all lighthouses which had previously existed on the English coast having been built by private individuals, under a patent from the Crown. It was not till the year 1854 that the private rights in light-dues were abolished, and the exclusive right of lighting and buoying the coast given over to the Trinity House Board. They also bind and enroll apprentices to the sea; examine the mathematical boys of Christ's

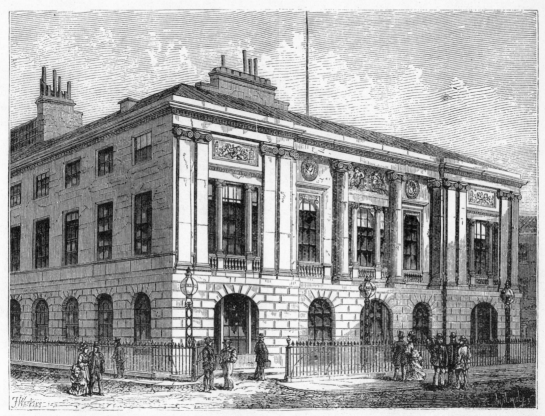

THE TRINITY HOUSE.

1671." Pepys, who lived close by, mentions going to see Tower Street on fire, from Trinity House on one side to the "Dolphin" Tavern on the other. This ancient and useful guild was founded by Sir Thomas Spert, Comptroller of the Navy to Henry VIII., and commander of the *Great Eastern* of that age, the *Harry Grace de Dieu*, a huge gilt four-master, in which Henry VIII. sailed to Calais, on his way to the Field of the Cloth of Gold. It was incorporated in 1529, by the name of "The Master, Wardens, and Assistants of the Guild, or Fraternity, or Brotherhood of the Most Glorious and Undividable Trinity, and of St. Clement, in the parish of Deptford Strond, in the county of Kent," and the mother house, pulled Hospital; examine mathematical masters for the navy; and place and alter all the buoys, beacons, and sea-marks along the English coast. By an Act passed in the 8th Elizabeth, they also survey the channel of the Thames and other ports. To them once belonged the power of ballasting all ships going out of the Thames, the ballast to be taken from the more dangerous shelves, and where the river needed deepening; and, at request of masters, they could also certify to goods "damnified" by evil stowing. They gave licences to poor, aged, and maimed mariners to row "upon the river of Thames" without licence from the Watermen's Company. They could prevent foreigners serving on board our ships without licence; they heard and determined complaints by officers and men in the merchant service; and, lastly, they could punish seamen for mutiny and desertion.

The Trinity House bye-laws of the reign of James II. contain some curious regulations. Every master homeward bound, for instance, was to un-shot his guns at Gravesend, on penalty of twenty nobles.

The corporation consists of a master, deputy-master, thirty-one elder brethren, and an unlimited number of humbler members. In Pennant's time it consisted of a master, four wardens, eight assist-ants, and eighteen elder brethren, and they seem to have been known as "the Thirty-one Brethren." The elder brothers are generally selected from old commanders in the navy and merchant service; and now and then a compliment is paid to a prince or a nobleman who could not, probably, steer a collier to Newcastle. The revenue of the corpora-tion, about £300,000 a year, arises from tonnage, ballastage, beaconage, and licensing pilots; and this sum, after defraying the expenses of light-houses, and paying off the portion of the debt in-curred by the purchase of all existing private rights in lighthouses, is chiefly expended in maintaining poor disabled seamen and their widows and orphans. The corporation hospital at Deptford, which the master and brethren used formerly to visit in their state yacht, in grand procession, on Trinity Monday, has been "disestablished."

The powers of the Trinity House in old times are fully described by Strype. They decided on mari-time cases referred to them by the Admiralty judges; they examined and gave certificates to masters of the navy; they examined pilots for the royal navy and for the merchant service. Bum-boats with fruit, wine, and strong waters were not permitted by them to board vessels. Every mariner who swore, cursed, or blasphemed on board ship, was by their rules to pay one shilling to the ship's poor-box. Every mariner who got drunk was fined one shilling. No mariner, unless sick, could absent himself from prayers without forfeiting sixpence.

The previous building is shortly dismissed by Pennant with the remark that it was unworthy of the greatness of its design. The present Trinity House was built in 1793–5, by Samuel Wyatt. It is of the Ionic order. On its principal front are sculptured the arms of the corporation (a cross between four ships under sail), medallions of George III. and Queen Charlotte, genii with nautical instruments, the four principal lighthouses on the coast, &c.

The interior contains busts of St. Vincent, Nelson, Howe, and Duncan; William Pitt, and Captain J.

Cotton, by Chantrey; George III., by Turnerelli, &c. The Court-room is decorated with imperso-nations of the Thames, Medway, Severn, and Humber; and among the pictures is a fine paint-ing, twenty feet long, by Gainsborough, of the elder brethren of Trinity House. In the Board-room are portraits of James I. and II., Elizabeth, Anne of Denmark, Earl Craven, Sir Francis Drake, Sir J. Leake, and General Monk; King William IV., the Prince Consort, and the Duke of Wellington, three of the past masters; and George III., Queen Charlotte, and Queen Adelaide.

Of one of the portraits Pennant gives a pleasant biography. "The most remarkable picture," says the London historian, "is that of Sir John Leake, with his lank grey locks, and a loose night-gown, with a mien very little indicative of his high courage and active spirit. He was the greatest commander of his time, and engaged in most actions of note during the reigns of King William and Queen Anne. To him was committed the desperate but success-ful attempt of breaking the boom, previous to the relief of Londonderry. He distinguished himself greatly at the battle of La Hogue; assisted at the taking of Gibraltar; and afterwards, as Commander-in-Chief, reduced Barcelona, took Carthagena, and brought Sardinia and Minorca to submit to Charles, rival to Philip for the crown of Spain. He was made a Lord of the Admiralty, but declined the offer of being the head of the commission; at the accession of George I., averse to the new family, he retired, but with the approving pension of £600 a year. He lived privately at Greenwich, where he died in 1720, and was buried in a manner suitable to his merits, in the church at Stepney."

The museum contains a flag taken from the Spanish Armada by Sir Francis Drake, a model of the *Royal William*, 150 years old, and two colossal globes, given by Sir Thomas Allan, admiral to Charles II.; pen-and-ink views of sea-fights (the same period), and models of lighthouses, floating lights, and lifeboats.

The office of the master of the corporation, at various times, has been held by princes and states-men. From 1816, when Lord Liverpool occupied the office of master, it was held in succession by the Marquis Camden, the Duke of Clarence (after-wards William IV.), Marquis Camden again, the Duke of Wellington, the Prince Consort, and Viscount Palmerston. The present master is the Duke of Edinburgh.

Behind the houses in Trinity Square, in George Street, Tower Hill, stands one of the four remaining portions of the old London wall. We have already mentioned it in our chapter on Roman London.

CHAPTER XIII.

ST. KATHARINE'S DOCKS.

St. Katharine's Hospital—Its Royal Benefactors in Former Times—The Fair on Tower Hill—Seizure of the Hospital Revenues at the Reformation —The Dreadful Fire of 1672—Three Luckless Gordon Rioters—St. Katharine's Church—The only Preferment in the Right of the Queen Consort—St. Katharine's Docks—Unloading Ships there—Labourers employed in them—Applicants for Work at the Docks—A Precarious Living—Contrasts.

BEFORE entering the gate of St. Katharine's Docks, where great samples of the wealth of London await our inspection, we must first make a brief mention of the old hospital that was pulled down in 1827, to make a fresh pathway for London commerce. This hospital was originally founded in 1148 by Matilda of Boulogne, wife of the usurper Stephen, for the repose of the souls of her son Baldwin and her daughter Matilda, and for the maintenance of a master and several poor brothers and sisters. In 1273, Eleanor, widow of Henry III., dissolved the old foundation, and refounded it in honour of the same saint, for a master, three brethren, chaplains, three sisters, ten bedeswomen, and six poor scholars. Opposed to this renovation, Pope Urban IV., by a bull, endeavoured in vain to reinstate the expelled prior and brotherhood, who had purloined the goods and neglected their duties. And here, in the same reign, lived that great alchemist, Raymond Lully, whom Edward III. employed in the Tower to try and discover for him the secret of transmutation.

Another great benefactress of the hospital was the brave woman, Philippa of Hainault, wife of that terror of France, Edward III. She founded a chantry and gave houses in Kent and Herts to the charity, and £10 in lands per annum for an additional chaplain.

In after years Henry V. confirmed the annual £10 of Queen Philippa for the endowment of the chantries of St. Fabian and St. Sebastian, and his son Henry VI. was likewise a benefactor to St. Katharine's Hospital. But the great encourager of the charity was Thomas de Bekington, afterwards Bishop of Bath and Wells, who, being master of the hospital in the year 1445, obtained a charter of privileges, to help the revenue. By this charter the precincts of the hospital were declared free from all jurisdiction, civil or ecclesiastical, except that of the Lord Chancellor. To help the funds, an annual fair was to be held on Tower Hill, to last twenty-one days from the feast of St. James. The district had a special spiritual and a temporal court.

Henry VIII. and Katharine of Arragon founded in this place the guild or fraternity of St. Barbara, which was governed by a master and three wardens, and included in its roll Cardinal Wolsey, the Dukes of Norfolk and Buckingham, the Earls of Shrewsbury and Northumberland, and their ladies. In 1526 the king confirmed the liberties and franchise of this house, which even escaped dissolution in 1534, in compliment, it has been supposed, to Queen Anne Boleyn, whom the king had then lately married.

In the reign of Edward VI., however, all the meshes of the Reformers' nets grew smaller. Now the small fry had all been caught, the lands of St. Katharine's Hospital were taken possession of by the Crown. Greediness and avarice soon had their eye on the hospital; and in the reign of Elizabeth, Dr. Thomas Wylson, her secretary, becoming the master, surrendered up the charter of Henry VI., and craftily obtained a new one, which left out any mention of the liberty of the fair on Tower Hill. He then sold the rights of the said fair to the Corporation of London for £466 13s. 4d. He next endeavoured to secure all the hospital estates, when the parishioners of the precinct began to cry aloud to Secretary Cecil, and stopped the plunderer's hand.

In 1672 a dreadful fire destroyed one hundred houses in the precincts, and another fire during a great storm in 1734 destroyed thirty buildings. During the Gordon riots of 1780 a Protestant mob, headed by Macdonald, a lame soldier, and two women—one a white and one a negro—armed with swords, were about to demolish the church, as being built in Popish times, when the gentlemen of the London Association arrived, and prevented the demolition. Macdonald and the two women were afterwards hanged for this at a temporary gallows on Tower Hill.

The church pulled down to make way for the docks (religion elbowed off by commerce) in 1825, was an interesting Gothic building, exclusive of the choir, 69 feet long, 60 feet broad. The altar was pure Gothic, and the old stalls, of 1340–69, were curiously carved with grotesque and fanciful monsters; the organ, by Green, was a fine one, remarkable for its swell; and the pulpit, given by Sir Julius Cæsar, already mentioned in our chapter on Chancery Lane, was a singular example of bad taste. Round the six sides ran the following inscription :—

" Ezra the scribe stood upon a pulpit of wood, which he had made for the preachin."—Neh. viii. 4.

The chief tombs were those of John Holland, Duke of Exeter, his duchess, and sister. This duke fought in France in the wars of Henry VI., and died in 1447. He was High Admiral of England and Ireland, and Constable of the Tower. We shall describe his tomb when we come to it in Regent's Park, in the transplanted hospital, where it now is. Gibbon, the herald, an ancestor of the great historian, was also buried here.

The Queen Consorts of England are by law the perpetual patronesses of this hospital, with unlimited power. This is the only preferment in the gift of the Queen Consort. When there is no Queen Consort, the Queen Dowager has the right of nomination. The business of the establishment and appointment of subordinate officers is transacted in chapter by the master, brothers, and sisters. Among the eminent masters of this hospital we may mention Sir Julius Cæsar, Sir Robert Ayton, a poet of the time of Charles I., and the Hon. George Berkeley, husband of Mrs. Howard, the mistress of George II. A curious MS. list of plate and jewels, in the Harleian Library, quoted by Dr. Ducarel, shows that the hospital possessed some altarcloths and vestments of cloth of gold and crimson velvet, green damask copes, and silken coats, for the image of St. Katharine. The Duke of Exeter left the church a beryl cup, garnished with gold and precious stones, a gold chalice, eleven silver candlesticks, &c., for the priests of his chantry chapel.

St. Katharine's Docks were begun in 1827, and publicly opened in 1828—a Herculean work, but performed with a speed and vigour unusual even to English enterprise.

The site of the docks, immediately below the Tower of London, is bounded on the north by East Smithfield, on the west and south by Tower Hill and Foss-side Road, while on the east they are separated from the London Docks by Nightingale Lane. The amount of capital originally raised by shares was between one and two million pounds, and was borrowed on the security of the rates to be received by the Company, for the liquidation of which debt a sinking fund was formed. Independently of the space actually occupied by the docks and warehouses, the Company possess freehold waterside property of the value of £100,000, which they were obliged to purchase by the terms of the Act of Parliament, and which yields a large annual rental, capable of very considerable improvement. In clearing the ground for this magnificent speculation, 1,250 houses and tenements were purchased and pulled down—no less than 11,300 inhabitants having to seek accommodation elsewhere.

The area thus obtained was about 24 acres, of which $11\frac{1}{2}$ acres are devoted to wet docks. The first stone was laid on the 3rd of May, 1827, and upwards of 2,500 men were employed on the work of construction from day to day.

The second ship that entered was the *Mary*, 343 tons, a Russian trader. She was laden with every description of Russian produce, and exhibited on board the pleasing spectacle of forty veteran pensioners from Greenwich, all of whom had served under Nelson at the battle of Trafalgar.

The permanent establishment of persons employed about the dock was for a long time only 100 officers and 120 labourers.

The last report of the Company in June, 1880, showed the earnings for six months had been £518,216 15s. 10d. ; the expenditure (exclusive of interest on debenture stock, &c.) to have been £352,829 14s. 9d. ; showing a half-year's balance of £165,387 1s. 1d. The number of loaded foreign ships which had entered the docks during the previous six months had been 785, measuring 754,503 tons. The goods landed had been 319,571 tons, and the stock of goods in the warehouses was 309,487 tons.

Mr. Mayhew, in his " London Labour," has some valuable notes on the unloading of ships in these docks, and on the labourers employed for that purpose :—

" The lofty walls," says Mr. Mayhew, " which constitute it, in the language of the Custom House, a place of special security, enclose an area capable of accommodating 120 ships, besides barges and other craft.

"Cargoes are raised into the warehouses out of the hold of a ship without the goods being deposited on the quay. The cargoes can be raised out of the ship's hold into the warehouses of St. Katharine's in one-fifth of the usual time. Before the existence of docks, a month or six weeks was taken up in discharging the cargo of an East Indiaman of from 800 to 1,200 tons burden ; while eight days were necessary in the summer, and fourteen in the winter, to unload a ship of 350 tons. At St. Katharine's, however, the average time now occupied in discharging a ship of 250 tons is twelve hours, and one of 500 tons two or three days, the goods being placed at the same time in the warehouse. There have been occasions when even greater dispatch has been used, and a cargo of 1,100 casks of tallow, averaging from 9 cwt. to 10 cwt. each, has been discharged in seven hours. This would have been considered little short of a miracle on the legal quays less than fifty years ago. In 1841, about 1,000 vessels and 10,000 lighters were accommodated at St. Katharine's Dock. The capital expended by the dock company exceeds £2,000,000 of money.

"The business of this establishment is carried on by 35 officers, 105 clerks and apprentices, 135 markers, samplers, and foremen, 250 permanent labourers, 150 preferable ticket labourers, propor‑ tioned to the amount of work to be done. The average number of labourers employed on any one day, in 1860, was 1,713, and the lowest number 515; so that the extreme fluctuation in the labour appears to be very nearly 1,200 hands. The lowest sum of money that was paid in 1848 for the day's work of the entire body of labourers employed was £64 7s. 6d., and the highest sum £214 2s. 6d.; being a difference of very nearly £150 in one day, or £900 in the course of the week. The average number of ships that enter the dock every week is 17; the highest number that entered in any one week in 1860 was 36, and the lowest 5, being a difference of 31. As‑ suming these to have been of an average burden of 300 tons, and that every such vessel would require 100 labourers to discharge its cargo in three days, then 1,500 extra hands ought to have been engaged to discharge the cargoes of the entire number in a week. This, it will be ob‑ served, is very nearly equal to the highest number of the labourers employed by the Company in the year 1848."

"Those persons," says Mr. Mayhew, "who are unable to live by the occupation to which they have been educated, can obtain a living there without any previous training. Hence we find men of every calling labouring at the docks. There are decayed and bankrupt master butchers, master bakers, publicans, grocers, old soldiers, old sailors, Polish refugees, broken-down gentle‑ men, discharged lawyers' clerks, suspended Go‑ vernment clerks, almsmen, pensioners, servants, thieves—indeed, every one who wants a loaf and is willing to work for it. The London dock is one of the few places in the metropolis where men can get employment without either character or recommendation; so that the labourers employed there are naturally a most incongruous assembly. Each of the docks employs several hundred hands to ship and discharge the cargoes of the numerous vessels that enter; and as there are some six or

seven of such docks attached to the metropolis, it may be imagined how large a number of indi‑ viduals are dependent on them for their sub‑ sistence."

The dock-work, says Mr. Mayhew, speaking of the dock labourers, whom he especially observed, may be divided into three classes. 1. Wheel-work, or that which is moved by the muscles of the legs and weight of the body. 2. Jigger, or winch-work, or that which is moved by the muscles of the arm. In each of these the labourer is stationary; but in the truck-work, which forms the third class, the labourer has to travel over a space of ground greater or less in proportion to the distance which the goods have to be removed.

The wheel-work is performed somewhat on the principle of the tread-wheel, with the exception that the force is applied inside, instead of outside, the wheel. From six to eight men enter a wooden cylinder or drum, upon which are nailed battens; and the men, laying hold of ropes, commence treading the wheel round, occasionally singing the while, and stamping time in a manner that is pleasant from its novelty. The wheel is generally about sixteen feet in diameter, and eight to nine feet broad; and the six or eight men treading within it will lift from sixteen to eighteen hundredweight, and often a ton, forty times an hour, an average of twenty-seven feet high. Other men will get out a cargo of from 800 to 900 casks of wine, each cask averaging about five hundredweight, and being lifted about eighteen feet, in a day and a half. At trucking, each man is said to go on an average thirty miles a day, and two-thirds of that time he is moving one and a-half hundredweight, at six miles and a-half per hour.

This labour, though requiring to be seen to be properly understood, must still appear so arduous, that one would imagine it was not of that tempting nature that 3,000 men could be found every day in London desperate enough to fight and battle for the privilege of getting two-and-sixpence by it; and even if they fail in "getting taken on" at the com‑ mencement of the day, that they should then retire to the appointed yard, there to remain hour after hour in the hope that the wind might blow them some stray ship, so that other gangs might be wanted, and the calling foreman seek them there. It is a curious sight to see the men waiting in these yards to be hired at fourpence an hour, for such are the terms given in the after part of the day. There, seated on long benches ranged round the wall, they remain, some telling their miseries and some their crimes to one another, whilst others doze away their time. Rain or sunshine, there

ST. KATHARINE'S DOCKS.

can always be found plenty to catch the stray shilling or eightpence. By the size of the shed you can tell how many men sometimes remain there in the pouring rain, rather than lose the chance of the stray hour's work. Some loiter on the bridges close by, and presently, as their practised eye or ear tells them that the calling foreman is in want of another gang, they rush forward in a stream towards the gate, though only six or eight at most can be hired out of the hundred or more that are waiting

vessels coming. It is a terrible proof how many of our population live on the very brink of starvation, and toil, like men in a leaky boat, only to keep off death.

In no single spot of London, not even at the Bank, could so vivid an impression of the vast wealth of England be obtained as at the Docks. Here roll casks of Burgundy, as they rolled in the reign of Edward III., on the eve of Poictiers; and there by their side are chests of tea, marked

ST. KATHARINE'S HOSPITAL.—THE BROTHERS' HOUSES IN 1781.

there. Again the same mad fight takes place as in the morning.

If you put the vessels belonging to the port of London at 3,000, and the steamers at 250 or 300, and the crews of which at 35,000 men and boys, it will be seen that the dock labourers required must be very numerous. Mr. Mayhew calculated that beside the great wealth of our docks there flows a parallel current of misery: a single day's east wind sometimes deprives 2,500 dock labourers of a day's living. He puts the men of this class at about 12,000 (it is, perhaps, even more now), and proves that their wages collectively vary from £1,500 a day to £500, and that 8,000 men are even thrown out of employ by a wind that prevents

all over with eastern characters, fresh from an empire where no English factory existed till the year 1680, after many unsuccessful efforts to baffle Portuguese jealousy; and near them are bales of exquisite silk from Yokohama—a place hardly safe for Englishmen till 1865. So our commerce has grown like the Jin, who arose from the leaden bottle, till it has planted one foot on Cape Horn and another on the Northern Pole. "How long will it continue to grow?" says the mournful philosopher. Our answer is, "As long as honour and truthfulness are the base of English trade; as long as freedom reigns in England; as long as our religion is heart-felt, and our Saxon nature energetic, patient, brave, and self-reliant."

CHAPTER XIV.

THE TOWER SUBWAY AND LONDON DOCKS.

London Apoplectic—Early Subways—The Tower Subway—London Breweries in the time of the Tudors—The West India, East India, and London Docks—A Tasting Order for the Docks—The "Queen's Pipe"—Curious "Treasure Trove."

IT has long been a question with English engineers, whether, as the wealth and population of the City increase, London must not some day or other be double-decked. The metropolis is growing plethoric, to use a medical metaphor—it makes so much blood; and if something is not done, a stoppage must ensue. A person disposed to fat sometimes grows larger the more depletive his diet; so increased railways (like the Metropolitan) seem rather to increase than lessen the general traffic. When that undertaking was opened in 1863 it was feared that the omnibuses from Paddington and Hyde Park would be driven off the line, for in the first year the railway carried 9,500,000 passengers. A little later it carried nearly 40,000,000 passengers; and since it began it has carried 150,000,000 persons to and fro. Yet at the present moment there are more omnibuses on this line of route from the West to the City than there were when the railway started, and they are earning one penny per mile a day more than they were before it was opened. These facts seem almost astounding; but the surprise disappears when we remember the fact, that in dealing with London passenger traffic we are dealing with a population greater than that of all Scotland, and more than two-thirds that of all Ireland; a population, too, which increases in a progressive ratio of about 42,000 a year. But with all this increase of numbers, which literally means increase of difficulty in moving about, the great streets most frequented grow not an inch wider. Fleet Street and "Old Chepe" are nearly as narrow as in the days of Elizabeth, when the barrier stood at Ludgate; and Thames Street, which is no wider than it was in the days of Alfred, is congested with its traffic twelve hours out of the twenty-four.

A few years ago Mr. Barlow, a very practical engineer, came forward to meet this crying want, and offered, at a cost of £16,000, in less than a year, to bore a subway through the bed of the Thames. The idea was not a new one. As early as 1799 an attempt had been made to construct a tunnel under the Thames between Gravesend and Tilbury; and in 1804 a similar work was actually begun between Rotherhithe and Limehouse, but after proceeding 1,000 feet, broke in; fifty-four engineers of the day deciding that such a work not only would never commercially pay, but was also impracticable.

Brunel's scheme of the Thames Tunnel cost half a million of money, and took twenty-one years' labour to complete.

Mr. Barlow's tunnel, from Tower Hill to Tooley Street, was of course looked upon as chimerical. Mr. Barlow, with less ambition and genius, but more common sense and thriftiness than his great predecessor, took good care to remember that the crown of Brunel's arches, in some places, came within four feet of the river water. In the Tower subway the average distance preserved is thirty feet, and in no place is there less than eighteen feet of sound London clay between the arch and the tideway. The cardinal principle of Mr. Barlow was to sink deep into the London clay, which is as impervious to water as stone, and in which no pumping would be required.

The works were begun on February 16, 1869, by breaking ground for the shaft on the north side of the river; in February, 1870, numerous visitors were conveyed from one shaft-head to the other. The tunnel commences, as we have said, at Tower Hill, where a hoarding encloses a small square of ground, not larger than an ordinary sitting-room, for which, however, the Government made the Company pay at the rate of about £240,000 an acre. In the centre of this is a little circular shaft, about fourteen feet diameter and sixty feet deep, and at the end of this, facing south, a clean, bright, vaulted chamber, which serves as a waiting-room. At the end of this chamber is the tunnel, a tube of iron not unlike the adit of a mine, which, in its darkness and silence, heightened by the knowledge that this grim-looking road runs down deeply below the bed of the river, gives it at first sight anything but an inviting appearance. The length of the whole tunnel is about 1,340 feet, or as nearly as possible about a quarter of a mile. From Tower Hill it runs in a south-west direction, and, passing under Barclay's brewery, opens under a shaft similar to that at entering, but only fifty feet deep, and out of this the passengers emerge within a few yards of Tooley Street, close to the railway station. From the Tower Hill shaft to the centre of the river the tunnel makes a dip of about one in thirty. From this point it rises again at the same incline to what we may call the Tooley Street station.

The method of constructing the tunnel, we need hardly remark, from its excessive cheapness, was simple in the extreme. It has been built in 18-inch lengths of cast-iron tubing, perfectly circular, each 18-inch circle being built up of three segments, with a key-piece at the top, which, fitting in like a wedge, holds the rest with the rigidity of a solid casting. The cast-iron shield used for excavation was less than two and a half tons weight. In front of the shield, which was slightly concave, was an aperture about two feet square, closed with a sliding iron water-tight door, and at the back of the shield were iron sockets, into which screw-jacks fitted, and, when worked by hand, forced the shield forward. The mode of advance was this. When a shaft on Tower Hill had been bored to a sufficient depth below the London clay, the shield was lowered and placed in its required position. The water-tight door we have spoken of as in the centre was then opened. Through this aperture sufficient clay, just of the consistency of hard cheese, was cut away by hand till a chamber was made large enough for a man, who entered and worked till there was room for two, and these soon made a circular space exactly the size of the shield and about two feet deep. This done, the miners came out, and with their screw-jacks forced the shield forward into the space which they had cut, but with the long telescope-like cap of the shield still over them. Under cover of this an 18-inch ring was quickly put in and bolted together; and while this was doing, the clay was being excavated from the front of the shield as before. Thus every eight hours, night and day, Sundays and week days, the shield went forward eighteen inches, and eighteen inches length of iron was added to the tube, which so advanced at the rate of 5 feet 4 inches every twenty-four hours.

The clay was so completely water-proof, that water had to be sent down to the workmen in cans to mix with the cement. No traces of fresh-water shells were found; but very large clay-stones and a great many sharks' teeth and marine shells. So perfect were Mr. Barlow's calculations, that the two opposite tunnels met within a quarter of an inch. The small interval between the iron and the clay was filled with blue lias cement, which coats the tube and protects it from oxidisation. The gain to the East-end of London by this successful and cleverly executed undertaking is enormous, and the intercourse between the north and south banks of the Thames is greatly facilitated; and the conception has been seized upon by Mr. Bateman as the basis of his well-known suggestion for a submarine tube to carry a railway from England to France. The Thames tube is 7 feet in clear internal diameter, and it originally carried a railway of 2 feet 6 inches gauge. On this railway formerly ran an omnibus capable of conveying twelve passengers. The omnibus was constructed of iron; it was light, but very strong, and ran upon eight wheels, and was connected with a rope of steel wire by means of a gripe that could be at any time tightened or relaxed at pleasure, and at each end of the tunnel this wire ran over a drum worked by means of a stationary engine.

If the carriage was stopped in the centre of the tunnel, the beat of the paddles of the steamers above could be heard, and even the hammering on board ships. In time there will be subways at Gravesend, Woolwich and Greenwich; and it has also been proposed to form one from St. George's Church in the Borough to Cannon Street. The Tower subway is now only used for foot-passengers, at a charge of one halfpenny.

On the river side, below St. Katharine's, says Pennant, on we hardly know what authority, stood, in the reign of the Tudors, the great breweries of London, or the "bere house," as it is called in the map of the first volume of the "Civitates Orbis." They were subject to the usual useful, yet vexatious, surveillance of the olden times; and in 1492 (Henry VII.) the king licensed John Merchant, a Fleming, to export fifty tuns of ale "called berre;" and in the same thrifty reign one Geoffrey Gate (probably an officer of the king's) spoiled the brew-houses twice, either by sending abroad too much beer unlicensed, or by brewing it too weak for the sturdy home customers. The demand for our stalwart English ale increased in the time of Elizabeth, in whose reign we find 500 tuns being exported at one time alone, and sent over to Amsterdam, probably, as Pennant thinks, for the use of our thirsty army in the Low Countries. The exportation then seems to have been free, except in scarce times, when it was checked by proclamation; but even then royal licences to brew could be bought for a consideration.

From the old brew-houses of Elizabeth in London, that have long since passed into dreamland, we must now guide our readers forward, under swinging casks and between ponderous wheels that seem to threaten instant annihilation, into the broad gateway of the London Docks, the most celebrated and central of all the semi-maritime brotherhood. The St. Katharine's Dock, with its twenty-four acres of water, can already accommodate 10,000 tons of goods, while the capital of the Company exceeds two million pounds. But all this dwindles into comparative insignificance beside the leviathan docks we have now to describe, which grasp an extent of 100 acres, and offer harbour-room for 500 ships and 34,000 tons of goods; the capital of the Company amounting to the enormous amount of four millions. Yet these again are dwarfed by the West India Docks, their richer neighbours, which are three times as extensive as the London Docks, having an area of no less than 295 acres, with water to accommodate 1,400 vessels, and warehouse-room for 180,000 tons of merchandise; the capital of the Company is more than six millions of pounds, and the value of goods which have been on the premises at one time twenty millions. Lastly, the East India Docks occupy 32 acres, and afford warehouse-room for 15,000 tons of goods.

The London Docks, built by Rennie, were opened in 1805. In 1858 two new docks were constructed for the larger vessels now built, and they have 28 feet depth of water. The wool floors were enlarged and glass-roofed in 1850. The annual importation is 130,000 bales. The vast tea warehouse, with stowage for 120,000 chests of tea, was completed in 1845, at a cost of £100,000. Six weeks are allowed for unloading a ship: a farthing a ton per week is charged for the first two weeks, then a halfpenny per week per ton. The great jetty and sheds, built in 1839, cost £60,000.

"As you enter the dock," says Mr. Mayhew, in a pleasant picture of the scene, "the sight of the forest of masts in the distance, and the tall chimneys vomiting clouds of black smoke, and the many-coloured flags flying in the air, has a most peculiar effect; while the sheds with the monster wheels arching through the roofs look like the paddle-boxes of huge steamers. Along the quay you see, now men with their faces blue with indigo, and now gaugers with their long brass-tipped rule dripping with spirit from the cask they have been probing. Then will come a group of flaxen-haired sailors, chattering German; and next a black sailor, with a cotton handkerchief twisted turban-like round his head. Presently a blue-smocked butcher, with fresh meat and a bunch of cabbages in the tray on his shoulder; and shortly afterwards a mate, with green paroquets in a wooden cage. Here you will see sitting on a bench a sorrowful-looking woman, with new bright cooking tins at her feet, telling you she is an emigrant preparing for her voyage. As you pass along this quay the air is pungent with tobacco; on that, it overpowers you with the fumes of rum; then you are nearly sickened with the stench of hides and huge bins of horns; and shortly afterwards the atmosphere is fragrant with coffee and spice.

Nearly everywhere you meet stacks of cork, or else yellow bins of sulphur, or lead-coloured copper ore. As you enter this warehouse the flooring is sticky, as if it had been newly tarred, with the sugar that has leaked through the casks; and as you descend into the dark vaults, you see long lines of lights hanging from the black arches, and lamps flitting about midway. Here you sniff the fumes of the wine, and there the peculiar fungus-smell of dry rot; there the jumble of sounds as you pass along the dock blends in anything but sweet concord. The sailors are singing boisterous nigger songs from the Yankee ship just entering; the cooper is hammering at the casks on the quay; the chains of the cranes, loosed of their weight, rattle as they fly up again; the ropes splash in the water; some captain shouts his orders through his hands: a goat bleats from some ship in the basin; and empty casks roll along the stones with a heavy, drum-like sound. Here the heavily-laden ships are down far below the quay, and you descend to them by ladders; whilst in another basin they are high up out of the water, so that their green copper sheathing is almost level with the eye of the passenger; while above his head a long line of bowsprits stretches far over the quay, and from them hang spars and planks as a gangway to each ship.

"This immense establishment is worked by from 1,000 to 3,000 hands, according as the business is either brisk or slack. Out of this number there are always 400 to 500 permanent labourers, receiving on an average 16s. 6d. per week, with the exception of coopers, carpenters, smiths, and other mechanics, who are paid the usual wages of those crafts. Besides these, there are many hundred—from 1,000 to 2,500—casual labourers, who are engaged at the rate of 2s. 6d. per day in the summer, and 2s. 4d. in the winter months. Frequently, in case of many arrivals, extra hands are hired in the course of the day, at the rate of 4d. an hour. For the permanent labourers a recommendation is required, but for the casual labourers no character is demanded. The number of the casual hands engaged by the day depends, of course, upon the amount of work to be done; and we find that the total number of labourers in the dock varies from 500 to 3,000 and odd. On the 4th of May, 1849, the number of hands engaged, both permanent and casual, was 2,794; on the 26th of the same month it was 3,012; and on the 30th it was 1,189. These appear to be the extreme of the variation for that year."

There are few Londoners with curiosity or leisure who have not at some time or other obtained "a tasting order for the docks." To all but the most prudent that visit has led to the same inglorious result. First there is "a coy, reluctant, amorous delay," a shy refusal of the proffered goblet, gradually an inquiring sip, then another; next arises a curious, half-scientific wish to compare vintages; and after that a determination, "being in for it," to acquire a rapid, however shallow, knowledge of comparative ages and qualities. On that supervenes a garrulous fluency of tongue that leads to high-flown remembrances of Spanish and French towns, illustrated by the songs of the peasantry of various countries. Upon that follows a lassitude and mute melancholy, which continues till the cooper seems suddenly to turn a screw which has long been evidently loose, and shoots you out into the stupefying open air. The chief features of such a visit are gravely treated by a writer in *Household Words :*—

"Proceeding down the dock-yard," says the writer in question, "you see before you a large area literally paved with wine-casks, all full of the most excellent wines. On our last visit, the wine then covering the ground was delicious Bordeaux, as you might easily convince yourself by dipping a finger into the bunghole of any cask; as, for some purpose of measurement or testing the quality, the casks were most of them open. This is, in fact, the great depôt of the wine of the London merchants, no less than 60,000 pipes being capable of being stored away in the vaults here. One vault alone, which formerly was seven acres, has now been extended under Gravel Lane, so that at present it contains upwards of twelve acres. These vaults are faintly lit with lamps, but, on going in, you are at the entrance accosted with the singular demand, 'Do you want a cooper?' Many people, not knowing its meaning, say, 'No, by no means.' The meaning of the phrase is, 'Do you want to taste the wines?' when a cooper accompanies you, to pierce the casks and give you the wine. Parties are every day, and all day long, making these exploratory and tasting expeditions. Every one, on entering, is presented with a lamp, at the end of a lath about two feet long, and you soon find yourselves in some of the most remarkable caving in the world. From the dark vaulted roof overhead, especially in one vault, hang strange figures, black as night, light as gossamer, and of a yard or more of length, resembling skins of beasts, or old shirts dipped in soot. They are fed to this strange growth by the fumes of the wine. For those who taste the wines the cooper bores the heads of the pipes, which are ranged throughout these vast cellars on either hand, in thousands and tens of thousands,

and draws a glassful. These glasses, though shaped as wine-glasses, resemble much more goblets in their size, containing each as much as several ordinary wine-glasses. What you do not drink is thrown upon the ground; and it is calculated that at least a hogshead a day is thus consumed."

In the centre of the great east vault of the wine cellars, you come to a circular building without any entrance; it is the root and foundation of the Queen's Pipe. Quitting the vault and ascending to the warehouse over it, you find that you are in the great tobacco warehouse, called the Queen's Warehouse, because the Government rent the tobacco warehouses here for £14,000 per annum. "This one warehouse has no equal," says a writer on the subject, "in any other part of the world; it is five acres in extent, and yet it is covered with a roof, the framework of which is of iron, erected, we believe, by Mr. Barry, the architect of the new Houses of Parliament, and of so light and skilful a construction, that it admits of a view of the whole place; and so slender are the pillars, that the roof seems almost to rest upon nothing. Under this roof is piled a vast mass of tobacco in huge casks, in double tiers—that is, two casks in height. This warehouse is said to hold, when full, 24,000 hogsheads averaging 1,200 pounds each, and equal to 30,000 tons of general merchandise. Each cask is said to be worth, duty included, £200, giving a sum total of tobacco in this one warehouse, when filled, of £4,800,000 in value! Besides this there is another warehouse of nearly equal size, where finer kinds of tobacco are deposited, many of them in packages of buffalo-hide, marked 'Giron,' and Manilla for cheroots, in packages of sacking lined with palmetto-leaves. There is still another warehouse for cigars, called the Cigar Floor, in which there are frequently 1,500 chests, valued at £100 each, at an average, or £150,000 in cigars alone."

The dock kiln, or "the Queen's Pipe," are objects of general curiosity not to be forgotten in our description of the London Docks. The kiln is the place where useless or damaged goods that have not paid duty are destroyed. It is facetiously called "the Queen's Pipe" by the Custom House clerks and tide-waiters.

"On a guide-post in the docks is painted in large letters, 'To the kiln.' Following this direction, you arrive at the centre of the warehouse, and at the Queen's Pipe. You enter a door on which are rudely painted the crown royal and the initials 'V. R.,' and find yourself in a room of considerable size, in the centre of which towers up the kiln, a furnace of the conical kind, like a glass-house or porcelain furnace; on the door of the furnace are again painted the crown and the 'V. R.' Here you find in the furnace a huge mass of fire, and around are heaps of damaged tobacco, tea, and other articles, ready to be flung upon it. This fire never goes out day or night from year to year. There is an attendant who supplies it with its fuel as it can take it, and some time ago set the chimney of the kiln on fire, is now rarely burnt ; and strange are the things that sometimes come to this perpetually burning furnace. On one occasion, the attendant informed us he burnt 900 Australian mutton-hams. These were warehoused before the duty came off. The owner

THE TOWER SUBWAY.

men, during the day-time, constantly come laden with great loads of tobacco, cigars, and other stuff, condemned to the flames. Whatever is forfeited, and is too bad for sale, be it what it will, is doomed to the kiln. At the other docks damaged goods, we were assured, are buried till they are partly rotten, and then taken up and disposed of as rubbish or manure. Here the Queen's Pipe smokes all up, except the greater quantity of the tea, which, having suffered them to remain till the duty ceased, in hopes of their being exempt from it ; but this not being allowed, they were left till so damaged as to be unsaleable. Yet a good many, the man declared, were excellent; and he often made a capital addition to his breakfast from the roast that, for some time, was so odoriferously going on. On another occasion he burnt 13,000 pairs of condemned French gloves." (*Household Words*, ii. 357.)

THE THAMES TUNNEL (*as it appeared when originally opened for traffic*).

"In one department of the place," says the same writer, "often lie many tons of the ashes from the furnace, which are sold by auction, by the ton, to gardeners and farmers, as manure and for killing insects, to soap-boilers, and chemical manufacturers. In a corner are generally to be found piled cart-loads of nails, and other pieces of iron, which have been swept up from the floors, or which have remained in the broken pieces of casks and boxes which go to the kiln. Those which have been sifted from the ashes are eagerly bought up by gunsmiths, sorted, and used in the manufacture of gun-barrels, for which purpose they are highly esteemed, as possessing a toughness beyond all other iron, and therefore calculated pre-eminently to prevent bursting."

CHAPTER XV.

THE THAMES TUNNEL, RATCLIFF HIGHWAY, AND WAPPING.

Sub-river Tunnels in the Coal-mining Districts—First Proposals for a Tunnel under the Thames—Its Commencement—A Dangerous Irruption—Brave Labourers—A Terrible Crisis—Narrow Escapes—The Last Irruptions—The Tunnel opened for Traffic—Ratcliff Highway—The Wild Beast Shops—The Marr and Williamson Murders—Swedenborg—Wapping—Hanging the Pirates in Chains—Townsend's Evidence—Capture of Jeffreys—Stag Hunting in Wapping—Boswell's Futile Exploration—The Fuchsia—Public-house Signs—Wapping Old Stairs—Shadwell and its Springs.

SUB-RIVER tunnels are not unfrequent in the coal-mining districts of the north of England. The beds of both the Tyne and the Wear are pierced in this manner; while at Whitehaven, and at the Botallack mines in Cornwall, the bed of the ocean has been penetrated for long distances, the tunnel at the former place extending upwards of a mile beneath the sea. At the close of the last century a North-country engineer proposed a sub-aqueous passage to connect North and South Shields, but the scheme was never carried out. The same gentleman then proposed the tunnel from Gravesend to Tilbury, mentioned by us in the preceding chapter; but it was soon abandoned as impracticable, as was also a Cornish miner's proposal to connect Rotherhithe with Limehouse.

In 1823, however, a bolder, more reckless, and far-seeing mind took up the project, and Mr. Brunel (backed by the Duke of Wellington and the eminent Dr. Wollaston) seriously submitted a plan of a tunnel to the public, and so practical a man soon obtained listeners. With his usual imaginative sagacity he had gone to Nature, and there found allies. The hard cylindrical shell of the soft-footed teredo (*Calamitas navium*, as Linnæus calls it), which eats its way, in small tubular tunnels, even through the tough timbers of men-of-war, had suggested to the great engineer a shield under which his workmen could shelter.

The communication between the Surrey shore and the Wapping side was most important, as the wharves for the coasting trade of England lay chiefly on the Surrey bank, and traffic had to be conveyed by carts to the Tower-side docks. In 1829, out of 887 wagons and 3,241 carts that passed over London Bridge southwards, 480 of the first and 1,700 of the second were found to turn down Tooley Street. It was also ascertained that the 350 watermen of the neighbourhood took over the Thames no less than 3,700 passengers daily.

In 1824 a company was formed to construct a tunnel, and an Act of Parliament was obtained. The preliminary step was three parallel borings, like cheese-tastings, made beneath the bed of the Thames, in the direction of the proposed tunnel. As to the level to be taken, Mr. Brunel consulted the geologists, who for once were not happy in their theories. They informed the engineer that below a certain depth a quicksand would be found, and he must therefore keep above it, and as close as possible to the stratum of firm clay forming the bed of the river. The Tower Subway has since shown the absurdity of this theory, and the folly of not making preliminary experiments, however costly. If the tunnel had been begun in a different place, and at the deep level of the Tower Subway, Mr. Brunel would have saved twenty years of labour, many lives, and about a quarter of a million of money.

In March, 1825, the laborious and for a long time unsuccessful work was begun, by erecting a round brick cylinder 42 feet high, 150 feet in circumference, and 150 feet distant from the river. The excavators then commenced on the inside, cutting away the earth, which was raised to the top of the shaft by a steam-engine placed there, which also relieved them from the water that occasionally impeded their progress. The engine raised 400 gallons a minute, and at a later stage served to draw carriages along the temporary tunnel railway, and also hoisted up and let down all things required by the masons. The bricklayers kept heightening their little circular fort as they themselves sank deeper in the earth. By this shaft Mr. Brunel congratulated himself he had evaded the bed of gravel and sand 26 feet deep, and full of land-water, which had annoyed his predecessors. When the shaft was sunk to its present depth of 65 feet, another shaft of 25 feet diameter was sunk lower; and at the depth of 80 feet the ground suddenly gave way, and sand and water were, as Mr. Saunders describes it, "blown up with some violence."

The tunnel itself was begun at the depth of 63 feet. Mr. Brunel proposed to make his tunnel 38 feet broad and $22\frac{1}{2}$ feet high, leaving room within for two archways each 15 feet high, and each wide enough for a single carriage-way and a footpath. The wonderful teredo shield, a great invention for a special object, consisted of twelve separate divisions, each containing three cells, one above another. When an advance was required, the men in their cells pulled down the top poling-board defences, and cut away the earth about six inches; the poling-boards in each division below were then *seriatim* removed, and the same amount of earth removed, and then replaced. "Each of the divisions," says a describer of the shield, "was then advanced by the application of two screws, one at its head and one at its foot, which, resting against the finished brick-work of the tunnel, impelled the shield forward into the new-cut space. The other set of divisions then advanced." As the miners were at work at one end of the cells, the bricklayers at the other were busy as bees forming the brick walls of the tunnel, top, sides, and bottom, the crushing earth above being fended off by the shield till the bricklayers had finished. Following the shield was a rolling stage in each archway, for the assistance of the men in the upper cells.

The difficulties, however, from not keeping to the stiff, firm, and impervious London clay, proved almost insuperable, even to Mr. Brunel. The first nine feet of the tunnel, driven through firm clay, in the early part of the year 1826, were followed by a dangerously-loose watery sand, which cost thirty-two anxious days' labour. From March to September all went well, and 260 feet of the tunnel were completed. On the 14th of September Brunel prophesied an irruption of the river at the next tide. It came, but the precautions taken had rendered it harmless. By the 2nd of January, 1827, 350 feet were accomplished, but loose clay forced itself through the shield. In April, the bed of the river had to be explored in a diving-bell. Bags of clay were used to fill up depressions.

A shovel and hammer, accidentally left in the river, were afterwards found in the shield during an influx of loose ground, eighteen feet below. In May, however, came the long-expected disaster, chiefly caused by two vessels coming in at a late tide, and mooring just above the head of the tunnel, causing a great washing away of the soil round them. Mr. Beamish, the resident assistant engineer, thus graphically describes the irruption:—

"As the water," he writes, "rose with the tide, it increased in the frames very considerably between Nos. 5 and 6, forcing its way at the front, then at the back; Ball and Compton (the occupants) most active. About a quarter before six o'clock, No. 11 (division) went forward. Clay appeared at the back. Had it closed up immediately. While this was going forward my attention was again drawn to No. 6, where I found the gravel forcing itself with the water. It was with the utmost difficulty that Ball could keep anything against the opening. Fearing that the pumpers would now become alarmed, as they had been once or twice before, and leave their post, I went upon the east stage to encourage them, and to choose more shoring for Ball. Goodwin, who was engaged at No. 11, where indications of a run appeared, called to Rogers, who was in the act of working down No. 9, to come to his assistance. But Rogers, having his second poling (board) down, could not. Goodwin again called. I then said to Rogers, "Don't you hear?" upon which he left his poling for the purpose of assisting Goodwin; but before he could get to him, and before I could get fairly into the frames, there poured such an overwhelming volume of water and sludge as to force them out of the frames. William Carps, a bricklayer, who had gone to Goodwin's assistance, was knocked down and literally rolled out of the frames on the stage, as though he had come through a mill-sluice, and would undoubtedly have fallen off the stage had I not caught hold of him, and with Rogers' assistance helped him down the ladder. I again made an attempt to get into the frames, calling upon the miners to follow; but all was dark (the lights at the frames and stage being all blown out), and I was only answered by the hoarse and angry sounds of Father Thames's roarings. Rogers (an old sergeant of the Guards), the only man left upon the stage, now caught my arm, and gently drawing me from the frames, said, 'Come away, pray, sir, come away; 'tis no use, the water is rising fast.' I turned once more; but hearing an increased rush at No. 6, and finding the column of water at Nos. 11 and 12 to be augmenting, I reluctantly descended. The cement casks, compo-boxes, pieces of timber were floating around me. I turned into the west arch, where the enemy had not yet advanced so rapidly, and again looked towards the frames, lest some one might have been overtaken ; but the cement casks, &c., striking my legs, threatened seriously to obstruct my retreat, and it was with some difficulty I reached the visitors' bar " (a bar so placed as to keep the visitors from the unfinished works), " where Mayo, Bertram, and others were anxiously waiting to receive me. . . . I was glad of their assistance ; indeed, Mayo fairly dragged me over it. Not bearing the idea of so precipitate a retreat, I turned once more ; but vain was the hope ! The wave rolled onward and onward ; the men retreated, and I followed. Met Gravatt coming down. Short was the question, and brief was the answer. As we approached I met I. [Isambard] Brunel. We turned round : the effect was splendid beyond description. The water as it rose became more and more vivid, from the reflected lights of the gas. As we reached the staircase a crash was heard, and then a rush of air at once extinguished all the lights. . . . . Now it was that I experienced something like dread. I looked up the shaft, and saw both stairs crowded ; I looked below, and beheld the overwhelming wave appearing to move with accumulated velocity.

" Dreading the effect of the reaction of this wave from the back of the shaft upon our staircase, I exclaimed to Mr. Gravatt, 'The staircase will blow up !' I. Brunel ordered the men to get up with all expedition ; and our feet were scarcely off the bottom stairs when the first flight, which we had just left, was swept away. Upon our reaching the top, a bustling noise assailed our ears, some calling for a raft, others for a boat, and others again a rope ; from which it was evident that some unfortunate individual was in the water. I. Brunel instantly, with that presence of mind to which I have been more than once witness, slid down one of the iron ties, and after him Mr. Gravatt, each making a rope fast to old Tillet's waist, who, having been looking after the packing of the pumps below the shaft, was overtaken by the flood. He was soon placed out of danger. The roll was immediately called—*not one absent.*"

The next step was to repair the hole in the river-bed. Its position being ascertained by the diving-bell, three thousand bags of clay, spiked with small hazel rods, were employed to effectually close it. In a few weeks the water was got under, and by the middle of August the tunnel was cleared of the soil that had washed in, and the engineer was able to examine his shattered fortifications. In all essentials the structure remained perfectly sound,

though a part of the brickwork close to the shield had been washed away to half its original thickness, and the chain which had held together the divisions of the shield had snapped like a cotton thread. The enemy—so powerless when kept at a distance, so irresistible at its full strength—had driven deep into the ground heavy pieces of iron belonging to the shield.

Amid all these dangers the men displayed great courage and perseverance. Brunel's genius had roused them to a noble and generous disregard of the opposing principles of nature. The alarms were frequent, the apprehension incessant. At any moment the deluge might come ; and the men worked, like labourers in a dangerous coal mine, in constant terror from either fire or water. Now and then a report like a cannon-shot would announce the snap of some portion of the overstrained shield ; sometimes there were frightened cries from the foremost workers, as the earth and water rushed in and threatened to sweep all before them. At the same time during these alarming irruptions, large quantities of carburetted and sulphuretted hydrogen would burst into fire, and wrap the whole place in a sudden sheet of flame. Those who witnessed these explosions describe the effect of the fire dancing on the surface of the water as singularly beautiful. The miners and bricklayers, encouraged by the steadfast hand at the helm, got quite accustomed to these outbursts, and, at the shout of " Fire and water !" used to cry, " Light your pipes my boys," reckless as soldiers in the trenches.

But still worse than these violent protests of Nature was a more subtle and deadly enemy. The air grew so thick and impure, especially in summer, that sometimes the most stalwart labourers were carried out insensible, and all the workmen suffered from headache, sickness, and cutaneous eruptions. It was a great struggle, nobly borne. They shared Brunel's anxieties, and were eager for a share of his fame, for he had inspired the humblest hodman with something of his own high impulse. " It was touching," writes a chronicler of the tunnel, " to hear the men speak of Brunel. As in their waking hours these men could have no thought but of the tunnel, so, no doubt, did the eternal subject constantly mingle with their dreams, and harass them with unreal dangers. One amusing instance may be mentioned. Whilst Mr. Brunel, jun., was engaged one midnight superintending the progress of the work, he and those with him were alarmed by a sudden cry of ' The water ! the water !—wedges and straw here !' followed by an appalling silence. Mr. Brunel hastened to the spot, where the men were found perfectly safe. They had fallen fast asleep from fatigue, and one of them had been evidently dreaming of a new irruption."

By January, 1828, the middle of the river had been reached, and no human life had yet been sacrificed. But, as if the evil principle had only retired to prepare for a fresh attack, a terrible crisis now came. " I had been in the frames," says Mr. Brunel, jun., in a letter written to the directors on the fatal Saturday, August 12th, 1828, "with the workmen throughout the whole night, having taken my station there at ten o'clock. During the workings through the night no symptoms of insecurity appeared. At six o'clock this morning (the usual time for shifting the men) a fresh set came on to work. We began to work the ground at the west top corner of the frame. The tide had just then begun to flow, and finding the ground tolerably quiet, we proceeded by beginning at the top, and had worked about a foot downwards, when, on exposing the next six inches, the ground swelled suddenly, and a large quantity burst through the opening thus made. This was followed instantly by a large body of water. The rush was so violent as to force the man on the spot where the burst took place out of the frame (or cell) on to the timber stage behind the frames. I was in the frame with the man; but upon the rush of the water I went into the next box, in order to command a better view of the irruption; and seeing there was no possibility of their opposing the water, I ordered all the men in the frames to retire. All were retiring except the three men who were with me, and they retreated with me. I did not leave the stage until those three men were down the ladder of the frames, when they and I proceeded about twenty feet along the west arch of the tunnel. At this moment the agitation of the air by the rush of the water was such as to extinguish all the lights, and the water had gained the height of the middle of our waists. I was at that moment giving directions to the three men, in what manner they ought to proceed in the dark to effect their escape, when they and I were knocked down and covered by a part of the timber stage. I struggled under water for some time, and at length extricated myself from the stage; and by swimming and being forced by the water, I gained the eastern arch, where I got a better footing, and was enabled, by laying hold of the railway rope, to pause a little, in the hope of encouraging the men who had been knocked down at the same time with myself. This I endeavoured to do by calling to them. Before I reached the shaft the water had risen so rapidly that I was out of my depth, and therefore swam to the visitors' stairs, the stairs of the workmen being occupied by those who had so far escaped. My knee was so injured by the timber stage that I could scarcely swim or get up the stairs, but *the rush of the water carried me up the shaft.* The three men who had been knocked down with me were unable to extricate themselves, and I grieve to say they are lost, and, I believe, also two old men and one young man in other parts of the work."

This was a crisis indeed. The alarmists grew into a majority, and the funds of the company were exhausted. The hole in the river-bed was discovered by the divers to be very formidable; it was oblong and perpendicular, and measured about seven feet in length. The old mode of mending was resorted to. Four thousand tons of earth (chiefly clay, in bags) were employed to patch the place. The tunnel remained as substantial as ever, but the work was for seven years suspended. Brunel, whose tenacity of purpose was unshakable, was almost in a state of frenzy at this accident. So far his plan had apparently failed, but the engineer's star had not yet forsaken him. In January, 1835, the Government, after many applications, agreed to make some advances for the continuation of the work, and it was once more resumed with energy. The progress was at first very slow; for, of sixty-six weeks, two feet four inches only per week were accomplished during the first eighteen, three feet nine inches per week during the second eighteen, one foot per week during the third eighteen, and during the last twelve weeks only three feet four inches altogether. This will excite little surprise when we know, says a clever writer on the subject, that the ground in front of the shield was, from excessive saturation, almost constantly in little better than a fluid state; that an entire new and artificial bed had to be formed in the river in advance; and brought down by ingenious contrivances till it was deep enough to occupy the place of the natural soil where the excavation was to be made, and that then there must be time allowed for its settlement, whenever the warning rush of sand and water was heard in the shield. Lastly, owing to the excavation being so much below that of any other works around the tunnel, it formed a drain and receptacle for all the water of the neighbourhood. This was ultimately remedied by the sinking of the shaft on the Wapping side. Yet it was under such circumstances that the old shield injured by the last irruption was taken away and replaced by a new one. This was executed by Brunel without the loss of a single life. But now fresh difficulties arose: the expenditure had been so great that the Lords of the Treasury declined to make further advances without the sanction of Parliament. The examination of Mr. Brunel and the assistant engineers before a Parliamentary Committee led, however, to favourable results, and the work was again renewed.

In August, 1837, a third irruption and several narrow escapes occurred. The water had gradu-

a platform constructed by Mr. Brunel in the east arch only a few weeks before. As the water still continued rising, after the men left, Mr. Page, the acting engineer, and four others, got into the boat, in order to reach the stages and see if any change had taken place; but after passing the 600 feet mark in

A WILD-BEAST SHOP. (*See page* 134.)

ally increased at the east corner, since two p.m. on the 23rd, rushing into the shield with a hollow roar, as though it fell through a cavity in the river-bed. A boat was then sent into the tunnel, to convey material to block up the frames. Notwithstanding, the water gained upon the men, and rapidly rose in the tunnel. About four p.m., the water having risen to within seven feet of the crown of the arch, it was thought wise for the men to retire, which they did with great courage, along

the tunnel the line attached to the boat ran out, and they returned to lengthen it. This accident saved their lives, for while they were preparing the rope the water surged up the arch ten or twelve feet. They instantly made their way to the shaft, and Mr. Page, fearing the men might get jammed in the staircase, called to them to go steadily; but they, misunderstanding him, returned, and could hardly be prevailed upon to go up. Had the line been long enough, all the persons in the boat must have perished, for no less than a million gallons of water now burst into the tunnel in a single minute. The lower gas-lights were now under water, and the tunnel was almost in darkness. The water had now risen to within fifty feet of the entrance of the tunnel, and was advancing in a wave. As Mr. Page and his assistants arrived at the second landing of the visitors' stairs, the waves had risen up to the knees of the last man.

The next irruption was in November, 1837, when the water burst in about four in the morning, and soon filled the tunnel. Excellent arrangements had been made for the safety of the men, and all the seventy or more persons employed at the time escaped, but one—he alone did not answer when the roll was called; and some one remembered seeing a miner going towards the shield when all he rest were escaping. The fifth and last serious irruption occurred on March 6, 1838. It was preceded by a noise resembling thunder, but no loss of life occurred.

The last feeble struggle of the river against its persistent enemy was in April, 1840. About eight a.m., it being then low water, during a movement of the poling-boards in the shield, a quantity of gravel and water rushed into the frame. The

ground rushed in immediately, and knocked the men out of their cells, and they fled in a panic; but finding the water did not follow, they returned, and by great exertions succeeded in stopping the run, when upwards of 6,000 cubic feet of ground had fallen into the tunnel. The fall was attended with a noise like thunder, and the extinguishing of all the lights. At the same time, to the horror of Wapping, part of the shore in that place sank, over an area of upwards of 700 feet, leaving a

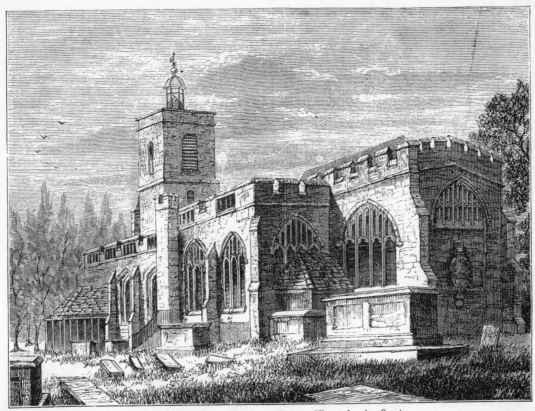

ST. DUNSTAN'S, STEPNEY.   (*From a View taken in* 1803.)

cavity on the shore of about thirty feet in diameter, and thirteen feet in depth. Had this taken place at high water, the tunnel would have been filled; as it was, men were sent over with bags of clay and gravel, and everything rendered secure by the return of the tide.

Sometimes sand, nearly fluid, would ooze through minute cracks between the small poling-boards of the shield, and leave large cavities in the ground in front. On one of these occasions the sand poured in all night, and filled the bottom of the shield. In the morning, on opening one of the faces, a hollow was discovered, eighteen feet long, six feet high, and six feet deep. This cavity was filled up with brickbats and lumps of clay. One of the miners was compelled to lay himself down in this cavity, for the purpose of building up the further end, though at the risk of being buried alive.

At last, on the 13th of August, 1841, Sir Isambard Brunel passed down the shaft on the Wapping side of the Thames, and thence, by a small drift-way through the shield, into the tunnel, and emerged on the opposite side. The difficulties of the great work had at last been surmounted.

The tunnel measures 1,200 feet. The carriageways were originally intended to consist of an immense spiral road, winding twice round a circular excavation 57 feet deep, in order to reach the proper level. The extreme diameter of this spiral road was to be no less than 200 feet. The road itself was to have been 40 feet wide, and the descent very moderate. The tunnel is now turned into a part of the East London Railway, and forms a junction between the Great Eastern Railway and the various branches of the Brighton Railway on the south of the Thames.

Ratcliff Highway, now called St. George Street, is the Regent Street of London sailors, who, in many instances, never extend their walks in the metropolis beyond this semi-marine region. It derives its name from the manor of Ratcliffe in the parish of Stepney. Stow describes it as so increased in building eastward in his time that, instead of a large highway, " with fair elm-trees on both the sides," as he had known it, it had joined Limehurst or Lime host, corruptly called Limehouse, a mile distant from Ratcliffe. In Dryden's miscellaneous poems, Tom, one of the characters, remarks that he had heard a ballad about the Protector Somerset sung at Ratcliff Cross.

The wild-beast shops in this street have often been sketched by modern essayists. The yards in the neighbourhood are crammed with lions, hyenas, pelicans, tigers, and other animals in demand among the proprietors of menageries. As many as ten to fifteen lions are often in stock at one time, and sailors come here to sell their pets and barter curiosities. The ingenious way in which animals are stored in these out-of-the-way places is well worth seeing.

Ratcliff Highway has not been the scene of many very memorable events. In 1811, however, it was startled by a series of murders that for a time struck all London with terror, and produced a deep conviction in the public mind that the old watchmen who then paraded the City were altogether insufficient to secure the safety of its inhabitants. Mr. Marr, the first victim, kept a lace and pelisse shop at No. 29, Ratcliff Highway. At about twelve at night on Saturday, December 7, 1811, he sent out his servant-girl to purchase some oysters for supper,

while he shut up the shop-windows. On the girl's return, in a quarter of an hour, she rang the bell, but obtained no answer. As she listened at the key-hole, she thought she could hear a person breathing at the same aperture ; she therefore gave the alarm. On the shop being broken open, Mr. Marr was found dead behind the counter, Mrs. Marr and the shop-boy dead in another part of the shop, and a child murdered in the cradle. The murderer had, it was supposed, used a ship-mallet, and had evidently come in on pretence of purchasing goods, as Marr had been reaching down some stockings when he was struck. Very little if any money was missed from the till. Twelve days after, before the horror and alarm caused by these murders could subside, other crimes followed. On the 19th of December, Williamson, the landlord of the King's Arms public-house, Old Gravel Lane, Ratcliff Highway, with his wife, and female servant were also murdered. An apprentice who lodged at the house, coming down-stairs in alarm at hearing a door slam, saw the murderer stooping and taking the keys out of the pocket of Mrs. Williamson. The murderer heard him, and pursued him upstairs ; but the lad, fastening his sheets to a bed, let himself down out of window into the street. The murderer, a sailor named Williams, escaped, though the house was almost instantly surrounded ; but was soon after captured at a sailors' boarding-house, where a knife stained with blood was afterwards found secreted. The wretch hanged himself in prison the night of his arrest. His body was placed on a platform in a high cart, with the mallet and ripping chisel, with which he had committed the murders, by his side, and driven past the houses of Marr and Williamson. A stake was then driven through his breast, and his carcase thrown into a hole dug for the purpose, where the New Road crosses and Cannon Street Road begins.

It was remembered afterwards by a girl to whom the murderer had been attached, that he had once asked her if she should be frightened if she awoke in the night and saw him standing with a knife by her bedside. The girl replied, " I should feel no fear, Mr. Williams, when I saw your face." Very little was discovered of the man's antecedents, but it is said that the captain of the East Indiaman in which he had sailed had predicted his speedy death by the gallows. These murders excited the imagination of De Quincey, the opium-eater, who wrote a wonderful though not strictly accurate version of the affair. Macaulay, writing of the alarm in England at the supposed murder of Sir Edmundbury Godfrey, says, " Many of our readers can remember the state of London just after the

murder of Marr and Williamson; the terror which
was on every face; the careful barring of doors;
the providing of blunderbusses and watchmen's
rattles. We know of a shopkeeper who on that
occasion sold 300 rattles in about ten hours.
Those who remember that panic may be able to
form some notion of the state of England after the
death of Godfrey."

In the Swedish Church, Princes Square, Ratcliff
Highway, lies buried that extraordinary man,
Emmanuel Swedenborg, who died in 1772, and
after whom the Swedenborgians—or New Jerusalem
Church—are called. The New Jerusalem Church
was organised in 1787, fifteen years after the
death of Swedenborg, by a few admirers of his
writings.

We now come to Wapping, that nautical hamlet of
Stepney, a long street extending from Lower East
Smithfield to New Crane. It was begun in 1571,
to secure the manor from the encroachments of the
river, which had turned this part of the north bank
of the Thames into a great wash or swamp; the
Commissioners of Sewers rightly imagining that
when building once began, the tenants would not
fail to keep out the river, for the sake of their own
lives and properties. Stow calls it Wapping-in-
the-Wose, or Wash; and Strype describes it as a
place "chiefly inhabited by seafaring men, and
tradesmen dealing in commodities for the supply
of shipping and shipmen."

It must have been a dirty, dangerous place in
Stow's time, when it was chiefly remarkable as being
the place of execution for pirates. Stow says
of it—"The usual place for hanging of pirates and
sea-rovers, at the low-water mark, and there to
remain till three tides had overflowed them; was
never a house standing within these forty years,
but since the gallows being after removed farther
off, a continual street, or filthy strait passage, with
alleys of small tenements or cottages built, inhabited by sailor's victuallers, along by the river
of Thames, almost to Radcliffe, a good mile from
the Tower."

Pirates were hung at East Wapping as early as
the reign of Henry VI., for in a "Chronicle of
London," edited by Sir Harris Nicolas, we read
that in this reign two bargemen were hung beyond
St. Katharine's, for murdering three Flemings and
a child in a Flemish vessel; "and there they
hengen till the water had washed them by ebbying
and flowyd, so the water bett upon them." And
as late as 1735 we read in the *Gentleman's
Magazine*, "Williams the pirate was hanged at
Execution Dock, and afterwards in chains at
Bugsby's Hole, near Blackwall." Howell, in his

"Londinopolis," 1657, says, "From the Liberties
of St. Katharine to Wapping, 'tis yet in the memory
of man, there never was a house standing but
the gallowes, which was further removed in regard
of the buildings. But now there is a continued
street, towards a mile long, from the Tower all
along the river, almost as far as Radcliffe,
which proceedeth from the increase of navigation,
mariners, and trafique." In one of those wild
romantic plays of the end of the Shakespearean
era, *Fortune by Land and Sea*, a tragi-comedy by
Thomas Heywood and William Rowley, the writer
fixes one scene near Execution Dock, where two
pirates, called Purser and Clinton, are brought to
die. One of these men delivers himself of a grand
rhapsody—

"How many captains that have aw'd the seas
Shall fall on this unfortunate piece of land !
Some that commanded islands; some to whom
The Indian mines paid tribute, the Turk vailed.
　　*　　　*　　　*　　　*
"But now our sun is setting; night comes on ;
The watery wilderness o'er which we reigned
Proves in our ruins peaceful. Merchants trade,
Fearless abroad as in the rivers' mouth,
And free as in a harbour. Then, fair Thames,
Queen of fresh water, famous through the world,
And not the least through us, whose double tides
Must overflow our bodies ; and, being dead,
May thy clear waves our scandals wash away,
But keep our valours living."

The audience, no doubt, sympathised with these
gallant filibusters, whose forays and piracies against
Spain would be thought by many present very
venial offences.

In 1816 Townsend, the celebrated Bow Street
runner, was examined before a Committee of the
House of Commons, on the decrease of highway-
men, and other questions connected with the police
of the metropolis. He was particularly questioned
as to the advantage of hanging men in chains.
The sturdy old officer, with the memorable white
hat, was strongly for the custom. "Yes," he said,
"I was always of that opinion, and I recommended
Sir William Scott to hang the two men that are
hanging down the river. I will state my reason.
We will take for granted that those men were
hanged, as this morning, for the murder of those
revenue officers. They are by law dissected. The
sentence is that afterwards the body is to go to
the surgeons for dissection. There is an end of
it—it dies. But look at this. There are a couple
of men now hanging near the Thames, where all
the sailors must come up; and one says to the
other, 'Pray, what are those two poor fellows there
for?' 'Why,' says another, 'I will go and ask.'
They ask. 'Why, these two men are hung and

gibbeted for murdering His Majesty's revenue officers.' And so the thing is kept alive."

In one of Hogarth's series of the Idle and Industrious Apprentices, the artist has introduced a man hanging in chains farther down the river ; and a friend of the author remembers seeing a pirate hung in chains on the Thames bank, and a crow on his shoulder, pecking his flesh through the iron netting that enclosed the body.

Wapping, it will be remembered, was in 1688 the scene of the capture of the cruel minister of James II., Lord Chancellor Jeffreys, who, trying to make his escape in the disguise of a common seaman, was surprised in a mean ale-house, called the "Red Cow," in Anchor-and-Hope Alley, near King Edward's Stairs, in Wapping. He was recognised by a poor scrivener, whom he had once terrified when in his clutches, as he was lolling out of window, confident in his security. The story of his capture is related with much vividness and unction by Macaulay :—

"A scrivener," says the historian, "who lived at Wapping, and whose trade was to furnish the seafaring men there with money at high interest, had some time before lent a sum on bottomry. The debtor applied to equity for relief against his own bond, and the case came before Jeffreys. The counsel for the borrower, having little else to say, said that the lender was a trimmer. The chancellor instantly fired. 'A trimmer! Where is he? Let me see him. I have heard of that kind of monster. What is it made like?' The unfortunate creditor was forced to stand forth. The chancellor glared fiercely on him, stormed at him, and sent him away half dead with fright. 'While I live,' the poor man said, as he tottered out of the court, 'I shall never forget that terrible countenance.' And now the day of retribution had arrived. The 'trimmer' was walking through Wapping, when he saw a well-known face looking out of the window of an ale-house. He could not be deceived. The eyebrows, indeed, had been shaved away. The dress was that of a common sailor from Newcastle, and was black with coal-dust ; but there was no mistaking the savage eye and mouth of Jeffreys. The alarm was given. In a moment the house was surrounded by hundreds of people, shaking bludgeons and bellowing curses. The fugitive's life was saved by a company of the Trainbands ; and he was carried before the Lord Mayor. The mayor was a simple man, who had passed his whole life in obscurity, and was bewildered by finding himself an important actor in a mighty revolution. The events of the last twenty-four hours, and the perilous state of the city which was under his charge, had disordered his mind and his body. When the great man, at whose frown, a few days before, the whole kingdom had trembled, was dragged into the justice-room begrimed with ashes, half dead with fright, and followed by a raging multitude, the agitation of the unfortunate mayor rose to the height. He fell into fits, and was carried to his bed, whence he never rose. Meanwhile, the throng without was constantly becoming more numerous and more savage. Jeffreys begged to be sent to prison. An order to that effect was procured from the Lords who were sitting at Whitehall; and he was conveyed in a carriage to the Tower. Two regiments of militia were drawn out to escort him, and found the duty a difficult one. It was repeatedly necessary for them to form, as if for the purpose of repelling a charge of cavalry, and to present a forest of pikes to the mob. The thousands who were disappointed of their revenge pursued the coach with howls of rage to the gate of the Tower, brandishing cudgels, and holding up halters full in the prisoner's view. The wretched man meantime was in convulsions of terror. He wrung his hands, he looked wildly out, sometimes at one window, sometimes at the other, and was heard, even above the tumult, crying, 'Keep them off, gentlemen! For God's sake, keep them off!' At length, having suffered far more than the bitterness of death, he was safely lodged in the fortress, where some of his most illustrious victims had passed their last days, and where his own life was destined to close in unspeakable ignominy and terror."

Strype records the fact that on July 24, 1629, King Charles I., having hunted a stag all the way from Wanstead, in Essex, ran him down at last, and killed him in Nightingale Lane, "in the hamlet of Wapping, in a garden belonging to a man who had some damage among his herbs, by reason of the multitude of people there assembled suddenly."

Dr. Johnson, in one conversation with that excellent listener, Boswell, talked much of the wonderful extent and variety of London, and observed that men of curious inquiry might see in it such modes of life as only few could imagine. "He in particular," says Boswell, "recommended us to 'explore' Wapping, which we resolved to do. We accordingly carried our scheme into execution in October, 1792; but, whether from that uniformity which has in modern times to a great degree spread through every part of the metropolis, or from our want of sufficient exertion, we were disappointed."

Joseph Ames, that well-known antiquary and lover of old books, who wrote "Typographical Antiquities, or the History of Printing in England," was a ship-chandler in a humble alley of Wapping, where he died in 1758. This worthy old student is described as a person of vast application and industry in collecting old printed books and prints, and other curiosities, both natural and artificial. His curious notices of Caxton's works, and of very rare early books, were edited and enlarged, first by Herbert, and lastly by that enthusiastic bibliomaniac, T. F. Dibdin. Another celebrated native of Wapping was John Day, a block and pump maker, who originated that popular festivity, Fairlop Fair, in Hainault Forest.

Amongst the ship and boat builders of Wapping, the rope makers, biscuit bakers, mast, oar, and block makers, many years ago, a prying nurseryman observed in a small window a pretty West Indian flower, which he purchased. It proved to be a fuchsia, which was then unknown in England. The flower became popular, and 300 cuttings from it were the next year sold at one guinea each.

Among the thirty-six taverns and public-houses in Wapping High Street and Wapping Wall, says Mr. Timbs, are the signs of the "Ship and Pilot," "Ship and Star," "Ship and Punchbowl," "Union Flag and Punchbowl," the "Gun," "North American Sailor," "Golden Anchor," "Anchor and Hope," the "Ship," "Town of Ramsgate," "Queen's Landing," "Ship and Whale," the "Three Mariners," and the "Prospect of Whitby."

Between 288 and 304, Wapping, are Wapping Old Stairs, immortalised by Dibdin's fine old song,

" ' Your Molly has never been false,' she declares,
' Since last time we parted at Wapping Old Stairs.' "

Going still further east we come to Shadwell, which, like Wapping, was a hamlet of Stepney, till 1669, when it was separated by Act of Parliament. It derives its name, it is supposed by Lysons, from a spring dedicated to St. Chad. Its extent is very small, being only 910 yards long, and 760 broad. In Lysons' time, the only land in the parish not built on was the Sun Tavern Fields, in which were rope-walks, where cables were made, from six to twenty-three inches in girth; the rest of the parish was occupied by ships' chandlers, biscuit bakers, ship-builders, mast-makers, sail-makers, and anchor-smiths. The church of St. Paul was built in the year 1656, but it was not consecrated till 1671. It was rebuilt in 1821 on the old site. There were waterworks established in Shadwell by Thomas Neale, Esq., in 1669.

About 1745 a mineral spring, which was called Shadwell Spa, was discovered by Walter Berry, Esq., when sinking a well in Sun Tavern Fields. It was said to be impregnated with sulphur, vitriol, steel, and antimony. A pamphlet was written by Dr. Linden, in 1749, to prove it could cure every disease. The water was found useful in cutaneous diseases. It was then employed for extracting salts, and for preparing a liquor with which the calico-printers fix their colours. The waters of another mineral spring in Shadwell resemble those of the postern spring on Tower Hill. Cook's almshouses at Shadwell are mentioned by the local historians.

CHAPTER XVI.

STEPNEY.

Derivation of the Name—Noble Families in Stepney—An Attack of the Plague—The Parish Church—Monuments—"The Cruel Knight"—Sir John Leake—Celebrated Incumbents—Colet—Pace—Roger Crab, "The English Hermit"—Dissenting Congregation at Stepney—Greenhill—Mead—Shadwell—Stepney "Parishioners."

AT Stepney, two and a half miles east of St. Paul's Cathedral, we reach the eastern boundary of the radius we have defined for our work. This parish was anciently called Stibenhede, Stebenhythe, or Stebunhethe. In 1299, probably because it was an out-of-the-way nook, between marshes and the river, it was the seat of a parliament summoned by Edward I. to meet at the mansion house of Henry Walleis, then Mayor of London. At an early date the manor was held by the Bishops of London, who had a palace, called Bishop's Hall, now in the parish of Bethnal Green. In the fourteenth century John de Pulteney, who was four times Mayor of London, owned property in this parish. From

the reign of Edward I. various injunctions were made at Stepney to prevent the frequent floods from the Thames, to inquire into the state of the banks and ditches, and to prevent all negligent tenants and delinquents.

Alienated by Bishop Ridley, the manor of Stepney was given by Edward VI. to the Wentworths. From Lord Wentworth it descended to Thomas, Earl of Cleveland, whose estates were confiscated in 1652, when Sir William Ellis, Cromwell's solicitor, was made steward of the manor, a place then valued at £200 per annum. After the Restoration the Earl of Cleveland recovered his manor, which continued in his family till the year 1720, when it was sold by the representatives of Philadelphia, Lady Wentworth, to John Wicker, Esq., whose son alienated it to his brother-in-law Sir George Colebrooke in the year 1754. In 1664, Charles II., at the Earl of Cleveland's request, instituted a weekly court of record at Stepney, and a weekly market at Ratcliffe Cross, afterwards transferred to Whitechapel, and an annual Michaelmas fair at Mile End Green, afterwards transferred to Bow. In the first year of Charles I., Stepney was ravaged by

of the Marquis of Worcester's house, where the famous Dr. Meade was born in 1673.

The parish church, dedicated to St. Dunstan and All Saints, was built in the fourteenth century. It has a low broad tower, strengthened with buttresses, and surmounted by a turret and dome. In it was buried the illustrious Sir Thomas Spert, Comptroller of the Navy in the time of Henry VIII., commander of the *Harry Grâce de Dieu*, and the founder of the Trinity House. Here also

OLD GATEWAY AT STEPNEY. (*From a View published by N. Smith, 1791.*)

the plague, which had broken out from time to time in London since Elizabeth's reign. This terrible disease carried off here 2,978 persons. At the commencement of the Civil War, Stepney, then a mere flat, extending to Blackwall, was strongly fortified for the defence of the City. In 1665 the plague again broke out in Stepney, and with such terrible effect that it swept off 6,583 persons in one year, besides 116 sextons and gravediggers. In 1794 a fire consumed more than half the hamlet of Ratcliffe, and spread to the shipping in the river. Stepney had a traditional reputation for healthiness till the cholera of 1849 and 1866, when many cases occurred in the neighbourhood. The Stratford College, founded in 1826, was built on the site

a writer to the *Spectator* discovered that remarkably absurd epitaph—

"Here Thomas Saffin lies interred—ah, why?
Born in New England did in London die.
Was the third son of eight, begot upon
His mother Martha by his father John.
Much favoured by his prince he 'gan to be,
But nipt by death at th' age of twenty-three.
Fatal to him was that we small-pox name,
By which his mother and two brethren came
Also to breathe their last, nine years before,
And now have left their father to deplore
The loss of all his children, with his wife,
Who was the joy and comfort of his life.
                    Deceased, June 18, 1687."

"On the outside of Stepney Church," says Lysons, "over the south porch, is a representation of the

PETTICOAT LANE. (*See p.* 144.)

Crucifixion, rudely carved; and on the west wall, an imperfect *basso relievo* (not better executed) of a figure adoring the Virgin Mary and the infant Jesus. Within the west porch is a stone, on which are these lines:—

> " 'Of Carthage wall I was a stone,
>   O mortals read with pity !
> Time consumes all, it spareth none,
>   Man, mountain, town, nor city.
> Therefore, O mortals ! now bethink
>   You whereunto you must,
> Since now such stately buildings
>   Lie buried in the dust.
>
> Thomas Hughes, 1663.'

"On the east wall of the chancel (on the outside)," says the same author, "is the monument of Dame Rebecca Berry, wife of Thomas Elton, of Stratford Bow, and relict of Sir John Berry, 1696. The arms on this monument are—Paly of six, on a bend three mullets (Elton) impaling, a fish, and in the dexter chief point an annulet between two bends wavy. This coat of arms has given rise to a tradition that Lady Berry was the heroine of a popular ballad called 'The Cruel Knight; or, Fortunate Farmer's Daughter;' the story of which is briefly this :—A knight, passing by a cottage, hears the cries of a woman in labour; his knowledge in the occult sciences informs him that the child then born was destined to be his wife. He endeavours to elude the decrees of fate, and avoid so ignoble an alliance, by various attempts to destroy the child, which are defeated. At length, when grown to woman's state, he takes her to the sea-side, intending to drown her, but relents; at the same time throwing a ring into the sea, he commands her never to see his face again, on pain of instant death, unless she can produce that ring. She afterwards becomes a cook, and finds the ring in a cod-fish, as she is dressing it for dinner. The marriage takes place, of course. The ballad, it must be observed, lays the scene of this story in Yorkshire. The incident of the fish and ring occurs in other stories, and may be found in the 'Arabian Nights' Entertainments.' "

Amongst the epitaphs in Stepney Church is that to Sir John Leake, 1720:—

"To the memory of the Honourable Sir John Leake, Knt., Rear-Admiral of Great Britain, Admiral and Commander-in-Chief of Her late Majesty Queen Anne's fleet, and one of the Lords Commissioners of the Admiralty. Departed this life the 21st of August, 1720, ætat 64 years, 1 month, 17 days; who, anno 1689, in the *Dartmouth*, by engaging Kilmore Castle, relieved the city of Londonderry, in Ireland; also, anno 1702, with a squadron at Newfoundland, he took and destroyed fifty-one sail of French, together with all their settlements. Anno 1704 he forced the van of the French fleet at the Malaga engagement; relieved Gibraltar twice,

burning and taking thirteen sail of French men-of-war. Likewise, anno 1706, relieved Barcelona, the present Emperor of Germany besieged therein by Philip of Spain, and took ninety sail of corn-ships; the same year taking the cities of Carthagena and Alicant, with the islands of Ivica, Majorca, Sardinia, and Minorca."

This celebrated officer was son of Captain Richard Leake, Master Gunner of England; he was born at Rotherhithe, in the year 1656. Whilst a captain he distinguished himself in several engagements. In Queen Anne's reign he was five times Admiral of the Fleet, and commanded with such undeviating success, that he acquired the appellation of "the brave and fortunate." On the accession of George I. he was dismissed from all employ, and retired into private life. The veteran died in 1720, and was buried in a family vault in Stepney Church. His son, Captain Richard Leake, who died a few months before him, seems to have been a worthless profligate, who married disgracefully, ran through his money, and then lived on his father. His nativity had, it is said, been cast by his grandfather, who pronounced that he would be very vicious, very fortunate, so far as prize-money was concerned, and very unhappy.

The living of Stepney was held by Archbishop Segrave, and by Bishop Fox, the founder of Corpus Christi College, Oxford. Of the Stepney district churches St. Philip's is said to have been the first district Gothic church built in the east of London. It was erected in 1829, at a cost of £7,000. There are also a synagogue and Jews' burial-ground at Stepney, and numerous almshouses and hospitals, such as Deacon's City Paupers' House, the German and Portuguese Jews' Hospitals, Drapers' Hospital, Trinity Almshouses, Gibson's, or Cooper's Almshouses.

In 1372 the rectory of Stepney was valued at sixty marks a year, and the vicarage at twelve. In the Parliamentary survey, taken in 1650, the vicarage is set down at the value of £70 per annum. The ancient rectory stood near the east end of the church; and in Lysons' time the brick wall which enclosed the site still remained.

Colet, the founder of St. Paul's School, and the sworn friend of Erasmus, was vicar here, and still resided in Stepney after being made Dean of St. Paul's. Sir Thomas More, writing to him, then abroad, says, "If the discommodities of the City offend you, yet may the country about your parish of Stepney afford you the like delights to those which that affords you wherein you now keepe." The dean's house was at the north end of White Horse Street, Ratcliffe. Upon his founding St. Paul's School he gave it to the head master as a country residence; but Stepney having in a great measure lost its rural delights, the masters have not resided there for many years. The site (now two messuages called Colet Place) was, in Lysons' time, still let for their advantage. In the front was a bust of the dean.

Richard Pace, who was presented to the vicarage in 1519, had been in the service of Cardinal Bainbridge, who having recommended him at Court, the king had made him Secretary of State, and employed him in matters of the highest importance. He was afterwards made Dean of St. Paul's, but kept the vicarage till 1527, when he was sent as ambassador to Venice. Whilst there he either thwarted some plan of Wolsey, or did not lend himself enough to the ambitious schemes of that proud cardinal, for he fell into disgrace, and at his return was thrown into the Tower for two years. These misfortunes affected his brain, and he suffered from mental disease, from which he never wholly recovered. After his release he retired to Stepney, where he died in 1532, and was buried in the church, near the great altar. Erasmus, who was a friend of Pace, speaks highly of his amiable character, his pleasant manner, and his integrity. He wrote a book on the unlawfulness of King Henry's marriage with the widow of his brother Arthur, a Preface to Ecclesiastes, and some Latin epistles and sermons. William Jerome, presented to the vicarage of Stepney in 1537, was executed in 1540 on a charge of heresy.

Roger Crab, gent., one of the old celebrities of Bethnal Green, and who was buried at Stepney, September 14, 1680, was one of the eccentric characters of the seventeenth century. The most we know of him is from a pamphlet, now very rare, written principally by himself, and entitled, "The English Hermit; or, the Wonder of the Age." It appears from this publication that he had served seven years in the Parliamentary army, and had his skull cloven to the brain in their service; for which he was so ill requited that he was once sentenced to death by the Lord Protector, and afterwards suffered two years' imprisonment. When he had obtained his release he set up a shop at Chesham as a haberdasher of hats. He had not been long settled there before he began to imbibe a strange notion, that it was a sin against his body and soul to eat any sort of flesh, fish, or living creature, or to drink wine, ale, or beer. Thinking himself at the same time obliged to follow literally the injunction to the young man in the Gospel, he quitted business, and disposing of his property, gave it to the poor, reserving to himself only a small cottage at Ickenham, where he resided, and a rood of land for a garden, on the produce of which he subsisted at the expense of three farthings a week, his food being bran, herbs, roots, dock-leaves, mallows, and grass; his drink, water. How such an extraordinary change of diet agreed with his constitution the following passage from his pamphlet will show, and give, at the same time, a specimen of the work :—" Instead of strong drinks and wines, I give the old man a cup of water; and instead of rost mutton and rabbets, and other dainty dishes, I give him broth thickened with bran, and pudding made with bran and turnip-leaves chopt together, and grass; at which the old man (meaning my body), being moved, would know what he had done, that I used him so hardly; then I show'd him his transgression: so the warres began; the law of the old man in my fleshly members rebelled against the law of my mind, and had a shrewd skirmish; but the mind, being well enlightened, held it so that the old man grew sick and weak with the flux, like to fall to the dust; but the wonderful love of God, well pleased with the battle, raised him up again, and filled him full of love, peace, and content of mind, and he is now become more humble; for now he will eat dock-leaves, mallows, or grass." The pamphlet was published in 1655. Prefixed to it is a portrait of the author, cut in wood, which, from its rarity, bears a very high price. Over the print are these lines—

"Roger Crab that feeds on herbs and roots is here;
But I believe Diogenes had better cheer.
Rara avis in terris."

A passage in this man's epitaph seems to intimate that he never resumed the use of animal food. It is not one of the least extraordinary parts of his history that he should so long have subsisted on a diet which, by his own account, had reduced him almost to a skeleton in 1655. It appears that he resided at Bethnal Green at the time of his decease. A very handsome tomb was erected to his memory in the churchyard at this place, which being decayed, the ledger-stone was placed in the pathway leading across the churchyard to White Horse Street. Strype says of the man, "This Crab, they say, was a Philadelphian, a sweet singer."

A congregation of Protestant Dissenters was established in Stepney in the year 1644 by William Greenhill, who was afterwards vicar of Stepney. He was ejected soon after the Restoration, and was succeeded by Matthew Mead. This eminent Puritan divine was appointed to the cure of the new chapel at Shadwell by Cromwell, but in 1662, being ejected for nonconformity, succeeded Greenhill as pastor of the Dissenting congregation at Stepney. In 1683, being accused of being privy to the Rye House Plot, he fled to Holland till the danger was over. He was author of the "Young Man's Remembrancer," "The Almost Christian Tried and Cast," "The Good of Early Obedience," "A Sermon on Ezekiel's Wheels," and several other single sermons. His son Richard, the celebrated physician, who for nearly half a century was at the head of his profession, author of several valuable medical treatises, and possessor of one of the most valuable collection of books, MSS., antiques, paintings, &c., that ever centered in a private individual, was born at Stepney, in the apartments over the ancient brick gateway opposite the rectory, August 11th, 1673. He first began practice in 1696, at his native place, in the very house where he was born, and met with that success which was a prognostic of his future eminence. Dr. Mead died in the year 1754, and was buried in the Temple Church. The meeting-house was erected in 1674 for Mr. Mead, who, in the ensuing year, instituted the May-day sermons, for the benefit of young persons.

Shadwell was separated from the parish of Stepney in the year 1669; St. George's-in-the-East, in the year 1727; Spitalfields, in 1729; Limehouse, in 1730; Stratford-Bow, the same year; and Bethnal Green, in 1743.

Sir Thomas Lake, who was afterwards Secretary of State to James I., resided at Stepney in 1595; Isabel, Countess of Rutland, had a seat there in 1596; Nathaniel Bailey, author of the useful and well-known English Dictionary, "An Account of London," and other works, lived at Stepney; Capt. Griffiths, an ancient Briton, who, by the gallant and extraordinary recovery of his fishing-boat from a French frigate, attracted the notice of King William IV., and became afterwards captain of a man-of-war, was an inhabitant of Stepney, and was buried there. He was known by the name of "Honour and Glory Griffiths," from the circumstance, it is said, of his addressing his letters to "their Honours and Glories at the Admiralty." There was also at Stepney, in Lysons' time, an old gateway of a large mansion that once belonged to Henry, the first Marquis of Worcester. An engraving of this very interesting specimen of old brickwork will be found on page 138.

It is an old tradition of the East End of London that all children born at sea belong to Stepney parish. The old rhyme runs—

> " He who sails on the wide sea
> Is a parishioner of Stepney."

This rather wide claim on the parochial funds has often been made by paupers who have been born at sea, and who used to be gravely sent to Stepney from all parts of the country; but various decisions of the superior courts have at different times decided against the traditional law.

CHAPTER XVII.

WHITECHAPEL.

Strype's Account—Mention of Whitechapel by Beaumont and Fletcher and Defoe—St. Mary Matfellon—Its Great Antiquity—Old Religious Custom—"Judas the Traytor"—Burials at Whitechapel—The Executioner of Charles I.—Rosemary Lane—Petticoat Lane and the Old Clothes Sales—Poverty in Whitechapel—The London Hospital The Danish Church—The Sailors' Home—Goodman's Fields Theatre.

"WHITECHAPEL," says Strype, "is a spacious fair street, for entrance into the City eastward, and somewhat long, reckoning from the laystall east unto the bars west. It is a great thoroughfare, being the Essex road, and well resorted unto, which occasions it to be the better inhabited, and accommodated with good inns for the reception of travellers, and for horses, coaches, carts, and wagons."

Whitechapel is mentioned by Beaumont and Fletcher, in their *Knight of the Burning Pestle.* "March fair, my hearts!" says Ralph. "Lieutenant, beat the rear up! Ancient, let your colours fly; but have a great care of the butchers' hooks at Whitechapel; they have been the death of many a fair ancient" (ensign).

"I lived," says Defoe, in his "Memoirs of the Plague," "without Aldgate, about midway between Aldgate Church and Whitechapel Bars, on the left-hand or north side of the street; and as the distemper had not reached to that side of the City, our neighbourhood continued very easy; but at the other end of the town the consternation was very great, and the richer sort of people, especially the nobility and gentry from the west part of the City, thronged out of town with their families and servants in an unusual manner; and this was more particularly seen in Whitechapel—that is to say, the broad street where I lived."

Although the church of St. Mary, Whitechapel, was at first only a chapel of ease to Stepney, it is of great antiquity, since there is record of Hugh de Fulbourne being rector there in the year 1329. As early as the 21st of Richard II., according to Stow, the parish was called Villa beatæ Mariæ de Matfellon, a name the strangeness of which has given rise to many Whitechapel legends. According to Stow, the name of Matfellon was given it about the year 1428 (6th Henry VI.), from the following circumstance :—A devout widow of the parish had long time cherished and brought up of alms a certain Frenchman or Breton born, who most "unkindly and cruelly," by night, murdered the said widow as she slept in her bed, and afterwards flew with such jewels and other stuff of hers as he might carry; but was so freshly pursued, that for fear he took sanctuary in the church of St. George, Southwark, and challenging the privileges there, abjured the king's land. Then the constables in charge of him brought him into London to convey him eastward, but as soon as he was come into Whitechapel, the wives there cast upon him so many missiles and so much filth, that notwithstanding all the resistance of the constables, they slew him out of hand ; and for this feat, it was said, the parish purchased the name of St. Mary Matfellon.

Now, that this event may have occurred in the reign of Henry VI. is very probable ; but as the parish was called Matfellon more than a hundred years before, it is very certain that the name of Matfellon did not arise from this particular felon. Strype thinks that the word Matfellon is somehow or other derived from the Hebrew or Syriac word "Matfel," which signifies a woman recently delivered of a son—that is, to the Virgin, recently delivered. Perhaps the church may have been dedicated to "Mary matri et filio," which in time was corrupted into Matfellon. The name of the White Chapel was probably given the new chapel in admiration of its stateliness, or from the whitewash that even in the Middle Ages was frequently used by builders.

The inhabitants of this parish, says Strype, were anciently bound, annually, at the feast of Pentecost, to go in a solemn procession to the cathedral church of St. Paul's, in the City of London, to make their oblations, as a testimony of their obedience to the Mother Church ; but upon the erection of the conventual church of St. Peter, Westminster, into a cathedral, and the county of Middlesex appropriated by Henry VIII. for its diocese, of which this parish being a part, the inhabitants were obliged to repair annually to St. Peter's, as they formerly did to St. Paul's ; which practice proving very troublesome, and of no service, Thomas Thirlby, bishop of the new see, upon their petition, agreed to ease them of that trouble, provided the rector and churchwardens

would yearly, at the time accustomed, repair to his new cathedral, and there, in the time of Divine service, offer at the high altar the sum of fifteen pence, as a recognition of their obedience.

The street, or way, says Strype, leading from Aldgate to Whitechapel Church, remaining in its original unpaved state, it became thereby so very bad that the same was almost rendered impassable, not only for carriages, but likewise for horses ; wherefore it, together with divers others on the west side of the City of London, was appointed to be paved by an Act of Parliament, in the year 1572.

In the year 1711 the advowson of Whitechapel was purchased by the principal and scholars of King's Hall and College, of Brasenose College, in Oxford. The Bishop of London is now patron.

Pennant, always vivacious and amusing, tells a story of a libellous picture of the Last Supper placed above the altar in this church, in the reign of Queen Anne, by the then High Church rector. Dr. White Kennet, at that time Dean of Peterborough, had given great offence to the Jacobites, by writing in defence of the Hanoverian succession, and in revenge the rector introduced the dean among the Apostles in the character of Judas. He clad him in a black robe, between cloak and gown, and a short wig, and, to brand him beyond mistake, put a black velvet patch on his forehead, such as the dean wore to hide a dreadful injury received in his youth ; beneath was written, "Judas, the traytor." The dean generously treated the matter with contemptuous silence ; but the Bishop of London interfered, and caused the obnoxious picture to be removed. It was afterwards replaced, but the libellous likeness was expunged.

The register of St. Mary Matfellon, Whitechapel, records the burial of two remarkable persons— Brandon, the supposed executioner of Charles I., and Parker, the leader of the Mutiny at the Nore. Brandon was a ragman, in Rosemary Lane. The entry is —" 1649. June 2. Richard Brandon, a man out of Rosemary Lane." And to this is added the following memorandum : " This R. Brandon is supposed to have cut off the head of Charles I." This man is said to have confessed that he had £30 for his work, and that it was paid him (why, we know not) in half-crowns, within an hour after the axe fell. He took an orange, stuck with cloves, and a handkerchief, out of the king's pocket, when the body was removed from the scaffold. For the orange he was offered twenty shillings by a gentleman in Whitehall, but he refused the sum, and afterwards sold the orange for ten shillings, in Rosemary Lane. This Brandon was the son of

Gregory Brandon, and claimed the headman's axe by inheritance. The first person he had beheaded was the Earl of Strafford; but, after all, there is still doubts as to who struck the death-blow at King Charles, and some say it was that Cornet Joyce who once arrested the king. Whitechapel Church was rebuilt in 1875—8, but was totally destroyed by fire, in August, 1880.

Rosemary Lane, now re-christened Royal Mint Street, is described by Mr. Mayhew as chiefly inhabited by dredgers, ballast-heavers, coal-whippers, watermen, lumpers, &c., as well as the slop-workers and "sweaters" employed in the Minories.

"One side of the lane," says Mayhew, in his "London Labour," "is covered with old boots and shoes; old clothes, both men's, women's, and children's; new lace, for edgings, and a variety of cheap prints and muslins, and often of the commonest kinds (also new); hats and bonnets; pots; tins; old knives and forks, old scissors, and old metal articles generally; here and there is a stall of cheap bread or American cheese, or what is announced as American; old glass; different descriptions of second-hand furniture, of the smaller size, such as children's chairs, bellows, &c. Mixed with these, but only very scantily, are a few bright-looking swag-barrows, with china ornaments, toys, &c. Some of the wares are spread on the ground, on wrappers, or pieces of matting or carpet; and some, as the pots, are occasionally placed on straw. The cotton prints are often heaped on the ground, where are also ranges or heaps of boots and shoes, and piles of old clothes, or hats or umbrellas. Other trades place their goods on stalls or barrows, or over an old chair or clothes-horse. And amidst all this motley display the buyers and sellers smoke, and shout, and doze, and bargain, and wrangle, and eat, and drink tea and coffee, and sometimes beer."

Rag Fair, or Rosemary Lane, Wellclose Square, is mentioned in a note to Pope's "Dunciad," as "a place near the Tower of London, where old clothes and frippery are sold." Pennant gives a humorous picture of the barter going on there, and says, "The articles of commerce by no means belie the name. There is no expressing the poverty of the goods, nor yet their cheapness. A distinguished merchant engaged with a purchaser observing me look on him with great attention, called out to me, as his customer was going off with his bargain, to observe that man, 'for,' says he, 'I have actually clothed him for fourteen pence.'" It was here, we believe, that purchasers were allowed to dip in a sack for old wigs—a penny the dip. Noblemen's suits come here at last, after undergoing many vicissitudes.

In the *Public Advertiser* of Feb. 17, 1756, there is an account of one Mary Jenkins, a dealer in old clothes in Rag Fair, selling a pair of breeches to a poor woman for sevenpence and a pint of beer. While the two were drinking together at a public-house, the lucky purchaser found, on unripping the clothes, eleven guineas of gold quilted in the waistband (eleven Queen Anne guineas), and a £30 bank-note, dated 1729, of which note the purchaser did not learn the value till she had sold it for a gallon of twopenny purl.

Petticoat Lane, according to Stow, was formerly called Hog Lane. It is now called Middlesex Street. The old historian gives a pleasant picture of it as it was forty years before he wrote. "This Hog Lane stretcheth north towards St. Mary Spittle," he says, "without Bishopsgate, and within these forty years it had on both sides fair hedge-rows of elm-trees, with bridges, and easy stiles to pass over into the pleasant fields, very commodious for citizens therein to walk about, and otherwise to recreate and refresh their dull spirits in the sweet and wholesome air which is now within a few years made a continual building throughout of garden-houses and small cottages; and the fields on either side be turned into garden-plots, tenter-yards, bowling-alleys, and such like."

Strype says that some gentlemen of the Court and City built their houses here for the sake of the fresh air. At the west of the lane, the same historian mentions, there was a house called, in Strype's boyhood, the Spanish ambassador's, who in the reign of James I. dwelt there, probably the famous Gondomar. A little way from this, down a paved alley on the east side, Strype's father lived, in a fair large house with a good garden before it, where Hans Jacobson, King James's jeweller, had dwelt. After that, French Protestant silk-weavers settled in the part of the lane towards Spittlefields, and it soon became a continuous row of buildings on both sides of the way.

"Petticoat Lane," says Mr. Mayhew, "is essentially the old clothes' district. Embracing the streets and alleys adjacent to Petticoat Lane, and including the rows of old boots and shoes on the ground, there is, perhaps, between two and three miles of old clothes. Petticoat Lane proper is long and narrow, and to look down it is to look down a vista of many-coloured garments, alike on the sides and on the ground. The effect sometimes is very striking, from the variety of hues, and the constant flitting or gathering of the crowd into little groups of bargainers. Gowns of every shade and every pattern are hanging up, but none, perhaps, look either bright or white; it is a vista of dinginess, but many-coloured dinginess, as regards female attire. Dress-coats, frock-coats, great-coats, livery and gamekeepers' coats, paletots, tunics, trowsers, knee-breeches, waistcoats, capes, pilot coats, working jackets, plaids, hats, dressing-gowns, shirts, Guernsey frocks, are all displayed. The predominant colours are black and blue, but there is every colour; the light drab of some aristocratic livery, the dull brown-green of velveteen, the deep blue of a pilot-jacket, the variegated figures

and shoes. Handkerchiefs, sometimes of a gaudy orange pattern, are heaped on a chair. Lace and muslins occupy small stands, or are spread on the ground. Black and drab and straw hats are hung up, or piled one upon another, and kept from falling by means of strings; while incessantly threading their way through all this intricacy is a mass of people, some of whose dresses speak of a recent purchase in the lane."

"Whitechapel," says Mr. Hollingshead, in his

KIRBY CASTLE, BETHNAL GREEN.   (THE BLIND BEGGAR'S HOUSE).

of the shawl dressing-gown, the glossy black of the restored garments, the shine of newly-turpentined black satin waistcoats, the scarlet and green of some flaming tartan—these things, mixed with the hues of the women's garments, spotted and striped, certainly present a scene which cannot be beheld in any other part of the greatest City in the world, nor in any other portion of the world itself.

"The ground has also its array of colours. It is covered with lines of boots and shoes, their shining black relieved here and there by the admixture of females' boots, with drab, green, plum, or lavender-coloured 'legs,' as the upper part of the boot is always called in the trade. There is, too, an admixture of men's 'button-boots,' with drab-cloth legs; and of a few red, yellow, and russet-coloured slippers; and of children's coloured morocco boots

"Ragged London," in 1861, "may not be the worst of the many districts in this quarter, but it is undoubtedly bad enough. Taking the broad road from Aldgate Church to Old Whitechapel Church—a thoroughfare in some parts like the high street of an old-fashioned country town—you may pass on either side about twenty narrow avenues, leading to thousands of closely-packed nests, full to overflowing with dirt, misery, and rags." Inkhorn Court is an Irish colony, with several families in one room. Tewkesbury Buildings is a colony of Dutch Jews. George Yard contains about one hundred English families; the inhabitants are chiefly dock-labourers. The other half of the residents are thieves, costermongers, stallkeepers, professional beggars, rag-dealers, brokers, and small tradesmen. The Jewish poor are independent and self-supporting, and keep up the ceremonies of their nation under the most adverse circumstances.

The London Hospital, situated in Whitechapel, and founded in 1740, is one of the most useful and extensive charities of the kind in the metropolis. The building was erected in 1752, from the designs of Mr. B. Mainwaring, and originally contained only thirty-five wards and 439 beds. The amount of fixed income is about £13,000, derived from funded property, voluntary donations, legacies, &c.

The School for the Children of Seamen, in Wellclose Square, occupies the site of the British and Foreign Sailors' Church, which was originally known as the Danish Church. The old building was erected in 1696, by Caius Gabriel Cibber, the sculptor, at the expense of Christian V., King of Denmark, for the use of the Danish merchants and sailors of London. Christian VII. visited the church in 1768, and both Caius Cibber, and his more celebrated son, Colley Cibber, were buried there.

Well Street is so named from a well in Goodman's Fields. In this street, and extending back to Dock Street, is the Sailors' Home, an institution founded in 1830, which unites as far as possible the advantages of a club with the comforts that home can give. Seamen are here lodged and boarded at a reasonable expense, and consequently shielded from the extortions of those "land sharks" who are ever ready to make a prey of them. The Home includes a library and recreation rooms, and also a school of navigation. The edifice covers the ground formerly occupied by the Royalty Theatre, which was opened in 1787, when Braham first appeared on the stage as "Cupid." The Royalty was burnt down in 1826, but was rebuilt in 1828, and reopened as the Royal Brunswick Theatre. During the rehearsal of *Guy Mannering*, a few days after opening, the roof fell in, when ten persons were killed and several seriously injured.

The original Goodman's Fields Theatre, once a throwster's shop, in Leman Street, or in Argyll Street, Goodman's Fields, was built in 1729, by Thomas Odell, a dramatic author, and the first licensee of the stage under Walpole's Licensing Act. A sermon preached at St. Botolph's Church, Aldgate, against the new theatre, frightened Odell, who sold the property to a Mr. Henry Giffard, who opened the new house in the year 1732. He, however, was soon scared away, and removed, in 1735, to Lincoln's Inn Fields; but he managed to return in 1741, bringing with him David Garrick, who had appeared in private at St. John's Gate, and now essayed the character of "Richard III." with enormous success. Horace Walpole writes his friend Mann about him, but says, "I see nothing wonderful in it. The Duke of Argyll says he is superior to Betterton." Gray the poet, in an extant letter, says, "Did I tell you about Mr. Garrick, the town are gone mad after? There are a dozen dukes of a night at Goodman's Fields, sometimes, and yet I am still in the opposition."

This theatre was pulled down, says Cunningham, about 1746; a second theatre was burnt down in 1802.

Goodman's Fields were originally part of a farm belonging to the Abbey of the Nuns of St. Clair. "At the which farm," says Stow, "I myself, in my youth, have fetched many a halfpenny-worth of milk, and never had less than three ale-pints for a halfpenny in summer, nor less than one ale-quart for a halfpenny in winter, always hot from the kine, as the same was milked and strained. One Trolop, and afterwards Goodman, were the farmers there, and had thirty or forty kine to the pail."

In 1720 Strype describes the streets as chiefly inhabited by thriving Jews. There were also tenters for clothworkers, and a cart-way out of Whitechapel into Well Close. The initials of the streets, Pescod, or Prescott, Ayliffe, Leman, and Maunsell, formed the word "palm." In 1678 a great many Roman funeral urns, with bars and silver money, and a copper urn, were found here, proving Goodman's Fields to have been a Roman burial-place.

CHAPTER XVIII.

BETHNAL GREEN.

Origin of the Name—The Ballad of the Blind Beggar of Bethnal Green—Kirby's Castle—The Bethnal Green Museum—Sir Richard Wallace's Collection—Nichol Street and its Population—The French Hospital in Bethnal Green and its present Site.

ACCORDING to Mr. Lysons, Bethnal Green probably derives its name from the old family of the Bathons, who had possessions in Stepney in the reign of Edward I.

The old ballad of "the Beggar of Bethnal Green," written in the reign of Elizabeth, records the popular local legend of the concealment under this disguise of Henry de Montfort, son of the redoubtable Earl of Leicester. He was wounded at Evesham, fighting by his father's side, and was found among the dead by a baron's daughter, who sold her jewels to marry him, and assumed with him a beggar's attire, to preserve his life. Their only child, a daughter, was the "Pretty Bessie" of the ballad in Percy.

"My father, shee said, is soone to be seene,
　The seely blind beggar of Bednall Green,
　That daylye sits begging for charitie,
　He is the good father of pretty Bessee.

"His markes and his tokens are knowen very well,
　He alwayes is led with a dogg and a bell ;
　A seely old man, God knoweth, is hee,
　Yet hee is the father of pretty Bessee."

The sign-posts at Bethnal Green have for centuries preserved the memory of this story; the beadles' staffs were adorned in accordance with the ballad; and the inhabitants, in the early part of the century, used to boldly point out an ancient house on the Green as the palace of the Blind Beggar, and show two special turrets as the places where he deposited his gains.

This old house, called in the Survey of 1703 Bethnal Green House, was in reality built in the reign of Elizabeth by John Kirby, a rich London citizen. He was ridiculed at the time for his extravagance, in some rhymes which classed him with other similar builders, and which ranked Kirby's Castle with "Fisher's Folly, Spinila's Pleasure, and Megse's Glory." It was eventually turned into a madhouse. Sir Richard Gresham, father of the builder of the Royal Exchange, was a frequent resident at Bethnal Green.

The opening, in 1872, of an Eastern branch of the South Kensington Museum at Bethnal Green was the result of the efforts of Mr. (now Sir) H. Cole, aided by Sir Antonio Brady, the Rev. Septimus Hansard, rector of Bethnal Green, Mr. Clabon, Dr. Millar, and other gentlemen interested in the district, and was crowned with success by the princely liberality of Sir Richard Wallace (the inheritor of the Marquis of Hertford's thirty years' collection of art treasures), who offered to the education committee the loan of all his pictures and many other works of art. The Prince and Princess of Wales were present at the opening of the Museum, which took place June 24, 1872.

Sir Richard Wallace's collection, which occupied the whole of the upper galleries, comprised not only an assemblage of ancient and modern paintings in oil, by the greatest masters of past or modern times, a beautiful gallery of water-colour drawings, miniatures, and enamels by French, German, and British artists, but also some fine specimens of bronzes, art porcelain and pottery, statuary, snuffboxes, decorative furniture, and jewellers' and goldsmiths' work. The collection was strongest in Dutch and modern French pictures. Cuyp was represented by eleven pictures, Hobbema by five, Maes by four, Metzu by six, Mieris by nine, Netscher by four, Jan Steen by four, Teniers by five, Vanderneer by six, A. Vandevelde by three, W. Vandevelde by eight, Philip Wouvermans by five, Rubens by eleven, Rembrandt by eleven, Vandyck by six. In the Italian school the collection was deficient in early masters, but there were excellent specimens of Da Vinci, Andrea del Sarto, Carlo Dolce, and Canaletto. Of the Spanish school there were fine specimens of Murillo and Velasquez. The French school was well represented—Greuze by twenty-two works, Watteau by eleven, Boucher by eleven, Lancret by nine, and Fragonard by five. There were forty-one works by Horace Vernet, thirteen by Bellangé, four by Pils, fifteen by Delaroche, five by Ary Scheffer, two by Delacroix, two by Robert Fleury, five by Géricault, six by Prud'hon, twelve by Roqueplan, thirty-one by Decamps, and fifteen by Meissonier.

In the English collection Sir Joshua Reynolds stood pre-eminent. His matchless portrait of "Nelly O'Brien" stood out as beautiful and bewitching as ever, though the finer carnations had to some extent flown. The childish innocence of the "Strawberry Girl" found thousands of admirers, though the picture has faded to a disastrous degree; and "Love me, Love my Dog," had crowds of East-end admirers.

Among the superb portraits by Reynolds, in his most florid manner, "Lady Elizabeth Seymour-Conway," and "Frances Countess of Lincoln," daughters of the first Marquis of Hertford, and one of "Mrs. Hoare and Son" (a masterpiece), were the most popular. The mildness and dignity of Reynolds was supplemented by the ineffable grace and charm of Gainsborough. Novices in art were astonished at the naïveté of "Miss Haverfield," one of the most delightful child-portraits ever painted. The fir e works of Bonington, a painter of genius little known, astonished those who were ignorant of his works. Among his finest productions at Bethnal Green were "The Ducal Palace at Venice," "The Earl of Surrey and the Fair Geraldine," and "Henri IV. of France and the Spanish Ambassador." This king, to the horror of the proud hidalgo, is carrying his children pick-a-back.

Among the French pictures there were eleven first-rate Bouchers. This protégé of Madame de Pompadour was a great favourite with the Marquis, and at Bethnal Green one saw him at his best. There was a portrait of "The Pompadour," quite coquettishly innocent, and those well-known pictures, "The Sleeping Shepherdess," the "Amphitrite," and the "Jupiter disguised as Diana." Three sacred pictures by Philippe de Champagne, showed us French religious art of the most ascetic kind, presenting a striking contrast to the gaiety and license of French art in general. In Greuze we find the affected simplicity and the forced sentiment of the age before the Revolution in its most graceful form. "The Bacchante," "The Broken Mirror," "The Broken Eggs," and the peerless portrait of "Sophie Arnould," enabled even those unacquainted with the charm of this painter to appreciate his merits. Lancret, the contemporary of Boucher, was represented by many works, among which the critics at once decided on the pre-eminence of "The Broken Necklace," and a portrait of the famous dancer, "Mdlle. Camargo." Lepicié was represented by his "Teaching to Read," and "The Breakfast," capital pieces of character. Watteau, that delightful painter of theatrical landscape, was a favourite of the Marquis, and at Bethnal Green appeared his fairy-like "Landscape with Pastoral Groups," his delightful "Conversation Humourieuse," and his inimitable "Arlequin and Colombine." What painter conveys so fully the enjoyment of a *fête champêtre* or the grace of coquettish woman? A dazzling array of twenty-six Decamps included the ghastly "Execution in the East," and that wonderful sketch of Turkish children, "The Breaking-up of a Constantinople School." The fifteen Paul Delaroche's comprised "The Repose in Egypt," one of the finest pictures in the collection; "The Princes in the Tower hearing the approach of the Murderers," and that powerful picture, "The Last Sickness of Cardinal Mazarin." Amongst the specimens of that high-minded painter, Ary Scheffer, we had the "Francesca da Rimini," one of the most touching of the painter's works, and the "Margaret at the Fountain." The contents of the Museum are occasionally varied by loan collections of works of art and industry; but that of Sir Richard Wallace has been the most important as yet brought together within its walls.

"Nichols Street," says a newspaper writer of 1862, writing of Bethnal Green in its coarser aspects, "New Nichols Street, Half Nichols Street, Turvile Street, comprising within the same area numerous blind courts and alleys, form a densely crowded district in Bethnal Green. Among its inhabitants may be found street-vendors of every kind of produce, travellers to fairs, tramps, dog-fanciers, dog-stealers, men and women sharpers, shoplifters, and pickpockets. It abounds with the young Arabs of the streets, and its outward moral degradation is at once apparent to any one who passes that way. Here the police are *certain* to be found, day and night, their presence being required to quell riots and to preserve decency. Sunday is a day much devoted to pet pigeons and to bird-singing clubs; prizes are given to such as excel in note, and a ready sale follows each award. Time thus employed was formerly devoted to cock-fighting. In this locality, twenty-five years ago, an employer of labour, Mr. Jonathan Duthiot, made an attempt to influence the people for good, by the hire of a room for meeting purposes. The first attendance consisted of one person. Persistent efforts were, however, made; other rooms have from time to time been taken and enlarged; there is a hall for Christian instruction, and another for educational purposes; illustrated lectures are delivered; a loan-library has been established, also a clothing-club and penny bank, and training-classes for industrial purposes."

Mr. Smiles, in his "Huguenots in London," has an interesting page on the old French Hospital in Bethnal Green:—"Among the charitable institutions founded by the refugees for the succour of their distressed fellow-countrymen in England," says Mr. Smiles, "the most important was the French Hospital. This establishment owes its origin to a M. de Gastigny, a French gentleman, who had been Master of the Buckhounds to William III., in Holland, while Prince of Orange. At his death, in 1708, he bequeathed a sum of £1,000 towards founding an hospital, in London, for the relief of distressed French Protestants. The money was placed at interest for eight years, during which successive benefactions were added to the fund. In 1716, a piece of ground in Old Street, St. Luke's, was purchased of the Ironmongers' Company, and a lease was taken from the City of London of some adjoining land, forming altogether an area of about four acres, on which a building was erected, and fitted up for the reception of eighty poor Protestants of the French nation. In 1718, George I. granted a charter of incorporation to the governor and directors of the hospital, under which the Earl of Galway was appointed the first governor. Shortly after, in November, 1718, the opening of the institution was celebrated by a solemn act of religion, and the chapel was consecrated amidst a great concourse of refugees and their descendants, the Rev. Philip Menard, minister of the French chapel of St. James's, conducting the service on the occasion.

"From that time the funds of the institution steadily increased. The French merchants of Toulon, who had been prosperous in trade, liberally contributed towards its support, and legacies and donations multiplied. Lord Galway bequeathed a thousand pounds to the hospital, in 1720, and in the following year Baron Hervart de Huningue gave a donation of £4,000. The corporation were placed in the possession of ample means, and they accordingly proceeded to erect additional buildings, in which they were enabled, by the year 1760, to give an asylum to 234 poor people."

The French Hospital has recently been removed from its original site to Victoria Park, where a handsome building has been erected as an hospital, for the accommodation of forty men and twenty women, after the designs of Mr. Robert Lewis Roumieu, architect, one of the directors, Mr. Roumieu being himself descended from an illustrious Huguenot family—the Roumieus of Languedoc.

CHAPTER XIX.

SPITALFIELDS.

The Priory of St. Mary, Spittle—A Royal Visit—The Spital Sermons—A Long Sermon—Roman Remains—The Silk Weavers—French Names, and Modern Versions of them—Riots in Spitalfields—Bird Fanciers—Small Heads—"Cat and Dog Money."

THE Priory of St. Mary of the Spittle was founded by Walter Brune and Rosia his wife, in the year 1197. It was surrendered at the dissolution to King Henry, and at that time the hospital which belonged to the priory was found to contain one hundred and eighty beds. In place of the hospital many large mansions were built, and among these Strype especially mentions that of Sir Horatio Pallavicini, an Italian merchant, who acted as ambassador to Queen Elizabeth; and in the reign of James I. we find the Austrian ambassador lodging there.

In the year 1559 Queen Elizabeth came in state to St. Mary Spittle, attended by a thousand men in harness, and ten great guns, with drums, flutes, and trumpets sounding, and morris-dancers bringing two white bears in a cart.

Long after the Dissolution of monasteries, part of the hospital churchyard remained, with a pulpit cross within a walled enclosure, at which cross, on certain days every Easter, sermons were preached. Opposite that pulpit was a small two-storeyed building, where the alderman and sheriffs came to hear the sermons, with their ladies at a window over them. Foxe, in his "Book of Martyrs," repeatedly mentions these Spital sermons.

The preaching at the Spittle seems to have been a custom of great antiquity. It is said that Dr. Barrow once preached a sermon on charity at the Spittle, before the Lord Mayor and aldermen, which occupied three hours and a half. Being asked, after he came down from the pulpit, if he was not tired, "Yes, indeed," said he, "I began to be weary with standing so long."

In 1594 a gallery was built near the pulpit for the governor and children of Christ's Hospital; and in 1617 we find many of the Lords of King James's Privy Council attending the Spital sermons, and afterwards dining with the Lord Mayor, at a most liberal and bountiful dinner at Billingsgate.

" It appears," says Bingham, speaking of the Spital sermons, "it was usual in those times that on Good Friday a divine of eminence should, by appointment, expatiate on Christ's Passion, in a sermon at Paul's Cross; on the three days next Easter, Monday, Tuesday, and Wednesday, a bishop, a dean, and a doctor of divinity, should preach at the Spital concerning the Resurrection; and on Low Sunday another learned divine was to rehearse the substance of the other four, in a fifth sermon. At this the Lord Mayor and Corporation always attended, robed in violet gowns, on Good Friday and Easter Wednesday, and on the other days in scarlet. This custom continued till the Great Rebellion, in 1642, when it was discontinued. However, it was revived after the Restoration, except that instead of being preached at Paul's Cross, which had been demolished, the sermons were in the choir of the cathedral. After the Great Fire they were discontinued, both at St. Paul's Church and at the Spital, and the Easter sermons were delivered at some appointed church, and at last at St. Bridget's, in Fleet Street, where they continued invariably till the late repairs of that church, when they were removed to Christ Church, Newgate Street, where they still continue."

In 1576, says Stow, in treating of a brick-field near the Spital churchyard, there were discovered many Roman funeral urns, containing copper coins of Claudius, Vespasian, Nero, Antoninus Pius, and

Trajan, lachrymatories, Samian ware lamps, and small images, also Saxon stone coffins. There was found there a skull, which some believed to be a giant's, though others took it for an elephant's. Some of these stone coffins are still preserved in the vaults of Christ Church.

Bagford, in Leland's "Collectanea," mentions the Priory of St. Mary Spittle as then standing, strongly built of timber, with a turret at one angle. Its ruins, says Mr. Timbs, were discovered early in the last century, north of Spital Square. The

of Nantes, settled here, and thus founded the silk manufacture in England; introducing the weaving of lustrings, alamodes, brocades, satins, paduasoys, ducapes, and black velvets. In 1713 it was stated that silks, gold and silver stuffs, and ribbons were made here, as good as those of French fabric, and that black silk for hoods and scarves was made actually worth three hundred thousand pounds. During the reigns of Queen Anne, George I., and George II., the Spitalfields weavers greatly increased; in 1832, 50,000 persons were entirely de-

ST. HELEN'S PRIORY, AND LEATHERSELLERS' HALL. (*From a View, by Malcolm,* 1799.)

pulpit, destroyed during the Civil Wars, stood at the north-east corner of the square. In the map of Elizabeth's reign the Spittle Fields are at the north-east extremity of London, with only a few houses on the site of the Spital. A map published a century later shows a square field bounded with houses, with the old artillery-ground, which had formerly belonged to the priory, on the west. Culpeper, the famous herbalist, occupied a house then in the fields, and subsequently a public-house at the corner of Red Lion Court.

This is the great district for silk-weavers. "Spital Square," says Mr. Timbs, "at the south-east corner, has been the heart of the silk district since 'the poor Protestant strangers, Walloons and French,' driven from France by the revocation of the Edict

pendent on the silk-manufacture, and the looms varied from 14,000 to 17,000. Of these great numbers are often unemployed; and the distribution of funds raised for their relief has attracted to Spitalfields a great number of poor persons, and thus pauperised the district. The earnings of weavers, in 1854, did not exceed ten shillings per week, working fourteen to sixteen hours a day. The weaving is either the richest, or the thinnest and poorest. The weavers are principally English, and of English origin, but the manufacturers, or masters, are of French extraction, and the Guillebauds, the Desormeaux, the Chabots, the Turquands, the Mercerons, and the Chauvets trace their connection with the refugees of 1685. Many translated their names into English, by which the

SIR PAUL PINDAR'S LODGE.

(From a View published by N. Smith, 1791.)

THE "SIR PAUL PINDAR."

(From an Original Sketch.)

ROOM IN SIR PAUL PINDAR'S HOUSE. *(From a Drawing by J. T. Smith, 1810.)*

(See p. 152.)

old families may still be known: thus, the Le-maîtres called themselves Masters; the Leroys, King; the Tonneliers, Coopers; the Lejeunes, Young; the Leblancs, White; the Lenoirs, Black; the Loiseaux, Bird."

Riots among the Spitalfields weavers, for many a century, were of frequent occurrence. Any de-cline of prices, or opposition in trade, set these turbulent workmen in a state of violent effer-vescence. At one time they sallied out in parties, and tore off the calico gowns from every woman they met. Perhaps the greatest riot was in 1765, when, on the occasion of the king going to Parlia-ment to give his assent to the Regency Bill, they formed a great procession, headed by red flags and black banners, to present a petition to the House, complaining that they were reduced to starvation by the importation of French silks. They terrified the House of Lords into an adjournment, insulted several hostile members, and in the evening attacked Bedford House, and tried to pull down the walls, declaring that the duke had been bribed to make the treaty of Fontainebleau, which had brought French silks and poverty into the land. The Riot Act was then read, and detachments of the Guards called out. The mob then fled, many being much hurt and trampled on. At a yet later date mobs of Spitalfields weavers used to break into houses and cut the looms of men who were working with improved machinery. Many outrages were com-mitted by these "cutters," and many lives were lost in scuffles and fights.

The older houses inhabited by the weavers have wide latticed windows in the upper storeys, to light the looms. Being nearly all bird-fanciers, the weavers supply London with singing-birds; and half the linnets, woodlarks, goldfinches, and green-finches sold in the metropolis are caught by Spital-fields weavers in October and March. They are fond of singing-matches, which they determine by the burning of an inch of candle.

Spitalfields weavers are said to have extremely small heads, $6\frac{1}{2}$ or $6\frac{3}{4}$ inches being the prevailing width, although the average size of the male head in England is 7 inches. We do not know whether the weavers still continue the old clothworkers' habit of singing at their looms, as mentioned by Shakespeare and Ben Jonson. "I would I were a weaver," says Falstaff; "I could sing all manner of songs." And Cutbeard, in Ben Jonson's *Silent Woman*, remarks, "He got his cold with sitting up late, and singing catches with clothworkers."

Spitalfields was a hamlet of Stepney until 1729, when it was made a distinct parish, and Christ Church was consecrated. Among the parochial charities, says Mr. Timbs, is "Cat and Dog Money," an eccentric bequest to be paid on the death of certain pet dogs and cats.

In one of the houses in Spital Square lived Pope's friend, the celebrated Lord Bolingbroke.

CHAPTER XX.

BISHOPSGATE.

The Old Gate—The "White Hart"—Sir Paul Pindar's House: its Ancient Glories and Present Condition—The Lodge in Half-moon Alley—St. Helen's and the Nuns' Hall—The Tombs—Sir Julius Cæsar—Sir John Crosby—Modern Improvements—The Windows—Crosby Hall and its History—Allusions to it in Shakespeare—Famous Tenants of Crosby Hall—Richard Crookback—Sir Thomas More.—Bonvici.

BISHOPSGATE, according to Stow, was probably built by good Bishop Erkenwald, son of King Offa, and repaired by Bishop William, the Norman, in the reign of the Conqueror. Henry III. confirmed to merchants of the Hanse certain privileges by which they were bound to keep Bishopsgate in repair, and in the reign of Edward IV. we find them rebuilding it. The gate was adorned with the effigies of two bishops, probably Bishop Erkenwald and Bishop William, and with effigies supposed to have represented King Alfred and Alred, Earl of Mercia, to whom Alfred entrusted the care of the gate. It was rebuilt several times. The latest form of it is shown on page 154. The rooms over the gate were, in Strype's time, allotted to one of the Lord Mayor's carvers. Pennant notices an old inn, the "White Hart," not far from this gate, which was standing until a few years back.

The old house where Sir Paul Pindar, a great City merchant of the reign of James I., lived, still exists in Bishopsgate Street, with some traces of its ancient splendour. This Sir Paul was am-bassador for James I. to the Grand Legion, and helped to extend English commerce in Turkey. He brought back with him a diamond valued at £30,000, which James wished to buy on credit, but prudent Sir Paul declined this unsatisfactory mode of purchase, and used to lend it to the monarch on gala days. Charles I. afterwards purchased the precious stone. Sir Paul was appointed farmer of the Customs to James I., and frequently supplied the cravings for money both of James and Charles. In the year 1639 Sir Paul was esteemed worth £236,000, exclusive of bad debts. He expended £10,000 in the repairing of St. Paul's Cathedral, yet, nevertheless, died in debt, owing to his generosity to King Charles. The king owed him and the other Commissioners of the Customs £300,000, for the security of which, in 1649, they offered the Parliament £100,000, but the proposition was not entertained. On his death affairs were left in such a perplexed state, that his executor, William Toomer, unable to bear the work and the disappointment, destroyed himself. Mr. J. T. Smith, in his "Topography of London," has a drawing of a room on the first floor of this house. The ceiling was covered with panelled ornamentations, and the chimney-piece, of carved oak and stone, was adorned with a badly-executed *basso-relievo* of Hercules and Atlas supporting an egg-shaped globe. Below this were tablets of stag hunts. The sides of the chimney-piece were formed by grotesque figures, the whole being a very splendid specimen of Elizabethan decorative art. In 1811 the whole of the ornaments, says Mr. Smith, were barbarously cut away to render the room, as the possessors said, "a little comfortable." The Pindar arms, "a chevron argent, between three lyon's heads, erased ermine crowned or," were found hidden by a piece of tin in the centre of the ceiling. The walls are covered with oak wainscoting, crowned with richly carved cornices. The house, No. 169, is now a public-house, "The Sir Paul Pindar's Head."

"The front towards the street," says Mr. Hugo, "with its gable bay windows, and matchless panel-work, together with a subsequent addition of brick on its northern side, is one of the best specimens of the period now extant. The edifice was commenced in one of the closing years of the reign of Elizabeth, on the return from his residence in Italy of its great and good master. It was originally very spacious, and extended for a considerable distance, both to the south side and to the rear of the present dwelling. The adjoining tenements in Half-moon Street, situated immediately at the back of the building, which faces Bishopsgate Street, though manifesting no external signs of interest, are rich beyond expression in internal ornament. The primary arrangement, indeed, of the mansion is entirely destroyed. Very little of the original internal woodwork remains, and that of the plainest character. But, in several of the rooms on the first floors of the houses just referred to, there still exist some of the most glorious ceilings which our country can furnish.

They are generally mutilated, in several instances the half alone remaining, as the rooms have been divided into two or more portions, to suit the needs of later generations. These ceilings are of plaster, and abound in the richest and finest devices. Wreaths of flowers, panels, shields, pateras, bands, roses, ribands, and other forms of ornamentation, are charmingly mingled, and unite in producing the best and happiest effect. One of them, which is all but perfect, consists of a large device in the centre, representing the sacrifice of Isaac, from which a most exquisite design radiates to the very extremities of the room. In general, however, the work consists of various figures placed within multangular compartments of different sizes, that in the centre of the room usually the largest. The projecting ribs, which in their turn enclose the compartments, are themselves furnished with plentiful ornamentation, consisting of bands of oak-leaves and other vegetable forms; and, in several instances, have fine pendants at the points of intersection. The cornices consist of a rich series of highly-ornamented mouldings. Every part, however, is in strict keeping, and none of the details surfeit the taste or weary the eye."

At a little distance, in Half-moon Alley, stood an old structure, now pulled down, ornamented with figures, which is traditionally reported to have been the keeper's lodge in the park attached to Sir Paul's residence; and mulberry-trees, and other park-like vestiges in this neighbourhood, grew almost within memory.

St. Helen's, Bishopsgate, occupies the site of Roman buildings. The ground in the neighbourhood is intersected with chalk foundations, and in 1836 a Roman tessellated pavement (red, white, and grey) was discovered under a house at the south-west angle of Crosby Square. A similar pavement was found in 1712 on the north side of Little St. Helen's gateway. There is mention of a church priory here, dedicated to the mother of Constantine, as early as 1180, when it was granted to the canons of St. Paul's Cathedral by one Ranulph and Robert his son. About 1210 a priory of Benedictine nuns was founded here by William Fitzwilliam, a goldsmith, and dedicated to the Holy Cross and St. Helen. The priory included a hall, hospital, dormitories, cloisters, and offices. The Nuns' Hall, at the north of the present church, was purchased by the Leathersellers' Company, who used it as a common hall till 1799, when it was pulled down to make room for St. Helen's Place.

A crypt extended from the north side of the church under Leathersellers' Hall, and in the wall which separated this crypt from the church were two ranges of oblique apertures, through which mass at the high altar could be viewed. A canopied altar of stone, affixed to the wall, indicates the position of one set of these "nuns' gratings." The priory of St. Helen's was much augmented in 1308 by William Basing, a London sheriff, and when it was surrendered to Henry VIII. its annual revenue was £376 6s. During the Middle Ages the church was divided from east to west by a partition, to separate the nuns from the parishioners; but after the dissolution this was removed. Sir Thomas Gresham, according to Stow, promised this church a steeple in consideration of the ground taken up by his monument.

However, architects praise this church as picturesque, with its two heavy equal aisles, and its pointed arches. There is a transept at the east end, and beyond it a small chapel, dedicated to the Holy Ghost. Against the north wall is a range of seats formerly occupied by the nuns. The church is a composite of various periods. St. Helen's, says Mr. Godwin, contains perhaps more monuments (especially altar-tombs) than any other parish church in the metropolis, and these give an especial air of antiquity and solemnity to the building. Here is the ugly tomb containing the embalmed body of Francis Bancroft. He caused the tomb to be built for himself in 1726. He is said to have made, by greedy exactions, a fortune of nearly £28,000, the whole of which he left to the almshouses and the Drapers' Company. In a small southern transept is a most singular table monument in memory of Sir Julius Cæsar, Privy Counsellor to James I., Chancellor of the Exchequer, and Master of the Rolls, who died about 1636. The epitaph, written by himself, engraved on a large deed, sealed and folded, the string to the seal represented as breaking, purports to be an engagement on the part of the deceased to pay the debt of Nature whenever God shall please and require it. The tomb, the work of Nicholas Stone, cost £110.

On the south side of the chancel, on a stone

BISHOPSGATE.

altar-tomb, are recumbent figures of a knight in armour, and a lady. The knight is Sir John Crosby, who died in the year 1475, the builder of Crosby Hall, who contributed largely to the church. Behind this is a large columned and canopied monument in memory of Sir William Pickering, famous for worth in learning, arts, and warfare. His effigy in armour reclines on a piece of sculptured matting, folded at one end to represent a pillow. Strype says he died in 1542. But the greatest of all the monuments at St. Helen's is that of Sir Thomas Gresham, a large sculptured altar-tomb covered with a marble slab. Another curious monument near Gresham's is that of Matthew Bond, captain of the London Trained Bands in the time of the Armada. He is represented sitting within a tent, with two sentries standing outside, and an attendant bringing up a horse. There were also buried here Sir John Lawrence, the good Lord Mayor who behaved so nobly in the Plague year, and Sir John Spencer, the rich Lord Mayor of Elizabeth's reign, whose daughter ran away with Lord Compton, escaping from her father's house in a baker's basket.

The charity-box in the church vestibule is supported by a curious carved figure of a mendicant. Mr. Godwin, writing in 1839, laments the ill-proportioned turret of St. Helen's, and the poor carvings of the mongrel Italian style.

The recent restorations and improvements have greatly increased the attractions of St. Helen's, while the magnificent stained-glass windows, that have been added to the sacred edifice, are modern works eminently worthy of the objects of ancient art, and the fine sculptures to be found within the walls. Of these windows one is in the memory of Sir Thomas Gresham, and has been contributed by the Gresham Committee, while two others have been erected at the expense of the family of Mr. McDougall. The magnificent window, in memory of the late Alderman Sir William Copeland, is a most striking work; but is not inferior in interest to the restoration, which was made at the expense of the churchwardens, Mr. Thomas Rolfe, jun., and Mr. George Richardson, of a beautiful window in stained glass, composed of the fragments of the ancient window, which was too dilapidated to remain. Several other fine memorial windows have been added to the building, amongst which are those contributed by the vicar, the Rev. J. E. Cox, and by Mr. W. Williams, of Great St. Helen's, who has taken a deep interest in the work of restoration. Some other splendid examples of stained glass were contributed by Mr. Alderman Wilson and Mr. Deputy Jones ; and the fine communion window was presented by the late Mr. Kirkman Hodgson, M.P., and his brother, Mr. James Stewart Hodgson. The tomb of Sir John Crosby has been renovated, as well as that of Sir John Spencer, which has been restored and removed under the direction of the Marquis of Northampton and Mr. Wadmore, who has himself contributed a window in memory of Bishop Robinson, and has superintended the entire restoration.

"Not a stone now remains," says Mr. Hugo, "to tell of the old priory of St. Helen's and its glories. A view of the place, as it existed at the close of the last century, which is happily furnished by Wilkinson in his 'Londina,' represents the ruins of edifices whose main portions and features are of the Early English period, and which were probably coeval with the foundation of the priory. These he calls the 'Remains of the *Fratry*.' He had the advantage of a personal examination of these beautiful memorials. 'The door,' he says, 'leading from the cloister to the Fratry, which the writer of this well remembers to have seen at the late demolition of it, was particularly elegant; the mouldings of the upper part being filled with roses of stone painted scarlet and gilt ; the windows of the Fratry itself, also, which were nearly lancet-shaped, were extremely beautiful.' He also gives two views of the beautiful 'crypt,' and one of the hall above it ; the former of which is in the Early English style, while the latter has ornamental additions of post-Dissolution times. It appears by his plan that there were at least two 'crypts,' one under the hall and another to the south, under what would be called the withdrawing-room."

Perhaps one of the most interesting old City mansions in London is Crosby Hall, now turned into a restaurant. It is one of the finest examples of Gothic domestic architecture of the Perpendicular period, and is replete with historical associations. It was built about 1470 by Sir John Crosby, grocer and woolstapler, on ground leased from Dame Alice Ashfield, Prioress of the Convent of St. Helen's. For the ground, which had a frontage of

110 feet in the "Kinge's Strete," or "Bisshoppesgate Strete," he paid £11 6s. 8d. a year. Stow says he built the house of stone and timber, "very large and beautiful, and the highest at that time in London." Sir John, member of Parliament for London, alderman, warden of the Grocers' Company, and mayor of the Staple of Elans, was one of several brave citizens knighted by Edward IV. for his brave resistance to the attack on the City made by that Lancastrian filibuster, the Bastard Falconbridge. Sir John died in 1475, four or so years only after the completion of the building. He was buried in the church of St. Helen's, where we have already described his tomb. The effigy is fully armed, and the armour is worn over the alderman's mantle, while round the neck there is a collar of suns and roses, the badge of the House of York, to which that knight had adhered so faithfully.

In 1470 Crosby Hall became a palace, for the widow of Sir John parted with the new City mansion to that dark and wily intriguer, Richard, Duke of Gloucester. "There," says Sir Thomas More, "he lodged himself, and little by little all folks drew unto him, so that the Protector's court was crowded and King Henry's left desolate."

Shakespeare, who was a resident in St. Helen's in 1598 (a fact proved by the parish assessments), has thrice by name referred, in his *Richard III.*, to this old City mansion, as if he found pleasure in immortalising a place familiar to himself. It was in the Council Chamber in Crosby Hall that the mayor, Sir Thomas Billesden, and a deputation of citizens, offered Richard the crown.

It was at the same place that Richard persuaded Anne to await his return from the funeral of the murdered King Henry :—

> *Gloucester.*   And if thy poor devoted servant may
> But beg one favour at thy gracious hand,
> Thou dost confirm his happiness for ever.
> *Anne.*   What is it ?   [designs
> *Gloucester.*   That it would please thee leave these sad
> To him that hath more cause to be a mourner,
> And presently repair to Crosby House.
>> *Richard III.*, Act i., Scene 2.

Other allusions also occur, as—

> *Gloucester.*   Are you now going to dispatch this deed ?
> *1st Murderer.*   We are, my lord; and come to have the warrant,
> That we may be admitted where he is.
> *Gloucester.*   Well thought upon ; I have it here about me.
>   [*Gives the warrant.*
> When you have done, repair to Crosby Place.
>> *Richard III.*, Act i., Scene 3.

> *Gloucester.*   Shall we hear from you, Catesby, ere we sleep ?
> *Catesby.*   You shall, my lord.
> *Gloucester.*   At Crosby House there shall you find us both.
>> *Richard III.*, Act iii., Scene 1.

On the 27th of June, 1483, Richard left Crosby Hall for his palace at Westminster.

In 1501 Sir Bartholomew Reed spent his brilliant mayoralty at this house at Crosby Place and here he entertained the Princess Katharine of Arragon two days before her marriage with Prince Arthur, and not long after the ambassadors of the Emperor Maximilian when they came to condole with Henry VII. on the death of the prince. Sir John Rest, Lord Mayor in 1516, was its next dis-

ing "their leisure to liberal studies and profitable reading, although piety was their first care. No wrangling, no idle word, was heard in it; every one did his duty with alacrity, and not without a temperate cheerfulness." In 1523 Sir Thomas More sold Crosby Hall to his "dear friend" Antonio Bonvici, a merchant of Lucca, the same person to whom, twelve years after, the chancellor sent an affecting farewell letter, written in the Tower with a piece of charcoal the night before his execution.

THE "WHITE HART," BISHOPSGATE STREET, IN 1810.

tinguished tenant, at whose show there appeared the grand display of "four giants, one unicorn, one dromedary, one camel, one ass, one dragon, six hobby-horses, and sixteen naked boys."

Then came a distinguished tenant, indeed, a man fit to stock it with wisdom for ever, and to purge it of the old stains of Richard's crimes. Between 1516 and 1523, says the Rev. Thomas Hugo, Crosby Hall was inhabited by the great Sir Thomas More, first Under Treasurer, and afterwards Lord High Chancellor of England. Here philosophy and piety met in quiet converse, and Erasmus compares More's house to the Academy of Plato, or rather to a "school and an exercise of the Christian religion;" all its inhabitants, male and female, apply-

After the dissolution of the Convent of St. Helen Bonvici purchased Crosby Hall and messuages of the king for £207 18s. 4d. In 1549 Bonvici forfeited the property by illegally departing the kingdom, and Henry VIII. granted Crosby Hall to Lord Darcy. Bonvici afterwards returned and resumed possession. By him the mansion was left to Germayne Cyoll, who had married a cousin of Sir Thomas Gresham, who lived opposite Crosby House. The weekly bequest of Cycillia Cyoll, wife of this same Cyoll, is still distributed at St. Helen's Church.

In 1566 Alderman Bond purchased the house for £1,500, and repaired and enlarged it, building, it is said, a turret on the roof. The inscription

on Bond's tomb in St. Helen's Church describes him as a merchant adventurer, and most famous in his age for his great adventures by both sea and land. Bond entertained the Spanish ambassador at Crosby Hall, as his sons afterwards did the Danish ambassador.

From the sons of Alderman Bond, Crosby Hall was purchased, in 1594, by Sir John Spencer, for £2,560. This rich citizen kept his mayoralty here in 1594; and during his year of office a house afterwards became a temporary prison for "malignants," like Gresham College and Lambeth Palace.

In 1672 the great hall of the now neglected house was turned into a Presbyterian chapel. Two years later the dwelling-houses which adjoined the hall, and occupied the present site of Crosby Square, were burnt down, but the hall remained uninjured. While used as a chapel (till 1769), twelve different ministers of eminence occupied the pulpit, the first

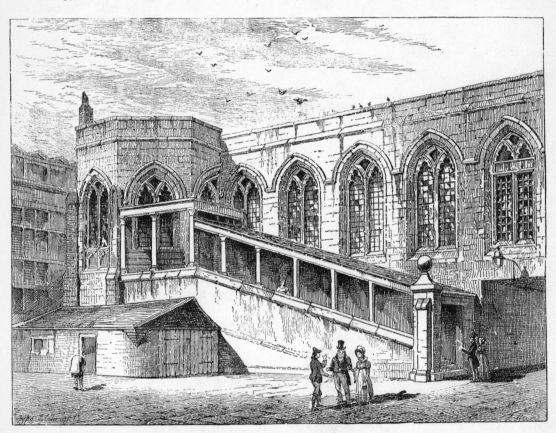

CROSBY HALL IN 1790.

masque was performed by the gentlemen students of Gray's Inn and the Temple, in the august presence of Queen Elizabeth. Spencer built a large warehouse close to the hall. It was during this reign that Crosby House was for a time tenanted by the Dowager Countess of Pembroke, "Sydney's sister, Pembroke's mother" (immortalised by Ben Jonson's epitaph); and at her table Shakespeare may have often sat as a welcome guest.

On the death of Sir John, in 1609, the house descended to his son-in-law, Lord Compton, afterwards Earl of Northampton, but whether he resided there is uncertain. The earl's son, Spencer, was killed, fighting for King Charles, in 1642. The being Thomas Watson, previously rector of St. Stephen's, Walbrook, and the author of the tract, "Heaven taken by Storm," which is said to have been the means of the sudden conversion of the celebrated Colonel Gardiner. In 1678 a sale was announced at Crosby Hall, of "tapestry, a good chariot, and a black girl of about fifteen." The Withdrawing-room and Throne-room were let as warehouses to the East India Company. It then was taken by a packer, and much mutilated; and in 1831 the premises were advertised to be let upon a building lease. It was greatly owing to the public spirit of Miss Hackett, a lady who lived near it, that this almost unique example of domestic Gothic architecture was ultimately preserved. In 1831 this lady made strenuous efforts for its conservation, and received valuable assistance from Mr. W. Williams, of Great St. Helen's, and other residents. In 1836 it was reinstated and partially restored by public subscription, after which it was re-opened by the Lord Mayor, W. T. Copeland, Esq., M.P., a banquet in the old English style being held on the occasion. From 1842 to 1860 Crosby Hall was occupied by a literary and scientific institute. It has since been converted into a restaurant.

It is conjectured that this fine old house was originally composed of two quadrangles, separated by the Great Hall, a noble room forty feet high.

The oriel of the hall is one of the finest specimens remaining; the timber roof is one of the most glorious which England possesses. The Throne-room and Council-room have suffered much. A fine oriel in one of these has been removed to Buckinghamshire, and both ceilings have been carried off. No original entrance to the hall now remains, except a flat arched doorway communicating with the Council-chamber. The main entrance, Mr. Hugo thinks, was no doubt under the minstrel's gallery, at the south end. In the centre of the oriel ceiling is still to be seen, in high relief, the crest of Sir John Crosby—a ram trippant, argent, armed and hoofed, or.

CHAPTER XXI.

BISHOPSGATE (continued).

Old Houses and Architectural Relics—St. Botolph's Church and its Records—St. Ethelburga—Sir Thomas Gresham's House—Gresham College—Sir Kenelm Digby—The New College—Jews' Synagogue in Great St. Helen's—The Leathersellers' Hall—The "Bull" Inn—Burbage—Hobson—Milton's Epitaph—Teasel Close and the Trained Bands—Devonshire Square—Fisher's "Folly"—Houndsditch and its Inhabitants—The Old-Clothes Men—Hand Alley—Bevis Marks—The Papey—Old Broad Street—The Excise Office—Sir Astley Cooper—A Roman Pavement Discovered—St. Peter-le-Poer—Austin Friars—Winchester House—Allhallows-in-the-Wall—London Wall—Sion College.

THE Ward of Bishopsgate having partially escaped the Great Fire, is still especially rich in old houses. In most cases the gable ends have been removed, and, in many, walls have been built in front of the ground floors up to the projecting storeys; but frequently the backs of the houses present their original structure. Mr. Hugo, writing in the year 1857, has described nearly all places of interest; but many of these have since been modified or pulled down. The houses Nos. 81 to 85 inclusive, in Bishopsgate Street Without, were Elizabethan. On the front of one of these the date, 1590, was formerly visible. In Artillery Lane the same antiquary found houses which, at the back, preserved their Elizabethan character. In No. 19, Widegate Street, there was a fine ceiling of the time of Charles I. The houses adjoining Sir Paul Pindar's, numbered 170 and 171, possessed ceilings of a noble character, and had probably formed part of Sir Paul Pindar's. The lodge in Half-moon Street, now destroyed, had a most noble chimney-piece, probably executed by Inigo Jones, besides wainscoted walls and rich ceilings. No. 26, Bishopsgate Street Without possessed two splendid back rooms, with decorations in the style of Louis XIV., full of flowing lines. In Still Alley, in 1857, there were several Elizabethan houses, since modernised. White Hart Court (though the old inn was gone before) boasted a row of four houses, of beautiful design, in the Inigo Jones manner.

In the house No. 18, at the corner of Devon-shire Street, Mr. Hugo discovered, as he imagined, a portion of the Earl of Devonshire's house, or that of Lord John Powlett. It was of the Elizabethan age, and one room contained a rich cornice of masks, fruit, and leaves, connected by ribands. In another there were, over the fireplace, the arms of Henry Wriothesley, Earl of Southampton, and Shakespeare's friend. At the corner of Houndsditch, No. 8, Bishopsgate Street Without, there was an Elizabethan house; and at the opposite corner, No. 7, was a house with fine staircases, and walls and ceilings profusely decorated à la Louis Quatorze. Just beyond, a tablet, surmounted with the figure of a mitre inserted in the wall, a little north of Camomile Street, marks the site of the old Bishops' Gate.

At 66, Bishopsgate Street Within, there was a finely-groined undercroft, of the fourteenth century. At the end of Pea Hen Court, Mr. Hugo, in his antiquarian tour of 1857, records a doorway of James I. In Great St. Helen's Place, the same antiquary found, at No. 2, a good doorway and staircase of Charles I.; and at Nos. 3 and 4, some Elizabethan relics. Nos. 8 and 9 he pronounced to be modern subdivisions of a superb house. On the front was the date, 1646. It was of brick, ornamented with pilasters, and contained a matchless staircase and a fine chimney-piece. Nos. 11 and 12, Great St. Helen's, Mr. Hugo noted as a red brick house, with pilasters of the same material. The simple but artistic doorways he had little hesitation in attributing to Inigo Jones: he supposed them to have been erected about 1633, the year Inigo designed the south entrance of St. Helen's Church.

At No. 3, Crosby Square, Mr. Hugo found a fine doorway (*temp.* Charles II.), in the style of Wren. This square was built in 1677, on the site of part of Crosby Hall. At Crosby Hall Chambers, No. 25, Bishopsgate Street Within, the street front had lost all ancient peculiarities, except two beautiful festoons of flowers inserted between the windows of the first and second floors.

The church of St. Botolph, Bishopsgate, stands on the banks of the City Ditch, and was rebuilt in 1725–28 by James Gold, an architect otherwise unknown. It contains a monument to the good and illustrious Sir Paul Pindar. The inscription describes him as nine years resident in Turkey, faithful in negotiations foreign and domestic, eminent for piety, charity, loyalty, and prudence; an inhabitant twenty-six years, and a bountiful benefactor to the parish, having left great bequests to many of the London hospitals and other institutions. Bishopsgate Church has proved a Bishop's Gate in more senses than one, for Dr. Mant, Dr. Grey, and Dr. Blomfield, successively its rectors, became bishops during the present century. The churchyard of St. Botolph's is adorned with a fountain.

The registers of the church (says Cunningham) record the baptism of Edward Alleyn, the player (born 1566); the marriage, in 1609, of Archibald Campbell, Earl of Argyll, to Ann Cornwallis, daughter of Sir William Cornwallis; and the burials of the following persons of distinction :—1570, Sept. 13, Edward Allein, poete to the Queene; 1623, Feb. 17, Stephen Gosson, rector of this church, and author of "The School of Abuse; containing a pleasant invective against Poets, Pipers, Plaiers, Jesters, and such-like Caterpillars of a Common-

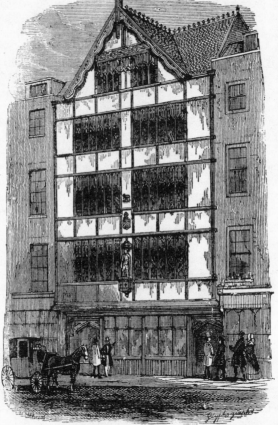

STREET FRONT OF CROSBY HALL. (*See page* 158.)

wealth," 4to, 1579; 1628, June 21, William, Earl of Devonshire (from whom Devonshire Square, adjoining, derives its name); 1691, John Riley, the painter.

St. Ethelburga, a church a little beyond St. Helen's, half hidden with shops, escaped the Great Fire, and still retains some Early English masonry. It was named from the daughter of King Ethelbert, and is mentioned as early as the year 1366; the advowson was vested in the prioress and nuns of St. Helen's, and so continued till the dissolution. One of Dryden's rivals, Luke Milbourne, was minister of this church. Pope calls him "the fairest of critics," because he exhibited his own translation of Virgil to be compared with that which he condemned.

The General Post Office, at first fixed at Sherborne Lane, was next removed to Cloak Lane, Dowgate, and then, till the Great Fire, to the Black Swan, Bishopsgate Street.

One of the glories of old Bishopsgate was the mansion built there by Sir Thomas Gresham, in 1563. It consisted (says Dean Burgon, his best biographer) of a square court, surrounded by a covered piazza, and had spacious offices adjoining. It was girdled by pleasant gardens, and extended from Bishopsgate Street, on the one side, to Broad Street on the other. The first plan of the college which afterwards occupied this house was to have seven professors, who should lecture once a week in succession on divinity, astronomy, music, geometry, law, medicine, and rhetoric. Their salaries, defrayed by the profits of the Royal Exchange, were to be £50 per annum, a sum equal to £400 or £500 at the present day. To the library of this college the Duke of Norfolk, in the latter part of the seventeenth century, presented two thousand volumes from his family library. From the meetings of scientific men at these lectures the Royal

Society originated, and was incorporated in 1663 by Charles II. The society afterwards removed to Arundel House, in the Strand. The Gresham College Lectures were commenced in 1597, the year after Lady Gresham's death, when the house became free. They were read in term-time, every day but Sunday, in Latin, at nine a.m., and in English at two p.m.

Aubrey mentions that that strange being, Sir Kenelm Digby, admiral, philosopher, and doctor, after the death of his beautiful wife, retired into Gresham College for two or three years, to avoid envy and scandal. He diverted himself with his chemistry, and the professors' learned talk. He wore, says the gossip, a long morning cloak, a high-crowned hat, and he kept his beard unshorn, and looked like a hermit, as signs of sorrow for his beloved wife, whom he was supposed to have poisoned by accident, by giving her vipers' flesh in broth, to heighten her beauty. In Johnson's time the attendance at the lectures had dwindled to nothing, and we find the terrible doctor telling Boswell, that ready listener, that if the professors had been allowed to take only sixpence a lecture from each scholar, they would have been "emulous to have had many scholars." Gresham College was taken down in 1768, the ground on which it stood made over to the Crown for a perpetual rent of £500 per annum, the lectures being read in a room above the Royal Exchange. A new college was subsequently erected in Gresham Street, and the first lecture read in it November 2, 1843. The music and other practical lectures are still well attended, but the Latin lectures are often adjourned, from there being no audience.

The new college, at the corner of Basinghall Street, is a handsome stone edifice, designed by George Smith. It is in the enriched Roman style, and has a Corinthian entrance portico. Over the entrance are the arms of Gresham, the City of London, and the Mercers' Company, in the last of which a demi-virgin, with dishevelled hair, is modestly conspicuous. The interior contains a large library and professors' rooms, and on the first floor a theatre, to hold 500 persons. The building cost upwards of £7,000. The professors' salaries have been raised, to compensate them for their rooms in the old college. In Vertue's print, in Ward's "Lives of the Gresham Professors," 1740, Dr. Woodward and Dr. Mead, Gresham professors, are represented as drawing swords. This refers to an actual quarrel between the two men, when Mead obtained the advantage, and commanded Woodward to beg his life. "No, doctor," said the vanquished man, "that I will not, till I am your patient." But he never-

theless at last wisely yielded, and Vertue has represented him tendering his sword to his conqueror.

One of the largest of the Jews' synagogues in London was built by Davies, in 1838, in Great St. Helen's, Bishopsgate. It is in rich Italian style, with an open loggia of three arches, resting upon Tuscan columns. The sides have Doric piers, and Corinthian columns above, behind which are the ladies' galleries, in the Oriental manner of the Jews, fronted with rich brass-work. There are no pews. The centre floor has a platform, and seats for the principal officers, with four large brass-gilt candelabra. At the south end is "the ark," a lofty semicircular-domed recess, consisting of Italian-Doric pilasters, with *verde antico* and porphyry shafts, and gilt capitals; and Corinthian columns with sienna shafts, and capitals and entablature in white and gold. In the upper storey the inter-columns are filled with three arched windows of stained glass, arabesque pattern, by Nixon, the centre one having "Jehovah," in Hebrew, and the tables of the Law. The semi-dome is decorated with gilded rosettes on an azure ground; there are rich festoons of fruit and flowers between the capitals of the Corinthian columns, and ornaments on the frieze above, on which is inscribed in Hebrew, "Know in whose presence thou standest." The centre of the lower part is fitted up with recesses for books of the Law, enclosed with polished mahogany doors, and partly concealed by a rich velvet curtain, fringed with gold; there are massive gilt candelabra, and the pavement and steps to the ark are of fine veined Italian marble, partly carpeted. Externally, the ark is flanked with an arched panel, that on the east containing a prayer for the Queen and Royal Family in Hebrew, and the other a similar one in English. Above the ark is a rich fan-painted window, and a corresponding one, though less brilliant, at the north end. The ceiling, which is flat, is decorated with thirty coffers, each containing a large flower aperture, for ventilation. This synagogue appears to have been removed from Leadenhall Street.

Leathersellers' Hall, at the east end of St. Helen's Place, was rebuilt about 1815, on the site of the old hall, which had formed part of the house of the Black Nuns of St. Helen's, taken down in 1799. The original site had been purchased by the Company soon after the surrender of the priory to Henry VIII. The old hall contained a curiously-carved Elizabethan screen, and an enriched ceiling, with pendants. Beneath the present hall runs the crypt of the Priory of St. Helen's, which we have already described. In the yard belonging to the hall is a curious pump, with a mermaid pressing her breasts, out of which, on festive occasions, wine used formerly to run. It was made by Caius Gabriel Cibber, in 1679, as payment to the Company of his livery fine of £25. The Leather-sellers were incorporated by the 21st of Richard II., and by a grant of Henry VII. the wardens were empowered to inspect sheep, lamb, and calf leather throughout the kingdom.

It was at the "Bull" Inn, Bishopsgate Street, that Shakespeare's friend, Burbage, and his fellows, obtained a patent from Queen Elizabeth for erecting a permanent building for theatrical entertainments. Tarlton, the comedian, often played here. The old inns of London were the first theatres, as we have before shown. Anthony Bacon (the brother of the great Francis), resided in a house in Bishops-gate Street, not far from the "Bull" Inn, to the great concern of his watchful mother, who not only dreaded that the plays and interludes acted at the "Bull" might corrupt his servants, but also objected on her own son's account to the parish, as being without a godly clergyman. The "Four Swans," and the "Green Dragon," lately pulled down, were fine old inns, with galleries complete. It was at the "Bull" that Hobson, the old Cambridge carrier eulogised by Milton, put up. The *Spectator* says that there was a fresco figure of him on the inn walls, with a hundred-pound bag under his arm, with this inscription on the said bag—

"The fruitful mother of an hundred more."

Milton's lines on this sturdy old driver are full of kindly regret, and are worth remembering—

"*On the University Carrier, who sickened in the time of the Vacancy, being forbid to go to London, by reason of the Plague.*

"Here lies old Hobson ; Death hath broke his girt,
And here, alas ! hath laid him in the dirt ;
Or else, the ways being foul, twenty to one,
He's here stuck in a slough, and overthrown.
'Twas such a shifter, that if truth were known,
Death was half glad when he had got him down ;
For he had, any time these ten years full,
Dodg'd with him, betwixt Cambridge and the 'Bull ;'
And surely Death could never have prevail'd,
Had not his weekly course of carriage fail'd ;
But lately finding him so long at home,
And thinking now his journey's end was come,
And that he had ta'en up his latest inn,
In the kind office of a chamberlain,
Show'd him his room, where he must lodge that night,
Pull'd off his boots, and took away the light ;
If any ask for him, it shall be said,
'Hobson has supt, and 's newly gone to bed.' "

The original portrait and parchment certificate of Mr. Van Harn, a frequenter of the house, were long preserved at the "Bull" Inn. This worthy is said to have drank 35,680 bottles of wine in this hostelry. In 1649 five Puritan troopers were sentenced to death for a mutiny at the "Bull."

The first Bethlehem Hospital was originally a priory of canons, with brothers and sisters, formed in 1246, in Bishopsgate Without, by Simon Fitz Mary, a London sheriff. Henry VIII., at the dissolution, gave it to the City of London, who turned it into an hospital for the insane. Stow speaks vaguely of an insane hospital near Charing Cross, removed by a king of England, who objected to mad people near his palace. The hospital was removed from Bishopsgate to Moorfields, in 1675, at a cost of "nigh £17,000."

The first Artillery Ground was in Teasel Close, now Artillery Lane, Bishopsgate Street Without. Stow describes Teasel Close as a place where teasels (the *tæsal* of the Anglo-Saxons, *Dipsacus fullonum*, or fullers' teasel of naturalists) were planted for the clothworkers, afterwards let to the cross-bow makers, to shoot matches at the popinjay. It was in his day closed in with a brick wall, and used as an artillery yard ; and there the Tower gunners came every Thursday, to practise their exercise, firing their "brass pieces of great artillery" at earthen butts. The Trained Bands removed to Finsbury in 1622.

Teasel Close was the practice-ground of the old City Trained Band, established in 1585, during the alarm of the expected Spanish Armada. "Certain gallant, active, and forward citizens," says Stow, "voluntarily exercising themselves for the ready use of war, so as within two years there was almost 300 merchants, and others of like quality, very sufficient and skilful to train and teach the common soldiers." The alarm subsiding, the City volunteers again gave way to the grave gunners of the Tower, warriors as guiltless of blood as themselves. In 1610, martial ardour again rising, a new company was formed, and weekly drill practised with renewed energy. Many country gentlemen from the shires used to attend the drills, to learn how to command the country Trained Bands. In the Civil Wars, especially at the battle of Newbury, these London Trained Bands fought with firmness and courage. Lord Clarendon is even proud to confess this. "The London Trained Bands," he says, "and auxiliary regiments (of whose inexperience of danger, or any kind of service beyond the easy practice of their postures in the Artillery Garden, men had till then too cheap in estimation) behaved themselves to wonder, and were in truth the preservation of that army that day. For they stood as a bulwark and rampire to defend the rest ; and when their wings of horse were scattered and dispersed, kept their ground so steadily, that though Prince Rupert himself led up the choice horse to charge them, and endured their storm of small shot, he could make no impression upon their stand of pikes, but was forced to wheel about; of so sovereign benefit and use is that readiness, order, and dexterity in the use of their arms, which hath been so much neglected."

Lord High Chamberlain to Queen Elizabeth, took it. The Queen lodged here during one of her visits to the City, and here probably the Earl presented his royal mistress with the first pair of perfumed gloves brought to England. The mansion afterwards fell to the noble family of Cavendish,

ST. ETHELBURGA'S CHURCH, 1870. (*See page* 159.)

Devonshire Square, a humble place now, was originally the site of a large house with pleasure-gardens, bowling-greens, &c., built and laid out by Jasper Fisher, one of the six clerks in Chancery, a Justice of the Peace, and a freeman of the Goldsmiths' Company. The house being considered far too splendid for a mere clerk in Chancery, much in debt, was nicknamed "Fisher's Folly. After Fisher's downfall, Edward, Earl of Oxford,

William Cavendish, the second Earl of Devonshire, dying in it about the year 1628. The family of Cavendish appear to have been old Bishopsgate residents, as Thomas Cavendish, Treasurer of the Exchequer to Henry VIII., buried his lady in St. Botolph's Church, and by will bequeathed a legacy for the repair of the building. The Earls of Devonshire held the house from 1620 to 1670, but during the Civil Wars, when the sour-faced preachers were all-powerful, the earl's City mansion became a conventicle, and resounded with the unctuous groans of the crop-eared listeners. Butler, in his "Hudibras," says the Rump Parliament resembled

> "No part of the nation
> But Fisher's Folly congregation."

About the close of the seventeenth century, when the Penny Post was started, one of the inventors, Mr. Robert Murray, clerk to the Commissioners of the Grand Excise of England, set up a Bank of Credit at Devonshire House, where men depositing their goods and merchandise were furnished with

in London—the Danish king cried, "I like the treason, but detest the traitor. Behead this fellow, and as he claims the promise, place his head on the highest pinnacle of the Tower." Edric was then drawn by his heels from Baynard's Castle, tormented to death by burning torches, his head placed on the turret, and his scorched body thrown into Houndsditch.

Stow speaks of the old City ditch as a filthy place, full of dead dogs, but before his time covered over and enclosed by a mud wall. On the side of the ditch over against this mud wall was a field at

SIR THOMAS GRESHAM'S HOUSE IN BISHOPSGATE STREET. (*See page* 159.)

bills of current credit at two-thirds or three-fourths of the value of the said goods.

Hatton, in 1708, calls the square "a pretty though very small square, inhabited by gentry and other merchants;" and Strype describes it as "an airy and creditable place, where the Countess of Devonshire, in my memory, dwelt in great repute for her hospitality."

Houndsditch, which may be called an indirect tributary of Bishopsgate, though not a dignified place, has a legend of its own. Richard of Cirencester says that here the body of Edric, the murderer of his sovereign Edmund Ironside, was contemptuously thrown by Canute, whom he had raised to the throne. When Edric, flushed with his guilty success, came to claim of Canute the promised reward of his crime—the highest situation

one time belonging to the Priory of the Holy Trinity, which being given, at the dissolution, to Sir Thomas Audley, was handed over by him to Magdalen College, Cambridge, of which he was the founder.

Brokers and sellers of disconsolate cast-off apparel took kindly to this place immediately after the Reformation, settling in this field of the priory; while the old dramatists frequently allude to the Jew brokers and usurers of this district, of the "melancholy" of which Shakespeare has spoken. "Where got'st thou this coat, I marle?" says Well-bred in Ben Jonson's *Every Man in his Humour;* to which Brainworm answers, "Of a Houndsditch man, sir; one of the devil's near kinsmen, a broker." And Beaumont and Fletcher call the place contemptuously Dogsditch :—

> "More knavery, and usury,
> And foolery, and brokery than Dogsditch."

In the reign of Henry VIII. three brothers named Owens set up in this field a foundry for brass ordnance, and the rest of the place was turned into garden ground. At the end of the reign of Edward VI. pleasant houses for respectable citizens began to be erected.

"This field," says Stow, "as all others about the City, was enclosed, reserving open passage thereinto for such as were disposed. Towards the street were some small cottages of two storeys high, and little garden plots, backward, for poor bedrid people (for in that street dwelt none other), builded by some Prior of the Holy Trinity, to whom that ground belonged.

"In my youth I remember devout people, as well men as women of this City, were accustomed oftentimes, especially on Fridays weekly, to walk that way purposely, and there to bestow their charitable alms, every poor man or woman lying in their bed within their window, which was towards the street, open so low that every man might see them; a clean linen cloth lying in their window, and a pair of beads, to show that there lay a bedrid body, unable but to pray only. This street was first paved in the year 1503."

The favourite localities of the Jew old-clothesmen were Cobb's Yard, Roper's Buildings, and Wentworth Street.

"The Jew old-clothesmen," says Mr. Mayhew, "are generally far more cleanly in their habits than the poorer classes of English people. Their hands they always wash before their meals, and this is done whether the party be a strict Jew or 'Meshumet,' a convert or apostate from Judaism. Neither will the Israelite ever use the same knife to cut his meat that he previously used to spread his butter, and he will not even put his meat upon a plate that has had butter on it; nor will he use for his soup the spoon that has had melted butter in it. This objection to mix butter with meat is carried so far, that, after partaking of the one, Jews will not eat of the other for two hours. The Jews are, generally, when married, most exemplary family men. There are few fonder fathers than they are, and they will starve themselves sooner than their wives or children should want. Whatever their faults may be, they are good fathers, husbands, and sons. Their principal characteristic is their extreme love of money; and, though the strict Jew does not trade himself on the Sabbath, he may not object to employ either one of his tribe, or a Gentile to do so for him.

"The capital required for commencing in the old clothes line is generally about £1. This the Jew frequently borrows, especially after holiday time, for then he has generally spent all his earnings, unless he be a provident man. When his stock-money is exhausted, he goes either to a neighbour or to a publican in the vicinity, and borrows £1 on the Monday morning, 'to strike a light with,' as he calls it, and agrees to return it on the Friday evening, with a shilling interest for the loan. This he always pays back. If he were to sell the coat off his back he would do this, I am told, because to fail in so doing would be to prevent his obtaining any stock-money in the future. With this capital he starts on his rounds about eight in the morning, and I am assured he will frequently begin his work without tasting food rather than break into the borrowed stock-money. Each man has his particular walk, and never interferes with that of his neighbour; indeed, while upon another's beat, he will seldom cry for clothes. Sometimes they go half 'rybeck' together—that is, they will share the profits of the day's business; and when they agree to do this, the one will take one street, and the other another. The lower the neighbourhood the more old clothes are there for sale. At the East-end of the town they like the neighbourhoods frequented by sailors; and there they purchase of the girls and the women the sailors' jackets and trousers. But they buy most of the Petticoat Lane, the Old Clothes Exchange, and the marine-store dealers; for, as the Jew clothes-man never travels the streets by night-time, the parties who then have old clothes to dispose of usually sell them to the marine-store or second-hand dealers over-night, and the Jew buys them in the morning. The first that he does on his rounds is to seek out these shops, and see what he can pick up there. A very great amount of business is done by the Jew clothes-man at the marine-store shops at the West as well as at the East-end of London."

Within a short distance of Houndsditch stood Hand Alley. built on the site of one of the receptacles for the dead during the raging of the great Plague in 1665. "The upper end of Hand Alley, in Bishopsgate Street," writes Defoe, "which was then a green, and was taken in particularly for Bishopsgate parish, though many of the carts out of the City brought their dead thither also, particularly out of the parish of St. Allhallows-in-the-Wall: this place I cannot mention without much regret. It was, as I remember, about two or three years after the Plague was ceased, that Sir Robert Clayton came to be possessed of the ground. It was reported, how true I know not, that it fell to the king for want of heirs, all those who had any right to it being carried off by the pestilence, and that Sir Robert Clayton obtained a grant of it from Charles II. But however he came by it, certain it is the ground was let out to be built upon, or built upon by his order. The first house built upon it was a large fair house, still standing, which faces the street or way now called Hand Alley, which, though called an alley, is as wide as a street. The houses, in the same row with that house northward, are built on the very same ground where the poor people were buried, and the bodies, on opening the ground for the foundations, were dug up; some of them remaining so plain to be seen, that the women's skulls were distinguished by their long hair, and of others the flesh was not quite perished, so that the people began to exclaim loudly against it, and some suggested that it might endanger a return of the contagion. After which the bones and bodies, as they came at them, were carried to another part of the same ground, and thrown all together into a deep pit dug on purpose, which now is to be known in that it is not built on, but is a passage to another house at the upper end of Rose Alley, just against the door of a meeting-house. . . . There lie the bones and remains of near 2,000 bodies, carried by the dead-carts to their graves in that one year."

A turning from Houndsditch, of unsavoury memory, leads to Bevis Marks. Here formerly stood the City mansion and gardens of the abbots of Bury. The corruption of Bury's Marks to Bevis Marks is undoubted, though not obvious. Stow describes it as "one great house, large of rooms, fair courts, and garden plots," some time pertaining to the Bassets, and afterwards to the abbots of Bury. Bury Street, where the old house stood, was remarkable for a synagogue of Portuguese Jews, and a Dissenting chapel, where the good Dr. Watts was for many years pastor.

Towards Camomile Street, close to London Wall, stood the Papey, a religious house belonging to a brotherhood of St. John and St. Charity (our readers will remember Shakespeare talks of "By Gis and by St. Charity"), founded in 1430, by three charity priests. The members were professional mourners, and are often so represented on monuments. The original band consisted of a master, two wardens, chaplains, chantry priests, conducts, and other brothers and sisters. Sir Francis Walsingham, Elizabeth's astute and wily secretary, afterwards inhabited the house.

Old Broad Street, as late as the reign of Charles I., was (says Cunningham) one of the most fashionable streets in London. In Elizabeth's reign, Gilbert Talbot, Earl of Shrewsbury, lived here, and, in Charles's time, Lords Weston and Dover. Here at the same time was a glass-house, where Venice glasses (then so prized) were made by Venetian workmen. Mr. James Howell, author of the "Familiar Letters" which bear his name, was (says Strype) steward to this house. When Howell, unable to bear the heat of the place, gave up his stewardship, he said, if he had stayed much longer, he should in a short time have melted to nothing among these hot Venetians. The place afterwards became Pinners' Hall, and then a Dissenting chapel. The Pinners, or Pinmakers, were incorporated by Charles I. In February, 1659-60 Monk drew up his forces in Finsbury, dined with the Lord Mayor, had conference with him and the Court of Aldermen, retired to the "Bull's Head," in Cheapside, and quartered at the glass-house, in Broad Street, multitudes of people following him, and congratulating him on his coming into the City, amid shouting, clashing bells, and lighted bonfires.

In Old Broad Street the elder Dance built the Excise Office in 1768, which was removed in 1848 to Somerset House. This Government Office originally stood on the west side of Ironmonger Lane, where was formerly the mansion of Sir J. Frederick. For £500 a year the trustees of the Gresham estates annihilated Gresham College. Dance's building, of stone and brick, was much praised for its simple grandeur. Charles I. seems to have intended to levy excise duties as early as 1626, but the Parliament stopped him. The Parliament, however, to maintain their forces, were compelled to found an Excise Office, in 1643, and ale, beer, cider, and perry were the first articles taxed, together with wine, silks, fur, hats, and lace. There were riots in London about the new system, and the mob burnt down the Excise House in Smithfield. The Excise revenue at first amounted to £1,334,532. The first act after the Restoration was to abolish excise on all articles except ale, &c., which produced an annual revenue of £666,383. The duties on glass and malt were first imposed in William's reign, and the salt duty was then re-imposed. Queen Anne's expensive wars led to duties on paper and soap; and her revenue from excise amounted to £1,738,000 a year. In the reign of George I. the produce of the Excise averaged £2,340,000. Sir Robert Walpole did all he could to extend the Excise, while Pitt carried out all Walpole had attempted. In 1793, no fewer than twenty-nine articles were subject to the Excise laws, and the gross revenue from them amounted to ten millions and a half. In 1797, the number of officers employed in England was 4,777. In the first twenty years after the peace, the reduction of duties led to the dismissal of 847 Excise officers.

One of the most distinguished inhabitants of Broad Street, many years ago, was the great surgeon, Sir Astley Cooper. "He was then," says "Aleph," "attached to Guy's Hospital, having a large class of pupils, and a numerous morning levee of City patients. His house was a capacious corner tenement in Broad Street, on the right-hand side of the wide-paved court leading by St. Botolph's Church into Bishopsgate Street. When patients applied they were ushered into a large front room, which would comfortably receive from forty to fifty persons. It was plainly furnished; the floor covered with a Turkey carpet, a goodly muster of lumbering mahogany horse-hair seated chairs, a long table in the centre, with a sprinkling of tattered books and stale periodicals, 'Asperne's Magazine,' and the 'British Critic,' and a dingy, damaged pier-glass over the chimney. Sir Astley Cooper's earnings during the first nine years of his practice progressed thus—First year, 5 guineas; second, £26; third, £64; fourth, £96; fifth, £100; sixth, £200; seventh, £400; eighth, £600; ninth, £1,100. But the time was coming when patients were to stand for hours in his ante-rooms waiting for an interview, and were often dismissed without being admitted to the consulting-room. His man Charles, with infinite dignity, used to say to the disappointed applicants when they reappeared next morning, 'I am not at all sure that we shall be able to attend to you, for we are excessively busy, and our list is full for the day; but if you'll wait, I'll see what can be done for you.'"

The largest sum Sir Astley ever received in one year was £21,000, but for a series of years his income was more than £15,000 per annum. As long as he lived in the City his gains were enormous, though they varied, the state of the money market having a curious effect on his fees. Most of his City patients paid their fee with a cheque, and seldom wrote for less than £5 5s. Mr. Coles, of Mincing Lane, for a long period paid him £600 a year. A City man, who consulted him in Broad Street, and departed without giving any fee, soon after sent a cheque for £63 10s. A West Indian millionaire gave Sir Astley his largest fee. He had undergone successfully a painful operation, and paid his physicians, Lettsom and Nelson, with 300 guineas each. "But you, sir," cried the grateful old man, sitting up in bed, and addressing Cooper, "shall have something better. There, sir, take that!" It was his nightcap, which he flung at the surprised surgeon. "Sir," answered Cooper, "I'll pocket the affront," and on reaching home he

found in the cap a draft for 1,000 guineas. When Sir Astley left Broad Street he established himself in Spring Gardens, and there, too, his practice was very considerable.

Cardinal Newman was born in Broad Street, where his father was a banker.

In 1854, on taking down the Excise Office, at about fifteen feet lower than the foundation of Gresham House, was found a pavement twenty-eight feet square. It is a geometrical pattern of broad blue lines, forming intersections of octagon and lozenge compartments. The octagon figures are bordered with a cable pattern, shaded with grey, and interlaced with a square border, shaded with red and yellow. In the centres, within a ring, are expanded flowers, shaded in red, yellow, and grey; the double row of leaves radiating from a figure called a truelove-knot, alternately with a figure something like the tiger-lily. Between the octagon figures are square compartments bearing various devices; in the centre of the pavement is Ariadne, or a Bacchante, reclining on the back of a panther; but only the fore-paws, one of the hind-paws, and the tail remain. Over the head of the figure floats a light drapery forming an arch. Another square contains a two-handled vase. In the demi-octagons, at the sides of the pattern, are lunettes; one contains a fan ornament, another a bowl crowned with flowers. The lozenge intersections are variously embellished with leaves, shells, truelove-knots, chequers, and an ornament shaped like a dice-box. At the corners of the pattern are truelove-knots. Surrounding this pattern, in a broad cable-like border, are broad bands of blue and white alternately.

The church of St. Peter le Poor, Old Broad Street, stands near the site of old Paulet House. Stow thinks this may once have been a poor parish, and so gives its name to the saint, "though at this present time there be many fair houses possessed by rich merchants and others." The church being in a ruinous condition, was pulled down in 1788, rebuilt by Jesse Gibson, and consecrated by Bishop Porteus in 1792.

Old Broad Street leads us into the interesting region of Austin Friars, a district rich in antiquities. Here once stood a priory of begging friars, founded, in 1243, by Humphrey Bohun, Earl of Hereford and Essex, and dedicated to St. Augustine, Bishop of Hippo, in Africa. The church was ornamented "with a fine spired steeple, small, high, and straight," which Stow admired. At the dissolution of the monasteries, Henry VIII. granted the friars' house and grounds to William Paulet, first Marquis of Winchester, Comptroller of the Household, and Lord High Treasurer, who made the place his town residence. The church was reserved, and given by Edward VI., to the Dutchmen of London, to have their services in, "for avoiding of all sects of Ana-Baptists, and such like." The decorated windows of the church are still preserved, but the spire and the splendid tombs mentioned by Stow are gone.

"Here," says Mr. Jesse, "lies the pious founder of the priory, Humphrey de Bohun, who stood god-father at the font for Edward I., and who afterwards fought against Henry III., with the leagued barons, at the battle of Evesham. Here were interred the remains of the great Hubert de Burgh, Earl of Kent, the most powerful subject in Europe during the reigns of King John and Henry III., and no less celebrated for his chequered and romantic fortunes. Here rests Edmund, son of Joan Plan-tagenet, 'the Fair Maid of Kent,' and half-brother to Richard II. Here lies the headless trunk of the gallant Fitzallan, tenth Earl of Arundel, who was executed in Cheapside in 1397. Here also rest the mangled remains of the barons who fell at the battle of Barnet, in 1471, and who were interred together in the body of the church; of John de Vere, twelfth Earl of Oxford, who was beheaded on Tower Hill with his eldest son, Aubrey, in 1461; and, lastly, of the gallant and princely Edward Stafford, Duke of Buckingham—'poor Edward Bohun'—who, having fallen a victim to the vin-dictive jealousy of Cardinal Wolsey, was beheaded on Tower Hill in 1521."

The Rev. Mr. Hugo says that the old conven-tual church of Austin Friars had all the magni-ficence of a cathedral; it consisted of the present nave, 153 feet in length, 183 broad, with ample transepts and choir. There are visible thirty-six monumental slabs; seventeen with one or more small figures, and sixteen with one or more shields and small inscriptions at the foot. The church suffered extensively by fire in 1862, and its roof and clerestory have been "restored" in a most singular manner.

In Austin Friars (1735) Richard Gough the antiquary was born; and here, at No. 18, lived James Smith, one of the authors of the "Rejected Addresses." A second James Smith coming to the place, after he had been many years a resident here, produced so much confusion to both, that the last comer waited on the author and suggested, to prevent future inconvenience, that one or other had better leave, hinting, at the same time, that he should like to stay. "No," said the wit, "I am James the First, you are James the Second; you must abdicate."

Lord Winchester died in 1572, and his son, having sold the monuments at Austin Friars for £100, took the lead off the roof, and made stabling of the church ground. In 1602 the fourth marquis was so poor as to be compelled to part with Austin Friars to John Swinnerton, a London merchant, afterwards Lord Mayor. Fulke Greville (Sir Philip Sidney's friend), who lived in Austin Friars, wrote in alarm at this change to the Countess of Shrewsbury, one of his neighbours. Lady Warwick seems to have been another tenant of the Friary.

In Winchester Street, adjoining Austin Friars, stood Winchester House, built by the first Marquis of Winchester, who also founded Basing House. This nobleman died in 1572, in his ninety-seventh year, having lived under nine sovereigns, and having 103 persons immediately descended from him. When this marquis was asked how he had retained royal favour and power under so many conflicting sovereigns, he replied, "By being a willow, and not an oak." Mr. Jesse visited the house before its demolition, in 1839, and found the old Paulet motto, "Aimez Loyaulte," on many of the stained-glass windows. This was the motto that the Marquis of Winchester, during the gallant defence of Basing House, engraved with a diamond on every window of his mansion. It was in apart-ments of this house in Austin Friars that Anne Clifford, daughter of the Countess of Cumberland, was married to her first husband, Richard, third Earl of Dorset, on the 25th of February, 1608–9. It was this proud lady (already mentioned by us) who returned the defiant answer to the election agents of Charles II., "Your man shall not stand."

In 1621, the Earl of Strafford (a victim of the sham Popish plot), when representing York, took up his residence in Austin Friars, with his young children and the fair wife whom he lost in the following year, and whom he alluded to in his trial as "a saint in heaven." In Austin Friars died, in 1776, James Heywood, who had been one of the popular writers in the *Spectator*. He is said to have been originally a wholesale linendraper in Fish Street Hill.

Nearly at the end of Little Winchester Street is the Church of Allhallows-in-the-Wall. It escaped the Great Fire, but, becoming ruinous, was taken down in 1764, and the present church built by the younger Dance. In the chancel is a tablet to the Rev. W. Beloe, the well-known translator of Herodotus, who died in 1817, after having held the rectory of the parish for twenty years. The altar-piece, a copy of Pietro di Cortona's "Ananias restoring Paul to Sight," was the gift of Sir N. Dance. The parish books, commencing 1455, record the benefactions of an anchorite who lived near the church.

London Wall, an adjoining street, is interesting, as indicating the site of that portion of the old City wall that divided the City Liberty from the Manor of Finsbury. The old Bethlehem Hospital, taken

Aldgate, Houndsditch, Bishopsgate, along London Wall, to Fore Street; through Cripplegate and Castle Street to Aldersgate; and through Christ's Hospital, by Newgate and Ludgate, to the Thames.

In this street stood, till 1880, Sion College, built on the site of the Priory of Elsing Spital. Elsing was

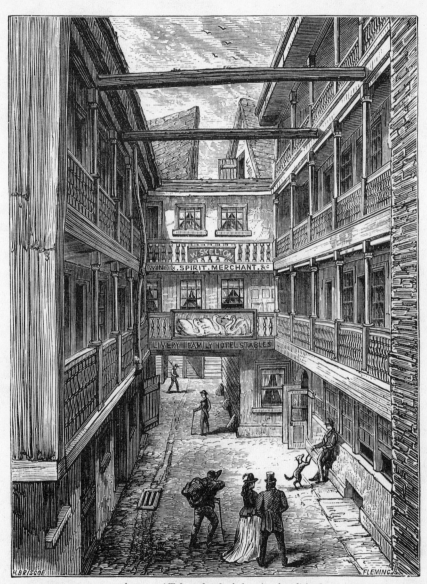

THE FOUR SWANS' INN. (*Taken shortly before its demolition.*) *See page 161.*

down in 1814, was built against the portion of the wall then removed. Hughson says the Roman work was found uncommonly thick, the bricks being double the size of those now used, and the centre filled in with large loose stones. The level of the street has been raised two feet within the last fifty years. The old Roman wall, it will be remembered, ran from the Tower through the Minories to

a London mercer, who, about 1329, founded an hospital for one hundred blind men on the site of a decayed nunnery. The house was subsequently turned into a priory, consisting of four canons regular, to minister to the blind, Elsing himself being the first prior.

The ground so long consecrated to charity was purchased, in pursuance of the will of Dr. Thomas

CORNHILL IN 1630. (From a View published by Boydell.)

White, vicar of St. Dunstan's-in-the-West, and in 1623 a college was erected, governed by a president, two deans, and four assistants. Dr. John Simson, rector of St. Olave's, Hart Street, and one of Dr. White's executors, founded a library. It contains the Jesuit books seized in 1679, and half the library of Sir Robert Cooke, the gift of George Lord Berkeley, in the reign of Charles II., but a third of the books were destroyed in the Great Fire. By the Copyright Act of Queen Anne, the library received a gratuitous copy of every work published, till 1836, when the college received instead a Treasury grant of £363 a year. The library contains more than 50,000 volumes, and is open to the public by an order from one of the Fellows. The College contains a curious old picture of the "Decollation of St. John the Baptist," with an inscription in Saxon characters, supposed to have come from Elsing's old priory. There are also a few good portraits.

Defoe, in his "Journey through England," 1722, speaks of Sion College as designed for the use of the clergy in and round London, where expectants could lodge till they were provided with houses in their own parishes. There was also a hospital for ten poor men and ten poor women. The College was transferred to a new site on the Thames Embankment purchased in 1880.

CHAPTER XXII.

CORNHILL, GRACECHURCH STREET, AND FENCHURCH STREET.

Mediæval Cornhill—The Standard—St. Michael's, Cornhill—St. Peter's—The First London Printsellers—A Comedian's Tragedy—Dreadful Fire in Cornhill—The First Coffee-house in London—"Garraway's "—Birchin Lane—St. Bennet Gracechurch—George Fox—Fenchurch Street—Denmark House—St. Dionis Backchurch—The Church of St. Margaret Pattens—Billiter Street—Ironmongers' Hall—Mincing Lane—The Clothworkers' Company—The Mark Lane Corn Exchange—The Corn Ports of London—Statistics and Curiosities of the Corn Trade—An Old Relic.

WHAT we have already written of the discovery of Roman antiquities on the site of the Royal Exchange will serve to show how completely Cornhill traverses the centre of Roman London.

A corn-market, says Stow, was, "time out of mind, there holden." Drapers were its earliest inhabitants. Lydgate speaks of it as a place where old clothes were bought, and sometimes stolen—

> " Then into Corn Hyl anon I yode,
> Where was mutch stolen gere amonge ;
> I saw where honge myne owne hoode,
> That I had lost amonge the thronge ;
> To buy my own hood I thought it wronge,
> I knew it well as I dyd my crede,
> But for lack of money I could not spede."

The two great ornaments of mediæval Cornhill were the Tun, a round house, or temporary prison; and the Standard, a water conduit, and point of measurement.

The Tun, says Stow, was built in the year 1282, by Henry Wallis, Mayor of London, as a prison for night offenders. For breaking open the prison and releasing prisoners, certain citizens, in the reign of Edward I., were fined 20,000 marks. Abandoned priests were sometimes locked up here. In 1401 the Tun was turned into a conduit, and a cage, stocks, and pillory added, for scolds and cheating bakers. Rascals of various kinds were, in Edward IV.'s reign, compelled to ride from Newgate to this pillory, in Cornhill, and there stand, with papers detailing their offences tied to their heads.

The Standard was a conduit, with four spouts, made by Peter Morris, a German, in the year 1582, and supplied with Thames water, conveyed by leaden pipes from the vicinity of St. Magnus' Church. It stood at the east end of Cornhill, at its junction with Gracechurch Street, Bishopsgate Street, and Leadenhall Street. The water ceased to run between 1598 and 1603, but the Standard itself remained long after. It was much used as a point of measurement of distances ; and Cunningham says that several of our suburban milestones are still inscribed with "so many miles from the Standard in Cornhill." There was a Standard in Cornhill as early as the 2nd of Henry V.

Cornhill, considering its commercial importance, is a street by no means full of old memories.

St. Michael's, Cornhill, is one of seven London churches dedicated to the Archangel Michael, the patron saint of France. It formerly faced Cornhill, but in the reign of Edward IV. it was blocked out by four houses, and it may now be described as standing on the east side of St. Michael's Alley. It is probable that a Saxon church first stood here ; but the earliest record of the fabric is previous to 1133. In that year the Abbot of Evesham granted it to Sparling, a priest, for the rent of one mark a year, and lodging, salt, water, and firing to the abbot, whenever he came to London.

In 1503 the Abbey of Evesham ceded it to the Drapers' Company for an annuity of £5 6s. 8d.

William Rous, sheriff of London in 1429, and who was buried in the chapel of St. Mary in this church, left £100 to found an altar in the chancel, and £40 towards a new tower, the old one having been burnt down in 1421. At the south side of the church there was originally a cloister, and in the churchyard a pulpit-cross, built by Sir John Rudston, Lord Mayor of London, who was buried beneath it. In the church is interred one of our old chroniclers, Alderman Fabian, who died in 1511. He is well known for his "Chronicles of England and France," which he termed "The Concordance of Histories." Here also rest the remains of the ancestors of another useful London chronicler, who was born in this parish, where his predecessors had resided for three generations. Stow's father and grandfather were both buried here. The grandfather, a tallow-chandler, with due remembrance of candles sold by him for such purposes, directs in his will that from All Hallows' Day till the Candlemas following a watching-candle burn on all the seven altars of the church from six o'clock till past seven, in worship of the seven sacraments. He also gave to a poor man and woman, every Sunday in one year, one penny to say five paternosters and aves and a credo for his soul.

The old church, all but the tower, was destroyed by the Great Fire, and Wren commenced the present building in 1672. The tower itself had to be rebuilt in 1721. The body of the church is in the Italian style, divided by Doric columns and arches. The tower is perpendicular, in imitation of the chapel tower at Magdalen College, Oxford, and it rises to the height of 130 feet. Wren spoiled his rival tower by a mixture of Italian details. This church was magnificently decorated in 1859, from designs by Sir G. G. Scott.

The chronicler Stow has the following legend, relating how the devil came down to St. Michael's belfry in a storm of lightning :—" Upon St. James's Night," says our venerable author, " certain men in the loft next under the bells, ringing of a peal, a tempest of lightning and thunder did arise : an ugly-shapen sight appeared to them coming in at the south window and lighted on the north. For fear whereof they all fell down, and lay as dead for the time, letting the bells ring and cease of their own accord. When the ringers came to themselves, they found certain stones of the north window to be raised and scratched, as if they had been so much butter printed with a lyon's claw ; the same stones were fastened there again, and so remain till this day. I have seen them oft, and have put a feather or small stick into the holes where the claws had entered three or four inches deep."

A brass slab preserved at St. Peter's, Cornhill, claims that building as the first Christian church founded in London. The legendary founder was Lucius, the first Christian king, A.D. 179. It is said to have remained the metropolitan church of the kingdom till the coming of St. Augustine, four hundred years after.

In the reign of Henry III. one Geoffrey Russell, who had been implicated in a murder said to have been committed by another man in St. Peter's Churchyard, fled for sanctuary to St. Peter's Church. In the year 1243, one of the priests attached to St. Peter's, Cornhill, was murdered. The patronage of the rectory came into the hands of Sir Richard Whittington, and others, who conveyed it, in 1411, to the Lord Mayor and Commonalty of London. Among the celebrated rectors we must not forget Dr. William Beveridge, afterwards Bishop of St. Asaph. Dr. Beveridge (died 1708) was an eminent theological writer, famous for his Syriac Grammar, and his laborious work on the Apostolical Canons. The old church was destroyed by the Great Fire, and the present edifice erected in 1686 by Sir Christopher Wren. The tower of brick is surmounted by a small leaden cupola and spire, crowned by an enormous key. The church contains a tablet recording the death, in a great fire, January 18th, 1782, of the seven children of James Woodmason, of Leadenhall Street. Leading from the church, it is said, is a subterranean passage, entered by a flight of steps from the belfry. Some " London tavern " apprentices are reported, many years ago, to have explored this passage, which is now bricked up. Many years ago a stone coffin and urn were found within the enclosure of the church.

One of the most celebrated taverns in Cornhill was the " Pope's Head," mentioned as early as the reign of Edward IV. Here, in the reign of Henry VI., wine was sold at a penny a pint, without charge for bread. Stow seems to think the " Pope's Head " had once been a royal palace. In his time the ancient arms of England (three leopards supported by two angels) were to be seen engraved in stone on the walls. It was here that the Alicant and English goldsmiths decided their wager, as we have already mentioned in our chapter on the Goldsmiths' Company. In 1615, Sir William Craven, father of the first Earl of Craven, left the " Pope's Head " to the Merchant Taylors' Company, for charitable purposes, and the Company had in 1849 nine houses on that spot. The first edition of Speed's "Great Britain" (folio, 1611) was sold by John Sudbury and George Humble in Pope's Head

Alley, at the sign of the "White Horse." This firm, says Cunningham, were the first printsellers established in London. Ben Jonson mentions the pamphlets of Pope's Alley, and Peacham, in his "Complete Gentleman," alludes to the printsellers. Before the Great Fire, the alley was famous for its traders in toys and turners' ware. In Strype's time (thirty years later) it was especially affected by cutlers. The "Pope's Head" tavern was the scene of a fray, in April, 1718, between Quin, the actor, and his fellow-comedian Bowen. The latter, a hot-headed Irishman, jealous of Quin's success, sent for him to the "Pope's Head." As soon as Quin entered, Bowen, in a transport of envy and rage, planted his back against the door, drew his sword, and bade Quin draw his. Quin in vain remonstrated, but at last drew in his own defence, and tried to disarm his antagonist. Bowen eventually received a mortal wound, of which he died in three days, confessing at last his folly and madness. Quin was tried, and honourably acquitted.

Cornhill has been the scene of two dreadful fires. The first, in 1748, commenced at a peruke-maker's, in Exchange Alley, and burnt from ninety to one hundred houses, valued at £200,000, and many lives were lost. This conflagration swept away a few historical houses, including the London Assurance Office, the "Fleece" and "Three Tuns" taverns, "Tom's" and the "Rainbow" coffee-houses, the "Swan" tavern, "Garraway's," "Jonathan's," and the "Jerusalem" coffee-houses, in Exchange Alley, besides the "George and Vulture" tavern. It likewise destroyed No. 41, Cornhill, a few doors from Birchin Lane, the house where, in 1716, the poet Gray had been born. Gray's father was an Exchange broker. The house was rebuilt, and was, in 1774, occupied by Natzell, a perfumer. In 1824 the occupant was also a perfumer. The second great fire, in 1765, also commenced at a peruke-maker's, in Bishopsgate Street, near Leadenhall Street. It made a clean sweep of all the houses from Cornhill to St. Martin Outwich; and the church parsonage, Merchant Taylors' Hall, and several houses in Threadneedle Street, were much damaged. The "White Lion" tavern, purchased the evening before for £3,000, all the houses in White Lion Court, five houses in Cornhill, and several houses in Leadenhall Street, were burnt, and several lives lost.

No. 15, Cornhill, with an old-fashioned front, is the shop of Messrs. Birch, the celebrated cooks and confectioners. We have already mentioned Mr. Birch, Lord Mayor in 1815-16, as the poet and orator, who wrote the "Adopted Child," and other dramatic works. He annually presented the mayor with a splendid cake, to keep Twelfth Night.

At a corner house half-way between Cornhill and Lombard Street, Thomas Guy, the wealthy stationer, commenced business. He was the son of a lighterman at Horsleydown, and was apprenticed to a Cheapside bookseller, as before mentioned by us. The "Lucky Corner" was subsequently Pidding's Lottery Office. There were other lottery offices in Cornhill, including that of Carroll, Lord Mayor in 1846.

Change Alley, Cornhill, recalls the days of the South Sea Bubble, and brings up recollections of Addison, Pope, and Gay. The latter poet mentions it in his verses to his friend Snow, the goldsmith and banker, near Temple Bar, who had been caught by the Bubble:—

"Why did 'Change Alley waste thy precious hours
　Among the fools who gaped for golden show'rs?
No wonder if we found some poets there,
Who live on fancy, and can feed on air;
No wonder they were caught by South Sea schemes,
Who ne'er enjoyed a guinea but in dreams."

In St. Michael's Alley, in the time of the Commonwealth, the first London coffee-house was established. It was opened, about the year 1652, by Bowman, the ex-coachman of Mr. Hodges, a Turkey merchant. His first partner was Pasque Rosee, a Levantine servant of the same merchant. Bowman afterwards dissolved partnership, and obtained leave to pitch a tent and sell the "sooty drink," at first so much villified by the jealous vintners, in St. Michael's churchyard. Four years after, Bowman's apprentice set up a coffee-house opposite St. Michael's Church. The novelty was soon over, in spite of the lampooners, who declared it made men unfruitful, and that to drink the new liquor was to ape the Turks and insult one's canary-drinking ancestors. "Were it the mode," says the writer of "Coffee in its Colours" (1663), "men would eat spiders."

"Garraway's," the coffee-house celebrated for two centuries, in Exchange Alley, is now pulled down. It was here that, after the Restoration, Garraway issued the following shop-bill:—"Tea in England hath been sold in the leaf for six pounds, and sometimes for ten pounds the pound weight, and in respect of its former scarceness and dearness it hath been only used as a regalia in high treatments and entertainments, and presents made thereof to princes and grandees, till the year 1657. The said Thomas Garway did purchase a quantity thereof, and first publicly sold the said tea in leaf, and drink made according to the directions of the most knowing merchants and travellers into those eastern countries; and upon knowledge and experience of the said Garway's continued care and industry in obtaining the best tea, and making drink thereof, very many noblemen, physicians, merchants, and gentlemen of quality, have ever since sent to him for the said leaf, and daily resort to his house, in Exchange Alley aforesaid, to drink the drink thereof. . . . . These are to give notice that the said Thomas Garway hath tea to sell from 16s. to 50s. a pound."

Defoe (1722) mentions Garraway's as frequented about noon by people of quality who had business in the City, and the more considerable and wealthy citizens. Dean Swift, in his ballad on the South Sea Bubble, calls Change Alley "a narrow sound though deep as hell," and describes the wreckers watching for the shipwrecked dead on "Garraway's cliffs." Two excellent anecdotes of Dr. Radcliffe, the eminent physician of the reigns of William III. and Queen Anne, connect him with Garraway's. The first relates to Dr. Hannes, a quack, who had ordered his servant to stop a number of gentlemen's coaches between Whitehall and the Royal Exchange, and inquire whether they belonged to Dr. Hannes, as if he was called to a patient. Not hearing of him in any coach, the fellow ran up into Exchange Alley, and entering Garraway's Coffee House, made the same interrogatories both above and below. At last, Dr. Radcliffe, who was usually there about Exchange time, and planted at a table with several apothecaries and chirurgeons that flocked about him, cried out, "Dr. Hannes was not there," and desired to know "Who wanted him?" The fellow's reply was, such a lord and such a lord; but he was taken up with the dry rebuke, "No, no, friend, you are mistaken; the doctor wants those lords."

"A famous physician (Dr. Radcliffe) ventured 5,000 guineas upon a project in the South Sea. When he was told at Garraway's that 'twas all lost, 'Why,' says he, ''tis but going up 5,000 pair of stairs more.' This answer deserved a statue."

Steele, in the *Tatler*, mentions receiving some French wine as a taster of 216 hogsheads, to be put up at £20 the hogshead at Garraway's.

Garraway's was closed after a joyous existence of 216 years. As a place of sale, exchange, auction, and lottery, it was never excelled. Here tea was first sold, and here the South Sea Bubblers met.

"Jonathan's" was another well-known Change Alley coffee-house of the old times. It is described in the *Tatler* as "the general mart for stock-jobbers;" and Addison, in the *Spectator*, No. 1, says, "I sometimes pass for a Jew in the assembly of stock-jobbers at 'Jonathan's.'" Mrs. Centlivre has laid one of the scenes of her *Bold Stroke for a Wife* at "Jonathan's." While the business goes on she makes the coffee-boys cry, "Fresh coffee, gentlemen! fresh coffee! Bohea tea, gentlemen!"

In Freeman's Court, Cornhill, taken down about 1848 to build larger houses, Defoe carried on the business of hose-factor in 1702.

In Cowper's Court is one of the oldest-established of the City coffee-houses and news-rooms, the "Jerusalem." It was originally located in Bishopsgate Street, but removed to its present site about two centuries ago. The house was rebuilt after the fire in 1748, and again in 1879. Its "subscription-room" is much frequented by merchants and others connected with the shipping interests. Here, in 1845, John Tawell, the Slough murderer, was captured. He had been in the habit of visiting the "Jerusalem" in pursuit of information respecting his property in Sydney; and to this haunt, after committing the murder, he was traced though the agency of the electric wires.

Finch Lane derived its name from Robert Finke, the worthy citizen who built St. Bennet-Finke, the church pulled down to enlarge the Exchange.

Birchin Lane is thus described by Stow, the Herodotus of old London:—"Then have ye Birchover Lane, so called of Birchover, the first builder and owner thereof, now corruptly called Birchin Lane. . . . This lane, and the High Street, near adjoining, hath been inhabited for the most part with wealthy drapers; from Birchin Lane, on that side the street down to the Stocks, in the reign of Henry VI., had ye for the most part dwelling fripperers or upholders, that sold old apparel and household stuffs."

Dekker, in his "Gull's Horn Book," speaks of the whalebone doublets of Birchin Lane; and one of Middleton's characters purchases there "a captain's suit, a valiant buff doublet, stuffed with points, and a pair of velvet slops scored thick with lace." In Strype's time Birchin Lane was still famous for old clothes. Garrick, always a strategist, kept up his interest in the City, says Sir John Hawkins, by appearing about twice a winter at Tom's Coffee House, Birchin Lane, the usual rendezvous of young merchants at 'Change time. Poor Chatterton, writing to his sister, May 30, 1770, with his usual air of feigned success, says, "There is such a noise of business and politics in the room (Tom's) that my inaccuracy in writing here is highly excusable. My present profession obliges me to frequent places of the best resort."

Some London streets seem determined never to distinguish themselves. No mediæval scuffle has ever occurred in them; no celebrated church hoards its monuments; no City hall cherishes its relics there; no celebrated person has honoured it by birth or death. Gracechurch Street is one of these unambitious streets. It derived its name, says Stow, from the grass or herb market there kept in old time, and which gave its name to the parish church of St. Bennet.

St. Bennet Gracechurch, described by Stow, was destroyed in the Great Fire, and another structure, recently pulled down, erected from Wren's designs in 1685. It is now united with the parishes of Allhallows, Lombard Street, and St. Leonard's,

"There was one Banks, in the time of Tarlton, who served the Earl of Essex, and had a horse of strange qualities, and being at the 'Crosse Keyes' in Gracious Streete, getting money with him, as he was mightily resorted to, Tarlton then, with his fellowes, playing at the 'Bel' by, came into the 'Crosse Keyes,' amongst many people, to see fashions, which Banks perceiving, to make the people laugh, saies, 'Signior,' to his horse, 'go fetch me the veriest fool in the company.' The

GARRAWAY'S COFFEE-HOUSE. (*From a Sketch taken shortly before its demolition.*) *See page* 172.

Eastcheap. The register, says Cunningham, records the following burial :—"1559, April 14, Robert Burges, a common player," probably from the theatre in the yard of the "Cross Keys." In Gracechurch Street, Tarlton, the favourite clown of Elizabeth's time, a droll, short, flat-nosed fellow, who sang comic songs to the music of a pipe and tabor (he was probably the representative of Touchstone, and others of Shakespeare's jesters), lodged at the sign of the "Saba," probably to be near the "Cross Keys." He was chosen scavenger by the ward, and was constantly complained of for not keeping the streets clean. In the old book called "Tarlton's Jests," an early "Joe Miller," the following story is told of this street :—

jade comes immediately, and with his mouth draws Tarlton forth. Tarlton, with merry words, said nothing but 'God a mercy, horse!' . . . . Ever after it was a by-word through London, 'God a mercy, horse!' and is to this day."

Taylor, the water poet, in his little Directory, the "Carriers' Cosmographie" (1637), mentions the "Tabard, near the Conduit," and the "Spread Eagle," both in "Gracious Street." In White Hart Court was a Quakers' meeting-house; and here, in 1690, at the house of Henry Goldney, died that strange, but honest fanatic, George Fox, the founder of the sect. Fox was the son of a Leicestershire weaver, and being "converted" at nineteen, betook himself to itinerant preaching. He was examined by Cromwell on one occasion, and kindly treated ; and on the rumour that Oliver was going to make himself king, Fox went to him and personally remonstrated. Fox preached at this meeting-house in White Hart Court only a few days before his death. Penn says of Fox that he had an extra-

" Throw but a stone, the giant dies." A happy image, in singularly small compass.

Fenchurch Street, another thoroughfare scanty in memories, and therefore still open for future fame, took its name from the marshy ground on the banks of the Langbourne. Indeed, even in Stow's

INTERIOR OF CLOTHWORKERS' HALL. (*See page* 178.)

ordinary gift in " opening " the Scriptures, and that above all he excelled in prayer. In Nag's Head Court died, in 1737, Matthew Green, the hypochondriacal author of " The Spleen." He held a post in the Custom House, and was nephew to a clerk of Fishmongers' Hall. His pleasant poem was posthumous, and was printed by " Leonidas " Glover. It was approved by Pope and Gray, and will certainly live, if only for the celebrated line—

time, the ward was called Langbourne or Fennieabout ; yet at that date some crotchety antiquaries insisted that it was called Fenchurch from *fœnum*, or hay sold there, as Gracechurch from its grass and herbs.

In this street, which runs from Gracechurch to Aldgate, formerly stood Denmark House, the residence, in the reign of Philip and Mary (1557), of the first Russian ambassador sent to England.

The Russian Company had just started, and our merchants, eager for barbaric furs, gold, and amber, treated the Muscovite duke's envoy with prudent respect. They met him, with their velvet gowns and gold chains, at Tottenham. At Islington Lord Montacute, the Queen's pensioner, welcomed his approach, and at the same place the Lord Mayor and aldermen, in a blaze of scarlet, came up, and accompanied him to Master Dimmocks' in Fenchurch Street.

Of all London saints perhaps St. Dionis or Dionysius, the Areopagite, is the least honoured; and yet St. Dionis was the St. Denis of France. St. Dionis is called Backchurch, as some think, from there having originally been a church to St. Gabriel in the centre of the roadway, behind which stood St. Dionis; but this is doubtful. This church, mentioned as early as 1288, was rebuilt in the reign of Henry VI., and again after the Great Fire under Wren's supervision. The church, which stood close by Lime Street, was pulled down in 1877-8 to make room for shops and warehouses, and the parish united with that of Allhallows, Lombard Street. Sir Arthur Ingram, a Spanish merchant, who was commemorated by a monument in the church of St. Dionis, gave his name to Ingram Court in this street, and was a great benefactor to the church.

At the "King's Head," now the "London Tavern," No. 53, Fenchurch Street, the Princess Elizabeth, when released from the Tower by her harsh sister Mary, is said to have dined, after attending divine service at the church of Allhallows Staining, in Mark Lane. The young lady, always a fair trencherwoman, exulting in freedom and fresh air, partook freely of pork and peas. This royal act of condescension was celebrated till quite recently by an annual dinner of the chief parishioners. In the coffee-room they still show, with honest pride, the metal dish and cover said to have been occupied by the afore-mentioned peas and pork. Another legend has it that the princess, on quitting Allhallows, gave the clerk a handsome fee, which he celebrated by an annual dinner given to his chief patrons. The old tavern was rebuilt, and its name altered, in 1877. The building, as it now stands, is one of the most extensive and elaborately-furnished establishments of its kind in London.

The Church of St. Margaret Pattens was so called, says Stow, because pattens were usually made and sold in this neighbourhood, but more probably, we think, from the church being specially decorated on its roof with such "patines of bright gold" as those to which Shakespeare, in the *Merchant*

of Venice, compares the stars. The venerable shade of Stow will forgive us this trifling rebellion to his dictum. This church is mentioned as early as 1344, was in Whittington's gift, and was rebuilt after the Great Fire. In 1538, the rood, having been left in the churchyard to receive oblations, was destroyed by some too zealous Reformer. The altar-piece is by Carlo Maratti. The great antiquary, Dr. Birch, rector of the parish nearly nineteen years, is buried here. Above the altar are some finely-carved flowers.

In Fenchurch Street, on the site of Northumberland Alley, stood the first town residence of the Earls of Northumberland. The gardens were afterwards converted into bowling-alleys for all comers.

St. Catherine Coleman, close to where Northumberland House once stood, derived its name from a large garden belonging to one Coleman (date uncertain). This church escaped the Great Fire, and was rebuilt in 1734.

Pepys has the following interesting allusion to Fenchurch Street, in connection with the Plague. "June 10, 1665," he says, "to my great trouble, hear that the Plague is come into the City (though it hath these three or four weeks since its beginning been wholly out of the City); but where should it begin but in my good friend and neighbour's, Dr. Burnett, in Fenchurch Street; which, in both points, troubles me mightily.

"June 11.—I saw poor Dr. Burnett's door shut; but he hath, I hear, gained great good-will among his neighbours, for he discovered it himself first, and caused himself to be shut up of his own accord; which was very handsome."

Out of respect to Fenchurch Street, we may mention its small tributary, Billiter Street, a name corrupted from Belzettar, a forgotten builder or owner. Strype describes the place as consisting of poor and ordinary houses, formerly inhabited by needy, beggarly people. The inhabitants were then brokers and chandlers, residing in very old and ruinous timber houses. The chief ornament of it was Billiter Square, which Strype describes as "a very handsome, open, and airy place, graced with good new-brick buildings very well inhabited."

Ironmongers' Hall in Fenchurch Street is a building with a history and traditions of its own. The iron that supplied London in the Middle Ages was chiefly worked in Sussex, Surrey, and Kent.

The earliest account, says Mr. Herbert, we have of the Ironmongers as a guild is in the 37th year of Edward III., when on occasion of the various Crafts or Mysteries making their offerings to the king for his French wars, the Ironmongers subscribed £6 18s. 4d. The same Company, in the 50th of Edward III., sent four of their members to the Common Council. Near this period, and for a long time afterwards, the Ironmongers appear to have united the professions both of merchant and trader, for, whilst they had large warehouses and yards, whence they exported and sold bar-iron and iron rods, they had also shops, wherein they displayed abundance of manufactured articles, which they purchased from the workmen in town and country, and of which they afterwards became the general retailers. Ironmonger Lane was one of the first spots on which the trade congregated. Many of the rich Ironmongers were buried in the church of the adjacent united parishes of St. Olave Jewry and St. Martin, Ironmonger Lane.

The Ironmongers were incorporated in the 3rd of Edward IV., their arms having been granted to them several years before. Their records are ancient; their first court-book commences in 1541, but they have documents and records of a still earlier date. Some of the entries are curious, and of these we select a few of the most interesting. In 1562, they provide 19 soldiers for the Queen's service; 1565, pay £75 towards building the Royal Exchange; 1566, provide three soldiers for the Queen's service, Ireland; 1575, they lend the Queen £60; 1577, supply 100 men as soldiers; 1578, provide seven seamen; 1579, provide 73 men for the defence of the kingdom; 1591, contribute £344 to help send forth ten ships of war and a pinnace; 1596, lend Government £172; 1630 pay £35 16s., being their proportion of a fine exacted from the City for not apprehending the murderers of John Lamb (see Vol. I., page 421); 1642, pay for the service of Parliament £3,400; 1643, pay Parliament £9 10s. every week for four months, and sell their plate to try to raise £1,700 to help Parliament.

The ancient livery hood was crimson and puce. In choosing wardens it was usual at the election dinner to bring in garlands, preceded by minstrels, and try them on each person, till they arrived at the stewards-elect. Worthy Mr. Evelyn (September 4, 1671) mentions this ceremony, and describes how the solemn procession came to the upper table and drank to the new stewards.

The present Ironmongers' Hall is the third or fourth building erected on the same site. The present hall was designed by T. Holden, in 1748. It was then a handsome stone building, with a rustic base and Ionic pilasters, balustraded roof, and carved tympanum. The vestibule was divided by six Tuscan columns, and the state room was adorned with Ionic ornaments, an orchestra and grand buffet. The master and wardens' chairs stood against the west wall, in front of the king's arms, while the blue semi-oval ceiling was stuccoed with heraldic bearings, satyrs' heads, cornucopias, palm-branches, flowers, and scrolls. The banqueting-hall has since been decorated in the Louis Quatorze taste, in papier-mache and *carton-pierre* imitative oak aided by oak carvings. The hall contains portraits of Mr. Thomas Betton, a Turkey merchant, who left £26,000, Sir Robert Jeffery (giver of the Company's almshouses in the Kingsland Road), Sir James Cambell, and other benefactors, and a fine full-length of Lord Hood, by Gainsborough, given by that admiral to the Company, in 1783, when his lordship was received into the Company without fee or previous nomination. The Ironmongers' arms are argent, on a chevron gules, three swivels or between three steel gads azure; crest on a wreath, two scaly lizards, erect, combatant proper (*i.e.*, vert); motto, "God is our strength." The lizards should properly be salamanders, but the Ironmongers insist on the lizards, and even named their Irish estate after them.

Mincing Lane was so called from houses there belonging to the "Minchuns," or nuns, of St. Helen's, Bishopsgate Street. Of old time, says Stow, there dwelt in this lane Genoese traders called "galleymen," because they brought their wines and other merchandise to Galley Wharf, in Thames Street. They used amongst themselves small silver halfpence called, in London, "galley halfpence," forbidden by Act of Parliament in the reigns of Henry IV. and Henry VI. These coins were broader than English halfpence, but not so thick and strong.

Mincing Lane is specially mentioned by Pepys, *àpropos* of the Great Fire :—"19th June, 1668," he says, "between two and three in the morning we were waked with the maids crying out, 'Fire, fire, in Marke Lane!' So I rose and looked out, and it was dreadful, and strange apprehensions in me and us all of being presently burnt. So we all rose, and my care presently was to secure my gold and plate and papers, and could quickly have done it, but I went forth to see where it was; and the whole town was presently in the streets; and I found it in a new-built house that stood alone in Minchin Lane, over against the Clothworkers' Hall, which burned furiously; the house not yet quite finished; and the benefit of brick was well seen, for it burnt all inward, and fell down within itself; so no fear of doing more hurt."

The original Clothworkers' Hall, in Mincing Lane, was purchased by the Fullers, in the year 1455

(Henry VI.), ever to remain in their fellowship. The spot is remarkable as the boundary of the Great Fire of London, which partly destroyed the hall. Pepys speaks of the building as being "in one body of flame for three days and nights, the cellars being full of oil."

The Clothworkers, says Herbert, seem to have sprung, like the Fullers, from the very ancient guild of Weavers. The trade had formerly several subdivisions, of which the Fullers, the Burrellers, and the Testers were the chief. The Burrellers were inspectors and measurers of cloth. In the reign of Edward IV. the Shearmen were separated from the Drapers and Tailors, and were incorporated. Henry VII. granted them additional privileges, and Henry VIII. united them with the Fullers, and gave the joint fraternity the name of Cloth-workers. There were endless disputes between the Clothworkers and Dyers for precedence, till at last the Clothworkers settled down as twelfth and last of the great companies, and the Dyers took rank as first of the minor ones. Shearmen, the old title of the Clothworkers, had no reference to re-moving the wool from the sheep, but applied to the manner of clipping the nap in the process of cloth manufacture. The Clothworkers are especially mentioned in a statute concerning the woollen manufacture, in the reign of Edward VI., which contained clauses requiring the clothiers' seal on cloth, and forbidding over-stretching, and adding chalk, or flour, or starch, and the use of iron cards. Queen Elizabeth confirmed the right of the Cloth-workers, and Charles I. (who, as well as his father, was a member of the fraternity) confirmed their charter. There were five degrees in the Com-pany—apprentices, freemen (also called yeomen and bachelors), householders, the fellowship, and wardens. The government consisted of a court of assistants, including only those who had been masters and wardens.

Pepys himself was a member of this Company, and left it a quaint and valuable old cup, which still shines out among the meaner plate on the occasion of grand dinners, "when beards wag all." The hall after the Great Fire seems to have been restored with green wood, which soon fell into decay. It must have been a fine building, for the banqueting-hall was a lofty wainscoted room, adorned with a great oak screen, with figures of James I. and Charles I., and two stained-glass windows. These windows contained, among other devices, the arms of Pepys and Sir John Robinson. The latter worthy was Lieutenant of the Tower, Pre-sident of the Artillery Company, and Lord Mayor in 1663, when he entertained, in Clothworkers' Hall,

Charles II. and his Queen, the Queen-Dowager, and the Duke and Duchess of York. Mr. Samuel Angell was the architect of the new hall, which occupies the old position in Mincing Lane. It was completed in 1860, and is now, with its fine oak carving and splendid mirrors, a good specimen of a Company's Hall—the ceiling, in white and gold, being ornamented in a rather unusual, but most tasteful manner, with life-size figures in relief. At one end of the hall stand the statues of James I. and Charles I., very dazzling in their covering of pure gilding. The ground on which the hall is built has been enlarged by the addition of a very large piece of land purchased by the Company quite recently. This is the site of the old church and graveyard of Allhallows Staining. The body of the church itself has been pulled down, and its place is occupied by houses built and let on lease to tenants. The churchyard is to remain as an open space, and will still admit air and light to the hall. But the old tower still remains ; the Company, by arrangement with the Ecclesiastical Commissioners, being bound not only not to de-molish it, but to keep it in repair. Anything more absurd than this restriction cannot be imagined. The crumbling old tower is not by any means ornamental, and it can serve no purpose on earth except that of obstructing and incommoding the property of the Company. The real estates held by this Company are very large, and comprise a great deal of valuable house property in London. The Irish estates were let as far back as 1769 for £600 per annum, and a fine of £28,000. They have, however, been sold since the last rebuilding of the hall. The Company have schools at Sutton Valence, in Kent, and in the Isle of Man, and almshouses at Sutton Valence, in Islington, and other places. The charities were estimated in 1836 at about £1,400 per annum, but they are now vastly increased. This Company has num-bered many royal personages among its members, and among them the Prince of Wales and the Duke of Cambridge. Prince Albert was also a member, and the Company have a large picture of his late Royal Highness, with a sister painting of Her Majesty, executed by Herrick in 1863. In proof of the honour in which the Clothworkers were held two centuries ago, we may quote the words of the panegyrist, Elkanah Settle :—"The grandeur of England is to be attributed to its golden fleece (which is the crest of this Company), the wealth of the loom making England a second Peru, and the back of the sheep, and not the entrails of the earth, being its chief mine of riches. The silkworm is no spinster of ours, and our wheel and web are wholly the Clothworkers'. Thus, as trade is the soul of the kingdom, so the greatest branch of it lies in the Clothworkers' hands, and though our naval commerce brings us in both the *or* and the *argent*, and indeed the whole wealth of the world, yet, when thoroughly examined, it will be found 'tis your cloth sends out to fetch them. And thus, whilst the Imperial Britannia is so formidable to her foes and so potent to her friends, . . . to the Clothworkers' honour it may justly be said, "'Tis your shuttle nerves her arm, and your wool that enrobes her glory.'"

Howes relates that "James I., being in the open Hall, inquired who was master of the Company; and the Lord Mayor answering, 'Sir William Stone,' to whom the king said, "Wilt thou make me free of the Clothworkers?' 'Yea,' quoth the master, 'and think myself a happy man that I live to see this day.' Then the king said, 'Stone, give me thy hand; and now I am a Clothworker.'"

The Clothworkers' arms, granted in the reign of Henry VIII., are sable, a chevron ermine between two habricks, in chief argent, and a thistle in base, or; crest, a ram passant, or; supporters, two griffins, or; pellette. Motto—"My trust is in God alone."

At the north-east corner of Mark Lane, says Stow, was the manor of a knight of Richard II., called by the pretty name of Blanch Appleton, afterwards corrupted into Blind Chapel Court. In the reign of Edward IV. basket-makers and wire-drawers were allowed to practise their trade in Blanch Appleton. Mark Lane was originally called Mart Lane, from some fair of uncertain date there established.

The Church of Allhallows, standing in Mark Lane, recently pulled down by the Clothworkers' Company to enlarge their hall, was given, in 1367, by the Bishop of London to the Abbey and Convent of our Lady of Grace, near the Tower of London. The right of presentation eventually came into the possession of the Grocers' Company. According to Stow, the church was called Stane or Stayning, to distinguish it at an early period when many London churches were erected of timber. The churchwardens' books of Allhallows are perfect from as far back as 1491, and abound with some interesting facts as to prices and manners and customs. In 1492 the great beam light of the church is mentioned as weighing more than 40 pounds, and cost 1d. the pound. In 1587 there is a shilling paid to the ringers for expressing joy at the execution of Mary Queen of Scots. In 1606 a shilling is paid for painting three red crosses on the doors of houses infected with the plague. In the Great Plague of 1665, 165 persons

died in the parish, and that year £3 17s. 6d. is paid for street fires to purify the air. In 1688, the ringers are paid for expressing joy at King James's return from Faversham, and two days after for more joy at the Prince of Orange's arrival, for the purpose of dethroning James! The church escaped the Great Fire, but, as if tired of standing, fell down suddenly in 1671, nearly burying a sexton who was digging a grave. The tower contains six bells, the greater number of which are dated 1682-3. Two of them, however, are much older. Malcolm says the date upon one is 1485.

The Corn Exchange in Mark Lane was projected and opened in 1747. A new Exchange was re-built by Mr. G. Smith in 1827, and opened the next year; and the old Exchange, which adjoined it, is now (1880) being rebuilt. On building the second Corn Exchange a fine Roman pavement was discovered. The old building had an open colonnade with modern Doric pillars, and the interior court has been compared to the *atrium*, or place of audience, of a Pompeian house. The New Corn Exchange is in the Grecian and Doric style. The portico is surmounted by the imperial arms, and the interior is lighted by a lantern with vertical lights in the centre space within the columns, and the compartments on each side have skylights in their ceilings. The stands of the corn-factors, to the number of eighty and upwards, are along the sides of the building. On them are placed small bags and wooden bowls, with samples of different kinds of grain, and behind is a desk for the factor or his clerk, with something of the convenience of a counting-house. Lightermen and granary-keepers have stands as well as corn-merchants, factors, and millers. The seed-market is held in another part of the building. In the north wing is a tavern and coffee-room, and an opening in the south side of the wing communicated with the old Corn Exchange.

As some London corn merchants were said, as far back as half a century ago, to turn over in a year nearly a million and a half of money, it may be supposed that Mark Lane is a strictly busy place, and that the factors there do not scoop up handfuls of corn or toss wheat up in the air for mere amusement. In two months alone in 1841 there arrived in London 787 vessels from foreign ports, laden with foreign corn, a fact which proves the ceaseless cry for bread of hungry England, unable to fully supply its own wants, and dependent on the energy of the Mark Lane dealers.

In the Middle Ages, London, a mere bantling then, with no great appetite, depended in simple faith for corn on Kent and Essex alone. In Stow's time Norfolk, Suffolk, Essex, Kent, and Sussex were the chief competitors in the London corn trade. Speculators in corn were looked upon in old times with suspicion, and even detestation; while regraters, or holders back of corn, were formerly branded as ruthless enemies of the human race. In 1542 corn-dealers were prohibited having more than ten quarters in their possession at one time, and justices could examine a farmer's barns and sell the superfluous stock. Heavy penalties

Simon Eyre, another Lord Mayor, established a public granary, such as Joseph did in Egypt, at Leadenhall. In 1521 a mayor found the City granaries nearly empty, and had to lay in a provision of wheat. In 1546 two aldermen were appointed weekly in rotation to see that the markets were well supplied. When prices rose the companies were compelled to send in for sale certain specified quantities of corn, and then to provide a fresh stock. In 1590, they were called on,

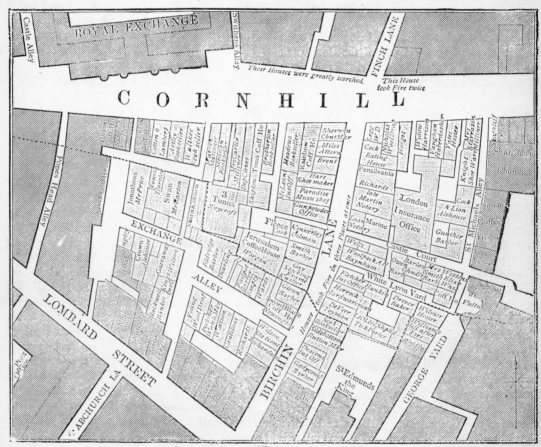

PLAN SHOWING THE EXTENT OF THE GREAT FIRE IN CORNHILL IN 1748. (*See page* 172.)

were inflicted two years afterwards on persons who bought corn to sell again. Farmers buying corn for seed were required to sell an equal quantity of store corn; while corn dealers were required to take out an annual licence, and not to engross or forestall, or buy out of open market, except under an express permission.

Dearths frequently occurring in the Middle Ages, the livery companies were required to keep stores of corn, as we have already mentioned in previous chapters. Sir Stephen Brown is the first Lord Mayor praised by Stow for sending to Dantzic for cheap corn in time of scarcity, and Sir

at two different periods, to purchase 18,000 quarters. The Bridgemaster had the charge of buying the corn, which was at one period entirely stored in the Bridge House. The money to purchase the grain for the City granaries was raised by loans and contributions from the mayor and aldermen, the City companies, and sometimes from the citizens. The companies often grumbled, clamoured for a return of their money, and were sometimes paid in store corn, which they by no means wanted. In 1596 the companies built their own granaries, and were allowed to keep their supply there. The difficulty with the companies grew worse and worse, and the refusals to buy corn became more frequent, till at last the Great Fire, that fierce reformer of many abuses, swept away the Bridge House and all the other granaries, and thus at last the custom of laying up corn and interfering with the natural balance of trade ceased altogether.

The German Steel Yard merchants were at one period the sole importers of foreign corn, and in times of scarcity were not allowed to sell either to bakers or brewers without the City's licence.

each of whom had three men under him. The chief corn-markets of London were Cornhill and Michael-le-Quern, at the west end of Cheapside. Bread Street was the mediæval bakers' market. The Fellowship of Bakers held four hall-motes during the year, to punish offences of their craft. In 1370 a Stratford baker, for selling loaves smaller than the assize, was drawn on a hurdle through London streets with a fool's cap on his head, while round his neck dangled his meagre loaves.

THE OLD INDIA OFFICE, LEADENHALL STREET, IN 1803. (*See page* 183.)

In one special year bakers were forbidden to buy any meal, except at the City's store, the Bridge House, where the quantity each might take, and the price, were fixed by the Lord Mayor. Such were the fetters in which trade had to move in the time of Queen Elizabeth, when so many feudal restrictions were still in existence. As an instance of the power of the City in the reign of her successor, it has been mentioned that in 1622 the Court tried to borrow thirty or forty quarters of wheat, and the City would only lend ten.

The ancient corn-ports of London were, as we have shown, Queenhithe and Billingsgate. The chief corn-warehouse was at Queenhithe. There was a principal meter there, and eight master porters,

The old assize of bread compelled bakers to regulate the size of thier loaves by the price of corn. The assize was regulated in Queen Anne's reign, and not finally abolished till 1815. The Bakers' Company used formerly to present two new-baked loaves to the Lord Mayor and Aldermen, to be fairly weighed. They were made out of wheaten corn, purchased by four "sworn and discreet men" at the markets of Grasschurch, St. Botolph, Bishopsgate, and Queenhithe. London bakers were formerly, except at Christmas, forbidden to sell household loaves at a higher price than twopence, or to sell by retail spice-cakes, buns, or biscuits, except for funerals, and at the festivals of Christmas and Easter.

The London corn-mills were latterly chiefly at London Bridge. Besides Leadenhall and the Bridge House there were granaries at one time at Bridewell and Christchurch. At the beginning of the last century the metropolitan corn-market was held at Bear Quay, in Thames Street. Queenhithe was at the same period the great market for flour and meal, and the "White Horse" Inn meal-market, situated near Holborn Bridge, was much frequented.

The system of factorage is only about 200 years old. Tradition has it that it began with a number of Essex farmers, who used to leave samples of corn with the landlord of an inn at Whitechapel where they put up, and to whom they paid commission, to save the trouble of attending the market every week. The ancestors of one of the oldest commission-houses began with a stand on Tower Hill :

" Such great events from little causes spring."

Kentish, Essex, and Suffolk corn arrives in sacks; foreign and Irish corn, and English oats and barley in loose bulk. The Kentish hoys sometimes bring joint-stock cargoes. The operation of unloading and measuring was, under the old system, very skilfully managed. Two fellow-ship porters all but filled the bushel with wooden shovels, the meter completed the bushel, and one of the men passed the strike over the surface. The sack was then filled and shot into the lighter. At purchase the grain was again measured.

By a recent Act of Parliament the City's rights of measuring corn, worth as much as £13,000 a year, were done away with. Corn is now sold by weight, the only charge being three-sixteenths of a penny per hundredweight, to pay for the ex-sworn meters, as compensation to the City; this charge to continue for thirty years.

The London terms of the factors are one month's open credit, and the buyer has to lodge any objection as to quality, bulk &c., at the factor's stand before eleven o'clock on the following market day, or else has to abide by his bargain. The centre of the market is devoted, at the entrance end, to shipbrokers of all classes, and also to masters of small craft, and lightermen ; in the middle assemble the great Greek merchants, who almost monopolise the importation of corn from every part of the world ; they here give directions to factors who are selling their arrived cargoes, and to agents who are negotiating with country merchants and factors from all parts of the kingdom, either personally or by telegraph, for the sale of cargoes shipping at foreign ports, or

on passage, or arrived on the coast at Plymouth or Queenstown. There are sometimes as many as 100 cargoes at ports of call, the size of each one being from 4,000 to 5,000 quarters up to 8,000 quarters, and sometimes as much as 13,000 quarters, waiting for a destination, which is notified to them by telegraph as soon as a contract is made. Not only is the United Kingdom supplied in this way, but also any part of the Continent where corn may be required.

The upper part of the market is the place of assembling for oil seed-crushers, and here the Greeks again are the great importers of all kinds of oil-seeds.

A strict and punctual system governs all the proceedings of the establishment. The market opens at eleven o'clock by ring of bell, and factors never name a price for goods till then. At two o'clock a notice bell is rung, and at half-past two the final bell, when the doors of the market are closed until three, when the sweepers begin to clear up the spilt samples, which bring in a good revenue to the company.

The next market adjoining, and in communication with the old Exchange, is the " London Corn Exchange," which is commonly called the New Corn Market, to distinguish it from the other. The exterior is much more imposing than the old market, which was very simple. Originally some dealers clubbed together and acquired some property opposite the old Exchange, and in opposition to it, and set up a few small stands, but they subsequently formed a company, and acquired the present site. This may be called the retail market, as the standholders are principally dealers, who sell corn lying in their own river-side warehouses to shopkeepers, livery-stables, &c., and they buy, generally from factors on the old market, the grain ex-ship. Some of these dealers are also factors in the old market. Here also the malt-factors and maltsters attend, as the Greeks do in the other market ; and also a great many country dealers, who sell home-grown barley. The stands are arranged round the interior, and smaller stands fill up the centre opening.

In the upper part of the old Exchange, and the property of the same company, was an apartment known as " Jack's Coffee House," the assembly for London and country millers, who examine their purchases, &c., after the market is over. The business is now transacted in another part of the Exchange. At the rear of the Exchange is a handsome building, which was erected in 1860 ; the upper storeys are divided into offices, and the ground-floor forms a large subscription-room.

Granaries are numerous about Bermondsey and Shad Thames, but they also abound on both sides of the river, from Greenwich to Vauxhall. The foreign corn is stored in bonded granaries near the Commercial Docks. In the times of the high duties corn-merchants have been known to throw 2,000 quarters of wheat into the river at one time rather than pay the high tax, or keep it subject to long granary rent.

The supply of foreign corn to this country has undergone many changes from time to time; formerly our supplies were chiefly from the Baltic and South Russian ports, but now the United States are the chief contributors, and we also get wheat from Australia, California, the Cape, and New Zealand.

The cultivation of grain has undergone a marvellous change since 1830, the English farmer preferring cattle-rearing to corn-growing: thus in 1830 the supply of foreign corn to the port of London, as measured by the sworn meters, was 1,132,580 quarters, and of English 3,154,270 quarters; whereas, in the year 1871 the quantities were, foreign, 2,471,394 quarters; English, 662,567 quarters. The total of foreign grain and flour imported into London during 1871 was 20,400,905 cwts., according to Custom House Returns.

In Mark Lane, opposite the Corn Exchange, stood till recently a large and very ancient house, with fine oak carving over the gateway, and inside. Horses used to be lodged inside the gateway, and the wooden pegs used for hanging up saddles were to be seen. This house must have been the residence of a rich City grandee.